Child Development Today and Tomorrow

William Damon, Editor

Child Development Today and Tomorrow

 Jossey-Bass Publishers
San Francisco • London • 1989

CHILD DEVELOPMENT TODAY AND TOMORROW
by William Damon, Editor

Copyright © 1989 by: Jossey-Bass Inc., Publishers
350 Sansome Street
San Francisco, California 94104

&

Jossey-Bass Limited
28 Banner Street
London EC1Y 8QE

Library of Congress Cataloging-in-Publication Data

Child development today and tomorrow.

(The Jossey-Bass social and behavioral science series)
Bibliography: p.
Includes index.
1. Child psychology.   I. Damon, William, date.
I. Series.
BF721.C5153   1989   155.4   88-42785
ISBN 1-55542-103-2

Manufactured in the United States of America

The paper in this book meets the guidelines for
permanence and durability of the Committee on
Production Guidelines for Book Longevity of the
Council on Library Resources.

JACKET DESIGN BY WILLI BAUM

FIRST EDITION

Code 8833   0183244894

The Jossey-Bass
Social and Behavioral Science Series

Contents

ix

Part Four: Social Development

Preface

The study of child development is by nature an expansive enterprise, long ago having burst the boundaries of anything that reasonably could be called a unified scholarly discipline. In recent years, child development has incorporated new approaches and expanded into new areas at a rapid rate. The academic fields of history, sociology, anthropology, psychology, and neuroscience, as well as the applied fields of education, law, and medicine, have all made contributions to contemporary child development theory and research. In turn, child development has become a recognized part of all these diverse fields. Previously unexplored territories in children's emotional, intellectual, and social lives have been opened up for scientific analysis. As a consequence, this field-in-motion has generated far-reaching new insights into children's behavioral and mental processes.

Perhaps because of the astonishing speed with which these changes have occurred, the expansion is not always recognized for what it is. Where we in the field see growth and progress, others throughout the scholarly community may perceive disarray and dissension. In my own discussions with colleagues and students from other academic specialties within and beyond psychology, I have often wished to convey the sense of movement and direction that characterizes child development today. That wish has been frustrated by the lack of a single up-to-date source covering the broad new areas of expansion within this multifaceted enterprise.

Child Development Today and Tomorrow is my response to this need. My purpose has been to bring together a collection of distinguished developmentalists to write forward-looking chapters that would convey the current excitement of this changing field. I have also wanted the chapters to present the many new ideas that have arisen out of contemporary research and theory on children's development. On both counts, I believe that this collection accomplishes its mission beyond my most optimistic initial expectations. The book's twenty contributions explicate the state of the art in child development's most central areas and also point the way to the field's future directions. In the process, the authors themselves make important strides toward this future by the original insights that they present here, often for the first time.

This book is addressed to scholars and practitioners from all disciplines who are concerned with children and their development. This includes, of course, developmental psychologists and others within the psychological sciences. But it also includes many others who want to read about recent trends in this field. I count here people from the range of disciplines noted above: historians, anthropologists, sociologists, educators, pediatric researchers, and many others. This book will also be a good source for graduate students planning their future careers in the child development area.

The book is organized into four parts. Part One presents important statements on the role of social and cultural context in development. This is an avenue of fundamental theoretical advance these days, and the positions presented here spring from insights that are already wielding considerable influence in the field. In Chapter One, James Wertsch shows how Vygotskian analysis offers us a way of understanding social and individual determinants of development without reducing one to the other. Wertsch also extends Vygotsky's theory into critical new areas. Chapter Two presents Harold Grotevant's resolution of choices about units and levels of analysis in studying the development of the child within a family context. In Chapter Three, Robert LeVine explains why our current developmental models have proven so insensitive to considerations of cultural context. He outlines the conceptual principles through which we can forge a new integration between developmental and cultural theory. In Chapter Four, Richard and Jacqueline Lerner, with their "goodness of fit" model, create a theoretical link between the dynamics of biological growth and the mediating influences of social context. In Chapter Five, Elliot Turiel warns against the intellectual and moral traps that have been posed by the social determinism now rampant in American social science.

The book's remaining three parts constitute major substantive areas in which innovative work on children's development is currently being accomplished. Part Two focuses on affective development, covering topics that range from empathy to pubertal emotions to affective disorders in childhood. In Chapter Six, Kurt Fischer, Phillip Shaver, and Peter Carnochan offer a new model that places the specifics of particular emotional experience in the context of an overarching developmental framework. Chapter Seven, by Nancy Eisenberg, gives us a state-of-the-art account of recent progress in exploring empathy as an affective system. In Chapter Eight, J. Brooks-Gunn examines adolescent emotional development. She casts doubt on "storm and stress" as a good description of the adolescent period but does identify a certain negative emotionality characteristic of the adolescent transition. Dante Cicchetti and Jennifer White, in Chapter Nine, explore the socialization of affect through attachment and self-theory and then extend their reach to related aspects of physiological and neuropsychological functioning.

Part Three focuses on intellectual achievement, exploring a pluralistic assortment of cognitive and artistic skills. In Chapter Ten, Ellen Winner discusses children's artistic development and shows the incompleteness of psychological accounts that ignore this critical area of human potential. Howard Gardner, in Chapter Eleven, presents his multifaceted approach to intelligence in all its many guises, from the artistic to the logical to the interpersonal. David Henry Feldman's chapter (Chapter Twelve) is a polemic that cuts the supports out from under the recent "development-is-an-

illusion" claims while presenting his own innovative transformational model. Chapter Thirteen, by Deanna Kuhn, poses ways of
closing the unnecessary gap between scientific and educational
approaches to children's cognitive development.

Part Four is devoted to social development. It looks into key
social relations during infancy, childhood, and adolescence and
probes the dynamics of the socialization process. It also presents
some educational and therapeutic interventions grounded in the
principles of children's social interactions with peers and adults. In
Chapter Fourteen, Ina Užgiris shows us how far we have come not
only in recognizing the fact of the infant's elaborate social self but
also in analyzing its precise features. Edward Mueller, in Chapter
Fifteen, focuses on shared meaning during toddlerhood, bringing
together individual and social sources of meaning. He presents new
links between early peer relations, parent-child relations, and the
development of social knowledge. In Chapter Sixteen, Thomas
Berndt examines friendship through the childhood and adolescent
years, focusing particularly on its role in the network of children's
other social relations. In Chapter Seventeen, Diana Baumrind
presents a comprehensive account of her ground-breaking categories
of child-rearing patterns and points out the directions toward which
her perspective is moving. James Youniss, in Chapter Eighteen,
explains the developmental legacy of productive parent-child
relations during adolescence. He employs sociological concepts like
social capital for his developmental analysis. In Chapter Nineteen,
Myrna Shure discusses her interpersonal cognitive problem solving
(ICPS) program and its promising successes in a wide range of social
settings. In Chapter Twenty, Robert Selman uses his "pair therapy"
method in the context of a new technique centering around a child's
computer game.

Beyond its main purposes, elaborated above, this book also
was conceived as a fitting way to celebrate the tenth year of the
Jossey-Bass series *New Directions for Child Development* (*NDCD*),
of which I am editor-in-chief. In fact, my first working plan was to
ask some of the people who had written for the series to provide
current position papers on their original topics. As the project began
shaping up, it became clear that the authors would go beyond
simply updating earlier statements. Many of the authors had not

only new things to say but also new targets of attention. This opened still further possibilities, and so I invited a few people who had not yet participated in *NDCD* to join in with chapters of their own. All this enhanced the book's main agenda of providing a coherent set of statements about the emerging contours of the field, about how the study of children's development is changing and growing. The realization that the book was becoming broadly inclusive as well as innovative gave birth to the title, *Child Development Today and Tomorrow*.

The book also preserves something of the flavor of the *New Directions* series: one thing I have always aimed for in the series is to come up with statements that are exploratory rather than definitive. Similarly here. I see this book as defining some—but by no means all—of developmental psychology's new frontiers. The field today supports many exciting and vital areas that I have not tried to cover. Still, the breadth of concern in the present chapters seems impressive to me; many chapters contain subject matter that will not be encountered in any developmental textbook or handbook. The question for the future, of course, is whether the material will prove to be enduring as well as new. My confidence on this score is firm. Readers will decide for themselves, and only the next generation of scholars can be the judge.

Acknowledgments

A central problem in life-span developmental psychology is determining how people continue learning well after they have reached maturity. My own reading of life-span studies tells me that certain enriching experiences play a key role. Specifically, these are experiences that engage an individual's interest and at the same time challenge the individual to confront ideas, goals, and strategies that go beyond the individual's current perspective. Editing *New Directions for Child Development* and *Child Development Today and Tomorrow* has been just such an experience for me. I am grateful to the people at Jossey-Bass for providing me with this opportunity. I am also fortunate to have had guest editors and authors who have exploited their confrontational possibilities to the fullest. Herewith I express my appreciation to all of them.

On the current project, Gracia Alkema not only took part in formulating the original conception but also has been supportive throughout. William E. Henry made some invaluable suggestions upon reading first drafts of the manuscripts. My secretary, Patricia Nash, assembled the many stray pieces into a coherent package and helped me (as she does on the series) fight the ever-impending threat of total disorganization. Anne Colby has given me much-needed advice and feedback, with patience as well as insight.

Worcester, Massachusetts   William Damon
October 1988

The Editor

William Damon is professor of psychology and chair of education at Clark University. He received his B.A. degree (1967) in social relations from Harvard and his Ph.D. degree (1973) in developmental psychology from the University of California, Berkeley. Damon also has been distinguished visiting professor at the University of Puerto Rico.

Damon's research has focused on several areas of social and cognitive development during childhood and adolescence. He has investigated social and self-understanding, moral development, and processes of peer learning. His books include *The Social World of the Child* (1977), *Social and Personality Development* (1983), *Self-Understanding in Childhood and Adolescence* (1988), and *The Moral Child* (1988). Damon was the founding editor of *New Directions for Child Development* and has served as its editor-in-chief since 1978.

Contributors

Diana Baumrind is research psychologist, University of California, Berkeley.

Thomas J. Berndt is professor of psychological sciences, Purdue University.

J. Brooks-Gunn is director, Adolescent Study Program, Educational Testing Service and St. Luke's–Roosevelt Hospital Center.

Peter Carnochan is a graduate student in psychology at the University of Denver.

Dante Cicchetti is professor of psychology and psychiatry, University of Rochester, and director, Mt. Hope Family Center.

Nancy Eisenberg is professor of psychology, Arizona State University.

David Henry Feldman is professor of child study, Tufts University.

Kurt W. Fischer is professor of education and psychology, Harvard University.

Howard Gardner is professor of education, Harvard University, and research psychologist, Boston Veterans Administration Medical Center.

Harold D. Grotevant is professor and head of the Division of Child Development and Family Relationships, University of Texas, Austin.

Deanna Kuhn is professor of psychology and education, Teachers College, Columbia University.

Jacqueline V. Lerner is associate professor of human development, Pennsylvania State University.

Richard M. Lerner is professor of child and adolescent development, Pennsylvania State University.

Robert A. LeVine is Roy E. Larsen Professor of education and human development and professor of anthropology, Harvard University.

Edward Mueller is associate professor of psychology, Boston University.

Robert L. Selman is director, Manville School, Judge Baker Children's Center.

Phillip R. Shaver is professor of psychology, State University of New York, Buffalo.

Myrna B. Shure is professor, Department of Mental Health Sciences, Hahnemann University.

Elliot Turiel is professor of education, University of California, Berkeley.

Ina Č. Užgiris is professor of psychology, Clark University.

James V. Wertsch is professor and chair of psychology, Clark University.

Jennifer White is a graduate student in psychology at the University of Wisconsin, Madison.

Ellen Winner is associate professor of psychology, Boston College, and research associate, Project Zero, Harvard Graduate School of Education.

James Youniss is professor of psychology, Catholic University of America.

Child Development Today and Tomorrow

Introduction:
Advances in
Developmental Research

William Damon

When I began studying child development in the late 1960s, the enterprise looked very much like a single scientific endeavor that bore characteristics of a Kuhnian theoretical paradigm. The dominant learning theory approach, grounded in assumptions of associationism and logical positivism, was fast being replaced by an emerging cognitivist paradigm focusing on meaning, psychological organization, and the special nature of the human organism. Chomsky had raised the new standard for language, Bruner for problem solving, Kohlberg for morality, and Piaget for intelligence in all its guises. Erikson and Loevinger, on the psychoanalytic front, were connecting deep-lying sectors of emotional life to general principles of structural development. Even social learning theorists like Bandura were beginning to call themselves "cognitive theorists." This was a satisfying time for those comforted by orderly progress in their science. The field of child development itself seemed to be developing, and in a straightforward and rational direction at that.

Of course it is always difficult to separate changes in one's own perspective from the shifting course of events through which one has lived; but, in any case, the whole story looks very different to me now. Rather than moving from one paradigm to the next, the field has been juggling several paradigms simultaneously—with

1

surprising tolerance. In fact, there has been far greater inclination to add new ones than to drop some out for the sake of consolidation.

Child development has been exposed to many jarring alternatives over the past twenty years. Anthropologists have challenged developmental universals and made us increasingly aware of cultural diversity. Ethologists and biologists have shown us the natural roots of basic behavioral and affective patterns and have forced us to question the ecological validity of much of our data base. Social historians and life-span theorists have oriented us toward the influence of large-scale historical forces. Feminists have challenged the generality of our methods and findings across the genders. Family theorists have drawn our attention to systematic properties of organizational units beyond the individual child. None of these views necessarily obviates any of the others; but neither do they blend easily into a seamless design.

One indication of this theoretical pluralism is the way in which data are presented. If my impression is correct, we see in child development these days fewer claims for having produced "critical experiments" testing between competing theories. Twenty years ago, the literature was rife with such accounts, generally with learning theory as the object of attack (though sometimes the tables were turned). Now, studies seem to be aimed more at introducing the value of a new vision than at discrediting an old one. The implication is that our old view was incomplete and perhaps therefore distorted; the challenge is to incorporate rather than to substitute the new for the old. This is not to say that incorporation is readily accomplished. A new perspective can have a jarring effect on existing sensibilities, particularly when the new perspective carries with it alternative assumptions about the nature of things. This can be as unsettling as it is intellectually delightful.

With this proliferation of theoretical approaches, child development seems to be evolving in a manner closer to that envisioned by Lakatos than to that envisioned by Kuhn (see Worral and Currie, 1978). Competing paradigms coexist, at times influencing, but rarely replacing, one another. Quite often this tolerant coexistence is made possible by minimal overlap in the behavior under consideration. As a result, child development has become less a discipline than a loosely associated set of problems drawing upon many disciplines for their answers. We are left with some interesting choices about how to approach developmental phenomena.

These choices, of course, do not come out of nowhere. Rather, they reflect the accumulated knowledge and wisdom established through the field's prior successes and failures. In this sense, there is a legacy of progress in the field, though not of the unidirectional and revolutionary sort envisioned by Kuhn. It is a legacy that has de-emphasized the directions which have proven unfruitful, while opening up or pointing the way to several others. The progressive legacy makes itself most apparent by gradual shifts in the research topics that attract interest as well as in the range of considerations that are brought to bear on these topics.

The present volume reflects such shifts. There are essays on topics that would have received scant attention in child development twenty years ago: artistic intelligence, empathy, toddler peer relations, family dynamics, infant communication, adolescent biosocial transitions, and the social construction of meaning, to name only a few. Further, and more important, these and other topics are given a conceptually richer and more satisfactory treatment than has been available in earlier analyses. The same conceptual themes and advances are evident throughout many of the chapters. For example, the authors strive for multiple levels of analysis in order to capture the interplay of biological, individual, and social forces in development. Social context is no longer considered a set of isolatable factors external to individuals, but rather an organized, intrinsic part of mental life. The child, too, has been reconceptualized in a far more sophisticated way—seen on the one hand, in a relational manner, as an integral part of family and societal networks; and on the other hand as a developing individual with complex and intertwining behavioral, affective, moral, and intellectual systems.

Above all, we have learned to pluralize both the social and the individual components of a child's development. There are many people in the child's social world, and there are many types of social influence, from parent to peer to cultural and transpersonal interactions. The child acquires multiple kinds of intelligence, value, and affect. There are qualitative differences between each of these forms of influence, knowledge, and feeling. These differences must be preserved and appreciated in any accurate account of a child's growth as a person. We are theoretically past the time when "society" could be considered a singular socialization agent (as in "society tells the child to . . .") or when "g" could be considered a sensible index of intellectual competence. Multiplicity is the word of the day.

But despite all such conceptual shifts, our choices in developmental study still remain centripetally bounded by a focal set of concerns. These concerns, which define the uniqueness of any enterprise that could ever be called child development, include most prominently the identification of processes responsible for the formation and transformation of human thought and action. Any analysis that we invoke, no matter how sweeping or elevated its level, must shed light on this problem in developmental psychology if it is to make a substantial contribution to our knowledge of child development. This is the center that must hold and does hold in each of the twenty contributions in the present volume.

At the same time, with respect to method and theory, our choices are centrifugally drawn in directions extended to virtually every scholarly discipline beyond psychology. This can happen to the degree that psychological analysis takes on a chameleon-like quality, ensconcing its own interpretive principles in the intellectual context of another scholarly discipline. As Erikson has written about people, such mergers of identity pose growth opportunities for those securely centered and risks of dissipation for those who are not. With regard to this problem, I must admit to some ambivalence in my overall assessment of the child development field at the current time. But again, in the present collection of papers I see many reasons to believe that interdisciplinary approaches can retain a firm conceptual coherence while opening up new issues and ideas.

The twenty chapters in this volume represent some of the best versions of the contemporary choices now extant in the study of child development. Moreover, beyond simply representing current choices in the field, the chapters show new extensions, integrations, and solutions that will define and redefine the shape of child development tomorrow. The title of this book, I believe, is not a stretch of the imagination. It is an emerging and almost tangible reality that becomes more and more apparent as one reads through the promising material presented here.

I have organized the book into four parts. The first contains comprehensive statements on the role of social and cultural context in development, a major focus of most real theoretical advances during the present epoch. The remaining three parts represent the main substantive areas in which innovative work is currently being accomplished: affective development, cognitive growth in its diverse forms, and children's social development. Within each part, a glance over the chapter topics reveals how far we have come over the past couple of decades. I venture to say that full-scale chapters on most of these topics could not have been written twenty—or even ten—years ago. Even in the few cases in which this may have been possible (such as on the subject of creativity), we would have seen a rather impoverished product from a developmental perspective.

The Social and Cultural Context of Development

The great contemporary appeal of Vygotsky's theory, I believe, is that it offers us a way of understanding social and individual determinants of development without reducing one to the other. This is no mean feat: It has, in fact, eluded most competing theoretical perspectives. Chapter One, by James Wertsch, shows us how Vygotskian analysis accomplishes this powerful conceptual bridge building. Most centrally, Vygotsky astutely chose units of analysis that simultaneously capture both social and psychological forces. Communication, with its interplay between shared social meaning and individual mental construction, is an ideal place to look for such units, and so speech and language reside at the heart of Vygotskian theory.

Chapter One does not confine itself merely to the Vygotskian linguistics with which we are already familiar. Wertsch introduces us to such notions as "voice" and "speech genre," which extend the theory's usefulness into critical new areas. As one example, these notions pose ways of resolving the tension between particular and universal forms of expression—a tension that has long frustrated accounts of cognitive development. As another example, these notions offer insights into how different forms of communication (such as adult-child and child-child) leave their distinct intellectual legacies in the mind of the individual learner. The value of Wertsch's analysis becomes apparent as one reads through the other chapters in this book: Developmentalists everywhere are encountering the same problems that he wrestles with so effectively.

Choices about units and levels of analysis are at the center of Chapter Two as well, and Harold Grotevant's resolution of this issue is astonishing in its sweep. Grotevant takes as his focal problem the development of the child within a family context. His solution is to take a multi-angle perspective on the child-family relationship, looking simultaneously at the principles of individual, dyadic, family and social-contextual functioning. Although Grotevant does not go so far as to incorporate these elements into a single systematic vision, his ambitious analysis succeeds on two grounds. First, he is able at each level of analysis to capture phenomena that would be inaccessible (in some cases even unobservable) at other levels of analysis. For example, the transitions in family regulation that Grotevant describes cannot be captured by focusing on child transitions alone; and yet once we are aware of both, it becomes clear that neither can be adequately understood or explained apart from the other. Second, through all the multiple levels, Grotevant keeps a firm fix on the central problem of the developing child. Thus Grotevant develops a coherent set of insights that support and enrich each other. This is exactly what earlier advocates of such multi-layered approaches have claimed possible; but few have realized the potential of Grotevant's comprehensive treatment.

"Developmental psychology is no longer oblivious to the challenge posed by cross-cultural evidence, but it has not yet engaged in a fundamental reevaluation of its theories and concepts in terms of data emerging from non-Western cultures and from the social history of Euro-American societies." With this challenge of his own, Robert LeVine goes on to explain in Chapter Three why our current developmental models have proven so insensitive to considerations of cultural context. In the process, LeVine outlines the conceptual principles through which we may forge a new integration between developmental and cultural theory. He shows how such an integration can be accomplished only by considering cultural influence as a central socializing process rather than as a set of contextual factors extrinsic to the developing child. Indeed, in LeVine's approach, cultural mediation is the primary process, guiding and giving shape to all of the child's learning experiences.

In Chapter Four, Richard and Jacqueline Lerner, with their "goodness of fit" model, create a theoretical link between the dynamics of biological growth and the mediating influences of social context. The biological thrust is a welcome extension of social-contextual theorizing. Beyond its obvious ability to handle reams of interesting data, the Lerners' model has many virtues: It is genuinely bidirectional rather than unidirectional in its causal predictions; it is organismic rather than mechanical in its assumptions; and it captures the interplay between physiological processes (such as pubertal growth), social processes (such as peer interaction), and psychological processes (such as self-conception). The Lerners convincingly argue that their model not only follows the natural contours of the developing person but also does justice to the complexity of psychological principles. Their original insights into adolescent personality and its key transformations lend further weight to their claims.

If Wertsch, Grotevant, LeVine, and the Lerners represent our theoretical protagonists on the side of social influence, Elliot Turiel singlehandedly provides our Greek chorus. In Chapter Five, Turiel methodically exposes the intellectual and moral traps that have been set by the rampant social determinism in current social science discourse. I believe that, by and large, the authors of this volume have worked hard to achieve a balanced perspective on the role of social forces in development. But, if a word to the wise is sufficient, Turiel's warnings may help prevent all of us from leaning too far over the collectivist precipice. I wish that Turiel's chapter could be made required reading for every graduate student who is entertaining relativistic ideas about developmental progress (which, in my experience, just about subsumes the set of graduate students). Turiel also suggests a positive alternative approach to understanding change through social influence, particularly in the area of moral development. His approach, perhaps more than any other in this book, retrieves individual initiative and free will for a socially sensitive science of psychology.

Affective Development

Complaints about models of emotional development generally claim that such models give short shrift either to emotions or to
development. The special features of affective responding are often
neglected in cognitively oriented models, whereas the developmental direction is difficult to discern in most physiologically oriented
models. (Even worse, emotions as a set of genuine phenomena
disappear entirely in some social constructivist accounts.) Kurt
Fischer, Phillip Shaver, and Peter Carnochan offer us a new model
in Chapter Six that fully attends to both parts of the phrase
"emotional development." The appeal of the model lies in its
ability to place the specifics of a particular emotional experience in
the context of an overarching developmental framework. The
model's reach is impressive, and the many behavioral examples the
authors provide are compelling. I believe that we will be seeing
much more of this new model as it is used and tested in future child
research.

Empathy is an affective system with profound social and
moral consequences. Even a decade ago, its origins and developmental course were still uncharted and its links to other psychological systems (such as cognition) were poorly understood. The
exploration of empathy and sympathy has been the locus of some of
the most exciting research in child development over the past few
years, and Nancy Eisenberg has been at the center of this work. In
Chapter Seven, she gives us a state-of-the-art account of recent
progress, covering everything from definitional issues to developmental trends, behavioral implications, and sex differences.
Eisenberg's abounding statement is in itself a microcosm of this
burgeoning research area.

Emotionality traditionally has been considered a hallmark of
the adolescent years: Every good *Bildungsroman* portrays a period
of stormy and moody youth. Physiologists have pointed at puberty
as the culprit, but without the support of particularly strong data.
In Chapter Eight, J. Brooks-Gunn takes a careful look at these
notions and at the true evidence bearing on them. She casts doubt
on "storm and stress" as a good descriptor for the adolescent period,
but she identifies a certain negative emotionality observed during

the adolescent transition. What are the cause and meaning of this postpubertal development? Brooks-Gunn's analysis of current biological and social explanations for this affective phenomenon reveals some unfinished business to which the field must attend. Her chapter suggests an important program of future research on adolescent emotional development.

Freud long ago showed us how normal and abnormal emotional processes can illuminate one another, but since his time advances in this area have been few and far between. Dante Cicchetti and Jennifer White, I believe, are on the verge of making such a landmark advance. In a real *tour de force,* they bring together in Chapter Nine a multi-level organizational approach to emotional development with their pioneering developmental approach to psychopathology. Their approach is reminiscent of the theoretical choices made by Grotevant and by the Lerners in Chapters Two and Four, further demonstrating the great scientific potential of such choices. Cicchetti and White explore the socialization of affect through attachment and self-theory and then extend their reach to related aspects of physiological and neuropsychological function. In the process, they arrive at intriguing new insights about bipolar illness and its etiology.

The Many Sides of Cognitive Growth

It was not long ago that "Intelligence—that's what the I.Q. test measures!" was a joke with some bite to it for psychologists. Researchers such as Ellen Winner (Chapter Ten) and Howard Gardner (Chapter Eleven) have made this a jest of the past. Winner paints an elaborate picture of children's artistic development, addressing all the special issues that arise when one considers artistic talent: What is the source of artistic competence? Of inspiration? Are there universals in artistic achievement, or is skill tailored to cultural taste? Is an artistic gift a unique quality, or is it an extension of competencies that any child may acquire? Winner's chapter shows the incompleteness of psychological accounts that ignore this critical area of human potential—as well as of those that reduce it to just another faceless manifestation of cognitive functioning.

Gardner's chapter presents his multi-faceted approach to

intelligence in all its many guises, from the artistic to the logical to the interpersonal. This is an important approach that already has become a contender among major theoretical positions on cognitive growth. It is also a highly generative position, and an eminently reasonable one at that. Gardner's chapter speaks volumes about the range of applications to which this wisely differentiated approach can be put. I see no constraints on the contribution it can make as it continues to evolve over the coming years.

David Henry Feldman's chapter (Chapter Twelve) is a polemic that not only takes all the right sides but also sets the stage for Feldman's own ground-breaking work on creativity. Just as Turiel in his chapter dismisses the "child-as-a-cultural-invention" rhetoric with impeccable logic, Feldman cuts the epistemological supports out from under the "development-is-an-illusion" claim. Both arguments, based on compatible though somewhat different types of evidence, are refreshingly clear sighted, solidly grounded, and difficult—if not impossible—to rebut. They both do great service to a field that sometimes swings too rapidly toward extreme critique positions. Beyond clearing up some distracting confusions remaining at large in the literature, Feldman shows how a developmental approach can capture the essence of the creative process. His innovative transformational model is, I believe, just what the oddly less-than-creative research tradition of creativity has long needed.

In the past, research on children's cognition has lurched unsteadily (if at all) toward application in educational settings. The transition has been neither as smooth nor as inevitable as it ought to be. Deanna Kuhn explains why this is so in a chapter (Chapter Thirteen) that poses ways of closing the unnecessary gap between basic and applied research. The principles Kuhn explicates could make an important difference for the future of research on children's thinking, as well as for the manner in which children are educated. As a result of applying those principles, scientific and educational approaches to children's cognitive development would become more closely intertwined and, in the process, would be strengthened together. Kuhn supports her case through an elegant integration of recent trends in cognitive-developmental and educational research.

Social Development

It is hard to believe that less than twenty years ago we needed to be convinced that infants were fundamentally social creatures. Between the blank-slate school and the egocentrism view, the infant's nascent sociability was not readily locatable. In Chapter Fourteen, Ina Užgiris shows us how far we have come not only in recognizing the fact of the infant's elaborate social life but also in analyzing its precise features. Užgiris finds the central elements of social transaction—communication, mutuality, reciprocity—deeply rooted in transactions between infant and parent. Her account goes beyond mere static description to show the developmental dynamics implicit in these early transactions. In keeping with the theoretical positions on social influence presented in this book's first part, Užgiris resists the tendency to treat the social context as just another set of extrinsic factors impinging upon the child. Instead, she sees social interaction as a core aspect of the infant's growing competence and as an inextricable part of the child's psychological experience.

Edward Mueller's chapter (Chapter Fifteen), too, brings to life many of the theoretical principles asserted by others in this book. Mueller's focus on shared meaning brings together individual and social sources of development in much the same way as do the Vygotskian units of analysis—although Mueller follows more in the American and Genevan psycholinguistic tradition of semantic acquisition. Mueller ventured to document toddlers' peer relations years before the rest of the field recognized their significance (or perhaps even their existence). In Chapter Fifteen, he forges new links between early peer relations, parent-child relations, and the development of social knowledge.

Peer relations evolve into friendships by the elementary school years, and many social scientists have taken friendship to be the centerpiece of a person's nonkinship social relations. In Chapter Sixteen, Thomas Berndt follows the developmental trajectory of friendship through the childhood and adolescent years, focusing particularly on its role in the complex network of children's other social relations. He accomplishes this by examining with un-matched precision the qualities and effects of children's friendship relations. Berndt's careful analysis enables him to shed light on intriguing but obscure problems of childhood, such as popularity and its psychological implications.

The parent-child relationship is at the heart of socialization, and no one has explored it more insightfully than Diana Baumrind. Her analytic categories of child-rearing patterns have come to dominate the field in a surprisingly brief period. As she takes fresh looks at her own and others' data, Baumrind's work is constantly evolving toward greater depth and expansiveness. In Chapter Seventeen, she provides us with a comprehensive account of her powerful perspective and the directions toward which it is moving.

Another perspective on parent-child relations can be found in James Youniss's chapter on adolescent socialization. In Chapter Eighteen, Youniss draws from sociology, and particularly from the work of James Coleman, to explain the developmental legacy of productive parent-child relations during adolescence. His chapter has explicit implications for understanding the problems faced by disadvantaged youth who have not had the benefit of a solid family structure. Youniss's innovative attempt to employ sociological notions, such as social capital, for developmental analysis is conceptually appealing but as yet empirically untested.

The final two chapters, by Myrna Shure and Robert Selman, respectively, present two of the most promising clinical applications of social-cognitive theory. Shure's interpersonal cognitive problem solving (ICPS) program has been successfully tried in a wide range of settings, and in Chapter Nineteen she shows us that this success is no accident. The approach is well grounded in developmental theory and carefully worked out methodologically. Selman's "pair therapy" method also has been widely emulated, and it also arises directly from developmental research and theory. In Chapter Twenty, Selman offers us a vital sense of his approach by presenting it in the context of a new technique centering around a child's computer game. Both Shure and Selman demonstrate the practical payoffs possible when scientific principles are both carefully and creatively applied. It does not take a crystal ball to see that more of this essential work surely lies in store for child development today and tomorrow.

Reference

Worral, J., and Currie, G. (eds.). *The Methodology of Scientific Research Programs: Imre Lakatos' Philosophical Papers.* Vol. 1. Cambridge, England: Cambridge University Press, 1978.

Chapter 1

A Sociocultural
Approach to Mind

James V. Wertsch

In the appendix to *Habits of the Heart: Individualism and Commitment in American Life,* Bellah and others (1986) make a plea for formulating social science as "public philosophy." This plea is largely motivated by the debilitating effects of the specialization and professionalization prevalent in the modern research university. In this setting, all too many social scientists have been led to believe that they must "exchange general citizenship in society for membership in the community of the competent" (Haskell, 1977, p. 31). In the view of Bellah and others, this belief has robbed social scientists of their ability to enter into dialogue with scholars from other areas of intellectual inquiry, let alone with the public at large.

The authors of *Habits of the Heart* also argue that "social science as public philosophy cannot be 'value free'" (Bellah and others, 1986, p. 302). In their view, "to attempt to study the possibilities and limitations of society with utter neutrality, as though it [society] existed on another planet, is to push the ethos of narrowly professional social science to the breaking point" (p. 302). These authors believe that, in contrast to such tendencies, we must regain our ability to see issues in terms of their hidden assumptions about "good persons and a good society" (p. 301). Among other

Note: The research reported in this chapter was assisted by the Spencer Foundation. The statements made and the views expressed are solely the responsibility of the author.

14

things, this means we must be able to recognize the ways in which the phenomena under investigation, as well as the investigation itself, are socially, culturally, and historically situated.

The observations Bellah and others make about social science are extremely pertinent to developmental psychology. We can continue to ignore them only at our own peril; failure to heed them could easily lead to the discipline becoming uninteresting and irrelevant to other areas of intellectual inquiry and to issues of public concern, and eventually we risk the discipline's degeneration into a set of arcane debates among specialized schools of thought. Avoiding these risks does not entail forgoing intellectual rigor or technical expertise; in many cases, quite the opposite would be the case. Rather, it means that in addition to the existing forms of technical expertise and rigor we bring to our research, we must be able to situate our efforts in broader sociocultural and philosophical milieus.

The set of issues raised by Bellah and others is very broad. Instead of attempting to address all of them in this chapter, I will focus on one: the issue of how we can study the mental functioning of individuals in such a way that we take into account their sociocultural situation. That is, rather than examining "the individual" or "the child" as if such entities exist in a sociocultural vacuum, the approach I will outline here strives to specify how mental functioning reflects and constitutes the sociocultural setting in which it occurs. The kind of analysis I have in mind is what I call a "sociocultural" approach to mind.

In general, the goal of a sociocultural approach to mind is to explicate what is historically and culturally specific to mental functioning. For example, such an account might be concerned with characterizing the mental functioning of a nineteenth-century British factory worker, a seventeenth-century Japanese peasant child, or a twentieth-century young, upwardly mobile professional in America. Although sociocultural analyses often involve a comparison between traditional and modern societies, they need not do so. Indeed, they need not involve explicit comparison at all, though the contrast implicit in claims about sociocultural specificity is always just below the surface. The main criterion that distinguishes a sociocultural analysis of mind is that it examines some aspect of mental functioning from the perspective of how it reflects and shapes the sociocultural setting.

Sociocultural approaches to mind contrast with the universalistic emphases that currently dominate so much of the theoretical discussion in developmental psychology. In many instances, this contrast is not so much one of contradiction as it is one of simply looking at different issues. The two types of theories often focus on such distinctly different questions and phenomena that for each type the other's findings are simply incomprehensible or irrelevant.

A final characteristic of the type of sociocultural perspective I will outline here is that it incorporates a self-critical moment. By this I mean that it seeks to clarify ways in which the approach itself is socioculturally specific (see Wertsch and Youniss, 1987). This is a major aspect of what Bellah and others (1986) see as the strength of "public philosophy," and in the end it is a straightforward extension of the basic claims of the approach made by the investigator formulating it.

There are several available foundations on which to build when trying to construct a sociocultural approach to mind. In what follows, I will outline ideas that owe a great deal to the work of Soviet semiotician and psychologist L. S. Vygotsky (1896–1934) and to one of his contemporaries—M. M. Bakhtin (1895–1975). Vygotsky lived and worked in a setting in which the search for sociocultural specificity of mental functioning was a clear desideratum. He was trying to formulate a Marxist psychology that would be relevant to and useful in dealing with the novel problems confronting social scientists as they tried to help carry out the first grand experiment in socialism. One of the principal criteria for this psychology was that it be capable of capturing the unique features of consciousness that characterized "the new Soviet man," who was supposed to differ from people of social formations prior to socialism.

Vygotsky's Theoretical Framework

It is possible to understand the basic framework of Vygotsky's ideas in terms of three general themes that run throughout his writings: (1) the employment of genetic, or developmental, analysis; (2) the claim that higher (that is, uniquely human) mental functioning in the individual derives from social activity; and (3) a focus on tools and signs that mediate human mental functioning.

In a nutshell, Vygotsky's claim about genetic analysis was that in order to understand any aspect of human mental functioning we must understand its origins and the transitions it has undergone. If we fail to do this, we will often be misled by the appearance of "fossilized" forms of behavior (Vygotsky, 1978)—that is, we will mistakenly focus on superficial characteristics of a mental process that do not reflect the underlying reality, which only a developmental account can provide.

The theoretical underpinnings of his genetic analysis derive in part from the ideas of Marx and Hegel, but Vygotsky was also heavily influenced by the writings of other psychologists and epistemologists, such as Baldwin, Piaget, Werner, and Blonskii (Wertsch, 1985a). For Vygotsky, the use of genetic analysis applied to several "genetic domains" (Wertsch, 1985b). In addition to the domain of ontogenesis, which provides much of the focus of developmental psychology, he was concerned with the roles of phylogenetic, social historical, and microgenetic forces in the formation of mental functioning. Among these, his concern with social history was so pronounced that in the Soviet Union his approach is often called the "sociohistorical" or "cultural historical" approach to mind (Smirnov, 1975).

In dealing with various genetic domains, Vygotsky explicitly ruled out recapitulationist notions (see Vygotsky and Luria, 1930). For him, each genetic domain was characterized by a unique set of transitions and forces of change. Given this, the crucial question becomes how the forces of change in various genetic domains interact in the concrete activity and development of an individual. For our purposes here, the specific issue is how processes of sociohistorical transition interact with ontogenetic change.

The second theme that runs through Vygotsky's writings is the claim that all higher mental functioning in the individual has its origins in social life. Here again, Vygotsky was influenced by some of Marx's ideas. In particular, he wished to outline the psychological correlates of the Sixth Thesis on Feuerbach. However, the writings of other contemporary scholars, such as Janet (1926-27), also had a major impact on his thinking.

The most general formulation of this theme can be found in what Vygotsky termed the "general genetic law of cultural development." According to this law, "any function in the child's cultural development appears twice, or on two planes. First it appears on the social plane, and then on the psychological plane. First it appears between people as an interpsychological category, and then within the child as an intrapsychological category. This is equally true with regard to voluntary attention, logical memory, the formation of concepts, and the development of volition. . . . [I]t goes without saying that internalization transforms the process itself and changes its structure and functions" (Vygotsky, 1981, p. 163).

The claims made here have several implications that are quite striking when made explicit. For example, Vygotsky used terms such as *attention, memory,* and *thinking* in such a way that they not only are predicated of individuals but apply equally appropriately to the interpsychological plane. This does not simply amount to a return to the notion of a group mind, which has been rejected in social psychology. Rather, it involves a coherent way of talking about mental functioning within the framework of Vygotsky's theoretical perspective. This usage underlies many of the rest of his ideas, such as the "zone of proximal development" (Vygotsky, 1978; Rogoff and Wertsch, 1984) and his claims about the transition from social to egocentric to inner speech (Vygotsky, 1987; Wertsch, 1985b).

The third theme in Vygotsky's work concerns the ways in which tools ("technical tools") and signs ("psychological tools") mediate human activity. As Wertsch (1985b) and Minick (1987) have noted, the notion of mediation played an increasingly important role near the end of Vygotsky's life in his ideas about mental functioning. His basic claim was that tools and signs shape the ways in which humans interact with the physical and social world. Instead of being used as props that simply facilitate the activities humans would otherwise carry out, mediational means reshape and redefine the tasks and the mental functioning involved. For this reason, it becomes important to examine the structure and function of the various mediational means employed.

The most important forms of mediation in Vygotsky's

approach are sign systems, such as natural language—that is, primary emphasis is given to "semiotic mediation" (Wertsch, 1985b). In accordance with the second theme that characterizes Vygotsky's work, semiotic mediation exists on the interpsychological as well as on the intrapsychological plane. Indeed, it is precisely because the *same* general mediational means are employed on the social and individual planes of functioning that the transition from the former to the latter is possible. This is not to say, however, that there is a strict isomorphism between interpsychological and intrapsychological mediational means. Rather, in accordance with the ideas Vygotsky developed about genetic transitions, a set of developmental transitions transforms the mediational means as they move from one developmental phase to another. This point is reflected in Vygotsky's comment about the impact of internalization in the general genetic law of cultural development.

As I have argued elsewhere (Wertsch, 1985b), the mediational theme in Vygotsky's approach analytically precedes the other two in the sense that each of the other two themes presupposes the mediational theme in some essential way. In a sense, this corresponds with the emergence of theoretical interests in Vygotsky's career. His first writings (Vygotsky, 1971) dealt with literary and philological issues raised by Potebnya, the Russian Formalists, and other theorists of language, and the ideas he developed during that period continued to influence his writings for the rest of his career (Ivanov, 1971; Leont'ev, 1971). In addition to its analytical priority, the role of the mediational theme in Vygotsky's writings is important for other reasons. It is in connection with this theme that he made his most unique contribution. Whereas one can find in other authors' writings ideas that are similar to his claims about genetic analysis (for example, Piaget) and about the social origins of individual mental functioning (for instance, Janet), Vygotsky's reinterpretation and extension of these themes in light of ideas about mediational means distinguish his theoretical approach from others.

Although Vygotsky provided the general theoretical framework for generating socioculturally situated accounts of mind, he did relatively little empirical research on the properties of mental functioning in specific settings. A comparison of chapters 5 and 6 in

Thinking and Speech (Vygotsky, 1987), however, reveals that this issue was becoming more important in his thinking near the end of his life. These chapters are concerned with differences between "everyday," or "spontaneous," concepts on the one hand and "scientific," or "genuine," concepts on the other. And in chapter 6, which was written three years after chapter 5, a new approach to these issues began to appear. In place of viewing concepts primarily in terms of the development of psychological functioning, Vygotsky's emphasis shifted to viewing them in terms of socioculturally situated forms of communication (that is, particular forms of interpsychological functioning) and associated forms of functioning on the intrapsychological plane. Specifically, he was interested in the form of speaking found in formal school settings (what Scribner and Cole [1981] call "literary practice") and in how it might influence individual mental functioning—in particular, reasoning or thinking. This shift is reflected in the appearance in chapter 6 of the term *nauchnoe ponyatie*. This term, which has usually been translated as *scientific concept,* could also be translated as *academic concept* or *scholarly concept.*

The new direction set out in chapter 6 of *Thinking and Speech* was obviously only a beginning for Vygotsky. As a result, it lacks detailed formulation. However, it does suggest a concrete way to extend his ideas about semiotic mediation. In short, it suggests that in formulating a sociocultural approach to mind one can identify historically and culturally situated forms of communication and specify how their mastery leads to particular forms of mental functioning on the intrapsychological plane. This amounts to extending Vygotsky's ideas such that semiotic mediation comes to be viewed as the essential theoretical link between society and the mental functioning of the individual.

Stated very simply, the project suggested by extending Vygotsky's ideas about semiotic mediation involves three basic ingredients: (1) an account of the historical, social institutional, and cultural setting of a society; (2) an analysis of the semiotic mediation that reflects and constitutes this setting; and (3) an account of the intrapsychological correlates that derive from mastering the forms of semiotic mediation. As anyone familiar with the literature of history, anthropology, semiotics, sociology, and psychology is aware, however, each of these ingredients is extremely complex. Following Vygotsky's lead in giving analytic priority to semiotic mediation, I will attempt to sort out some of the issues, beginning with the second ingredient.

Pursuing this course is no accident. It accords with Vygotsky's basic methodological tenets about the role of a unit of analysis in a sociocultural approach to mind. As Zinchenko (1985) and Wertsch (1985b) have noted, a unit of analysis in Vygotsky's account must meet two primary criteria. First, it must be a genuine "unit" as opposed to an "element": That is, by focusing on a unit of analysis, one must not fragment or reduce the phenomena under consideration. As Lee (1985) has noted, Vygotsky's concern with this issue in psychology parallels Marx's ideas on exchange value as a unit of analysis in political economy. In general, the point here is that an appropriate unit of semiotic mediation can serve an essential role because it allows one to deal simultaneously with the mental functioning of the individual and the sociocultural setting in a nonreductionistic way.

The second criterion that a Vygotskian unit of analysis must meet is that it must be finite and manageable. The whole idea of identifying a *unit* is to avoid the dilemma of having to say everything about everything before analyzing any particular phenomenon. As noted earlier, each of the three basic ingredients of a sociocultural approach to mind is extremely complex. If one had to specify all the phenomena involved in each before beginning to analyze any particular issue, it would be virtually impossible to get any concrete research under way; there would be no practical way "into" a program of inquiry. To avoid being put into such a paradoxical situation, one needs to use some kind of unit that is manageable and yet not exclude or reduce key phenomena under investigation. Building on the ideas of Zinchenko (1985), Wertsch (1985b) has argued that a semiotically mediated, goal-directed action (as opposed to Vygotsky's [1987] ideas about word meaning) is just such a unit. It can be studied in concrete detail in such a way that it can relate social and historical processes on the one hand and intrapsychological functioning on the other, reducing neither in the process. In a sense, this ingredient is itself a form of mediation, since it provides the link between the first and third ingredients of the sociocultural approach.

Bakhtin's Contribution

It is in connection with units of analysis that the ideas of M. M. Bakhtin (1981, 1984, 1986; Voloshinov, 1973) are relevant. Throughout his writings, Bakhtin emphasized the need to examine the concrete *utterance,* as opposed to linguistic forms and meanings abstracted from use. He readily accepted the need to examine such decontextualized forms and meanings, noting that this is the traditional province of linguistics. However, he argued that if we are to make progress in understanding many aspects of human communication and consciousness, we must examine the properties of concrete utterances in real linguistic and extralinguistic contexts. Bakhtin (1984) used the term *metalinguistics* to refer to studies in this realm. Metalinguistics is concerned with "the *utterance* as a unit of speech communication" as opposed to "the *sentence* as a *unit of language"* (Bakhtin, 1986, p. 73).

The affinity between Bakhtin's metalinguistic analysis of the utterance and Vygotsky's ideas about speech is striking. Both authors were concerned with a wide range of issues under the heading of communicative activity (a point that has been somewhat obscured in Vygotsky's case by the mistranslation of the word *rech'* as *language* instead of *speech* in his best-known book, *Thought and Language,* [1934] 1962). Indeed, a close reading of both authors reveals that they were concerned with a general theory of human communication grounded in what would be seen as a radical version of pragmatics in the contemporary parlance of linguistics and sociolinguistics.

While such affinities highlight the similarities between Vygotsky's and Bakhtin's ideas, there are several respects in which they differ from and hence complement one another. Some of the most important points at which this is evident are in Bakhtin's account of voice, dialogicality, and social speech types. Strong parallels to each of these can be found in Vygotsky's writings; but by invoking Bakhtin's ideas major new implications begin to emerge for a more powerful and comprehensive analysis of issues in a sociocultural approach to mind.

For Bakhtin, the notion of voice—"the speaking personality, the speaking consciousness" (Holquist and Emerson, 1981, p. 434)—is closely tied to that of utterance. For him, "speech is always cast in the form of an utterance belonging to a particular speaking subject [that is, voice], and outside this form it cannot exist" (Bakhtin, 1986, p. 71). This concern with the concrete particularity of speech utterances did not lead Bakhtin to view them in terms of the randomness linguists have traditionally seen in "parole" or "performance." Instead, he developed several theoretical constructs to examine the organizational principles that shape the flow of utterances.

The most fundamental of these constructs—dialogicality—is grounded in the observation that "any utterance is a link in the chain of speech communication" (Bakhtin, 1986, p. 84). Associated with this is the claim that every utterance responds in some way to previous utterances and anticipates the responses of other, succeeding ones. Such responses and anticipations, which create the inherent dialogicality of an utterance, are tied not only to utterances that immediately precede or follow in the speech situation; they also can involve a sensitivity to a much broader range of voices—that is, a more extensive historical and cultural sensitivity. It was in this connection that Bakhtin explored a variety of types of dialogicality, including the relation between the voices of author and hero in novelistic discourse and the history of the relation between reporting and reported voices in reported speech.

One of the most fundamental ways in which dialogicality, or "multi-voicedness," appears in everyday speech as well as in artistic texts concerns what Holquist (1981) has termed *ventriloquism*. This involves one voice's inhabiting another. One way in which ventriloquism can give rise to multi-voicedness, a way that has major implications for a sociocultural approach to mind, concerns Bakhtin's notion of social speech types. In this case, a speaking consciousness, or voice, does not interanimate another individual, concrete voice. Instead, the process is one in which a voice takes on the properties of a generalized type. Bakhtin (1981, pp. 262-263) identified several kinds of social speech types, including "social dialects; characteristic group behavior; professional jargons; generic languages; languages of generations and age groups; tendentious languages; languages of the authorities, of various circles, and of passing fashions; and languages that serve the specific sociopolitical purposes of the day."

In what follows, I will focus on only one of the social speech types Bakhtin examined—"speech genres," which involve "relatively stable and normative forms of the utterance" (Bakhtin, 1986, p. 81). According to Bakhtin, "A speech genre is not a form of language, but a typical form of utterance; as such the genre also includes a certain typical kind of expression that inheres in it. In the genre the word acquires a particular typical expression. Genres correspond to typical situations of speech communication, typical themes, and, consequently, also to particular contacts between the *meanings* of words and actual concrete reality under certain typical circumstances" (1986, p. 87).

With regard to the use of speech genres, Bakhtin asserted that "we speak only in definite speech genres; that is, all our utterances have definite and relatively stable typical *forms of construction of the whole*. . . . Like Molière's Monsieur Jourdain, who, when speaking in prose, had no idea that was what he was doing, we speak in diverse speech genres without suspecting they exist" (1986, p. 78).

Bakhtin's account of speech genres reveals another way in which all utterances are inherently multi-voiced: Even though every utterance involves a unique voice in a concrete situation, it also simultaneously involves a speech genre. The speaking subject must ventriloquate, or invoke a type of voice (that is, a speech genre), in order to produce any token utterance. Bakhtin noted that there are undoubtedly hundreds of speech genres, most of which have not been the object of concrete investigation. In order to give some sense of the notion, however, he listed a few, among which he included everyday narration, the brief standard military command, writing (in all its various forms), the various forms of business documents, and the diverse world of political and social commentary.

The implications of Bakhtin's notions of social speech type in general and of speech genre in particular for a sociocultural approach to mind of the sort outlined in this chapter are enormous.

With regard to the mental functioning of the individual, these notions provide an entirely new dimension of phenomena whose implications remain to be worked out in terms of the three major themes in Vygotsky's approach. The notion of semiotic mediation involved in the socialization of mind needs to be enriched by explicating the implications of social speech types, the major implication being that by participating in and mastering social speech types, such as speech genres, on the interpsychological plane, intrapsychological functioning is shaped.

The notion of social speech type also has obvious possibilities for helping us understand the institutional, cultural, and historical processes that organize a society. Specifically, it suggests that a concrete way to explicate these processes is to examine the particular, systematic forms of activity reflected and constituted by social speech types. In short, the notion of social speech type provides a major analytic tool for extending the fundamental theme of semiotic mediation and for specifying a unit of analysis in a Vygotskian sociocultural approach to mind.

In order for the notion of a social speech type to fulfill this potential, some of its concrete properties must be explicated. Bakhtin began this process by claiming that among the major features of the utterance are "the relation of the utterance to the *speaker himself* (the author of the utterance)" and "[the relation of the utterance] to the *other* participants in speech communication" (1986, p. 84). Under the heading of the former, he argues that "each utterance is characterized primarily by a particular referentially semantic content" (p. 84) and that the "*expressive* aspect," or "the speaker's emotional evaluation of the referentially semantic content" (p. 84), also must be taken into account.

When he turned to the relationship between the speaker and other participants in speech communication (that is, the dimension of dialogicality), Bakhtin argued that "utterances are not indifferent to one another and are not self-sufficient; they are aware of and mutually reflect one another" (p. 91). This reflection may occur in many forms: "others' utterances can be repeated," "they can be referred to," "they can be silently presupposed," or "one's responsive reaction to them can be reflected only in the expression of one's own speech" (p. 91).

Among the implications of these comments is that one cannot analyze utterances or social speech types in terms of a single dimension. Instead, multiple analytic dimensions must be invoked in tandem. To date, little research in developmental psychology has been done along these lines. However, there are several existing studies that bear on one or another of the dimensions of utterances and social speech types (and perhaps even on their relationships). A quick review of some of these can begin to clarify the implications of Bakhtin's ideas for a developmental, sociocultural approach.

As already noted, in his account of the relation of the utterance to the speaker, Bakhtin distinguished between the referentially semantic content (or "sphere" or "theme") and the expressive aspect. Under the heading of referentially semantic content, it is possible to make a basic distinction between two types of objects—namely, nonlinguistic and linguistic. Among nonlinguistic objects one can make a further distinction between objects that are assumed to exist independently of the utterance in the extralinguistic context and objects that are assumed to exist independently of the utterance but not in the immediate extralinguistic context. The former case is grounded primarily on "extralinguistic indexical relationships," whereas the latter relies on "intralinguistic indexical relationships" (Wertsch, 1985b). The distinction between these two types of relationships and the nonlinguistic objects they involve has been shown to be extremely important in a variety of lines of developmental research. For example, Hickmann (1985) and Karmiloff-Smith (1979) have conducted extensive studies documenting the complexity of mastering anaphora (a type of intralinguistic indexical relationship), and Wertsch (1987b) has argued that anaphoric relationships are one of the basic building blocks of the "text-based realities" that characterize the discourse of formal instructional settings.

When one turns to linguistic objects as the referentially semantic content, yet another set of speech settings emerges. In particular, it is important to consider the kinds of reflective activity found in formal instructional settings. This was the point of much of Vygotsky's writing on the emergence of scientific concepts in adult-child discussion in this institutional setting, and it has been the object of research for several investigators concerned with related issues (see Olson, 1977; Olson and Bruner, 1974; Scribner, 1977; Wertsch and Minick, 1987). Among the analytic tools needed to explicate this dimension of social speech types are the distinction between sign tokens (individual utterances) and sign types (such as dictionary definitions) as objects and the distinction between focusing on linguistic form as opposed to linguistic meaning.

While Bakhtin focused on the "speaker's subjective emotional evaluation" in his account of the expressive aspect of the utterance, it is useful when outlining a sociocultural approach to mind to use a more general account of perspective or point of view (Uspensky, 1973) on the referentially semantic content of an utterance. This is still quite consistent with Bakhtin's observation that "there can be no such thing as an absolutely neutral utterance" (1986, p. 84), but it allows one to deal with a wider set of issues than were of interest to Bakhtin. For example, it allows one to deal with issues such as the "referential perspective" (Wertsch, 1980, 1985b), which plays such an important role in the dynamics of interpsychological functioning in the zone of proximal development.

Turning to the utterance's relation to other utterances, several additional issues emerge. It is in connection with this aspect of speech genres that Bakhtin will make his most important contribution to sociocultural approaches to mind, both because it is tied to his mostly highly developed construct—dialogicality—and because semiotic approaches in the social sciences are weakest on this point. What is striking in this connection is that some insightful observations are available on this issue, but to date we have not been able to deal with them within a systematic social scientific account. Two such observations can serve as illustrations.

It has often been observed that certain complexities of adult-child communication in testing and instructional settings arise because children are asked questions to which the interlocutor obviously has the answer. This contrasts with many forms of peer interaction and with certain adult questions (Did you have milk at lunch today? Does your stomach hurt?) where this is not the case. The difference between these two speech situations is a difference between ways in which an utterance can relate to another utterance, and it probably is closely related to phenomena such as those Damon and Phelps (1987) have recently outlined concerning the intrapsychological correlates of different forms (adult-child versus child-child) of interpsychological functioning. The issue here concerns different ways a speaking subject, or voice, may conceptualize another speaker (for instance, as omniscient or not). In Bakhtin's view, this involves a difference in speech genres, because "each speech genre in each area of speech communication has its own typical conception of the addressee, and this defines it as a genre" (1986, p. 94).

As a second example of this phenomenon, consider some recent findings of Ochs (1984). Through careful ethnographic analysis of speaking patterns among Samoans, she has shown that their pattern of responding to requests for clarification (for example, What?) differs markedly from that of American English speakers in assumptions about who can and should make clarifications. Ochs has been able to document associated differences in folk theories' ontological assumptions about where information resides and who has the ability and the right to clarify it. Whereas Americans tend to assume that clarification is incumbent on the speaker because he or she "has" the original intention or meaning, Samoans' patterns of clarification reflect and create the assumption that meaning does not reside in individuals, including the speaker.

When considered from the perspective of Bakhtin's account of social speech types, especially speech genres, findings such as these suggest a much broader set of issues to incorporate into an analysis of semiotic mediation in a sociocultural approach to mind. Not only do they suggest important new aspects of interpsychological functioning to take into account when trying to understand the genesis of intrapsychological processes; they also may provide key insights into the ways in which institutional and cultural contexts reflect and are created by semiotic practices.

Tomorrow

The general picture suggested by the Bakhtinian extension of Vygotsky's ideas outlined here is one in which it is necessary to invoke the notions of voice, dialogicality, and social speech type to explicate the theme of semiotic mediation. Ultimately, we must also confront the issue of how and why certain voices and social speech types come to be "privileged" (Wertsch, 1987a) or to dominate others in various spheres of discourse. This will take us into other areas Bakhtin (1981) examined under the headings of "authoritative" and "internally persuasive" discourse.

When thinking about the path that developmental psychology should pursue in order to deal with these matters, it is essential to recognize that this discipline alone cannot explicate the forces that give rise to voices and result in the privileging of some voices over others. In order to deal with the issues at hand, we are going to have to be more serious about collaborating with those who study history, culture, and social organization. This will call for at least some members of the discipline to become much more familiar with the ideas and methods of other areas of scholarly inquiry. For example, more of us will need to utilize, and in some cases conduct, ethnographic analyses of cultural and institutional settings.

This by no means suggests, however, that the findings of developmental psychology can be reduced to the findings of other disciplines. There remains a real, unique object of study for the discipline. In particular, the processes whereby individuals master voices and patterns of privileging are prime candidates for specialized study by developmental psychologists interested in a sociocultural approach to mind. The products of such research will be essential to understanding the ways in which institutional and cultural forces shape individuals and how individuals might come to control and shape these forces, thereby developing the capacity for emancipating themselves from unwanted effects.

Finally, in accordance with the comments of Bellah and others (1986) on the impossibility of a value-free social science, it will become important for developmental psychologists to recognize and examine the voices we use in carrying out our studies. What assumptions about "good persons and a good society" shape our voices? Do the social speech types we use preclude our voices from coming into contact with those of scholars from other disciplines and with those of the general public? Do the social speech types we use implicitly reflect perspectives to which we would object if they were made explicit to us? These are the kinds of questions that must be addressed in a public philosophy of social science, and they are the kinds of questions that developmental psychologists must be ready to answer if we hope to avoid becoming an overspecialized, arcane, and eventually irrelevant field of study.

References

Bakhtin, M. M. *The Dialogic Imagination: Four Essays by M. M. Bakhtin.* (M. Holquist, ed. C. Emerson and M. Holquist, trans.) Austin: University of Texas Press, 1981.

Bakhtin, M. M. *Problems of Dostoevsky's Poetics.* (C. Emerson, trans.) Minneapolis: University of Minnesota Press, 1984.

Bakhtin, M. M. *Speech Genres and Other Late Essays.* (C. Emerson and M. Holquist, eds. V. McGee, trans.) Austin: University of Texas Press, 1986.

Bellah, R. N., and others. *Habits of the Heart: Individualism and Commitment in American Life.* New York: Harper & Row, 1986.

Damon, W., and Phelps, E. "Peer Collaboration as a Context for Cognitive Growth." Paper presented at Tel-Aviv annual workshop in human development: "Culture, Schooling, and Psychological Development." Tel-Aviv University, June 1987.

Haskell, T. L. *The Emergence of Professional Social Science: The American Social Science Association and the Nineteenth-Century Crisis in Authority.* Urbana: University of Illinois Press, 1977.

Hickmann, M. "The Implications of Discourse Skills in Vygotsky's Developmental Theory." In J. V. Wertsch (ed.), *Culture, Communication, and Cognition: Vygotskian Perspectives.* New York: Cambridge University Press, 1985.

Holquist, M. "The Politics of Representation." In S. Greenblatt (ed.), *Allegory in Representation: Selected Papers from the English Institute.* Baltimore, Md.: Johns Hopkins University Press, 1981.

Holquist, M., and Emerson, C. "Glossary." In M. M. Bakhtin, *The Dialogic Imagination: Four Essays by M. M. Bakhtin.* (M. Holquist, ed. C. Emerson and M. Holquist, trans.) Austin: University of Texas Press, 1981.

Ivanov, V. V. "Afterword." In L. S. Vygotsky, *The Psychology of Art.* (Scripta Technica, Inc., trans.) Cambridge, Mass.: MIT Press, 1971.

Janet, P. "La pensée intérieure et ses troubles" [Internal thought and its disturbances]. Course given at the College de France, 1926-27.

Karmiloff-Smith, A. *A Functional Approach to Child Language: A Study of Determiners and Reference.* Cambridge, England: Cambridge University Press, 1979.

Lee, B. "The Intellectual Origins of Vygotsky's Semiotic Analysis." In J. V. Wertsch (ed.), *Culture, Communication, and Cognition: Vygotskian Perspectives.* New York: Cambridge University Press, 1985.

Leont'ev, A. N. "Preface." In L. S. Vygotsky, *The Psychology of Art.* (Scripta Technica, Inc., trans.) Cambridge, Mass.: MIT Press, 1971.

Minick, N. "Introduction." In L. S. Vygotsky, *Thinking and Speech.* (N. Minick, trans.) New York: Plenum, 1987.

Ochs, E. "Clarification and Culture." In D. Schiffrin (ed.), *The Georgetown Roundtable.* Washington, D.C.: Georgetown University Press, 1984.

Olson, D. R. "From Utterance to Text: The Bias of Language in Speech and Writing." *Harvard Educational Review,* 1977, *47,* 257-281.

Olson, D. R., and Bruner, J. S. "Learning Through Experience and Learning Through Media." In D. R. Olson (ed.), *Media and Symbols: The Forms of Expression, Communication, and Education.* Chicago: National Society for the Study of Education, 1974.

Rogoff, B., and Wertsch, J. V. (eds.). *Children's Learning in the "Zone of Proximal Development."* New Directions for Child Development, no. 23. San Francisco: Jossey-Bass, 1984.

Scribner, S. "Modes of Thinking and Ways of Speaking: Culture and Logic Reconsidered." In P. N. Johnson-Laird and P. C. Wason (eds.), *Thinking: Readings in Cognitive Science.* New York: Cambridge University Press, 1977.

Scribner, S., and Cole, M. *The Psychological Consequences of Literacy.* Cambridge, Mass.: Harvard University Press, 1981.

Smirnov, A. N. *Razvitie i sovremennoe sostoyanie psikhologicheskoi nauki v SSSR* [The development and present status of psychology in the U.S.S.R.]. Moscow: Izdatel'stvo Pedagogika, 1975.

Uspensky, B. *A Poetics of Composition.* Berkeley: University of California Press, 1973.

Voloshinov, V. N. *Marxism and the Philosophy of Language.* (L. Matejka and I. R. Titunik, trans.) New York: Seminar Press, 1973.

Vygotsky, L. S. *Thought and Language.* Cambridge, Mass.: MIT Press, 1962. (Originally published 1934.)

Vygotsky, L. S. *The Psychology of Art.* (Scripta Technica, Inc., trans.) Cambridge, Mass.: MIT Press, 1971.

Vygotsky, L. S. *Mind in Society: The Development of Higher Psychological Processes.* (M. Cole, V. John-Steiner, S. Scribner, and E. Souberman, eds.) Cambridge, Mass.: Harvard University Press, 1978.

Vygotsky, L. S. "The Genesis of Higher Mental Functions." In J. V. Wertsch (ed.), *The Concept of Activity in Soviet Psychology.* Armonk, N.Y.: M. E. Sharpe, 1981.

Vygotsky, L. S. *Thinking and Speech.* (N. Minick, trans.) New York: Plenum, 1987.

Vygotsky, L. S., and Luria, A. R. *Etyudy po istorii povedeniya: Obez'yana, primitiv, rebenok* [Essays in the history of behavior: Ape, primitive, child]. Moscow and Leningrad: Gosudarstvennoe Izdatel'stvo, 1930.

Wertsch, J. V. "Semiotic Mechanisms in Joint Cognitive Activity." Paper presented at the Joint U.S.-U.S.S.R. Conference on the Theory of Activity, Institute of Psychology, U.S.S.R. Academy of Sciences, Moscow, 1980.

Wertsch, J. V. "Introduction." In J. V. Wertsch (ed.), *Culture, Communication, and Cognition: Vygotskian Perspectives.* New York: Cambridge University Press, 1985a.

Wertsch, J. V. *Vygotsky and the Social Formation of Mind.* Cambridge, Mass.: Harvard University Press, 1985b.

Wertsch, J. V. "Modes of Discourse in the Nuclear Arms Debate." *Current Research on Peace and Violence,* 1987a, *2,* 33–41.

Wertsch, J. V. "Sociocultural Setting and the Zone of Proximal Development: The Problem of Text-Based Realities." Paper presented at the Tel-Aviv annual workshop in human develop-

ment: "Culture, Schooling, and Psychological Development."
Tel-Aviv University, June 1987b.

Wertsch, J. V., and Minick, N. "Negotiating Sense in the Zone of
Proximal Development." Paper presented at the "Conference on
Thinking and Problem Solving in the Developmental Process:
International Perspectives." Rutgers University, 1987.

Wertsch, J. V., and Youniss, J. "Contextualizing the Investigator:
The Case of Developmental Psychology." *Human Development,*
1987, *30,* 18-31.

Zinchenko, V. P. "Vygotsky's Ideas About Units for the Analysis of
Mind." In J. V. Wertsch (ed.), *Culture, Communication, and
Cognition: Vygotskian Perspectives.* New York: Cambridge
University Press, 1985.

Chapter 2

Child Development
Within the Family Context

Harold D. Grotevant

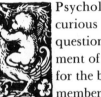Psychologists, novelists, historians, geneticists, and curious laypersons share an interest in several intriguing questions: In what ways do families affect the development of children who grow up in them? What accounts for the basic similarities that are typically shared among members of the same family? Yet what causes two children who grow up in the same family to be so different? The answers to these seemingly straightforward questions are anything but simple. Social scientists have struggled with these issues for many years, but some important changes that have been made in the last decade in ways of understanding the family have opened the door for significant new advances. The purpose of this chapter is to provide a brief overview of recent conceptual advances in our understanding of the family as a context for development and to discuss several current research trends that promise to yield important new information.

In the 1950s and 1960s, the predominant approach to the study of family socialization was to examine parents' effects on their children. Hartup (1978) has referred to this view as the "social mold" approach, because it assumes that the primary direction in socialization is through parents' shaping of their children's behavior. Sears (1951) urged psychologists to abandon "monadic"

Note: I gratefully acknowledge the helpful comments of colleagues Ted Huston and Deborah Jacobvitz on an earlier version of this chapter.

views of socialization in favor of dyadic, interactive ones, but the impact of his message was not fully realized until almost twenty years later. Bell's (1968) seminal reconceptualization of the direction of effects in socialization set the stage for a major shift in thinking about family influences. During the 1970s, developmental research began to acknowledge bidirectionality of effects and to study ways in which children elicit behavior from their parents (Bell and Harper, 1977; Lewis and Rosenblum, 1974). Further consideration of indirect effects in development (for example, how the father's presence in a room might alter mother-infant interaction: Clarke-Stewart, 1978) led to a broader conceptualization of the child embedded within a family system (see, for example, Belsky, 1981). This more inclusive view was also stimulated by the need to understand the increasing diversity of family forms and structures in contemporary society and the new ways in which family members participated in the larger social and economic system.

Although the view of the family as an interactive system is intuitively appealing and comes closer to acknowledging the complexities of family functioning than do unidirectional models, the conceptual and methodological problems associated with the adoption of systems models are significant. As the field attempts to make this shift, I fully concur with Maccoby and Martin (1983, p. 4) that "choosing the most meaningful level of analysis remains one of the most challenging problems in the studies of parent-child interaction." Several different ways of distinguishing among levels of analysis have been proposed. Maccoby and Martin (1983) contrasted molar and molecular approaches with studies of family interaction. For example, one researcher might assess members' evaluations of "family cohesion," whereas another might count frequencies of discourse units in which a husband expresses acknowledgment to his wife. Using a somewhat different contrast, Scarr (1985) has compared proximal (behavioral) and distal (sociocultural or background) variables. Perhaps the most comprehensive taxonomy of levels of analysis has been offered by Bronfenbrenner (1979, 1986) in his discussion of the four levels of settings in which development takes place: the microsystem (the experiences of the individual in the settings in which he or she interacts directly), the mesosystem (interrelations among settings in which the individual interacts), the exosystem (effects of settings in which the individual does not directly participate), and the macrosystem (effects at the level of the culture, ideology, and belief system).

Child Development Within the Family: Four Levels of Analysis

For purposes of this chapter, I will be discussing the family's role in child development at four levels of analysis: the individual, dyadic relationships within the family, the whole family system, and the interface of the family and its contexts. These levels were chosen in order to highlight the relational contexts of development (see, for example, Grotevant and Cooper, 1986; Hartup and Rubin, 1986; Kelley and others, 1983; Sroufe and Fleeson, 1986) rather than the physical contexts. Following a brief presentation of the four levels of analysis, I will explore how these relational/contextual issues can be considered developmentally. The chapter will conclude with a brief discussion of research trends focused on the developing child within the family context.

Individual Contributions. Much of the research undertaken at this level of analysis has focused on the effects of individual characteristics of children, such as temperament or physical attractiveness, on parent-child relations. For example, temperament is commonly viewed as an aspect of personality. However, in contrast to a static trait characterization, contemporary scholars acknowledge that temperament is shaped both by biology and by family experience. Furthermore, temperament has an impact on interactions in which the child is involved, which, in turn, affect subsequent development (Goldsmith and others, 1987). Langlois and Casey (1984) have described the effects of infant physical attractiveness on maternal behavior. From the parents' side, researchers have debated the degree to which attitudes about child rearing are reflected in parents' behavior toward their children. Becker and Krug (1965) concluded that scores on the Parental Attitude Research Instrument had "some small relations" with assessments of parental behavior. However, Broussard and Hartner (1971) and Walker (1980) found relations between mothers' attitudes and their behavior toward their newborns. The "new look" in parenting research has moved beyond a singular focus on global child-rearing attitudes to examine how parents' attributions about what causes their children's behavior mediate cognitive and affective responses to their children (Dix and Grusec, 1985). Clearly, individual characteristics of both children and parents contribute to the family's context. However, these individual qualities are embedded within human relationships, thus necessitating conceptualization and investigation at a higher level of analysis as well.

Dyadic Relationships. Research at this level may address two questions: What are the relationships like in which the child participates, and what are the relationships like that the child observes? Obviously, children participate in relationships with both parents and siblings. A large body of socialization research is devoted to parent-child relationships (for reviews, see Maccoby and Martin, 1983, and Martin, 1975), and a growing literature addresses sibling relationships (Dunn, 1983) and only children (Falbo, 1984).

Consideration of the child's participation in dyadic relationships within the family introduces the question of whether problems in one relationship can be compensated for in another, either within or outside the family. Can the child's exposure to intense conflict in his or her parents' marriage be buffered by a supportive and nurturing relationship with another family member or by a relationship in the extended family? Rutter (1979), for example, cited evidence that a good relationship with one parent can protect children from the negative consequences of being brought up in a conflict-ridden household.

The second question acknowledges that children may be affected by relationships in which they are not the focal participants and settings in which they themselves are not involved. The most extensive discussion of the effects of family relationships in which the child is not the focal member is found in the literature on family therapy (see, for example, Haley, 1980; S. Minuchin, 1974; P. Minuchin, 1985). Family therapists have been particularly influential in demonstrating the impact of marital pathology on the development of children, especially on adolescents who are facing the task of individuating from the family (Haley, 1980). In a complementary study that examined the flip side of this issue, Kleiman (1981) demonstrated a link between health in the marital relationship of an adolescent's parents and positive psychological adjustment in the adolescent. The effects of settings in which the child does not directly participate were recently reviewed in Bronfenbrenner's (1986) discussion of exosystem models, studies addressing effects of the parents' workplace, the parents' social networks, and the community.

The Family System. Even though many of the transactions of daily family life are accomplished within dyadic relationships, there is also a sense in which the whole family has a distinctive character that affects the members within it and their relations with the outside world. David Reiss (1981, 1982) has developed the concept of the family paradigm, which refers to the family's shared assumptions about the world in which it lives. His work suggests that family health is related to the conservation of the family's paradigm and that disorganization occurs when the paradigm falls apart. Family systems therapists have also discussed the impact of the family's structure and interactive processes on individual development (Steinglass, 1987).

In addition, family therapists have called attention to a neglected area for consideration: intergenerational relations within the family and their impact on individual development. The importance of this topic has especially been registered in the study of adolescent development by researchers, theorists, and clinicians, who have noted that the adolescent's ability to individuate from the family is affected not only by relationships with his or her parents but also by his or her middle-aged parents' relationships with their aging parents (Carter and McGoldrick, 1980). Adolescence is an unusually dynamic phase in the family life cycle in that three generations may be undergoing major life transitions simultaneously. The adolescent is dealing with issues of identity formation and major transformations in relationships with parents and peers (Grotevant and Cooper, 1986). Middle-aged parents may be reconsidering life choices concerning relationships and/or careers (Levinson, 1986). The adolescent's grandparents may be dealing with the transition to retirement, health issues, and possibly major changes in their marriage due to the death of a spouse (Carter and McGoldrick, 1980). A systems perspective suggests that the adolescent's ability to deal with his or her own developmental tasks depends, at least in part, on how developmental issues in the other relationships within the family are being handled.

Interface of the Family and Its Contexts. Exploration of the relation of the developing family to its changing contexts evokes consideration of two important questions. First, what are the demands and the supports in the family's environment that might affect the functioning of the family unit or its members? Much of the "stress and coping" literature (for example, McCubbin and Boss, 1980) focuses on specific challenges that arise in normative transitions, such as the birth of a first child, or nonnormative family transitions, such as divorce or remarriage.

Second, what are the specific processes by which individuals and contexts interface? Three approaches to this question have recently received significant research attention. First, a number of researchers have been interested in children's social networks— those people outside the child's immediate family who are involved with affective or material interactions with the family. Social network research typically focuses on the impact of such qualities as network size, interconnectedness, and diversity on developmental outcomes (Cochran and Brassard, 1979). In a provocative study, Kitchens (1984) found a relation between sociometric status of preschool children and characteristics of their families' social networks. For example, "popular" children had parents who tended to include them in interactions with family social network members, whereas "rejected" children had more adult-oriented and less responsive social networks. Although these results are open to differing interpretations, the link between child development and social networks is worth pursuing further.

Second, a growing number of scholars have investigated the interface between work and family environments. As an increasing number of American husbands and wives both participate in the workplace, it has become critically important to understand how their work activities affect the functioning of their families and the individuals within them. Current research is addressing the effects of "spillover" from work to family, typically of negative affect associated with stress or anxiety (see, for example, Billings and Moos, 1982), and the reciprocal spillover from family to work, often through the effects of child-care needs on employee turnover and morale (see, for example, Bronfenbrenner and Crouter, 1982). In a more process-oriented approach to the work-family interface, Crouter, Perry-Jenkins, Huston, and McHale (1987) examined how the work roles of parents (dual-earner versus single-earner families) create different family contexts in which the parental roles are related to both marital conflict and love.

A third area of interest has concerned the impact of the sociopolitical context on children's development. Such effects were most strongly investigated during the 1960s, but the works of Baumrind (1987) and sociologists such as Bellah and others (1986) have emphasized the need to continue considering this sphere of influence in order to understand the development of values in children and adolescents.

Awareness of these four different levels of analysis poses challenges for family scholars. How is one to choose an appropriate level of analysis? Must all levels be studied? How is one to face the formidable task of integrating knowledge gained from studies targeted at different levels? As Cowan (1987) has noted, family functioning is likely a product of events occurring in individual, dyadic, whole family, and outside-the-family domains. Cowan's research on the adaptation to parenthood (see Cowan and Cowan, 1987) has shown that "each level of the family system adds unique explanatory power to the understanding of individual, couple, and family adaptation" (Cowan, 1987, p. 49). Family research will be enhanced when more models for effective integration across levels become available.

A Developmental Perspective

The early sociological work on family development (Duvall, 1957) emphasized the family's progression through a series of stages, typically marked by events involving the addition (usually through birth) or departure (through leaving home or death) of family members. Although this approach rightfully contributed to the view that the family as a unit develops and changes, its emphasis on normative family structures and its lack of attention to process have made other conceptualizations of development more useful for research.

Two complementary but compatible approaches characterize current developmental family work. On the one hand, researchers are searching for continuity and coherence in development over time. One of the strongest representatives of this type of work concerns the consequences of mother-infant attachment for later development of the child. An impressive body of work whose conclusions nicely converge suggests, for example, that security of attachment in infancy is predictive of the child's later effectiveness in problem solving (Matas, Arend, and Sroufe, 1978), in peer relations (Lieberman, 1977), and in independent exploration of spatial environments (Hazen and Durrett, 1982).

On the other hand, there is a great deal of current interest in studying family transitions—points in the family's history at which important shifts take place. Among the transitions currently being studied are the child's transition into early adolescence (Hauser and others, 1985); the adolescent's "leaving home" transition (Grotevant and Cooper, 1986); and the structural changes in the family associated with such transitions as marriage (Huston, McHale, and Crouter, 1986), first-time parenthood (Cowan and Cowan, 1987), adoption (Grotevant and McRoy, forthcoming), divorce (Hetherington and Camara, 1984), and remarriage (Hetherington, 1987).

Earlier work on family transitions was primarily concerned with describing differences in families across time or comparing families with different structures. More current work is focused on process: What are the processes that occur as families experience transitions? How do family processes differ before and after transitions? Shifts in parent-child relations occur in the direction of increasing reciprocity involving coregulation as the child matures (Youniss, 1980). Understanding how this shift occurs and why some families have difficulty with it is currently of great interest to developmentalists. In current research on adolescent development, attention is being focused on the dynamic tension in families between individuality (expression of one's sense of self) and connectedness (expressions of one's relating to others) and how the interplay between them changes over time (Grotevant and Cooper, 1986; Cooper and others, 1987).

Trends in Family Research

As we think ahead to the nature of child development tomorrow, several research trends appear to hold unusual promise. First, research about the family contexts of child development requires improved integration of biological and social-psychological perspectives. Until very recently, biological perspectives on the family (for example, Scarr and Kidd, 1983; Strayer, 1984) have largely developed outside the mainstream of family research. The important contributions of behavior geneticists and ethologists have had limited impact on developmentalists operating within social learning and cognitive-developmental paradigms.

Behavior genetic research in the 1970s devoted so much attention to apportioning variance into environmental and genetic bins that family processes were largely ignored. However, as Scarr (1987) recently pointed out, the biological perspective has slowly but surely found its way into mainstream developmental psychology. The recent work on nonshared family environments (Rowe and Plomin, 1981) has pointed to ways in which the perspectives of geneticists and socialization researchers can complement one another. For example, both genetic (Rowe and Plomin, 1981) and socialization (Dunn, 1983) perspectives now acknowledge the importance of studying parents' relationships with multiple children in the family rather than relying solely on parental relations with one target child per family. This work may finally yield a satisfactory answer to the paradoxical question raised in the introduction concerning how siblings who grow up in the same family are both similar and different.

A second important trend in this area concerns the emergence of new subdisciplines concerned with family studies within both sociology and psychology. During the past decade, sociologists have attempted to define a new discipline that would cross traditional academic boundaries (Burr and Leigh, 1983). Although the viability of "famology" is yet to be established, the dialogue that has begun among family scholars from varied backgrounds is likely to have a major impact on family theory and research. Within psychology, a significant number of family systems-oriented therapists and family researchers also have experienced frustration with traditional paradigms. Their efforts have contributed to a new field—"family psychology" (L'Abate, 1985)—whose impact is too recent to be assessed fairly. In attempting to define family psychology, Kaye (1985, p. 39) stated that "a psychology of the family means a science whose unit of study is no longer the individual mind/body/person but a developing social system of physically separate people." If this definition is to be taken seriously, a "new look" in both theory and research will be required. Despite the newness of this field, two indicators of the interest in it include its recent elevation to the status of a division within the American Psychological Association and the launching of the *Journal of Family Psychology* (Liddle, 1987).

A third trend, in line with the shifting disciplinary boundaries discussed above, involves the vigorous development of academic units and programs around the United States concerned with development in context. Although these programs come with various labels (such as child development and family relationships, human development and family studies, family and human development, human ecology, and home economics, to name a few), their common denominator is acknowledgment of the interface between developing individuals and their changing contexts. Such programs share a commitment to formulating more effective conceptualizations of these relations and to developing new research techniques that are appropriate for studying relationships and families.

A fourth new perspective that has emerged from an integration of social, developmental, and clinical psychology is the "close relationships" model (Kelley and others, 1983). The authors' goal has been to provide a conceptual schema that could be used by scholars to analyze ongoing relationships and to highlight the importance of interpersonal relationships in linking the individual to larger groups, such as the family. The model's conceptualization is already proving to be a valuable tool for researchers interested in child development within family and peer contexts (Losoff, 1988).

A final trend involves the increasing interest in investigating the "links" between the family system and other systems outside the family. There is a great deal of current research activity in two areas, and several other possibilities may be envisioned. In one of these areas, the links between the child's family and peer relations are being studied. For example, recent work suggests that adolescents develop interactional skills and attitudes within the family and carry these into other relationships and arenas outside the family (Cooper, Grotevant, and Ayers-Lopez, forthcoming). A second area of research interest concerns the links between family relations and the work environment (Hoffman, 1984). General models of parenting are now appropriately adding the parents' work environment as an element that must be considered (for example, Belsky and Vondra, 1985).

Tomorrow

Scholars wishing to understand child development within the family context have several challenges ahead. The first involves a greater understanding of the role of biology in regulating individual development. Progress in understanding the role of biology has begun, especially in the areas of puberty, hormones, and depression. However, much more research on the biological underpinnings of normal behavior remains to be undertaken. The second challenge involves conceptualizing and understanding how development is affected by specific contexts and relationships and how development, in turn, modifies the contexts and relationships in which subsequent development takes place. This is an area in which substantial progress is currently being made. The third challenge involves understanding the interdependencies among the various relationships in which the child is directly or indirectly involved. We currently know very little about this topic.

In order to accomplish these goals, the study of the family will need to become more interdisciplinary. Biologists, sociologists, developmentalists, and clinicians will need to become more comfortable crossing traditional disciplinary boundaries. One of the most promising avenues for collaboration should involve family researchers and clinicians. Clinicians often have the experience of working with complex relationship issues and seeing firsthand the interdependencies among family relationships; however, they often lack the interest and training in research to translate their insights into empirically verifiable terms. Many researchers have a stronger theoretical and empirical bent but often have an oversimplified view of human relationships. Effective collaboration between these two professional worlds could contribute new and important insights.

Methodological tools in the family field will also need updating. Assessment of family functioning at different levels of analysis and theoretically guided integration of the findings will be essential, but the development of appropriate observational and self-report techniques necessarily lags behind the need for them. (For further discussion of family research methodology, see Larzelere and Klein, 1986; for further discussion of family assessment techniques, see Grotevant and Carlson, forthcoming.)

The past ten years have seen a strong and renewed interest in understanding the family as a context for child development. What makes this burst of interest distinctive is that advances in conceptualization and methodology have both contributed to this vital research area. Research journals that traditionally have focused on individual development now acknowledge the importance of the contexts of development; new subdisciplines, such as family psychology and behavior genetics, are making contributions to the mainstream; and academic units dealing with the interface between individual development and the contexts in which development occurs are enjoying vigorous activity. It is anticipated that the next decade will bring substantive contributions to our understanding of the family as a context for development.

References

Baumrind, D. "Authoritative Parenting in the Adolescent Transition." Paper presented at the Family Research Consortium Second Annual Summer Institute, Santa Fe, N.Mex., June 1987.

Becker, W. C., and Krug, R. S. "The Parent Attitude Research Instrument—A Research Review." *Child Development*, 1965, *36*, 329–361.

Bell, R. Q. "A Reinterpretation of the Direction of Effects in Studies of Socialization." *Psychological Review*, 1968, *75*, 81–95.

Bell, R. Q., and Harper, L. V. *Child Effects on Adults*. Hillsdale, N.J.: Erlbaum, 1977.

Bellah, R. N., and others. *Habits of the Heart: Individualism and Commitment in American Life.* New York: Harper & Row, 1986.

Belsky, J. "Early Human Experience: A Family Perspective." *Developmental Psychology,* 1981, *17,* 3-23.

Belsky, J., and Vondra, J. "Characteristics, Consequences, and Determinants of Parenting." In L. L'Abate (ed.), *Handbook of Family Psychology and Therapy.* Vol. 1. Homewood, Ill.: Dorsey Press, 1985.

Billings, A., and Moos, R. "Work Stress and the Stress-Buffering Role of Work and Family Resources." *Journal of Occupational Behavior,* 1982, *3,* 215-232.

Bronfenbrenner, U. *The Ecology of Human Development: Experiments by Nature and Design.* Cambridge, Mass.: Harvard University Press, 1979.

Bronfenbrenner, U. "Ecology of the Family as a Context for Human Development: Research Perspectives." *Developmental Psychology,* 1986, *22,* 723-742.

Bronfenbrenner, U., and Crouter, A. "Work and Family Through Time and Space." In S. B. Kamerman and C. D. Hayes (eds.), *Families That Work: Children in a Changing World.* Washington, D.C.: National Academy Press, 1982.

Broussard, E. R., and Hartner, M. S. "Further Considerations Regarding Maternal Perception of the First Born." In J. Hellmuth (ed.), *Exceptional Infant: Studies in Abnormalities.* Vol. 2. New York: Brunner/Mazel, 1971.

Burr, W., and Leigh, G. K. "Famology: A New Discipline." *Journal of Marriage and the Family,* 1983, *45* (3), 467-481.

Carter, E. A., and McGoldrick, M. *The Family Life Cycle: A Framework for Family Therapy.* New York: Gardner Press, 1980.

Clarke-Stewart, K. A. "And Daddy Makes Three: The Father's Impact on Mother and Young Child." *Child Development,* 1978, *49* (2), 466-478.

Cochran, M. M., and Brassard, J. A. "Child Development and Personal Social Networks." *Child Development,* 1979, *50,* 601-616.

Cooper, C. R., and others. "Developmental Patterns in Individuation: Family Interaction in Early and Late Adolescence." Paper presented at the Family Research Consortium Second Annual Summer Institute, Santa Fe, N.Mex., June 1987.

Cooper, C. R., Grotevant, H. D., and Ayers-Lopez, S. "Links Between Patterns of Negotiation in Adolescents' Family and Peer Interaction," forthcoming.

Cowan, C. P., and Cowan, P. A. "Becoming a Family: Implications for Marital Quality and Child Development." Paper presented at the Family Research Consortium Second Annual Summer Institute, Santa Fe, N.Mex., June 1987.

Cowan, P. A. "The Need for Theoretical and Methodological Integrations in Family Research." *Journal of Family Psychology,* 1987, *1,* 48-50.

Crouter, A. C., Perry-Jenkins, M., Huston, T. L., and McHale, S. M. "Processes Underlying Father Involvement in Dual-Earner and Single-Earner Families." *Developmental Psychology,* 1987, *23,* 431-440.

Dix, T. H., and Grusec, J. E. "Parent Attribution Processes in the Socialization of Children." In I. Sigel (ed.), *Parental Belief Systems: Their Psychological Consequences for Children.* Hillsdale, N.J.: Erlbaum, 1985.

Dunn, J. "Sibling Relationships in Early Childhood." *Child Development,* 1983, *54* (4), 787-811.

Duvall, E. M. *Family Development.* Philadelphia: Lippincott, 1957.

Falbo, T. "Only Children: A Review." In T. Falbo (ed.), *The Single Child Family.* New York: Guilford Press, 1984.

Goldsmith, H. H., and others. "Roundtable: What Is Temperament? Four Approaches." *Child Development,* 1987, *58* (2), 505-529.

Grotevant, H. D., and Carlson, C. I. *Family Assessment: A Guide to Methods and Measures.* New York: Guilford Press, forthcoming.

Grotevant, H. D., and Cooper, C. R. "Individuation in Family Relationships: A Perspective on Individual Differences in the Development of Identity and Role-Taking Skill in Adolescence." *Human Development,* 1986, *29,* 82-100.

Grotevant, H. D., and McRoy, R. G. "Adopted Adolescents in Residential Treatment: The Role of the Family." In D. Brodzinsky and M. Schechter (eds.), *The Psychology of Adoption.* New York: Oxford University Press, forthcoming.

Haley, J. *Leaving Home: The Therapy of Disturbed Young People.* New York: McGraw-Hill, 1980.

Hartup, W. W. "Perspectives on Child and Family Interaction: Past, Present, and Future." In R. M. Lerner and G. B. Spanier (eds.), *Child Influences on Marital and Family Interaction: A Life-Span Perspective.* Orlando, Fla.: Academic Press, 1978.

Hartup, W. W., and Rubin, Z. (eds.). *Relationships and Development.* Hillsdale, N.J.: Erlbaum, 1986.

Hauser, S. T., and others. "Family Contexts of Pubertal Timing." *Journal of Youth and Adolescence,* 1985, *14* (4), 317–337.

Hazen, N., and Durrett, M. E. "Relationship of Security of Attachment to Exploration and Cognitive Mapping Abilities in Two-Year-Olds." *Developmental Psychology,* 1982, *18,* 751–759.

Hetherington, E. M. "Divorce and Remarriage." Paper presented at the Family Research Consortium Second Annual Summer Institute, Santa Fe, N.Mex., June 1987.

Hetherington, E. M., and Camara, K. A. "Families in Transition: The Processes of Dissolution and Reconstitution." In R. D. Parke (ed.), *Review of Child Development Research.* Vol. 7: *The Family.* Chicago: University of Chicago Press, 1984.

Hoffman, L. W. "Work, Family, and the Socialization of the Child." In R. D. Parke (ed.), *Review of Child Development Research.* Vol. 7: *The Family.* Chicago: University of Chicago Press, 1984.

Huston, T. L., McHale, S. M., and Crouter, A. "When the Honeymoon's Over: Changes in the Marriage Relationship over the First Year." In R. Gilmour and S. Duck (eds.), *The Emerging Field of Personal Relationships.* Hillsdale, N.J.: Erlbaum, 1986.

Kaye, K. "Toward a Developmental Psychology of the Family." In L. L'Abate (ed.), *Handbook of Family Psychology and Therapy.* Vol. 1. Homewood, Ill.: Dorsey Press, 1985.

Kelley, H. H., and others. *Close Relationships.* New York: W. H. Freeman, 1983.

Kitchens, E. "Family Social Networks and Their Influence on Social Acceptance in Preschool Children." Unpublished master's thesis, Department of Home Economics, University of Texas, Austin, 1984.

Kleiman, J. J. "Optimal and Normal Family Functioning." *American Journal of Family Therapy*, 1981, *9*, 37-44.

L'Abate, L. (ed.). *Handbook of Family Psychology and Therapy.* Homewood, Ill.: Dorsey Press, 1985.

Langlois, J. H., and Casey, R. J. "Baby Beautiful: The Relationship Between Infant Physical Attractiveness and Maternal Behavior." Paper presented at the fourth biennial International Conference on Infant Studies, New York, April 1984.

Larzelere, R. E., and Klein, D. M. "Methodology." In M. B. Sussman and S. K. Steinmetz (eds.), *Handbook of Marriage and the Family.* New York: Plenum, 1986.

Levinson, D. J. "A Conception of Adult Development." *American Psychologist*, 1986, *41* (1), 3-13.

Lewis, M., and Rosenblum, L. A. *Origins of Behavior.* Vol. 1: *The Effect of the Infant on Its Caregiver.* New York: Wiley, 1974.

Liddle, H. A. "Family Psychology: The Journal, the Field." *Journal of Family Psychology*, 1987, *1*, 5-22.

Lieberman, A. F. "Preschoolers' Competence with a Peer: Relations with Attachment and Peer Experience." *Child Development*, 1977, *48*, 1277-1287.

Losoff, M. "Responsiveness in Adolescent Friendships." Unpublished doctoral dissertation in progress, Department of Psychology, University of Texas, Austin, 1988.

Maccoby, E. E., and Martin, J. A. "Socialization in the Context of the Family: Parent-Child Interaction." In P. Mussen (ed.), *Handbook of Child Psychology.* (4th ed.) Vol. 4. New York: Wiley, 1983.

McCubbin, H. I., and Boss, P. G. (eds.). *Family Relations: Special Issue on Family Stress, Coping, and Adaptation*, 1980, *29.*

Martin, B. "Parent-Child Relations." In F. D. Horowitz (ed.), *Review of Child Development Research.* Vol. 4. Chicago: University of Chicago Press, 1975.

Matas, L., Arend, R. A., and Sroufe, L. A. "Continuity of Adaptation in the Second Year: The Relationships Between Quality of Attachment and Later Competence." *Child Development*, 1978, *49*, 547-556.

Minuchin, P. "Families and Individual Development: Provocations from the Field of Family Therapy." *Child Development*, 1985, *56* (2), 289–302.

Minuchin, S. *Families and Family Therapy*. Cambridge, Mass.: Harvard University Press, 1974.

Reiss, D. *The Family's Construction of Reality*. Cambridge, Mass.: Harvard University Press, 1981.

Reiss, D. "The Working Family: A Researcher's View of Health in the Household." *American Journal of Psychiatry*, 1982, *11*, 1412–1420.

Rowe, D., and Plomin, R. "The Importance of Nonshared (E1) Environmental Influences in Behavioral Development." *Developmental Psychology*, 1981, *17* (5), 517–531.

Rutter, M. "Maternal Deprivation, 1972–1978: New Findings, New Concepts, New Approaches." *Child Development*, 1979, *50*, 283–305.

Scarr, S. "Constructing Psychology: Making Facts and Fables for Our Times." *American Psychologist*, 1985, *40*, 499–512.

Scarr, S. "Three Cheers for Behavior Genetics: Winning the War and Losing Our Identity." *Behavior Genetics*, 1987, *17*, 219–228.

Scarr, S., and Kidd, K. K. "Developmental Behavior Genetics." In P. Mussen (ed.), *Handbook of Child Psychology*. (4th ed.) Vol. 2. New York: Wiley, 1983.

Sears, R. R. "A Theoretical Framework for Personality and Social Behavior." *American Psychologist*, 1951, *6*, 476–482.

Sroufe, L. A., and Fleeson, J. "Attachment and the Construction of Relationships." In W. W. Hartup and Z. Rubin (eds.), *Relationships and Development*. Hillsdale, N.J.: Erlbaum, 1986.

Steinglass, P. "A Systems View of Family Interaction and Psychopathology." In T. Jacob (ed.), *Family Interaction and Psychopathology*. New York: Plenum, 1987.

Strayer, F. F. "Biological Approaches to the Study of the Family." In R. D. Parke (ed.), *Review of Child Development Research*. Vol. 7: *The Family*. Chicago: University of Chicago Press, 1984.

Walker, L. O. "Early Parental Attitudes and the Parent-Infant Relationship." In D. B. Sawin, R. C. Hawkins, L. O. Walker, and J. H. Penticuff (eds.), *Exceptional Infant*. Vol. 4: *Psychoso-*

cial Risks in Infant-Environment Transactions. New York: Brunner/Mazel, 1980.

Youniss, J. *Parents and Peers in Social Development: A Sullivan-Piaget Perspective.* Chicago: University of Chicago Press, 1980.

Chapter 3

Cultural Environments
in Child Development

Robert A. LeVine

Cross-cultural diversity in the environmental conditions of infancy and childhood has been documented with increasingly detailed evidence over the past fifty years, but its implications for our understanding of child development remain unclear. Developmental psychology is no longer oblivious to the challenge posed by cross-cultural evidence, but it has not yet engaged in a fundamental reevaluation of its theories and concepts in terms of data emerging from non-Western cultures and from the social history of Euro-American societies. This chapter explores the implications of cross-cultural evidence for conceptions of child development and illustrates the ways in which those conceptions will have to be altered to fit the human species as a whole. The question of whether there will be a "cross-cultural revolution" in thinking about child development is considered in the concluding section.

Attitudes concerning the relevance of anthropological information on environmental diversity to the scientific understanding of child development have fluctuated over the last half century. The early work of Mead (1928, 1930, 1936), Benedict (1938), and John Whiting (1941), among others, convinced many psychologists and psychiatrists that the conditions of early development in non-Western societies differed from those of the West in ways that limited the generalizability of findings from American and European studies to the human species as a whole. Universal generalizations were only possible by the incorporation of cross-cultural evidence into child development research (J.W.M. Whiting, 1954). The evidence could be provided by comparative analysis of the existing ethnographic literature and by new field observations of parent and child behavior in diverse cultural settings.

Cross-cultural research was established within the child development field by John and Beatrice Whiting and their colleagues (Whiting and Child, 1953; B. B. Whiting, 1963; Whiting and Whiting, 1975). Their work, influenced by psychoanalysis as well as by stimulus-response psychology, was an outgrowth of Hullian learning theory, the dominant school of American academic psychology from the mid 1930s to about 1960. Starting with Hull's model of habit formation, the Whitings and their colleagues defined child development in terms of socialization and social learning as the acquisition of responses under the varied stimulus conditions of the world's cultures. This approach was welcomed during the 1950s as relevant to theories of child development—so long as the exotic data had been systematically collected or analyzed according to the methodological canons of psychological research. It appeared that cross-cultural studies were becoming an integral part of the child development research enterprise.

All this changed in the following decade, when the child development field was redefined as a developmental psychology dedicated to basic research on cognitive processes and applied research on practical problems of compensatory education and mental retardation. The environments of children in New Guinea, Africa, and Japan seemed largely irrelevant to these research interests. Like all academic fields, child development research expanded enormously during the 1960s, and few of the students who were trained then or later—now comprising the vast majority of investigators in the field—were exposed to cross-cultural studies in more than a perfunctory fashion. Thus the cross-cultural study of child development underwent a setback during the 1960s in terms of its claims on the attention of child development specialists.

Paradoxically, however, many important cross-cultural studies were carried out during the 1960s (see LeVine, 1970, 1980, for reviews), and comparative research on child rearing and development began to constitute a separate specialty—marginal to psychol-

ogy and anthropology but with its own vitality. During the 1970s
and 1980s, ethologists (Blurton-Jones, 1972; Konner, 1977a, 1977b;
Chisholm, 1983) and linguists (Ochs and Schieffelin, 1984, 1987)
became involved, producing fine-grained descriptions of early
childhood environments in non-Western societies. Non-Western
behavioral scientists, most notably in Japan, began publishing
systematic studies of child development in the environmental
conditions of their own societies (Stevenson, Azuma and Hakuta,
1985). Thus we know more than ever about the diverse conditions in
which human offspring are raised, as research findings have not
only accumulated but deepened in their analytic sophistication
concerning the interaction of the infant and child with culture-
specific environmental patterns.

Why Cross-Cultural Evidence Is Discounted

Given the amount that is known about the diversity of
childhood environments in humans, it is remarkable how rarely
this is taken into account in the mainstream of child development
theory and research. Investigators are not necessarily unaware of the
cross-cultural evidence, but they tend to discount its significance on
the basis of assumptions that constitute crucial issues for the future
integration of such evidence into theories of human development.
The following three assumptions are representative.

The Optimality Assumption. Many child development
specialists implicitly assume that the conditions of infants and
children among educated middle-class Anglo-Americans represent,
or at least approximate, the optimal environment for individual
development in humans—in terms of parental commitment, health
care, nutrition, living space, domestic facilities, physical protection,
emotional warmth, cognitive stimulation, communicative responsiveness, and social stability. Deviations from this pattern are
interpreted not as alternative pathways for normal child development but as conditions of deficit or deprivation, representing less
adequate environments in which to raise children, like those of poor
families in our own society.

Given this assumption, there is little point in investigating
the environments of deprived children in far-flung places when they

are present here at home. Furthermore, if the aim of developmental psychology is to identify the *capacities* of children as they mature, it makes more sense to study them in contexts that favor the emergence of their capacities than in those that might suppress or retard them due to exogenous factors, such as malnutrition. From this point of view, cross-cultural evidence offers nothing new in terms of developmental patterns—only more examples of deficiencies already known from domestic research.

The Assumption of Endogenous Development. Another premise that is widespread among developmental psychologists is that the major trends in human behavioral development are sturdy maturational patterns developing according to a pre-set schedule and sequence, requiring only minimal (or "average expectable") environmental stimulation to facilitate their emergence. Any environment to which humans can adapt, from the Arctic to the tropical rain forest, urban or rural, is presumed to provide the triggers that release the pre-organized capacities of children as they age. Environmental variations within this normal range may affect the ways in which these patterns are expressed but not their eventual emergence or their influence on mature psychic functioning. This is the premise of Chomsky's model of language development, Piaget's conception of cognitive development, and (to a large extent) Bowlby's theory of attachment in emotional development.

From this point of view, cross-cultural evidence is relatively trivial or epiphenomenal because the complex organization that guides behavior is genetically transmitted in all humans and virtually immune in its main developmental course to environmental influence under normal conditions present in any human society. Language development is an example: Every human language has a complex grammar that is mastered by each neurologically intact child who is consistently exposed to it through speech during the first years of life, regardless of whether or not the child is deliberately trained to speak. A child is so prepared to acquire grammar by the maturation of its central nervous system that purposely organized instruction is unnecessary. Anthropologists have not discovered a society in which some children grow up without learning to speak according to the rules of their immediate environments, despite lack of training, social isolation, or other environmental factors in their early lives. Thus cross-cultural variations in the speech environments of infants and children are of little developmental significance. The same reasoning can be applied to cognitive and emotional development.

The Assumption of Methodological Rigor. Many child development specialists believe in restricting their view of what is known to the findings from replicated research studies conducted under controlled conditions approximating those of the laboratory experiment. Thus information on exotic environments—from ethnographic reports on customs of child rearing, ethological or linguistic observations on small samples of children, and large-scale demographic surveys—can be discounted or ignored as not meeting the scientific standards of developmental psychology. At best it can be regarded as indirect and suggestive evidence of variations deserving future investigation. Whatever challenge it might potentially represent to existing developmental theories is not worth taking seriously until its validity and reliability approach those of the standard research literature in the field.

Challenging the Assumptions. Each of these assumptions has been called into question by recent research. The optimality assumption is challenged, for example, by evidence from Japan (Stevenson, Azuma, and Hakuta, 1985; White, 1987), an affluent, urbanized society in which the average quality of child health and education is outstanding in the context of the industrialized world but the goals and strategies of child rearing are demonstrably different. It has proven possible, in other words, to organize an "optimal" environment for children on the basis of alternative cultural premises and with divergent effects on development. Thus cultural difference from Western norms is not equivalent to inferiority.

The assumption of endogenous development is challenged by a pragmatic analysis of language, cognitive, and emotional development, from which it can be seen that the child's acquisition of meanings attached to culture-specific symbols is as important for performance in these domains as is the emergence of innate abilities. Language again provides the clearest example. The universals of language acquisition are necessary but insufficient for a child to communicate effectively in a given environment. A child does not develop through maturation a general competence in human language but must learn to speak a particular language, with its culture-specific representational forms and rules of use. In other words, learning Turkish does not provide competence in Chinese. If language universals are the hardware, the basic circuitry of human communication, then particular languages are the software, the programs that actualize communicative potentials in usable, complex, and flexible forms. Far from being trivial or epiphenomenal, the particular language in a child's first speech environment is, together with its local rules of communication, a powerful influence on psychosocial development (Ochs and Schieffelin, 1987).

Cognitive development and emotional development, similarly based on universally emerging hardware, are also organized by culture-specific programs into individually acquired competencies or dispositions. How a child thinks about and uses an intellectual ability depends on cultural models of competence, while how a child feels about and acts toward persons to whom he or she is attached depends on cultural models of interpersonal relations. Cultural models of competence and interpersonal relations are, like languages, variable across human populations, creating divergent pathways for the behavioral and psychological development of the child.

The assumption of methodological rigor as a basis for discounting cross-cultural evidence is equally dubious. At its most extreme, it represents a failure to integrate results from field studies with laboratory evidence, though such integration has become established in the more advanced life sciences. Darwin's discoveries might well be excluded as scientific knowledge on the basis of this assumption. In any event, more systematically collected data are becoming available from non-Western societies, and Japanese psychologists are now conducting developmental studies in the laboratory (see, for example, Miyake, Chen, and Campos, 1985). It is no longer true that the only systematic and controlled research has been conducted on Euro-American children, and it will be even less true in the future.

Environmental Variations

Taking account of environmental diversity in child development requires a conception of what varies and how environmental

variations influence development. Three kinds of environmental
variations can be roughly distinguished: material, social, and
cultural. *Material* factors include the child's diet, physical sur-
roundings, clothing and holding devices, toys and other personal
possessions, exposure to disease and other environmental risks, and
access to medical care. *Social* variables include the age, gender, kin
relationships, and number of persons in contact with the child and
the organization of interpersonal contacts in situations, relationships, groups, and networks that are stabilized in space and time.
Cultural factors include beliefs, concepts, rules, preferences, and
other ideas in the child's environment and their organization as
codes of communication, bodies of knowledge, standards of competence and enjoyment, and models of virtue and vice. These three
sets of dimensions are rarely distinct in the child's experience but
are useful to distinguish in an analysis of cross-cultural variations.

The variability in these dimensions can be illustrated by
comparing the typical American child-rearing environment with
that of many contemporary agrarian peoples of Africa, Asia, and
Latin America. In terms of material conditions, there is a dramatic
difference in survival risks and economic resources in the two
environments, beginning with an infant mortality rate of less than
10 per thousand live births on the one hand to a rate of about 200
per thousand (in the poorest countries) on the other. Child
mortality rates are equally discrepant, due to less adequate diet,
sanitary facilities, and health care for children in agrarian
communities of the Third World. Babies in those communities are
often breast-fed for one to two years, compared with less than six
months in the United States. In many agrarian societies, children
grow up without living space or possessions assigned to them alone;
they sleep first with their mothers and then with others in their
families, sharing resources rather than acquiring goods identified
with themselves.

Social conditions are even more varied. While many children
in the United States grow up as the only child, or as one of two
children, in a residence with one or two parents, many agrarian
children grow up as one of six or ten children of a mother who
shares domestic facilities with numerous adult kin in a compound
residence; these children have access to daily social contact with

men, women, and children of all ages. The social experience of a child who is part of a multi-age group of siblings from the early years and whose routine interaction includes grandparents and parents' siblings is quite different from the nuclear family experience of a child in a modern low-fertility industrial society. There are many possible ways of characterizing the difference, but it is not implausible to claim that the agrarian experience is a richer one in terms of opportunities for easily acquiring a variety of social skills useful in adulthood.

Variations in the cultural environments of children are no less pronounced for being less visible than their material and social conditions. In many agrarian communities, for example, a traditional code of social hierarchy based on ranking by age and gender governs conduct in the domestic group and shapes the directions of learning during childhood: Children after infancy are expected to be respectful of and obedient to their elders and to acquire skills of interpersonal responsiveness and accommodation as their basic repertoire of adaptive behavior. This contrasts sharply with the American emphasis on personal autonomy as a goal of individual development and the explicit expectation that each child will, from infancy onward, acquire cognitive and verbal skills and self-reliant social behavior as means toward that end. Thus the influence of cultural values on the child's opportunities, models, and incentives for learning sets behavioral development on a culture-specific course.

Culture also constitutes the subjective framework within which material and social conditions are experienced by parent and child. In this perspective, neither parents nor children experience the environment directly, but only as mediated by the local categories, beliefs, and norms that reflect their cultural traditions and guide the design of the man-made environments in which offspring are raised. Domestic economic resources, for example, might appear to be objective conditions determining the diet and living space of children, but close examination usually shows that the child is allocated food and housing according to a cultural model of distribution based on traditional, not necessarily utilitarian, preferences. Thus the best food may be reserved for adults in agrarian families, in accordance with hierarchical values, regardless of its current abundance and potential availability to children. Similarly, the sharing of sleeping and other living spaces by children in such families often reflects a cultural preference, not a housing shortage.

Social relationships are also culturally mediated, in the sense that each culture's conception of what it means to be a mother, father, or sibling endows that relationship with its primary meaning in the experience of the child. An older sibling can be conceptualized as a nurturant caretaker, an authority figure, or a competitor for family resources; cultures provide models that emphasize one or more of these potentials for realization in a child's social life, often with an evident influence on the course of later relationships. The emotional content of routine social interaction, though comprised at base of universal affects, reflects cultural display rules that specify which affects will be displayed, which masked, and which suppressed in situations endowed with social significance. The child must learn this code of conduct in order to adapt to the conventions of the community. Thus the social as well as the material conditions of a child's life in a particular society can only be understood in terms of the culture-specific meanings of those conditions for parents and children alike.

Implications for Child Development

What are the implications for our understanding of child development of cultural variations in child environments among humans? Given the growing evidence that such variations are wide ranging (more than developmental theories have anticipated), multi-dimensional (in terms of material, social, and cultural conditions), and potent (in setting culture-specific priorities for behavioral development from infancy through adolescence), will there be a "cross-cultural revolution" in thinking about child development? In fact, a significant change has already occurred, and the building of developmental models that take account of environmental diversity across cultures will probably become established during this century. The pace of change is gradual rather than revolutionary, limited not only by the entrenched attitudes of psychologists but also by the very small number of child development specialists working outside of North America and Western Europe to produce the kind of evidence that would force reevaluation of fundamental assumptions.

In the remainder of this chapter I will give examples of changes in thinking about child development that are taking place and others that are called for by the growing awareness of cultural variation in the environments of children. My examples fall under three headings: (1) revised claims of universality, (2) microsocial processes, and (3) connections with macrosocial features and processes.

Revised Claims of Universality. As cross-cultural evidence concerning cognitive development, social attachment, and child language becomes available, theorists are becoming more cautious about claiming universality for findings based exclusively on Western samples. In studies of cognitive development, it had become evident more than a decade ago that Piaget's model, though offered as universal, could not be replicated among children of all cultures (Dasen, 1977). The neo-Piagetian formulations that have arisen since then all have a conceptual place for culturally organized variations in the child's experience that affect cognitive competence (Dasen and de Ribaupierre, forthcoming). While little cross-cultural research has been conducted so far within the neo-Piagetian frameworks, the theorists have responded to the earlier findings by building models that anticipate variation rather than uniformity.

Attachment research is at an earlier stage in what might be the same process of revision. Bowlby (1969) and Ainsworth (1977) have claimed that the pattern of infant-mother attachment they identified in Britain and the United States as being the majority condition ("secure attachment") is a human universal (produced by natural selection among the earliest human populations) and a requisite for nonpathological emotional development. But evidence from North Germany (Grossman and others, 1985) and Japan (Miyake, Chen, and Campos, 1985; Takahashi, forthcoming) shows a different distribution of babies among the three attachment categories: in North Germany "avoidant attachment" is the majority condition; in Japan it is "anxious attachment." Are the Germans and Japanese pathological or just different? Or is there something wrong with the measuring instrument—that is, the strange situation, a structured observation in which a mother leaves her child and is soon reunited?

One interpretation is that the North German babies are simply more habituated to being left alone by their mothers, and the Japanese less, than are their American counterparts. This idea is consistent with reports of their respective practices, but it needs to be studied more carefully through naturalistic observations. Meanwhile, the question of whether the problem posed by the cross-cultural findings is methodological or theoretical has not been resolved. It seems likely, however, that more anomalous findings from other cultures will force a retreat on earlier claims to universality.

Certain other proposed universals of social development have not survived comparative examination. Stern (1974, 1977), for example, proposed that the interaction he observed between mothers and their young infants in New York, involving reciprocal play and proto-conversation, represented a biologically designed choreography necessary for normal emotional development. Linguistic anthropologists Ochs and Schieffelin (1984) found no evidence of this kind of interaction in Papua New Guinea and Samoa, casting doubt on its status as a universal feature or requisite for development. In his more recent extended theoretical account of infancy, Stern (1985) has dropped the claim of universality and presents a model that is consistent with cultural variation in early environments.

The role of cross-cultural data in puncturing inflated claims of universality is valuable so long as theorists continue to make such claims—that is, so long as they *presume* patterns of child development to be universal instead of seeking to discover universals through empirical research (Dasen, Berry, and Sartorius, forthcoming). But the more important role for cross-cultural research is in describing the processes by which children and their parents adapt to varying environments, and the outcomes of those adaptations.

Microsocial Processes. Culture can be thought of as setting priorities for behavioral development, guiding parents to select some potentials for realization while neglecting others. Parental goals are translated into creating learning environments for their children so that the latter will acquire the skills deemed valuable in their culture. Those skills will receive environmental support during the learning process, will probably become overlearned and habitual as well as elaborated and refined, and are likely to form an important part of the child's growing representation of self. Parents may not think of themselves as trainers or transmitters of knowledge; they may simply take it for granted that their children will acquire the valued skills in the domestic and community environment. While we know that there are cultural variations in what is learned and in the processes and outcomes of learning, these have not yet been described in sufficient detail to change our understanding of child development as a general human phenomenon.

One example of how psychological understanding of development might be altered by cross-cultural data comes from sub-Saharan Africa. As Gay and Cole (1967) describe childhood learning among the Kpelle of Liberia, and as I observed it among the Gusii of Kenya and other peoples, children grow up without experiencing praise from their parents or others for behaving in a socially approved way or for learning a desirable skill. In contrast with the familiar American sequence of a child's performing well, calling the performance to adult attention, and being praised by the adult, the African child learns through another sequence: observe the approved task (as performed by an older sibling), imitate it spontaneously, and receive corrective feedback only for inadequate performance. There is no expectation of recognition for good performance in learning or for carrying out a task, yet tasks are learned and performed with skill.

This raises basic questions for a view of learning based on response-reinforcement: Where is the external reward in the African sequence, and, if it is entirely missing, what is it that accounts for the acquisition of skills? Furthermore, what are the emotional lessons learned from parents who do not praise or even display recognition of a child's good behavior? And what is it like to grow up without having people around you who provide contingent verbal approval but with siblings and others whose relationships you nevertheless enjoy? As these questions suggest, the context of

learning in an African community differs radically from the context
assumed in formulating extant theories of learning.

Connections with Macrosocial Features and Processes. The
observable environments of children in a given population reflect
the demographic, socioeconomic, and ideological features characteristic of that population. These parameters of reproduction,
subsistence, social organization, and communication vary more
widely at the population level in homo sapiens than in other
species—so much so that population-level behavioral variation
itself must be considered a species-specific characteristic of humans.
The study of population-specific social and cultural patterns as
adaptive strategies and traditional symbol systems in their complexities of organization, functional stability, and historical change is
the province of the institutional social sciences. Rarely are the links
to childhood social experience traced in any detail, although the
Whitings (Whiting and Whiting, 1975) have shown how important
such connections can be in explaining the cultural design of child
environments.

One way of conceptualizing these links is to assume that in
any given society at a particular time there is an optimal parental
investment strategy for bearing and raising children under the local
conditions in which parents can realistically expect to find
themselves. The strategy is optimal in the sense of maximizing the
benefits that parents of that society desire while minimizing the
risks they perceive in obtaining such benefits. Once embedded in
folk models of reproduction and child care, such a strategy becomes
a guide to the allocation of domestic resources, including their own
time and attention, for young parents beginning their reproductive
careers.

In an agrarian society, children are regarded as an economic
benefit because they contribute to domestic production when they
are young and they are expected to continue helping their parents
when they grow up; yet the cost of raising a child when the family
grows its own food and shares living space (and where children do
not attend school) is relatively slight. Thus, on the one hand, the
benefits to parents of bearing many children far outweigh the costs.
Furthermore, since the survival risks for each newborn are great,
parents may need to bear many children if they are to have a few live

to maturity. On the other hand, many other labor-intensive tasks—cultivation, food processing, local defense, and governance—compete with child care for the parents' time. Thus folk models direct mothers to concentrate their caretaking efforts on the earliest part of the child's life (when the mothers are on call for breast-feeding anyway), coping with the risk of infant mortality, and to delegate subsequent caretaking to other children, older women, and others in the domestic group. The focus on survival rather than on social interaction during infancy leads to an emphasis on physical nurturance (feeding, soothing) in infant care practices, a low-intensity pattern that leaves mothers relatively free to attend to other tasks in the subsistence economy of the household.

In an urban-industrial society, survival risks are low and children do not contribute to production, so those incentives for high fertility are missing. Furthermore, the competitiveness of the labor market and the need for increasing levels of schooling to compete effectively demand a larger contribution from the parents, both economically and in managing their offsprings' careers, to the preparation of each child for adult life. Thus the optimal strategy of parental investment, assuming that a couple wants children at all, is to keep the number of offspring low and invest a good deal of domestic resources, including parental attention, in each one from infancy onward—a model that makes each child even more costly in economic terms. The parental investment strategy of a population is not culturally formulated as an economic cost-benefit calculation, but it reflects local economic and demographic conditions and enters into parental thinking as an implicit set of expectations that "every sensible person" makes.

Tomorrow

That parental behavior following a particular strategy of investment affects the psychological development of the child can hardly be doubted and will be empirically demonstrated before long. Perhaps the most obvious outcomes of this concern academic performance. It is clear that children who have acquired school-like skills at home, through a greater intensity and prolongation of parental attention than is typical in high-fertility, agrarian societies, are more likely to do well in school. This seems to hold within and between societies. Cross-national studies, however, show that parental investment strategies vary among urban-industrial societies and, in concert with policies of public investment, can make a substantial difference in academic performance. Japan and the United States, for example, do not differ greatly in birth and death rates and are both industrialized and highly urbanized societies. The stronger performance of Japanese children in mathematics is associated with more time and effort devoted to it by the pupils, their teachers (in the classroom), and their mothers (at home); this investment is the indirect consequence of private and public agencies working together for educational outcomes (LeVine and White, 1986; Stevenson, Azuma, and Hakuta, 1985; White, 1987).

This example makes clear a final point about the importance of taking macrosocial features of childhood environments into account: When the developmental outcome of interest is a skilled performance that can be improved by training, all the social forces facilitating that training in a given population are relevant to the explanation of the outcome. A major task in future research on child development will be to bring a greater variety of social science perspectives to bear on variations in the environments of children around the globe.

References

Ainsworth, M.D.S. "Attachment Theory and Its Utility in Cross-Cultural Research." In P. H. Leiderman, S. Tulkin, and A. Rosenfeld (eds.), *Culture and Infancy*. Orlando, Fla.: Academic Press, 1977.

Benedict, R. F. "Continuities and Discontinuities in Cultural Conditioning." *Psychiatry*, 1938, *1*, 161–167.

Blurton-Jones, N. (ed.). *Ethological Studies of Child Behaviour*. Cambridge, England: Cambridge University Press, 1972.

Bowlby, J. *Attachment*. New York: Basic Books, 1969.

Chisholm, J. *Navajo Infancy*. Hawthorne, N.Y.: Aldine, 1983.

Dasen, P. R. *Piagetian Psychology: Cross-Cultural Contributions*. New York: Gardner Press, 1977.

Dasen, P. R., Berry, J. W., and Sartorius, N. (eds.). *Health and Cross-Cultural Psychology: Toward Applications.* Beverly Hills, Calif.: Sage, forthcoming.

Dasen, P. R., and de Ribaupierre, A. "Neo-Piagetian Theories: Cross-Cultural and Differential Perspectives." *International Journal of Psychology,* forthcoming.

Gay, J., and Cole, M. *The New Mathematics in an Old Culture.* New York: Holt, Rinehart & Winston, 1967.

Grossman, K., and others. "Maternal Sensitivity and Newborns' Orientation Responses as Related to Quality of Attachment in Northern Germany." In I. Bretherton and E. Waters (eds.), *Growing Points in Attachment Theory and Research.* Monographs of the Society for Research in Child Development, 1985, *50* (209).

Konner, M. "Evolution of Human Behavior Development." In P. H. Leiderman, S. Tulkin, and A. Rosenfeld (eds.), *Culture and Infancy.* Orlando, Fla.: Academic Press, 1977a.

Konner, M. "Infancy Among the Kalahari Desert San." In P. H. Leiderman, S. Tulkin, and A. Rosenfeld (eds.), *Culture and Infancy.* Orlando, Fla.: Academic Press, 1977b.

LeVine, R. A. "Cross-Cultural Study in Child Psychology." In P. Mussen (ed.), *Carmichael's Manual of Child Psychology.* Vol. 2. (3rd ed.) New York: Wiley, 1970.

LeVine, R. A. "Anthropology and Child Development." In C. M. Super and S. Harkness (eds.), *Anthropological Perspectives on Child Development.* New Directions for Child Development, no. 8. San Francisco: Jossey-Bass, 1980.

LeVine, R. A., and White, M. I. *Human Conditions: The Cultural Basis of Educational Development.* London: Routledge & Kegan Paul, 1986.

Mead, M. *Coming of Age in Samoa.* New York: William Morrow, 1928.

Mead, M. *Growing Up in New Guinea.* New York: William Morrow, 1930.

Mead, M. "Research on Primitive Children." In L. Carmichael (ed.), *Manual of Child Psychology.* New York: McGraw-Hill, 1936.

Miyake, K., Chen, S., and Campos, J. "Infant Temperament,

Mother's Mode of Interaction, and Attachment in Japan: An Interim Report." In I. Bretherton and E. Waters (eds.), *Growing Points in Attachment Theory and Research*. Monographs of the Society for Research in Child Development, 1985, *50* (209).

Ochs, E., and Schieffelin, B. "Language Acquisition and Socialization: Three Developmental Stories and Their Implications." In R. Shweder and R. LeVine (eds.), *Culture Theory*. New York: Cambridge University Press, 1984.

Ochs, E., and Schieffelin, B. (eds.). *Socialization and Language Acquisition*. New York: Cambridge University Press, 1987.

Stern, D. N. "Mother and Infant at Play: The Dyadic Interaction Involving Facial, Vocal and Gaze Behaviors." In M. Lewis and L. A. Rosenblum, *Origins of Behavior*. Vol. 1: *The Effect of the Infant on Its Caregiver*. New York: Wiley, 1974.

Stern, D. N. *The First Relationship: Infant and Mother*. Cambridge, Mass.: Harvard University Press, 1977.

Stern, D. N. *The Interpersonal World of the Infant*. New York: Basic Books, 1985.

Stevenson, H., Azuma, H., and Hakuta, K. (eds.). *Child Development and Education in Japan*. Philadelphia: W. H. Freeman, 1985.

Takahashi, K. "The Japanese Attachment Studies in Cross-Cultural Perspective." *Human Development*, forthcoming.

White, M. I. *The Japanese Educational Challenge: A Commitment to Children*. New York: Free Press, 1987.

Whiting, B. B. *Six Cultures: Studies of Child Rearing*, New York: Wiley, 1963.

Whiting, B. B., and Whiting, J.W.M. *Children of Six Cultures*. Cambridge, Mass.: Harvard University Press, 1975.

Whiting, J.W.M. *Becoming a Kwoma*. New Haven, Conn.: Yale University Press, 1941.

Whiting, J.W.M. "The Cross-Cultural Method." In G. Lindzey (ed.), *Handbook of Social Psychology*. Reading, Mass.: Addison-Wesley, 1954.

Whiting, J.W.M., and Child, I. L. *Child Training and Personality*. New Haven, Conn.: Yale University Press, 1953.

Chapter 4

Organismic and Social-Contextual Bases of Development: The Sample Case of Early Adolescence

Richard M. Lerner
Jacqueline V. Lerner

Over the past two decades, developmental psychology has been undergoing radical changes in its intellectual agenda. These changes may presage similarly profound alterations in the field of psychology as a whole. A model of the human life course has emerged that portrays development as occurring through bidirectional relationships among biological, psychological, and social (including historical) processes (Baltes, 1987; Featherman, 1983). The implication of this model, and of the growing body of research that supports it, is that an exclusively psychological interpretation of psychological functioning and development must be rejected in favor of one derived from a multidisciplinary perspective (R. M. Lerner, 1984). The genesis of these changes in developmental psychology derives from a relatively recently "rediscovered" conception of the means by which biology influences human behavior and development.

Note: The authors' work on this chapter was supported in part by a grant from the William T. Grant Foundation and by a grant from the National Institute of Mental Health (MH 39957).

Since its inception as a specialization within the discipline, developmental psychology—or, as it was initially termed, "genetic psychology" (see Hall, 1904)—has been dominated by a biological model of change. Indeed, the concept of development is biological in its scientific origin (Harris, 1957). Although the particular version of biological change that has influenced developmental psychology has been and remains Darwinian in character (White, 1968), this common heritage nevertheless has led to the formation of quite distinct models of development (Dixon and Lerner, 1988). For instance, mechanistic-behavioral conceptions of developmental change (see Bijou, 1976) and organismic-dynamic (see Freud, 1949) and organismic-structural (see Piaget, 1950) theories may be interpreted as having derived from this Darwinian heritage (Dixon and Lerner, 1988).

However, despite this range of interpretations of the contribution of biology to psychological development, the organismic versions have been predominant in developmental psychology and in fact have been termed "strong" developmental models (see Reese and Overton, 1970). Thus, in the field of psychology in general, and perhaps in the scholarly community as a whole, the organismic theories of Freud (1949), Erikson (1959), and Piaget (1950) are typically held to be the classic, prototypic, or exemplary theories within developmental psychology (for example, see Lerner, 1986).

These instances of organismic theory, especially those of Freud and Erikson, have been labeled "predetermined epigenetic" (Gottlieb, 1983). In this type of theory, biology is seen as the prime mover of development: Intrinsic (for example, maturational) changes are seen to essentially unfold; although environmental or experiential variables may speed up or slow down these progressions, they can do nothing to alter the sequence or quality (for instance, the structure) of these hereditarily predetermined changes (see Hamburger, 1957). In other words, this view, "as it applies to behavior, means that the development of behavior in larvae, embryos, fetuses, and neonates can be explained entirely in terms of neuromotor and neurosensory maturation ([that is,] in terms of proliferation, migration, differentiation, and growth of neurons and their axonal and dendritic processes). In this view, factors such as the use or exercise of muscles, sensory stimulation, mechanical agitation, environmental heat, gravity, and so on, play only a passive role in the development of the nervous system. Thus, according to predetermined epigenesis . . . structural maturation determines function, and not vice versa" (Gottlieb, 1983, p. 11).

Victor Hamburger's organismic position epitomizes this view. He notes that "the architecture of the nervous system and the concomitant behavior patterns result from self-generating growth and maturation processes that are determined entirely by inherited, intrinsic factors, to the exclusion of functional adjustment, exercise, or anything else akin to learning" (Hamburger, 1957, p. 56).

However, another view of biological functioning exists, one that sees biological and contextual factors as reciprocally interactive; as such, developmental changes are probabilistic with respect to normative outcomes due to variation in the timing of the biological, psychological, and social factors that provide interactive bases of ontogenetic progressions (see Schneirla, 1957). This view has been labeled as "probabilistic epigenetic" by Gottlieb (1970) and was developed by him (Gottlieb, 1983) and earlier by Schneirla (1957).

The term *probabilistic epigenesis* was used by Gottlieb to indicate that individual behavioral development is not invariant or inevitable. Instead, "the sequence or outcome of individual behavioral development is probable (with respect to norms) rather than certain" because "probabilistic epigenesis necessitates a bidirectional structure-function hypothesis. The conventional version of the structure-function hypothesis is unidirectional in the sense that structure is supposed to determine function in an essentially nonreciprocal relationship. . . . The bidirectional version of the structure-function relationship is a logical consequence of the view that the course and outcome of behavioral epigenesis is probabilistic: It entails the assumption of reciprocal effects in the relationship between structure and function whereby function (exposure to stimulation and/or movement of musculo-skeletal activity) can significantly modify the development of the peripheral and central structures that are involved in these events" (Gottlieb, 1970, p. 123).

Thus, within the probabilistic-epigenetic view of development, or—as it is termed within the area of life-span-developmental psychology—the developmental-contextual (Lerner, 1986) view of development, variables from biological, psychological, and social-contextual levels of analysis bidirectionally interact to provide the bases of behavior and development. It is important to stress that, in this literature, levels are conceived of as integrative organizations. That is, "the concept of integrative levels recognizes as equally essential for the purpose of scientific analysis both the isolation of parts of a whole and their integration into the structure of the whole. It neither reduces phenomena of a higher level to those of a lower one, as in mechanism, nor describes the higher level in vague nonmaterial terms which are but substitutes for understanding, as in vitalism. Unlike other 'holistic' theories, it never leaves the firm ground of material reality. . . . The concept points to the need to study the organizational interrelationships of parts and whole" (Novikoff, 1945, p. 209). Moreover, Tobach and Greenberg (1984, p. 2) stress that "the interdependence among levels is of great significance. The dialectic nature of the relationship among levels is one in which lower levels are subsumed in higher levels so that any particular level is an integration of preceding levels. . . . In the process of integration, or fusion, *new* levels with their own characteristics result." If the course of human development is the product of the processes involved in the "fusions" (or "dynamic interactions"; R. M. Lerner, 1984) among integrative levels, then the processes of development are more plastic than was often previously believed (see Brim and Kagan, 1980).

This probabilistic-epigenetic, or developmental-contextual, view of development provides the theoretical underpinning of the life-span view of human development (Lerner, 1986). In addition, it is this particular organismic view, or, better, this organismic-contextual view, that constitutes the new intellectual agenda of developmental psychology: This is the case because this conception of human development "differs from most Western contemporary thought on the subject" (Brim and Kagan, 1980, p. 1) and as such redirects "the burden of proof to those who hold more static, deterministic views" (Sherrod and Brim, 1986, p. 575)—that is, predetermined epigenetic conceptions.

Nevertheless, such redirection does not obviate the need to demonstrate the empirical utility of models or hypotheses derived from developmental-contextual views of biological-psychological-social interaction. In point of fact, there *is* a quite extensive literature presenting such empirical support (for reviews of this literature, see, for example, Hetherington, Lerner, and Perlmutter, 1988; Sorensen, Weinert, and Sherrod, 1986). Review of this large literature is not possible in this chapter. Fortunately, however, one area of research in which such support exists may be used as a representative case of this larger literature. This area is early adolescence, and it in fact is an exemplar of the use of developmental contextualism across the life span (Lerner, 1987).

The Developmental-Contextual Study of Early Adolescence

We have noted that the study of early adolescence exemplifies the theoretical and empirical issues involved in the use of the developmental-contextual perspective at any point in the life span. Indeed, the distinctions between probabilistic epigenesis and predetermined epigenesis, distinctions that divide developmental-contextual views of biological functioning from alternative conceptions, are "translated" directly into theoretical divisions that exist within the early adolescent literature—that is, at least two theoretical perspectives exist about the effects of biological variables on early adolescent psychosocial functioning. One—a "direct effects" view (see A. Freud, 1969; Kestenberg, 1967)—specifies that the intraindividual changes associated with early adolescent biological or organismic development directly influence other intraindividual ("psychic") characteristics. This first view obviously is akin to a predetermined-epigenetic position. A second view—termed the "moderated," "mediated," or "dynamic-interactional effects" view (Lerner, 1987; Petersen and Taylor, 1980)—is akin to a probabilistic-epigenetic position. Here the influence of early adolescent organismic changes on individual functioning is seen to be moderated by the social context. There are several instances of this general idea (see Brooks-Gunn, 1987; Lerner, 1987; Petersen and Taylor, 1980); however, all instances share the belief that characteristics of organismic individuality influence and are influenced by the psychosocial context within which they are expressed; and it is this bidirectional relation between organismic individuality and the context that moderates any link between the organismic changes of early adolescence and other, individual behaviors and developments.

In short, then, the direct-effects view of early adolescent development specifies that direct—that is, noncontextually mediated—relations should exist between the individual's organismic (biological) and psychological characteristics. In turn, the dynamic-interactional view specifies that the social context moderates any links among organismic and psychological characteristics. As noted previously, there are considerable empirical data supporting the developmental-contextual, dynamic-interactional view of early adolescent behavior and development. Much of these data have been generated in the context of tests of our "goodness of fit" model of person-context relations (see J. V. Lerner, 1984; Lerner and Lerner, 1987). It is useful, then, to review the nature of this developmental-contextually derived model and some of the data supporting it.

The Goodness of Fit Model. All people have significant characteristics of individuality (R. M. Lerner, 1984). Moreover, the context surrounding each person is singular as well (Bronfenbrenner, 1979; Lerner, 1987; Schneirla, 1957). In other words, each person and his or her context are individually distinct as a consequence of the unique combination of genotypic and phenotypic features of that person and of the specific attributes of his or her context. The presence of such individuality is central to understanding the goodness of fit model. As a consequence of characteristics of physical individuality (for example, in regard to physical attractiveness) and/or of psychological individuality (for instance, in regard to behavioral style or temperament), children promote differential reactions in their socializing with others; these reactions may feed back to children, increase the individuality of their developmental milieu, and provide a basis for their further development. T. C. Schneirla (1957) termed these relations "circular functions." It is through the establishment of such functions in ontogeny that people may be conceived of as producers of their own development (Lerner, 1982). However, this circular functions idea needs to be extended. In and of itself, the notion is mute regarding the specific characteristics of the feedback (for example, its positive or negative valence) an adolescent will receive as a consequence of his or her individuality. What may provide a basis of the feedback?

Just as an adolescent brings his or her singular characteristics to a particular social setting, there are specific demands that are placed on the adolescent by virtue of the physical and/or social (significant others) components in the setting (Lerner and Lerner, 1987). It is these demands that provide the functional significance for a given characteristic of individuality; if congruent with the demands of a significant other (such as a parent), this characteristic should produce a positive adjustment (adaptation). If that same attribute is incongruent with such demands, a negative adjustment is expected.

To illustrate, consider the case of the adolescent in his or her family context and of the psychosocial and physical climate promoted by the parents. Parents can vary in their cognitive and behavioral attributes (for example, in regard to their child-rearing attitudes and parenting styles; Baumrind, 1971); they can vary, too, in the physical features of the home they provide. These parent-based psychosocial and physical characteristics constitute presses for, or demands on, the adolescent for adaptation. Simply put, parent characteristics are "translated" or "transduced" into demands on the adolescent.

First, these demands may take the form of attitudes, values, or expectations held by parents (or, in other contexts, by teachers or peers) regarding the adolescent's physical or behavioral characteristics. Second, demands exist as a consequence of the behavioral attributes of parents (or, again, of teachers or peers); these people are significant others with whom the adolescent must coordinate, or fit, his or her behavioral attributes in order for adaptive interactions to exist. Third, the physical characteristics of a setting (such as the noise level of the home or the presence or absence of access ramps for people with motor disabilities) constitute contextual demands. Such physical presses require the adolescent to possess certain behavioral attributes in order for the most efficient interaction within the setting to occur.

The adolescent's individuality in differentially meeting these demands provides a basis for the feedback he or she gets from the socializing environment. For example, considering the demand "domain" of attitudes, values, and expectations, teachers and parents may have relatively individual and distinct expectations about behaviors desired of their students and children, respectively. Teachers may want students who are not easily distracted, since they do not want attention diverted from a lesson by the activity of children in the classroom. Parents, however, might desire their adolescents to be moderately distractible—for example, when they require their adolescents to move from television watching to the dinner table or to bed. Adolescents whose behavioral individuality is either generally distractible or generally not distractible will thus differentially meet the demands of these two contexts. Problems of adjustment to school demands or to those at home might thus develop as a consequence of an adolescent's lack of match, or "goodness of fit," in either or both settings.

Tests of the Model. Our tests of this goodness of fit model have been quite extensive, and our results have been summarized in several articles and chapters (for example, J. V. Lerner, 1984; Lerner and Lerner, 1987). Thus this chapter will only present briefly some recently obtained findings derived from the Pennsylvania Early Adolescent Transitions Study (PEATS), a short-term longitudinal study of approximately 150 northwestern Pennsylvania early adolescents, from the beginning of sixth grade across the transition to junior high school and to the end of the seventh grade.

In one study derived from the PEATS, East, Lerner, and Lerner (forthcoming) determined the overall fit between adolescents' temperament (as measured by the Revised Dimensions of Temperament Survey, or DOTS-R; Windle and Lerner, 1986) and the demands of their peers regarding desired levels of temperament. Based on the circular functions notion involved in the goodness of fit model, East, Lerner, and Lerner predicted that while no significant direct paths would exist between adjustment and either temperament measured alone or temperament-demands fit, fit would influence adolescent-peer social relations, which, in turn, would influence adjustment; in short, significant mediated paths, but insignificant direct paths, were expected. These expectations were supported. For nine of the twelve measures of adjustment employed (involving parents' ratings of behavior problems; teachers' ratings of scholastic competence, social acceptance, athletic competence, conduct adequacy, and physical appearance; and students' self-ratings of scholastic competence, social acceptance, athletic competence, conduct adequacy, physical appearance, and self-worth), both of the two mediated paths (between adolescent-peer group fit and peer relations and between peer relations and adjustment) were significant; in no case, however, was a significant direct path found. Figure 4.1 presents diagramatically one representative finding, involving the adjustment outcome of self-rated (or perceived) self-worth, from the East, Lerner, and Lerner (forthcoming) study.

Nitz, Lerner, and Lerner (1987) found similar results regarding temperamental fit with parental demands and adolescent adjustment. Although at the beginning of sixth grade the number of significant relations between the adjustment measures and temperament-demands fit did not exceed the number of significant relations between temperament alone and adjustment, at both the middle and the end of sixth grade the percentage of significant relations between fit and adjustment scores was significantly greater than the corresponding percentages involving temperament alone.

In a related study, Talwar, Nitz, Lerner, and Lerner (1988) found that poor fit with parental demands (especially in regard to the attributes of mood and approach-withdrawal) at the end of sixth

Figure 4.1. Path Analysis of Early Adolescent-Peer Group Fit, Peer Relations, and Perceived Self-Worth.

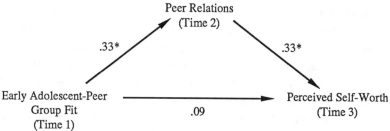

*p < .01

Note: Higher scores reflect a good fit, positive peer relations, and favorable perceived self-worth.
Source: East, Lerner, and Lerner, forthcoming.

grade was associated in seventh grade with low teacher-rated academic and social competence and negative peer relations. Corresponding relations were found in regard to fit with peer demands. Moreover, and again underscoring the importance of considering the context within which organismic characteristics are expressed, goodness of fit scores (between temperament and demands) were more often associated with adjustment than were temperament scores alone; this was true for both peer and parental contexts at the end of sixth grade and for the peer context after the transition to junior high school (at the beginning of seventh grade). Finally, Talwar, Nitz, Lerner, and Lerner grouped the PEATS subjects into high versus low overall fit groups (by adding fit scores across all temperament dimensions). Adolescents in the low-fit group in regard to peer demands received lower teacher ratings of scholastic competence and higher parent ratings for conduct and school problems than did the adolescents in the high-fit group in regard to peer demands. Comparable findings were found in regard to low versus high fit in regard to parent demands.

In regard to physical attractiveness, Lerner, Jovanovic, Delaney, and Hess (1987) found that the circular functions component of the goodness of fit model was supported in regard to academic achievement. Based on the presence of a "what is beautiful is good" stereotype (Langlois, 1986), teachers were expected to differentially evaluate adolescents who differed in their physical attractiveness (PA). These differential evaluations were expected to influence the achievements of adolescents as well as their self-evaluations of their academic competence; these self-perceptions, in turn, were expected to influence achievement. In both cases, however, it was expected that these indirect paths between PA and achievement would be significant while direct paths between PA and achievement would not. The results of Lerner, Jovanovic, Delaney, and Hess (1987) confirm these expectations with respect to two indexes of achievement—grade point average (GPA) and scores on a standardized achievement test, the California Achievement Test/Form C (CAT/C)—at the beginning, middle, and end of sixth grade. An illustration of these findings, using data from the beginning of the sixth grade, is displayed in Figure 4.2.

Figure 4.2. Results of Path Analyses from Time 1 (Beginning
of Sixth Grade) of the PEATS: Direct and Indirect Effects of Physical
Attractiveness on GPA and CAT/C Score.

Time 1

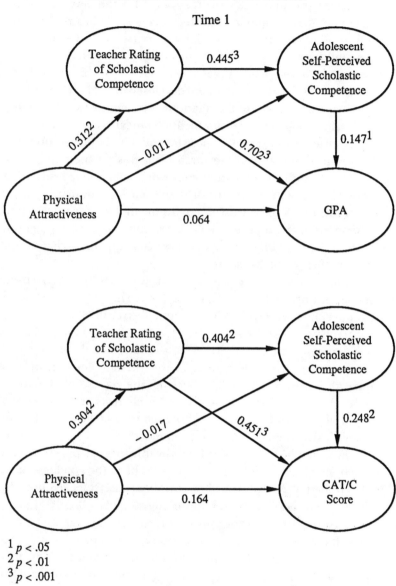

[1] $p < .05$
[2] $p < .01$
[3] $p < .001$

Source: Lerner, Jovanovic, Delaney, and Hess, 1987.

Tomorrow

Given this above-described support for the developmental-contextually derived goodness of fit model, as well as the support found in other studies from our laboratory (see J. V. Lerner, 1984; Lerner and Lerner, 1987), it is useful to make some final statements regarding the developmental-contextual view of the biological and social-contextual bases of human development. The concepts of biology, of context, and of the relations between the two found in a probabilistic-epigenetic, developmental-contextual perspective are, as a set, quite complex; they impose formidable challenges on those who seek to derive feasible research from this perspective. As we have argued, this developmental-contextual perspective leads to an integrated, multi-level concept of development, one in which the focus of inquiry is the organism-environment dynamic interaction. Furthermore, such an orientation places emphasis on the potential for intraindividual change in structure and function—that is, for plasticity—across the life span.

The data we have reviewed here, as well as those derived from other laboratories (for reviews, see Hetherington, Lerner, and Perlmutter, 1988; Sorensen, Weinert, and Sherrod, 1986), underscore the current use—across the life span—of a developmental-contextual orientation. Nevertheless, the future challenge for this perspective, as we have noted, is the further derivation and empirical testing of models reflecting the nature of dynamic, interlevel interactions across time. Such tests will profit by triangulation of the constructs within each level of analysis thought to dynamically interact within a given model.

For instance, in regard to the biological-psychosocial interactions of early adolescence assessed within the goodness of fit model, pubertal changes could be simultaneously indexed both by molecular, hormonal changes and by more molar, bodily appearance measures; similarly, demands (for example, of parents) could be simultaneously appraised by assessing both attitudes/expectations about behavior and actual behavioral exchanges. Not only would such triangulation provide convergent and discriminant validation information, but, in addition, better insight would be gained about whether all modalities of functioning within a level of analysis are of similar import for adaptive functioning in particular person-context interactions. For instance, it may be that because of the power of age-graded expectations regarding early adolescent social (and, particularly, heterosexual) behavior, internal, hormonal changes are less important in the young person's interactions with peers and adults than are external, bodily appearance variables—variables that may make a person look older to significant others (Lerner, 1987). While there is some evidence to support this particular example (Dornbusch and others, 1981), involving the age grading of dating behavior in adolescence, this particular data set is not developmental, and its existence—rather than obviating the need for further triangulation efforts—underscores the importance of such work. Moreover, the standard incorporation of multiple measures into future research is important not only because of the new information it would provide about the developmental-contextual model but also because this information would provide insight into the most useful targets of interventions aimed at enhancing the social behavior of the developing person.

As we have indicated, one reasonably successful path we have taken in exploring the usefulness of a developmental-contextual perspective involves the testing of the goodness of fit model of person-context relations. Nevertheless, our own work would profit from the sort of triangulation for which we call. In addition, of course, the goodness of fit model is not the only conception of person-context relations that may be derived from a contextual orientation: There are perhaps an infinite number of possible interlevel relations that may occur and a potentially similarly large array of ways to model them. In the future, those testing these perspectives should consider incorporation of multiple measures within each of the levels modeled. Indeed, since current tests of other models derived from a developmental-contextual or life-span perspective also have found considerable empirical support (see Baltes, 1987), we can expect that such extensions will be important additions to an already significant foundation.

In sum, the relative plasticity of human development across the life span—a plasticity deriving from the dynamic interactions between organism and context that characterize human functioning—is already well documented (see Baltes, 1987; Brim and Kagan,

1980; Featherman, 1983; Hetherington, Lerner, and Perlmutter, 1988; R. M. Lerner, 1984; Sorensen, Weinert, and Sherrod, 1986). Thus a future including the sorts of directions we suggest should enrich greatly our understanding of the precise conditions promoting and constraining human plasticity and development. Given the present literature and the promise we see for tomorrow, we believe there is reason for great optimism about the future scientific use of the developmental-contextual view of the biological and social-contextual bases of development.

References

Baltes, P. B. "Theoretical Propositions of Life-Span Developmental Psychology: On the Dynamics Between Growth and Decline." *Developmental Psychology*, 1987, *23*, 611–626.

Baumrind, D. "Current Patterns of Parental Authority." *Developmental Psychology Monographs*, 1971, *4* (no. 1, part 2).

Bijou, S. W. *Child Development: The Basic Stage of Early Childhood*. Englewood Cliffs, N.J.: Prentice-Hall, 1976.

Brim, O. G., Jr., and Kagan, J. "Constancy and Change: A View of the Issues." In O. G. Brim, Jr., and J. Kagan (eds.), *Constancy and Change in Human Development*. Cambridge, Mass.: Harvard University Press, 1980.

Bronfenbrenner, U. *The Ecology of Human Development: Experiments by Nature and Design*. Cambridge, Mass.: Harvard University Press, 1979.

Brooks-Gunn, J. "Pubertal Processes and Girls' Psychological Adaptation." In R. M. Lerner and T. T. Foch (eds.), *Biological-Psychosocial Interactions in Early Adolescence: A Life Span Perspective*. Hillsdale, N.J.: Erlbaum, 1987.

Dixon, R. A., and Lerner, R. M. "A History of Systems in Developmental Psychology." In M. H. Bornstein and M. E. Lamb (eds.), *Developmental Psychology*. (2nd ed.) Hillsdale, N.J.: Erlbaum, 1988.

Dornbusch, S. M., and others. "Sexual Development, Age, and Dating: A Comparison of Biological and Social Influences upon One Set of Behaviors." *Child Development*, 1981, *52*, 179–185.

East, P. L., Lerner, R. M., and Lerner, J. V. "Early Adolescent-Peer

Group Fit, Peer Relations, and Adjustment." *Journal of Youth and Adolescence,* forthcoming.

Erikson, E. H. "Identity and the Life-Cycle." *Psychological Issues,* 1959, *1,* 18–164.

Featherman, D. L. "Life-Span Perspectives in Social Science Research." In P. B. Baltes and O. G. Brim, Jr. (eds.), *Life-Span Development and Behavior.* Vol. 5. Orlando, Fla.: Academic Press, 1983.

Freud, A. "Adolescence as a Developmental Disturbance." In G. Caplan and S. Lebovici (eds.), *Adolescence.* New York: Basic Books, 1969.

Freud, S. *Outline of Psychoanalysis.* New York: Norton, 1949.

Gottlieb, G. "Conceptions of Prenatal Behavior." In R. Aronson, E. Tobach, D. S. Lehrman, and J. S. Rosenblatt (eds.), *Development and Evolution of Behavior: Essays in Memory of T. C. Schneirla.* New York: W. H. Freeman, 1970.

Gottlieb, G. "The Psychobiological Approach to Developmental Issues." In P. Mussen (ed.), *Handbook of Child Psychology.* (4th ed.) Vol. 2. New York: Wiley, 1983.

Hall, G. S. *Adolescence: Its Psychology and Its Relations to Physiology, Anthropology, Sociology, Sex, Crime, Religion, and Education.* 2 vols. East Norwalk, Conn.: Appleton-Century Crofts, 1904.

Hamburger, V. "The Concept of Development in Biology." In D. B. Harris (ed.), *The Concept of Development.* Minneapolis: University of Minnesota Press, 1957.

Harris, D. B. (ed.). *The Concept of Development.* Minneapolis: University of Minnesota Press, 1957.

Hetherington, E. M., Lerner, R. M., and Perlmutter, M. (eds.). *Child Development in Life Span Perspective.* Hillsdale, N.J.: Erlbaum, 1988.

Kestenberg, J. "Phases of Adolescence with Suggestions for a Correlation of Psychic and Hormonal Organization. Part One: Antecedents of Adolescent Organizations in Childhood." *Journal of the American Academy of Child Psychiatry,* 1967, *6,* 426–463.

Langlois, J. H. "From the Eye of the Beholder to Behavioral Reality: The Development of Social Behaviors and Social

Relations as a Function of Physical Attractiveness." In C. P. Herman (ed.), *Physical Appearance, Stigma, and Social Behavior: The Ontario Symposium on Personality and Social Psychology*. Hillsdale, N.J.: Erlbaum, 1986.

Lerner, J. V. "The Import of Temperament for Psychosocial Functioning: Tests of a 'Goodness of Fit' Model." *Merrill-Palmer Quarterly*, 1984, *30*, 177–188.

Lerner, R. M. "Children and Adolescents as Producers of Their Own Development." *Developmental Review*, 1982, *2*, 342–370.

Lerner, R. M. *On the Nature of Human Plasticity*. New York: Cambridge University Press, 1984.

Lerner, R. M. *Concepts and Theories of Human Development*. (2nd ed.) New York: Random House, 1986.

Lerner, R. M. "A Life-Span Perspective for Early Adolescence." In R. M. Lerner and T. T. Foch (eds.), *Biological-Psychosocial Interactions in Early Adolescence: A Life Span Perspective*. Hillsdale, N.J.: Erlbaum, 1987.

Lerner, R. M., Jovanovic, J., Delaney, M., and Hess, L. E. "Early Adolescent Physical Attractiveness and Academic Competence." Unpublished manuscript, College of Health and Human Development, Pennsylvania State University, 1987.

Lerner, R. M., and Lerner, J. V. "Children in Their Contexts: A Goodness of Fit Model." In J. B. Lancaster, J. Altmann, A. S. Rossi, and L. R. Sherrod (eds.), *Parenting Across the Life Span: Biosocial Dimensions*. Hawthorne, N.Y.: Aldine, 1987.

Nitz, K., Lerner, R. M., and Lerner, J. V. "Temperament, Parental and Peer Demands, and Goodness of Fit During Early Adolescence." Unpublished manuscript, College of Health and Human Development, Pennsylvania State University, 1987.

Novikoff, A. B. "The Concept of Integrative Levels of Biology." *Science*, 1945, *62*, 209–215.

Petersen, A. C., and Taylor, B. "The Biological Approach to Adolescence: Biological Change and Psychological Adaptation." In J. Adelson (ed.), *Handbook of Adolescent Psychology*. New York: Wiley, 1980.

Piaget, J. *The Psychology of Intelligence*. San Diego, Calif.: Harcourt Brace Jovanovich, 1950.

Reese, H. W., and Overton, W. F. "Models of Development and

Theories of Development." In L. R. Goulet and P. B. Baltes (eds.), *Life-Span Developmental Psychology: Research and Theory.* Orlando, Fla.: Academic Press, 1970.

Schneirla, T. C. "The Concept of Development in Comparative Psychology." In D. B. Harris (ed.), *The Concept of Development.* Minneapolis: University of Minnesota Press, 1957.

Sherrod, L. R., and Brim, O. G., Jr. "Epilogue." In A. B. Sorensen, F. E. Weinert, and L. R. Sherrod (eds.), *Human Development in the Life Course: Multidisciplinary Perspectives.* Hillsdale, N.J.: Erlbaum, 1986.

Sorensen, A. B., Weinert, F. E., and Sherrod, L. R. (eds.). *Human Development in the Life Course: Multidisciplinary Perspectives.* Hillsdale, N.J.: Erlbaum, 1986.

Talwar, R., Nitz, K., Lerner, J. V., and Lerner, R. M. "Temperamental Individuality, Fit with Parent and Peer Demands, and Personal and Social Adjustment Across the Transition to Junior High School." Paper presented at fifty-ninth annual meeting of the Eastern Psychological Association, Buffalo, N.Y., April 21–24, 1988.

Tobach, E., and Greenberg, G. "The Significance of T. C. Schneirla's Contribution to the Concept of Levels of Integration." In G. Greenberg and E. Tobach (eds.), *Behavioral Evolution and Integrative Levels.* Hillsdale, N.J.: Erlbaum, 1984.

White, S. H. "The Learning-Maturation Controversy: Hall to Hull." *Merrill-Palmer Quarterly,* 1968, *14,* 187–196.

Windle, M., and Lerner, R. M. "Reassessing the Dimensions of Temperamental Individuality Across the Life-Span: The Revised Dimensions of Temperament Survey (DOTS-R)." *Journal of Adolescent Research,* 1986, *1,* 213–230.

Chapter 5

The Social Construction of Social Construction

Elliot Turiel

 In the early part of 1987, a federal judge from Alabama made national headlines by ordering a large number of textbooks in such fields as home economics, history, and social studies removed from the elementary and secondary public schools of that state. The judge's ruling stemmed from a suit brought by a group of Christian parents who claimed that the books violated their constitutional rights by promoting a religious orientation different from their own. In essential agreement with the parents, the judge banned the books on the grounds that they promoted the "religion" of secular humanism at the expense of traditional religions. The judge's decision held that: "For purposes of the First Amendment, secular humanism is a religious belief system, entitled to the protection of, and subject to the prohibitions of, the religious clauses. It is not a mere scientific methodology that may be promoted and advanced in the public schools" ("U.S. Judge Bans Thirty-Six Textbooks," 1987). This ruling followed an equally publicized but more limited ruling by a judge in Tennessee who had ordered public schools to excuse children from classes so they would not be forced to read books that were objectionable to their religions. The objectionable books and stories included *Macbeth*, "Cinderella," *The Wizard of Oz*, Hans Christian Andersen's fairy tales, and the *Diary of Anne Frank*. It is likely that these cases will be taken to the United States Supreme Court, since both rulings have been overturned in courts of appeals.

Disputes over the teaching of science and religion are not new, of course. These recent cases are reminiscent of the famous Scopes trial of 1925, which pitted William Jennings Bryan against Clarence Darrow in arguments regarding Tennessee's ban on the teaching of evolution. On the contemporary scene, however, we see efforts to blur distinctions between religious propositions and knowledge of ideas that stem from secular sources—as in the treatment of secular humanism as a type of religion. These distinctions are blurred through the notion that various types of secular ideas are part of a system of thought that represents an ideology or world view tantamount to an alternative nontraditional religious perspective. In recent times, the continuing arguments regarding the teaching of evolution have developed a new twist that serves to blur the distinction between religion and science: It is maintained by some religious groups that evolution should not be taught as the only credible theory of the origin of life because creationism represents a legitimate scientific rival to the theory of evolution (at the same time these groups assert that evolution is a dogma of the religion of secular humanism). Indeed, laws mandating the teaching of creationism do exist in several states.

These controversies and trends regarding religion, science, and so-called secular humanism are relevant to this volume's major themes regarding the state of the field of child development "today and tomorrow" because they are paralleled in current—and, no doubt, future—controversies and trends regarding the nature and development of children's thinking. Whereas in the past it could be assumed that the social scientific community was at odds with attempts to equate religion, science, and secular academic thought, this is no longer the case. An increasingly influential school of social scientific thought now exists with its basis in the fundamental propositions that (1) all forms of practice and thinking are primarily culturally determined, (2) therefore, all ideas, propositions, and theories are equally mythical and/or ideological, and (3) there can be no grounds for determining their relative validity or adequacy. Accordingly, a relativistic position is taken through the proposition that all ideas and theories are social constructions particular to the cultural and historical context from which they emanated.

The proposition that morality—a main topic of this chapter—is relative and determined by culture is not new in social science, nor is it likely to be unfamiliar to the readers of this volume. One long-standing explanation of the development of morality is that children learn the values of their society or culture as taught to them by adults. Psychological explanations of this sort seek to specify mechanisms of learning or acquisition (for example, the effects of reward and punishment and the process of modeling and imitation) that account for children's incorporation of moral behaviors, values, or traits of character. The search for specific social learning mechanisms has waned in recent years because of inconsistent empirical support and because of a recognition that cognitive processes are not detached from social development. In recent accounts, the realm of morality is seen to be embedded in general uniform ways of thinking, or world views, that represent broad cultural schemes encompassing many areas of thought, including religion, physical science, social science, the humanities, lay social orientations, and much more. The very topic of this volume is subsumed under general cultural orientations, since it has been proposed that the concept of childhood, as well as psychologists' explanations of development, are "cultural inventions" (Kessen, 1979, 1983).

It follows, then, that as social constructions, creationism and evolutionary theory or religion and secular humanism all have the same sources and status (Shweder, 1986). This is not to say that all proponents of social construction would necessarily take the same political and educational positions as those who support the teaching of creationism or restricting the use of books in the public schools. It should also be noted that those who support the teaching of creationism and the restriction of books would not necessarily take the same position on how children learn as would social constructionists. However, they all share similar epistemological assumptions regarding commonalities and differences in world views as reflected in religion, science, and other forms of secular thought.

Individualism, Collectivism, and Culture as Context

As should become evident shortly, proponents of social construction often speak as if it is the only valid perspective and, certainly, the wave of the future. Some boldly and categorically preempt the validity of theoretical perspectives with an environmentalism that renders culture the source of *all* forms of human behavior and thought. An interesting commentary on all this is that the environmentalism of social construction is in direct opposition to other recent categorical assertions as to the *biological* determinism of human behavior and thought. A fair amount of attention and notoriety was garnered by the movement of sociobiology (Dawkins, 1976; Trivers, 1971; Wilson, 1975, 1978), with its claims that most social behaviors and patterns of social interaction are genetically determined. The view that the future of social scientific explanation is already settled was evident in statements made by one of the leading proponents of sociobiology, as quoted in a popular national magazine (R. Trivers in *Time*, August 1, 1977): "Sooner or later, political science, law, economics, psychology, psychiatry and anthropology will all be branches of sociobiology." One need only transpose the terms *anthropology* and *sociobiology* in that statement to capture the opposite but equally categorical view of much of the social construction movement. (Both environmental and innatist positions continue to be pursued; for examples of the latter, see Bower, 1979; Fodor, 1983; Gelman, 1979; Keil, 1986.)

These are not the only opposing claims demonstrating that matters are far from settled in the study of human development and behavior. Commenting favorably on the social constructionist movement, Gergen (1985, p. 271) predicted that it would "inevitably confront strong resistance within psychology" and that "few are prepared for such a wrenching, conceptual dislocation." Social constructionists consider their perspective to be at odds with the "positivism" of the behavioristic movement (although they share an environmentalistic perspective). Commenting favorably on behaviorism, B. F. Skinner (1987, pp. 782–783) recently asserted that "many people find the implications of a behavioral analysis disturbing" and that "some long-admired features of human behavior are then threatened."

One symptom of the all-encompassing perspective on culture is the accusation often leveled by social constructionists that the explanations or theories of social scientists are "culturally biased."

The types of biases presumed to exist are related to the orientation presumed to encompass the culture of North America and perhaps more generally of the Western world. The term used most frequently to characterize this cultural orientation is *individualism*. Within this perspective, individualism is an organizing feature of Western morality (this particular aspect of social construction is dealt with in greater detail below). Individualism is also regarded as a pervasive cultural orientation that not only explains the everyday activities of members of the culture but also heavily influences (biases) the explanations of social scientists (since they are members of the culture).

Examples from some of its proponents can serve to illustrate the social construction position on culture and its ramifications for psychological and other social scientific research and explanation. As already noted, the claim is that the overarching cultural and historical context shapes the behaviors and perspective of everyone (Gergen, 1978, 1985, 1986; Hogan, 1975; Kessen, 1979, 1983; Sampson, 1977, 1978, 1981). Knowledge and types of thought, whether they be held by the layperson or by social scientists, are a consequence of social processes that produce consensus. Meanings and accepted truths are not based on inferences about events or on evidence independent of the social construction of meanings (Gergen, 1986; Shweder, 1986). Construction has a special and limited connotation here: It is not that a given group of people negotiate and construct meanings anew; the construction is located at a more general level of culture and its tradition or history. Accordingly, the sources of knowledge and thought are tied to specific but broadly conceived historical and cultural contexts. It follows that the child's development would also be a process of social construction in this sense. Again, it is not that particular groups of children or children and adults negotiate and create or recreate new (or perhaps old) ways of thinking; rather, it is a prior historical and cultural construction that shapes development.

Most frequently, the general ethos of this culture is identified as, in Sampson's (1977, p. 769) phrase, one of "self-contained individualism," with its self-sufficiency, detachment, and independence from other persons. Individualistic cultures are contrasted with collectivistic cultures that stress attachment and interdependence. Furthermore, the central ethos of individualism is sufficiently pervasive as to represent the dominant mode of American psychology. That psychological theories reflect the cultural ethos follows from the premise of social construction: that all systems of thought are determined by cultural context and are not due to verification from evidence.

In asserting that explanations in psychology and other disciplines are guided by individualism, the social constructionist turns critic. The thrust of that criticism, however, is a labeling of alternative positions as biased, without critical scrutiny, analysis, or consideration of the weight of evidence. Broad claims about cultural influences on social scientific thought include the assertion that the "dominant temper of American psychology . . . is wedded to an individualistic psychology" (Hogan, 1975, p. 534). In this regard, psychological theories idealize individual separation, independence, and transcendence of society. Perhaps the most sweeping claims have been made by Sampson, who has incrementally (1977, 1978, 1981) embedded more and more of American psychology into the individualistic rubric to the point of encompassing just about all areas—social, developmental, personality, and cognitive psychology. This is consistent with the assertion that children and child psychology are cultural inventions (Kessen, 1979). The reason for this state of affairs, according to Sampson, is that "we are blinded by our own cultural heritage"—hence the bias. Moreover, in keeping with the notion that "secular humanism" is an alternative type of religious system, Sampson (1977, p. 774) generalizes the influence of individualism: "Perhaps this is not so much a psychological thesis as it is a dominant perspective within which most academics do their work. Thus it serves as the background culture, which undoubtedly plays a part in the conceptions we formulate."

There are components central to these positions that are directly antipathic to traditional concerns in child development. The antidevelopmental components are twofold. First is a rejection of the general notion that changes in individuals' psychological functioning are nonarbitrary and progressive. Many in child development have been concerned with how changes broadly associated with age might represent shifts in levels of functioning.

Developmentalists have attempted to describe such levels in a variety of domains and to provide criteria by which types or structures of functioning are more adaptive or advanced than previous ones in the child's growth. The whole idea of an order or sequence in development is antithetical to the assumption that individuals are shaped by external cultural forces.

Second, there is a rejection of specific explanations of moral and social development (for example, see Kohlberg, 1969; Piaget [1932] 1965) that social constructionists interpret to assert that advanced development entails the ability to think in terms that transcend the culture and collectivity. In this particular interpretation of the moral judgments proposed by developmentalists (actually, there are serious misinterpretations of the position that we need not go into here), in the most advanced types of moral reasoning, individuals are able to separate themselves and make judgments that are at odds with the group or culture. Placing moral judgments that transcend the group at the most advanced level is regarded as an example of the idealization of individualism in this culture. In more collectivistic cultures, the individualistic separation from the group would be regarded as less morally desirable than group embeddedness.

Culture and Development

Several hard questions about culture, development, and the use of evidence emerge from the various ideas in the social constructionist position. These include questions about the validity of a general proposition underlying the entire enterprise: namely, that culture is *the* context that organizes psychological acquisition. A related issue is whether cultures and individual members can be characterized through general overarching social orientations (such as individualism or collectivism). Questions are also raised as to the validity of the assumption that psychological explanations are reflections of the cultural ethos. This proposition, of course, conflicts with what many in the social sciences and other fields of scholarly study assume are their nonrelativistic aims and procedures—that they are seeking to provide unbiased explanations with logic, reason, and evidence.

These and other issues can be examined in two ways. One is through consideration of internal contradictions in social construction, which show that the position actually does not adhere (for good reasons) to its own key propositions that (1) culture organizes the conceptual orientations of its members, including physical scientists, social scientists, and other scholars, and (2) one cannot point to validity, truth value, or more and less adequate forms of knowledge. The other means of examining these questions is to consider data regarding cultural orientations and the social judgments of individuals, particularly in the realm of morality.

Contradictions and Paradoxes. The basic claims of social constructionism have one of two possible implications: Either social construction has no greater validity than any other viewpoint, or it is self-contradictory in that it asserts the very propositions it is designed to reject.

One basic claim of social constructionism, as we have seen, is that thought, including that of social scientists, mirrors the historical and cultural orientation. This means that the evaluations and explanations of social construction theorists themselves are subject to historical and cultural forces. Hence social construction explanations are culturally determined (they are cultural inventions) and biased for the same reasons as other explanations, and there is no basis for determining their validity or comparative adequacy. Social construction is a social construction! In other words, we have a vicious cycle in which the idea that thought is culturally determined is itself culturally determined and thus no more valid than any other idea regarding the sources of thought. Accordingly, one implication is that the tenets of the theory are the basis for the deconstruction of social construction.

However, other tenets of social constructionism imply that the position is self-contradictory. In spite of their seeming cultural relativism, social constructionists do take the position that it is possible to reason in ways that go beyond the historical and cultural context in order to provide more truthful and valid positions than those biased by cultural context. The most obvious manifestation of this notion is in the presentation of the theoretical structure of social construction not as just another cultural invention but as a correct explanation of culture, knowledge, and individual development. Social constructionists do not merely describe this culture as individualistic; they criticize psychological explanations and propose an alternative explanation. Some couple that with moralizations about the individualism of the culture. As one example, Hogan (1975) criticizes the dominant temper of psychology by labeling it as individualistic and egocentric. He dismisses the positions of Dewey, Piaget, and Kohlberg as presenting various versions of "romantic individualism" and Freud's position as a form of "egoistic individualism." Hogan moralizes about psychological explanations and cultural individualism in asserting that they are "symptomatic of a sick society." He proposes an alternative explanation (referred to as role theory) believed to correct shortcomings in psychology and improve the condition of society. Similarly, Sampson (1977) goes beyond individualism to consider explanations based on collectivism and interdependence. Moreover, collectivism and interdependence are regarded as correctives to the social problems caused by individualism that would improve human welfare. Invoked are notions of progress for society and of more adequate explanations for the social sciences.

Whether it be with regard to psychological explanations or the moral status of society, by invoking notions of progress and adequacy, social constructionists affirm the propositions they presumably reject. In addition, their ability to provide a psychology of collectivism and interdependence renders them free of the cultural constraints to which they claim most everyone else is subject. Unlike others, their viewpoints are not "blinded by the cultural heritage." Therefore, social constructionists assert just the type of individualism and transcendence they criticize in mainstream psychology. Because of the implicit assertion of rejected propositions, this is a more serious problem than the previously mentioned negation of the validity of social construction by the very premise of social construction. It is asserted that knowledge consists of shared meanings and is acquired through cultural influences; but a version of intellectual and moral progress is presented. It is asserted that psychological explanations are biased and incomplete because of the idealization of individual transcendence of the group; but an explanation at odds with the group norm is presented, whose validity requires that its proponents transcend their culture's biases.

Moral and Social Development. The idea that cultures can be characterized as globally individualistic or collectivistic and that these orientations unknowingly influence social scientists' explanations has a large bearing on characterizations of the more specific realm of morality and its development. According to this idea, if science and religion or evolution and creationism have similar status as forms of knowledge—each culturally determined and of equal evidential value—surely morality must be viewed as culturally determined and variable. It follows from this cultural perspective that if our society's general orientation is individualistic, its morality must also be individualistic in nature. This means that moral values and judgments mainly revolve around concerns with rights, equality, and personal liberties or freedoms. It also follows that research and theory on moral development by members of this culture reflect a liberal, rights-oriented, egalitarian bias. Although they are not explicit about it, some of the social constructionists mentioned above assume that a morality of collectivism, connectedness, and interdependence is uncharacteristic of this culture because of its emphasis on individual freedoms and rights. (It is also implied that collectivism and interdependence form a more adequate morality in their belief that individualism has produced societal decay.) An explicit statement comes from a group that has conducted cross-cultural research in the United States and India (Shweder, 1986; Shweder, Mahapatra, and Miller, 1987). They maintain that Western morality is "rights based," while Indian Hindu morality is "duty based." Duty-based morality, in contrast with self-interested rights-based morality, emphasizes tradition, social hierarchy, and the performance of particular duties defined by the codes of the social order. For instance, a duty-based system of morality contrasts sharply with rights and equality, since it is tied to the affirmation and maintenance of unequal distribution (for example, in health, wealth, or status) based on hierarchical roles. These researchers also maintain that most Western developmental explanations of morality are culturally biased by a liberal individualism that is not representative of any general or universalizable moral reasoning.

However, this idea of general, homogeneous moral orientations that divide up by culture is not very well sustained by the

varying positions held by different members of the society. There
are many more disagreements, conflicts, and debates over morality
than would be expected if the society were adequately characterized
as individualistic and rights oriented. Deep disagreements and
conflicts are evident from at least three sources: from the ways social
scientists and other scholars characterize the society, from public
legal and political positions, and from data from large representative samples of laypersons.

First consider some scholarly characterizations of morality in
the society. A particularly informative example comes from the
propositions put forth by some who have been concerned with
problems of what they refer to as "character education" in the
schools (Bennett, 1980; Bennett and Delattre, 1978, 1979; Sommers,
1984; Wynne, 1986). Like social constructionists, this group holds
that the society is in a state of moral decay and that there is a liberal,
secular bias in some psychological explanations of moral development. However, they also claim that those liberal biases are
representative not of the dominant morality of this society but of a
minority group with an ideology of secular humanism (at times
John Dewey has been referred to as the high priest of secular
humanism). The claim is that the morality of this society is more
adequately represented by its traditions, with concerns for virtuous
acts, conformity to duties, and upholding the moral codes of the
social order. Notice that such a characterization of this society is
inconsistent with the idea that Western morality is individualistic
or rights oriented and more consistent with the characterizations of
Hindu morality (which supposedly is diametrically opposed to
Western morality). Matters are further complicated by findings from
the research of one of those supposedly presenting a liberal and
secular view (Kohlberg, 1969). It turns out that the majority of adult
Americans studied display the type of moral reasoning that
Kohlberg refers to as oriented toward duties, authority, and
maintenance of the social order.

Other recent discussions bring another set of differences into
the picture. It has been asserted that moral orientations in the
society differ by gender (Gilligan, 1982). Concerns with rights,
equality, and justice represent an orientation mainly favored by
males; females, in contrast, have a relational orientation that

emphasizes connectedness and interdependence. The dichotomy based on gender is, in turn, questioned by researchers whose emphasis on cultural determination leads to the view that these orientations divide up by culture, such that justice is characteristic of both genders in the United States, while relational concerns are characteristic of males and females in cultures like those of India. This proposition also complicates the characterization of Indian morality by adding the relational orientation to the duty orientation.

These few examples show that we have a dizzying situation in terms of social scientists' portrayals of our culture's moral orientations and its differences from other cultures. These disagreements parallel disagreements and debates over moral issues within the society. There is hardly a consensus over many issues, including those bearing on personal rights and freedoms (affirmative action, women's rights, equal pay, the death penalty, the rights of homosexuals, and so on). Even at the level of constitutional decisions, it cannot be said that individual rights and freedoms are always supported. Whereas some Supreme Court decisions uphold individual rights, others do not. As examples, in three recent cases (in 1986 and 1988), the Supreme Court ruled against the right to engage in private, consensual acts of homosexuality and the right to free speech when it violates school rules.

The variability in characterizations of morality in this society and the apparent lack of consensus on important issues suggest the need for a reconceptualization of the intersection of culture and morality. For this society, at least, it does not appear that general, homogeneous characterizations accomplish the task of describing moral and social orientations. It could be argued that this society is sufficiently large and varied in the backgrounds of the participants that more than one general cultural orientation appear to be represented. However, this reconceptualization would not be sufficient to capture the nature of the heterogeneity of social orientations—as evidenced by survey findings, dating back to the 1930s, on Americans' attitudes toward rights and liberties.

The survey findings show individuals holding a mixture of attitudes toward moral and social issues that are not by any means solely tied to rights and liberties. A heterogeneity of moral and social concerns is evident within individuals, which calls for a reconceptualization of culture and morality to account for differentiations made regarding different aspects of social interaction. Perhaps the most comprehensive of the surveys was conducted in the 1970s, with large samples of adults (McClosky and Brill, 1983) responding to a large number of survey items (about 300) dealing with issues that would normally be regarded to be at the heart of individualism: rights and liberties (freedom of speech, press, assembly, and religion, as well as academic freedom and the right to dissent, to have privacy, and to choose one's own life-style). The results were clear-cut in their diversity: Members of this society sometimes uphold personal rights and liberties, and sometimes they do not. In the abstract, rights and freedoms are supported. They are also supported when they are not in strong conflict with other moral goals (such as preventing harm) or concerns with cultural traditions and maintaining social order. It is important to stress that the same respondents who endorsed rights and freedoms in some contexts failed to do so in other contexts. In many contexts, freedom of speech, religion, privacy, and assembly, to cite a few examples, were not upheld (for details, see McClosky and Brill, 1983; Turiel, Killen, and Helwig, 1987). These findings do not portray Americans as having an "ethos of self-contained individualism."

Heterogeneity in Social Judgments

Explaining diversity in social judgments and practices is a long-standing problem struggled with by philosophers, anthropologists, and psychologists. All too often, however, the observation of diversity of some kind is taken as proof of (or at least evidence for) cultural determinism as the explanatory principle for acquisition. An explanatory leap from observed diversity is made in the far-reaching assertion, noted earlier, that explanations of child development are cultural inventions. One of several grounds for this assertion is that there are diverse explanations of child psychology. The variety of theories of development is regarded as an indication that there is no true explanation to be obtained and that extant views are defined by culture. However, the diversity of theories can be taken to suggest just the opposite: The lack of agreement among theorists could just as well be an indication that culture has a minimal influence and that theorists are trying to uncover or discover ways of explaining complicated phenomena. The complexity and obscurity of psychological-developmental issues may be a major source of diversity in explanations.

It is this observed diversity that has been capitalized upon in order to ban books from public schools or treat evolutionary theory as just another viewpoint equal with creationism. A principle of different but equal seems to be at work here. The existence of differences in viewpoints is equalized by, for instance, labeling secular humanism another form of religion.

Frequently, cross-cultural observations of diversity have been translated into the assumption that moral acquisition is the learning of cultural codes. Often-cited examples include cultural practices of infanticide, patricide, and polygamy. Also cited are variations in acceptable sexual practices and the existence in some cultures of rigid hierarchical role differentiations (such as in caste systems). Citing dramatic examples of this sort only serves to catalogue possible variations and provide what has been referred to as sociological information (Asch, 1952). As has been extensively discussed elsewhere, variations should not be automatically translated into an explanatory mechanism (Asch, 1952; Duncker, 1939; Hatch, 1983; Schmidt, 1955; Spiro, 1986; Wertheimer, 1935). Variations can stem from a number of sources and constitute data requiring explanation.

The survey findings on Americans' attitudes toward rights and freedoms complicate the problem considerably by showing that explaining diversity is not a straightforward matter of comparing different groups. Diversity exists within individuals' thinking. One avenue for dealing with diverse social attitudes comes from recent research on the development of children's social reasoning showing that children make distinctions among different aspects of social relationships and social regulations. A very well documented proposition is that children and adolescents are, all at once, oriented toward interdependence, collectivism, tradition, and individualism (for a review and details, see Turiel, Killen, and Helwig, 1987). These concerns with social matters are not of one kind only. The research shows that children form moral judgments pertaining to harm, welfare, justice, and rights, which are distinguishable from their concepts of social convention pertaining to uniformities that coordinate social interactions and are part of systems of social organization. Through their moral judgments, children display understandings of interdependence. Through their concepts of convention, children display understandings of social organization and collectivity. Individualism is part of the picture, since children and adolescents are also concerned with personal choice and prerogative (Nucci, 1981; Smetana, 1988).

The coexistence of different types of social judgments and the lack of a unitary cultural orientation are consistent with the survey findings on the application of rights and freedoms. Although rights and freedoms are of concern to Americans, other social issues, such as custom, convention, and cultural traditions, are also of concern. This is evidenced by both studies of attitudes toward rights and examinations of the development of different realms of social reasoning. And it is not solely in Western societies that children develop distinct forms of social judgment: Although the majority of studies were conducted in the United States, similar findings were obtained in Nigeria (Hollos, Leis, and Turiel, 1986), Korea (Song, Smetana, and Kim, 1987), and Indonesia (Carey and Ford, 1983).

This should not be taken to mean that cultural affiliation is unimportant or that there is always uniformity between cultures. One point already stressed is that cross-cultural variability in social judgments and practices requires explanation and should not be taken as direct evidence for the learning of cultural norms or values. Another point is that cultures are not homogeneous entities imposed upon individuals in a top-down fashion. Developing children deal with a variety of types of social experiences, including direct relationships with others, that influence their development. It is also no small matter that individuals are able to reflect upon those experiences and their cultural constructions. It may well be that individuals have the dual relationship to the group of being part of it and being able to stand apart from it through critical reflection. A homogeneous conception of culture is too broad to account for the different social contexts forming part of individuals' experiences.

More detailed conceptual and empirical analyses than are currently available are needed in order to better explain cross-cultural variations and commonalities in social judgments and practices. One useful direction for such analyses advanced by psychologists (Asch, 1952; Duncker, 1939) and anthropologists (Hatch, 1983; Spiro, 1986) bears on the role of information about persons and assumptions about reality. A central point is that even when moral concepts are similar, differences in accepted facts or beliefs about the natural and supernatural can produce different moral decisions or conclusions. Similarly, assumptions made about psychological or biological reality can bear upon when, how, and to whom moral principles apply (decision about abortion is a case in point). As stated by Hatch (1983, p. 67): "For the anthropologists to establish the claim about the radical differences in values among the world's populations, they would have to eliminate these differences in factual belief and compare pure moral values uncontaminated by existential ideas."

The distinction between assumptions or beliefs regarding reality, on the one hand, and moral concepts or principles, on the other, is an important one that helps explain some apparent differences in cultural practices. It is likely that beliefs and information regarding matters that are neither of direct access nor based on observable knowledge would differ by context and influence moral decisions. Some examples taken from Asch, Duncker, and Hatch illustrate this point. In some societies, for instance, it is common practice for sons to put their elderly parents to death while the parents are still in good health. Underlying this practice is the belief, among others, that a person's state of health at the time of death is carried into the next world (Asch, 1952). Accordingly, varying assumptions about an afterlife can lead to different conclusions as to what furthers another's welfare. As another example, moral decisions may be influenced by beliefs or knowledge that illnesses are caused by spirits or by germs and viruses. The current debate over abortion often hinges on differences in biological assumptions about the beginning of life (Smetana, 1982). In our recent history, decisions regarding social hierarchies and equality among persons have been influenced by assumptions regarding psychology, physiology, and heredity (Gould, 1981).

These considerations bear directly on a study comparing Hindus from an orthodox temple town in India with secular

Americans (Shweder, Mahapatra, and Miller, 1987), from which it was presumed that cross-cultural variations were obtained in moral and conventional concepts. It was concluded that because moral judgments among Indians are duty based and tied to role differentiations, they do not distinguish between morality (for example, justice concerns) and convention (for example, social order maintenance). It was further argued that the distinction between morality and convention is specific to a rights-based cultural orientation tied to individualism. Those data, however, provide a good context for examining how differences in assumptions about the natural and supernatural produce varying conclusions. Reinterpretations of the data (Turiel, Killen, and Helwig, 1987) indicated that the primary variations were not in moral concepts but in cultural beliefs in an afterlife, the transmigration of souls, and assumptions about cause-effect relations between earthly and unearthly events.

Tomorrow

Currently, there is a great deal of stereotyping of social orientations. Perhaps we can avoid this particular kind of stereotyping in the future by looking to the recent past. Whereas Americans are now being characterized as oriented to self-contained individualism, it was not too long ago that social scientists were portraying a culture whose ethos was conformity, bureaucracy, and dependence. During the 1950s and beyond, many were alerting us to how Americans were faceless types who were other directed (Riesman, Glazer, and Denney, 1953), "organization men" (Whyte, 1956), or white-collar people who "are the interchangeable parts of the big chains of authority that bind the society together" (Mills, 1956, p. xvii). In contrast to individualism, the culture was characterized as constituted of persons lacking freedom, personal control over their lives, assertiveness, or creativity.

These relatively fast shifts in social scientific characterizations of the society (which, it should be stressed, do not represent analyses of current changes in society) are further illustrations of the inadequacies of one-dimensional portrayals. That such opposite characterizations of the same culture exist suggests the need for an alternative approach that avoids stereotypical portrayals. In order to go beyond a stereotyping of the social orientations of cultures and individuals, it is necessary to account for the coexistence of social judgments, the variety of contexts for individuals' social interactions within societies, and distinctions between social or moral concepts and fundamental assumptions about reality. Such a program of research would be consistent with a perspective, also put forth in the 1950s, referred to as "relational determination" (Asch, 1952). Rather than viewing culture as the only relevant context that determines fixed moral values and judgments through its codes, the idea of relational determination has the virtue of attempting to account for the circumstances and conditions to which social and moral judgments are applied. The basic premise is interactional—that in their social judgments individuals apply their concepts in ways that account for particular circumstances and social conditions. Accordingly, it is essential to consider the meanings attributed to a situation and the belief and information available to persons. With regard to the example already mentioned, killing one's parents to ensure their well-being in an afterlife would not have the same meaning as would doing it to inherit their wealth, even though the acts are the same in a literal sense. Furthermore, if we do not assume that individuals hold one general social orientation, then competing moral, social, and personal goals and their potential conflicts would contribute to explanations of variations within and between cultures.

References

Asch, S. E. *Social Psychology.* Englewood Cliffs, N.J.: Prentice-Hall, 1952.

Bennett, W. J. "The Teacher, the Curriculum, and Values Education Development." *New Directions in Higher Education,* 1980, *8,* 27–34.

Bennett, W. J., and Delattre, E. J. "Moral Education in the Schools." *The Public Interest,* 1978, *50,* 81–98.

Bennett, W. J., and Delattre, E. J. "A Moral Education: Some Thoughts on How Best to Achieve It." *American Educator: The*

Professional Journal of the American Federation of Teachers, 1979, *3,* 6-9.

Bower, T.G.R. *Human Development.* New York: W. H. Freeman, 1979.

Carey, N., and Ford, M. "Domains of Social and Self-Regulation: An Indonesian Study." Paper presented at the annual meeting of the American Psychological Association, Los Angeles, August 1983.

Dawkins, R. *The Selfish Gene.* New York: Oxford University Press, 1976.

Duncker, K. "Ethical Relativity? (An Inquiry into the Psychology of Ethics)." *Mind,* 1939, *48,* 39-53.

Fodor, J. *The Modularity of Mind.* Cambridge, Mass.: MIT Press, 1983.

Gelman, R. "Preschool Thought." *American Psychologist,* 1979, *34,* 900-905.

Gergen, K. J. "Toward Generative Theory." *Journal of Personality and Social Psychology,* 1978, *36,* 1344-1360.

Gergen, K. J. "The Social Constructionist Movement in Modern Psychology." *American Psychologist,* 1985, *40,* 266-275.

Gergen, K. J. "Correspondence Versus Autonomy in the Language of Understanding Human Action." In D. W. Fiske and R. A. Shweder (eds.), *Metatheory in Social Science: Pluralisms and Subjectivities.* Chicago: University of Chicago Press, 1986.

Gilligan, C. *In a Different Voice: Psychological Theory and Women's Development.* Cambridge, Mass.: Harvard University Press, 1982.

Gould, S. J. *The Mismeasure of Man.* New York: Norton, 1981.

Hatch, E. *Culture and Morality: The Relativity of Values in Anthropology.* New York: Columbia University Press, 1983.

Hogan, R. "Theoretical Egocentrism and the Problem of Compliance." *American Psychologist,* 1975, *30,* 533-539.

Hollos, M., Leis, P., and Turiel, E. "Social Reasoning in Ijo Children and Adolescents in Nigerian Communities." *Journal of Cross-Cultural Psychology,* 1986, *17,* 352-376.

Keil, F. "On the Structure-Dependent Nature of Stages of Cognitive Development." In I. Levin (ed.), *Stage and Structure: Reopening the Debate.* Norwood, N.J.: Ablex, 1986.

Kessen, W. "The American Child and Other Cultural Inventions." *American Psychologist,* 1979, *34,* 815–820.

Kessen, W. "The Child and Other Cultural Inventions." In F. S. Kessel and A. W. Siegel (eds.), *The Child and Other Cultural Inventions.* New York: Praeger, 1983.

Kohlberg, L. "Stage and Sequence: The Cognitive-Developmental Approach to Socialization." In D. A. Goslin (ed.), *Handbook of Socialization Theory and Research.* Skokie, Ill.: Rand McNally, 1969.

McClosky, H., and Brill, A. *Dimensions of Tolerance: What Americans Believe About Civil Liberties.* New York: Russell Sage Foundation, 1983.

Mills, C. W. *White Collar: The American Middle Class.* New York: Oxford University Press, 1956.

Nucci, L. P. "The Development of Personal Concepts: A Domain Distinct from Moral or Societal Concepts." *Child Development,* 1981, *52,* 114–121.

Piaget, J. *The Moral Judgment of the Child.* New York: Free Press, 1965. (Originally published 1932.)

Riesman, D., Glazer, N., and Denney, R. *The Lonely Crowd: A Study of the Changing American Character.* New York: Doubleday, 1953.

Sampson, E. E. "Psychology and the American Ideal." *Journal of Personality and Social Psychology,* 1977, *35,* 767–782.

Sampson, E. E. "Scientific Paradigms and Social Values: Wanted— A Scientific Revolution." *Journal of Personality and Social Psychology,* 1978, *36,* 1332–1343.

Sampson, E. E. "Cognitive Psychology as Ideology." *American Psychologist,* 1981, *36,* 730–742.

Schmidt, P. M. "Some Criticisms of Cultural Relativism." *Journal of Philosophy,* 1955, *52,* 780–791.

Shweder, R. A. "Divergent Rationalities." In D. W. Fiske and R. A. Shweder (eds.), *Metatheory in Social Science: Pluralism and Subjectivities.* Chicago: University of Chicago Press, 1986.

Shweder, R. A., Mahapatra, M., and Miller, J. G. "Culture and Moral Development." In J. Kagan and S. Lamb (eds.), *The Emergence of Morality in Young Children.* Chicago: University of Chicago Press, 1987.

Skinner, B. F. "Whatever Happened to Psychology as the Science of Behavior?" *American Psychologist*, 1987, *42*, 780–786.

Smetana, J. G. *Concepts of Self and Morality: Women's Reasoning About Abortion*. New York: Praeger, 1982.

Smetana, J. G. "Concepts of Self and Social Convention: Adolescents' and Parents' Reasoning About Hypothetical and Actual Family Conflicts." In M. R. Gunnar (ed.), Minnesota Symposia on Child Psychology. Vol. 21. Hillsdale, N.J.: Erlbaum, 1988.

Sommers, C. H. "Ethics Without Virtue: Moral Education in America." *American Scholar*, 1984, *53*, 381–389.

Song, M., Smetana, J. G., and Kim, S. "Korean Children's Conceptions of Moral and Conventional Transgressions." *Developmental Psychology*, 1987, *23*, 577–582.

Spiro, M. E. "Cultural Relativism and the Future of Anthropology." *Cultural Anthropology*, 1986, *1*, 259–286.

Trivers, R. L. "The Evolution of Reciprocal Altruism." *Quarterly Review of Biology*, 1971, *46*, 35–57.

Trivers, R. L. "Why You Do What You Do: Sociobiology—A New Theory of Behavior." *Time*, Aug. 1, 1977.

Turiel, E., Killen, M., and Helwig, C. C. "Morality: Its Structure, Functions and Vagaries." In J. Kagan and S. Lamb (eds.), *The Emergence of Moral Concepts in Young Children*. Chicago: University of Chicago Press, 1987.

"U.S. Judge Bans Thirty-Six Textbooks." *San Francisco Chronicle*, Mar. 5, 1987.

Wertheimer, M. "Some Problems in the Theory of Ethics." *Social Research*, 1935, *2*, 353–367.

Whyte, W. H. *The Organization Man*. New York: Simon & Schuster, 1956.

Wilson, E. O. *Sociobiology: The New Synthesis*. Cambridge, Mass.: Harvard University Press, 1975.

Wilson, E. O. *On Human Nature*. Cambridge, Mass.: Harvard University Press, 1978.

Wynne, E. A. "The Great Tradition in Education: Transmitting Moral Values." *Educational Leadership*, 1986, *43*, 4–9.

Chapter 6

A Skill Approach to Emotional Development: From Basic- to Subordinate-Category Emotions

Kurt W. Fischer
Phillip R. Shaver
Peter Carnochan

 There is an enormous difference between the anger of a seven-month-old whose hands are held against her will and a forty-year-old's "smoldering resentment" caused by a boss's favoritism toward a rival worker (Campos and others, 1983). There is also a strong similarity: Both are cases of anger. Although it strains the imagination to describe the seven-month-old as experiencing smoldering resentment, the forty-year-old's resentment does bear some resemblance to the infant's anger. What do the two forms of behavior have in common that causes people to see them as examples of essentially the same emotion—as episodes of anger, not of sadness or joy? What accounts for the difference in sophistication between the two?

Note: Preparation of this chapter was supported by a fellowship from the Cattell Fund and by a grant from the Spencer Foundation. The authors would like to thank Joseph Campos, Helen Hand, Susan Harter, Susie Lamborn, and Judy Schwartz for their contributions to the arguments presented here.

The similarities and differences can be explained by a developmental theory that integrates research on cognitive and emotional development. Such a skill theory of emotional development should explain how infants can experience primitive anger but not the anger of an adult, especially not such complex forms of anger as resentment. It should explain how, with development, resentment gradually grows out of early forms of anger. The theory should address both the "basic" emotions—such as anger, fear, sadness, joy, and love—and the wide range of sophisticated emotions, such as resentment, jealousy, pride, and guilt.

The skill theory of emotional development proposed here is an integration of a theory of the development of cognitive skills (Fischer, 1980) and a composite of recent theories about the organization and function of emotions. The skill theory explains how emotions are activated and how they organize behavior. It also places emotions in a developmental context and explains how emotion-related skills are gradually transformed as infants develop into adults.

Need for a Developmental Perspective

The study of emotions has made great progress in recent years. The cultural universality of a number of basic emotions has been documented, including anger, sadness, fear, joy, and love or attachment (for love/attachment, see Bretherton and Waters, 1985; Sroufe, 1979; for other emotions, see Ekman, Friesen, and Ellsworth, 1982; Izard, 1977). These emotions have been shown to be present in infants by the middle of the first year, if not earlier; and they are universal across human cultures.

At the same time, the massive diversity of human emotions has been documented. When all emotion categories are considered, people in different cultures show a wide range and complexity of emotions, with some languages (including English) naming hundreds of them (Averill, 1975). These complex emotions are part of the fabric of literature and art (Schwartz and Shaver, forthcoming).

The evidence for both the universality of basic emotions and the cultural diversity of complex emotions has stirred controversy in the field of emotion research. Are emotions innate (Ekman, 1984), or are they socially constructed (Harre, 1986b)? Are emotions present in infants in their full-blown, mature form, or are they constructed later in development? Can the basic nature of emotions be seen in the way people talk about them, or are behavior and physiology the only legitimate indexes of emotions? Do emotions precede cognitions (Zajonc, 1984), or do cognitions precede emotions (Lazarus, 1984)?

Although these controversies have been fruitful in generating new research, they cannot be resolved on one side or the other. Nature does not honor human dichotomies. For example, the evidence used to argue for cross-cultural universality has come from facial and vocal expressions of basic emotions, such as fear, anger, and joy. The evidence for cultural relativity has come from adult descriptions of sophisticated emotions, such as *loneliness* in English-language culture (Levy, 1973), *accidie* in medieval European culture (Harre, 1986a), and *amae* in Japanese culture (Doi, 1973; Morsbach and Tyler, 1986). The evidence for basic emotions concerns fundamental emotional behaviors evident from early infancy, whereas the evidence for cultural relativity stems from the sophisticated, complex utterances of adults who are capable of conceptualizing their emotions. There is no real dichotomy here.

To resolve the *apparent* dichotomies, the field needs a theory that explains how emotions develop. Such a theory would provide rules for explaining how the simpler processes of early basic or core emotions are transformed, in steps along a continuum, into the complex processes of later, more sophisticated emotions (see Campos and others, 1983; Fox and Davidson, 1984; Izard, 1978, Leventhal and Scherer, 1987).

As suggested by the example of the seven-month-old who is angry about being restrained, there *are* emotions in infancy. They are the same ones for which it is easiest to document cross-cultural universality of expression and recognition. At the same time, there are many sophisticated emotions which no one would attribute to infants. For example, infants do not have identities to protect, complex social comparisons to weigh, or decisions to make about justice and injustice, so they do not experience shame, envy, or indignation.

The issue is not whether innate or socially constructed emotions exist but how the sophisticated and socially constructed emotions are built upon a foundation of early-appearing basic emotions. Similarly, the issue is not whether emotion depends on cognition or vice versa, since both are always present, but how the organization of emotion and cognition develops from rudimentary to sophisticated forms. What is needed, then, is (1) a theory of *emotions* that is compatible with development and that includes both the basic emotions and the more sophisticated ones and (2) a theory of *development* that includes emotions as well as cognitions and that explains how the organization of behavior (including cognition, emotion, and action) changes systematically over time. We believe that recent theories of emotion and of skill development fill these needs. They provide the tools necessary for explaining how emotions are integrated with cognitive development and how they develop from rudimentary to sophisticated forms.

Organization of Emotions

We detect an emerging consensus among emotion researchers and theorists concerning the nature of emotions as organized processes (see Campos and others, 1983; Frijda, 1986; Scherer, 1984; Shaver, Schwartz, Kirson, and O'Connor, 1987). The consensus view of emotions includes four components: a definition of emotion emphasizing functionally organized action tendencies, the structure of emotion categories, the event scripts that define each category, and the processes that produce specific emotional responses fitting these categories and scripts. Our formulation of the consensus view is outlined in Figures 6.1 and 6.2 and in Table 6.1, which provide a focus for the discussion that follows.

What Is an Emotion? In searching for the referent of an emotion term like *anger*, three facets demand attention. First, there are physical signs of anger—facial expressions, clenched fists, bulging arteries, loud voice, and so on. Second, there is a subjective side to anger—the way anger feels when we ourselves are angry. Third, there is an organization of anger episodes that is implicitly understood in terms of functions, goals, action tendencies, and so on. When we see that a person is becoming angry, we know what kinds of events may have caused this and what kinds of actions may follow. All three of these facets contribute to what people mean by "emotion" and by specific emotion labels, such as "fear" or "anger."

Particularly at the early stages of development, the three aspects are closely interrelated. The physiological, expressive, and gestural components of anger all serve anger's primary function: to remove or destroy an obstacle that is interfering with the satisfaction of an intention or desire. With the onset of anger, blood pressure rises as oxygen is pumped to tensing muscles, the jaw clenches, and the teeth may be shown as the body prepares for a struggle. The characteristic feeling of anger, which we have to assume is present in some form in infants' consciousness as it is in adults', is partly due to feedback from this kind of physiological and gestural change (Frijda, 1986). Ever since Darwin analyzed emotions from an evolutionary perspective ([1872] 1975), it has been possible to view the relations among the three components of basic emotions as products of natural selection (Ekman, 1973; Izard, 1977; Plutchik, 1980).

Within the first few months of life, human infants exhibit the genetically determined organization of expressions and actions associated with the basic emotions (Izard, 1978). People refer to these infantile response systems as emotions for at least two reasons: They contain certain biological markers associated in adulthood with, for example, anger and sadness. And they seem to serve the same general functions as adult responses (linking blocked progress with attempts to destroy an obstacle and linking failed efforts with goal abandonment, respectively).

With development, both goals and actions become more complex, but certain functions, viewed abstractly, are still realized. We therefore use the same basic-emotion terms for different developmental levels, even though the genetically determined organizations of these emotions may have become elaborated or partially restructured. The components of the basic-emotion systems can be extended, elaborated, detached, and suppressed, to form new socially and personally constructed combinations.

A Hierarchy of Emotion Categories. The relation between basic and sophisticated emotions is reflected in the growth of the emotion lexicon between age two and early adulthood. Two-year-olds talk about the basic emotions, using terms such as *mad, scared,* and *happy.* Adults, in addition, talk about nonbasic emotions, such as scorn, disappointment, and anxiety. Figure 6.1 represents the organized knowledge of emotion categories exhibited by adult subjects in recent studies (for example, Scherer, 1984; Shaver,

Schwartz, Kirson, and O'Connor, 1987). The categories are organized hierarchically into three levels of specificity. The superordinate categories involve a split between positive and negative
emotions. The basic categories, nested within the two superordinate
groups, are a small set of common, core emotions, including love,
joy, anger, sadness, and fear. At the subordinate level, there are
scores of emotion terms, such as adoration, resentment, and loneliness, which mark specific forms of the basic-category emotions.

    The categories generally fit a prototype model (Rosch, 1978).
Those in the middle of the hierarchy are the most basic in Rosch's
sense: They are the categories people agree upon most easily and use
most frequently in everyday discourse. The first emotion terms
learned by American and British children seem to name these
categories (Bretherton, Fritz, Zahn-Waxler, and Ridgeway, 1986;
Dunn, Bretherton, and Munn, 1987). And these are the same
categories that have been identified as universal across human
cultures and that are evident in infants' facial expressions (see
Campos and others, 1983; Ekman, Friesen, and Ellsworth, 1982;
Izard, 1977). The close correspondence between what is "basic" in
the language of emotion and what is "basic"—that is, first to
emerge—in emotional development suggests that the linguistic
categories are organized around actual core emotion systems.

    The positive-negative distinction is superordinate, integrat-
ing across basic categories: Love and happiness are "good" feelings;
anger, sadness, and fear are "bad" feelings. Certain forms of these
broad categories seem to be as accessible and easily used as the basic
categories. For example, terms for positive and negative qualities—
nice and *mean*, *good* and *bad*, *like* and *don't like*—seem to develop
as early as do terms for the basic-emotion categories (see Bretherton,
Fritz, Zahn-Waxler, and Ridgeway, 1986; Fischer and others, 1984;
Fischer and Pipp, 1984a). This fact makes the emotion hierarchy
different from the typical prototype hierarchies described by Rosch
(1978), in which superordinate categories (for example, animal,
furniture) are less accessible than basic categories (for example, dog,
chair). In the case of emotions, the tangible experience of desirability versus undesirability ("Give me that." "Let me do it." "No, I
don't want to.") seems to provide an extra source of support for
using emotion terms at a superordinate level.

Figure 6.1. A Simplified Version of the Emotion Hierarchy Reported by Shaver, Schwartz, Kirson, and O'Connor (1987).

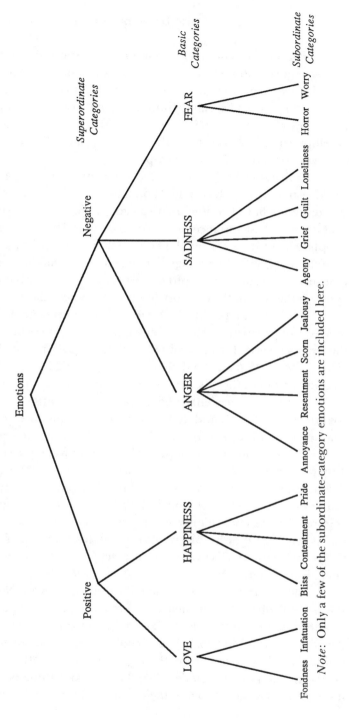

Note: Only a few of the subordinate-category emotions are included here.

The subordinate-category emotions are specific forms of the basic-category emotions. These emotions and a person's knowledge of them seem to develop relatively late and to depend more on specific contexts and social definitions than do categories higher in the hierarchy. As we will show, a skill theory of emotional development can be used to predict how such subordinate emotions as resentment and jealousy develop.

Prototypic Scripts for Basic Emotions. Prototype theory specifies not only the hierarchical organization of categories shown in Figure 6.1 but also how each category is defined in terms of a prototype—a best instance of the category that designates its core. People generally agree on the name for a prototypical emotion episode. They will often disagree, however, on classifying instances that share only some of the prototype's characteristics. That is, they agree on the core of the category but not on its boundaries.

Adult prototypes for the basic-emotion categories have been derived from written accounts of emotional experiences or episodes (Shaver, Schwartz, Kirson, and O'Connor, 1987; see also de Rivera, 1981; Scherer, Walbott, and Summerfield, 1986). For each basic-category emotion, there is a typical script for emotion episodes that includes both antecedents and responses, the latter including cognitive, behavioral, and bodily reactions. For the three negative emotions, there are also typical self-control or coping strategies.

Table 6.1 shows the empirically derived prototypic script for anger. Anger occurs when a person perceives something as threatening harm or interfering with his or her goals in a way that is unfair to him or her. In response, the person becomes energized for aggression, looks and moves angrily, and focuses on the situation that is causing his or her anger. To control this emotional reaction, the person may try to cover it up or redefine the situation so that anger is no longer called for.

Clearly, this situation is described in adult terms. Nevertheless, several of the key elements are present even in infant anger. Infants of seven months become angry when their arms are held so that they cannot move or when a cookie they are about to eat is suddenly taken away from them (Campos and others, 1983; Stenberg, Campos, and Emde, 1983). Because something is interfering with their goal of moving their arms or eating the cookie, they

Table 6.1. Prototypic Script for Anger.

Antecedents:

Something interferes with the person's plans or goals or threatens to harm him or her.
This interference or harm is illegitimate or unfair.

Responses:

The person becomes energized to fight or verbally attack or imagine attacking the agent causing the anger so that he or she can rectify the injustice or physical harm.
The person looks angry and moves in a heavy, tight, or exaggerated way.
The person focuses on the anger-inducing situation, convinced that he or she is right.

Self-Control Procedures:

The person may try not to show his or her emotion or attempt to redefine the situation so that it no longer makes him or her angry.

Source: Adapted from Shaver, Schwartz, Kirson, and O'Connor, 1987.

become energized to remove the interference, focus on the distressing situation, and look angry. There is no evidence, however, of several other adult components, including imagining attack, trying to hide their anger, or mentally redefining the situation. These components await the further development of the child's capacities.

Presumably, similar scripts could be written for subordinate-category emotions, although we would expect much less agreement across cultural groups on these scripts. In fact, different cultures might construct not only different versions of the subordinate emotions but novel, culturally specific emotions as well.

Emotion Processes. The third component of the emotion theory specifies the processes that produce the different emotional responses fitting these categories and scripts. As shown in Figure 6.2, emotions begin with the perception of *notable change*. When events lead to a perception of change or the violation of expectations, this acts as a signal to continue processing the input for its affective significance.

The second step in the appraisal process is relating the event to *concerns* (Frijda, 1986). The term *concerns* refers both to the

Figure 6.2. Composite Model of the Emotion Process.

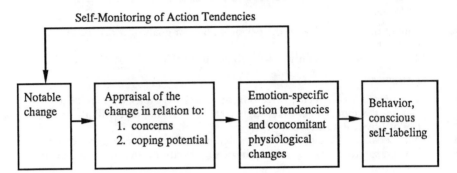

current goals and desires of the individual and to his or her implicit goals. The outcome of this step in emotion processing creates a general positive or negative evaluation, producing the superordinate division shown in Figure 6.1. Events that interfere with wish fulfillment or goal attainment lead to negative emotions, while events that facilitate wish fulfillment or goal attainment lead to positive emotions.

Beyond the superordinate distinction between positive and negative emotions, the specific emotional consequences of noting change depend upon the appraisal of the change in relation to *coping potential*. The basic emotions are the result of the individual's appraisal of how he or she can cope with or alter the event. If, according to the appraisal, the events are desirable or are even going surprisingly well, the emotional reaction is joy: The person feels good—smiling, laughing, or otherwise expressing positive feelings—and allows the events to continue. If, according to the appraisal, the events jeopardize a major goal and the individual feels that he or she has the means to overcome the obstacle, the emotion is anger and the anger script is activated. If an individual makes the appraisal that events threaten a goal, that these events are dangerous, and that he or she has little capacity to prevent the negative events, the resulting emotion is fear. If the individual makes the appraisal that events interfere with an important goal and the interference cannot be reversed, the goal must be abandoned, and the emotion experienced is sadness. For other basic emotions as well, there is a specific appraisal leading to a particular emotional reaction.

These different emotions, each following from a particular set of appraisals, can be viewed as patterned *action tendencies* (Frijda, 1986). Action tendencies are organized plans for bringing about a change in the person's relation to the appraised events. As they gain what Frijda calls control precedence—that is, top priority in the control of behavior—then the body is prepared physiologically to take the indicated actions. The action tendency accounts for measurable changes in heart rate, blood pressure, posture, and expression, which give rise to the subjective feelings associated with particular emotions.

With infants, the distinction between action tendencies and action itself is superfluous. With social experience and the development of cognitive capacity, children become able to represent actions apart from acting, which allows them to modulate their emotion responses. In studies of adults, such modulating tendencies have been referred to as coping or self-control efforts (see Lazarus, 1984; Shaver, Schwartz, Kirson, and O'Connor, 1987).

These self-control efforts arise as part of the *self-monitoring of action tendencies*. We propose that they involve an additional loop through the previously discussed appraisal process, as shown in Figure 6.2. That is, they are not a separate part of the emotion process (as proposed by Shaver, Schwartz, Kirson, and O'Connor, 1987; Frijda, 1986; and Leventhal and Scherer, 1987) but a re-application of the process from which the emotional action tendencies were generated. In this second pass through the appraisal process, which we call an emotion loop, emotional action tendencies themselves become the events to be appraised, causing an *emotion about an emotion.*

If the initial pass generated anger, for instance, then the self-perception of emerging action becomes a notable change that in turn is appraised. The result of this emotion loop, based on considerations such as relative social status or power, may be fear of counterattack. The action tendencies for fear then act upon the action tendencies for anger. Fear, when enacted behaviorally, involves freezing or fleeing. When carried out representationally, with anger action tendencies as the target, the result is suppression of anger. What emerges from this process—fear of anger or conflict between anger and fear—can sometimes be observed in behavior, physiological reactions, or self-labeling: "It scares me when I get so mad." This process is an inherent part of such complex emotions as resentment, jealousy, and exasperation.

As discussed so far, the emotion process may sound implausibly cognitive, conscious, and deliberate. Emotional appraisals and loops involving emotions about emotions are very frequently repeated, however, and like other skills, they become automatic (Shiffrin and Schneider, 1977). As a result of this automaticity, emotions seem to happen to us, or wash over us, without thought, even though the process that causes them is, or once was, quite complex.

With development, all the components of the emotion process represented in Figure 6.2 undergo reorganization. There are developments in the kinds of environmental and internal changes that get noticed, the kinds of appraisals that get made, the perceived potential to cope with changes, the organization and complexity of action tendencies, self-monitoring, and emotion labeling. The concerns of the infant are relatively simple: satisfaction of biological needs, being reliably cared for by an attachment figure, exploring the physical environment. As the infant grows, develops cognitively, and experiences socialization pressures, he or she also develops complex and automatic emotion loops and accumulates emotion-related concerns, such as not wanting to make an attachment figure angry or not wanting to "cry like a baby." Changes in the complexity and form of emotional processes create a need for more complex emotion concepts and categories, as reflected in Figure 6.1, and for new emotion scripts (such as for resentment, envy, and pride).

Skill Development

Skill theory (Fischer, 1980) is designed to explain the changes in skill acquisition and organization that occur with development. The theory, when integrated with the consensus model of emotions presented above, becomes a general skill theory of cognitive and emotional development. The basic components of the emotion process are present in rudimentary form early in infancy. Infants construct the basic-category emotions in action in the first half year of life. The skill theory of emotional development specifies the processes of integration and differentiation that produce first the basic emotions of infancy and later the more complex emotional organizations of adulthood. With skill theory, the investigator can predict detailed developmental sequences for emotion skills in any domain.

Developing Organization of Skills. According to skill theory, any voluntary or operant (Skinner, 1969) behavior develops progressively through a series of changes in organization. That is, what a person can control changes systematically and predictably with development. Emotions, understood as complex mixtures of thought and action processes, are amenable to the same developmental analysis applied in earlier work to tasks more traditionally conceptualized as cognitive.

In developing from birth to adulthood, people pass through four major reorganizations in their ability to control skills. These reorganizations, called *tiers,* involve reflexes, sensorimotor actions, representations, and abstractions, respectively. The tiers eventually progress from simple, concrete behaviors to abstract mental skills far removed from their origins in action (for example, thinking about personal identity, doing mathematical proofs, arguing about democracy). Within each tier, development proceeds through a series of four levels, summarized in Table 6.2. Note that these developmental levels are not the same as the categorical levels in prototype theory shown in Table 6.1.

The first level of each tier is the ability to control single sets, which are the elementary building blocks of that tier. For the four tiers, these sets are, respectively, reflexes, sensorimotor actions, representations, and abstractions. For example, with single representations, two- or three-year-olds can represent meanness, making a doll act mean in several ways, or separately, they can represent niceness, making it act nice in several ways; but they cannot coordinate two such representations. The second level within each tier is the ability to map single sets onto each other. With the dolls, four- and five-year-old children can map one representation for nice behavior onto another, so as to understand

Table 6.2. Levels of Skill Development.[a]

Level	Name of Structure	Tier[b] Reflex	Sensorimotor	Representational	Abstract	Estimated Age Region of Emergence
Rf1	Single reflex sets	[A] or [B]				3–4 weeks[c]
Rf2	Reflex mappings	[A —— B]				7–8 weeks[c]
Rf3	Reflex systems	$[A_{E,F} \longleftrightarrow B_{E,F}]$				10–11 weeks[c]
Rf4/S1	Systems of reflex systems, which are single sensorimotor sets	$\begin{bmatrix} A \rightarrow B \\ \downarrow \\ C \rightarrow D \end{bmatrix} \equiv$	[G]			4 months
S2	Sensorimotor mappings		[G —— H]			7–8 months
S3	Sensorimotor systems		$[G_{K,L} \longleftrightarrow H_{K,L}]$			11–13 months
S4/Rp1	Systems of sensorimotor systems, which are single representational sets		$\begin{bmatrix} G \rightarrow H \\ \downarrow \\ I \rightarrow J \end{bmatrix} \equiv$	[M]		20–24 months

Rp2	Representational mappings	$[M \, \text{—} \, N]$	4–5 years
Rp3	Representational systems	$[M_{Q.R} \longleftrightarrow N_{Q.R}]$	6–7 years
Rp4/A1	Systems of representational systems, which are single abstract sets	$\begin{bmatrix} M & \longrightarrow & N \\ & \downarrow & \\ O & \longrightarrow & P \end{bmatrix} \equiv [S]$	10–12 years
A2	Abstract mappings	$[S \, \text{—} \, T]$	14–16 years
A3	Abstract systems	$[S_{W.X} \longleftrightarrow T_{W.X}]$	18–20 years
A4	Systems of abstract systems, which are single principles	$\begin{bmatrix} S & \longleftrightarrow & T \\ \updownarrow & & \downarrow \\ U & \longrightarrow & V \end{bmatrix}$	24–26 years[c]

[a]Plain capital letters designate reflex sets; boldface capital letters designate sensorimotor sets; italic capital letters designate representational sets; and script capital letters designate abstract sets. Multiple subscripts designate differentiated components of a set; whenever there is a horizontal arrow, two or more subsets exist by definition, even when they are not expressly shown. Long, straight lines and arrows designate a relation between sets or systems. Brackets designate a single skill.

[b]Reflex structures continue at higher levels, as do sensorimotor and representational structures, but the formulas become so complex that they have been omitted. For example, to fill in the sensorimotor structures in the representational tier, simply replace each representational set with the sensorimotor formula for level S4.

[c]Since little research has been done on development at these levels, these regions must be considered highly tentative.

mean reciprocity: One doll is mean to another because that other doll was previously mean to it. Similarly, they can make a doll be nice because the other doll was previously nice. The third level within each tier is the ability to form a system of sets. Children six and seven years of age can coordinate the mappings of nice and mean behavior in the two dolls, making one be simultaneously nice and mean to the other because it was previously nice and mean. The fourth level involves the capacity to form a system of these systems, which constitutes the single set of the next tier. For example, the abstraction "intentionality" is based on a coordination of a system for nice and mean overt behaviors with a system for nice and mean intentions (Fischer, Hand, and Russell, 1984; Fischer and Pipp, 1984a).

Each level specifies an upper limit, or optimal level, for the complexity of skills a person can build and control. When a new optimal level emerges, it produces a cluster of spurts in performance under optimal performance conditions for a wide range of familiar domains. Table 6.2 indicates for each level the approximate age at which these spurts begin to occur for middle-class American children.

In any domain, skills develop through these levels and tiers. However, the structures of the small steps within each level vary widely and so cannot be shown in a single table. These steps are specified by a set of transformation rules for building more complex structures upon the basic structure for the level. Using the structures and transformation rules, one can predict developmental sequences of skills in great detail for any specific domain.

A skill is essentially a scheme or procedure for controlling variations in behavior within a context. The sets indicated by the letters in the skill structures in Table 6.2 specify sources of variation that a person can control, and the lines and arrows specify relations between those sources of variation. Emotions involve control of a number of such sources of variation, as suggested by the process model of emotions in Figure 6.2. Infants detect changes, appraise their significance, and react to that significance. Later in development, the sources controlled become even more numerous as people loop back through the emotion process: They detect their own emotional reaction, appraise its significance, and react to it.

For the purposes of this chapter, we will focus primarily on the largest developmental changes in Table 6.2: the tiers. In this way, we will be able to lay out the general outline of development of anger, resentment, and jealousy. The mechanisms of skill theory can be used to fill in the details and variations in this pattern. (For further explanation of these basic structural mechanisms and descriptions of how to use them, see Fischer, 1980; Fischer and Farrar, forthcoming; Fischer and Pipp, 1984b.)

Most theories that include concepts such as stage or level focus primarily on the organismic bases of changes in organization. That is, they characterize a person as changing from one stage or level to the next. According to skill theory, however, a skill is a characteristic not of a person but of a *person in a context*. The skill changes when either the person or the context changes. For example, people exhibit skills indicative of their optimal level only when there is environmental support for high-level performance. A child who has the organismic capacity to form representational mappings will be able to act out a story about nice reciprocity only if he or she has had experience with that sort of interaction and if the context provides support for that particular behavior.

In general, a child's functional level rises and falls with variations in many different contextual and organismic factors specified by a set of functional mechanisms (Fischer and Hogan, forthcoming; Fischer and Lamborn, forthcoming). In most situations, children do not perform at optimal level, but their level varies systematically, as specified by the functional mechanisms.

Emotions as Organizers. Emotions make an important contribution to these functional mechanisms, partly determining the level and content of people's skills at any moment. In everyday usage, emotions are sometimes thought of as taking a person over, eliminating his or her self-control. Although they do have a preemptive character, emotions do not eliminate control; instead, they affect its direction. As explained earlier, emotions have script-like properties that direct the organization of behavior.

An example from the behavior of three-and-a-half-year-old Seth Fischer illustrates how fear organizes behavior by directing control rather than eliminating it (Fischer and Elmendorf, 1986). On a visit to the Will Rogers Museum on Cheyenne Mountain in

Colorado Springs, Colorado, he became afraid as he and his father approached the narrow and eerie stone tower of the museum. Immediately he asked if there were any monsters there, showing the normal preschool tendency to externalize fear as a concern about monsters. As he and his father began to walk up the stone stairs, he asked to be carried. At each door they encountered in the tower, he asked if there were any monsters or bad guys behind the door. The organizing effect of fear also affected his perception of an audiotape of Will Rogers that was being played in the tower. When Rogers used the word "try," Seth immediately asked, "Who's dying?" Then when Rogers said "got," Seth asked, "Who's getting shot?" A few minutes later, when they left the tower, his fear quickly dissipated, along with his concern with monsters and injury.

This example illustrates how the organization of a particular emotion facilitates some behaviors and interferes with others. Seth became sensitized to detecting potential threats, while at the same time he became less able to explore the tower or learn about Will Rogers. The organizing effect was so powerful that it even led him to mishear Rogers's speech.

In this way, emotions do not simply disorganize or disrupt behavior, as has sometimes been claimed. They shift its organization toward a specific script, and one of the effects of that shift is on the level of performance. When an activated emotion script facilitates the demands of a task, level of performance on the task improves. When the script interferes with task demands, performance level deteriorates. Anger, for instance, facilitates detecting obstacles or affronts and acting assertively to remove them, and it interferes with behaviors that are incompatible with this script.

Development from Anger to Resentment and Jealousy

The skill theory of emotional development combines the organizing effects of emotions with the mechanisms for specifying developmental changes in skill organization. With this combination, many aspects of emotional development can potentially be predicted and explained. In this chapter, we are focusing on how basic-category emotions are gradually transformed into subordinate-category emotions, and especially on how anger is transformed into resentment and jealousy.

Anger develops in the reflex tier to gradually become a sensorimotor control structure called an action. This anger-action structure in turn is differentiated and integrated with other actions in the sensorimotor tier until a child can represent anger as occurring independently in the self and in others. In the representational tier, the representation of anger is then combined with other representations. The result is relations of concrete representations about anger, as when a child tells a story about a fight he or she had with a friend or begins to understand sophisticated subordinate emotions, such as resentment and jealousy. Then, at about the onset of adolescence, the complexities of representations produce the ability to construct abstractions about anger. Many of the subtleties of adult emotions involve abstractions and relations among abstractions.

Anger: Sensorimotor Action, Representation, and Abstraction. In the first few months of life, the relatively helpless newborn gradually develops the capacity to skillfully control single sensorimotor actions (Fischer and Hogan, forthcoming). This development involves movement through the levels of the reflex tier (Table 6.2). Early in this period, many of the components of action are present: The newborn baby can look at lines or edges, grasp objects placed into his or her hand, and make facial expressions. But these action components, called reflexes, can seldom be skillfully organized.

By three or four months, the infant has constructed sensorimotor actions: She can skillfully control her eyes, looking into her mother's eyes when she is talking (Haith, Bergman, and Moore, 1977) and then systematically scanning her face. She can reach out to grasp an object touching her hand. She can produce a full-blown angry facial expression in reaction to interference with an action goal, as when a cookie she is about to eat is taken away (Stenberg, Campos, and Emde, 1983). And when she sees her mother's angry face, she can organize what she sees into a perception of anger (Campos and others, 1983).

The presence of these organized anger actions (expression and perception of anger) provides the foundation for further development of emotions related to actions. By seven or eight months, the infant can coordinate one action with another in a sensorimotor mapping. In one instance of such a mapping, he can relate looking with reaching, using what he sees to skillfully guide where he reaches. Consequently, when the baby is angry at having a cookie grabbed from his hand, his action script leads him to try to get the cookie back: He can look to see where the cookie is and reach out to try to take it back. Similarly, he can relate looking at his mother's angry face to looking at another person in what is called social referencing (Campos and others, 1983). When the infant sees his mother's angry face following his older brother's entry into the room, he can relate the emotion of anger to the brother's appearance.

The relations among sensorimotor actions involving anger grow more and more complex, until at eighteen to twenty-four months the baby puts together her action systems to form the first representations for anger. This is the first major step in moving from a script for anger in action to a script for anger in thought or story. In pretend play, children can make a doll act angry or mean (Fischer, Hand, and Russell, 1984). In speech, they can describe someone as angry: "Mommy mad" (Bretherton, Fritz, Zahn-Waxler, and Ridgeway, 1986; Dunn, Bretherton, and Munn, 1987).

With this change, children begin to be able to deal with anger symbolically, and the gradual development of this representational capacity has far-reaching consequences. Over several years, they come to relate representations to each other, for example, when they relate two representations for mean actions to understand that mean actions merit mean responses: "She was mean to me—she hit me! So I was mean to her—I hit her back!" And this capacity even allows them to reinterpret apparently angry acts in terms of intention: When one girl shoves another to save her from being hit in the head by a baseball, then the second one should not be angry with the first; the apparently angry act was based on a positive intention. By age five, children can understand this sort of script in pretend play (Fischer and Elmendorf, 1986).

Representation also gradually brings with it a change in the potential retributions in anger scripts. By the preschool years, a new form of aggressive act enters the repertoire—the insult, or symbolic attack. Instead of carrying out a direct physical act, the child understands that he or she can hurt the other person's feelings: "I hate you!" "You're dumb." Children relate a representation of their own statement with a representation of the other child's hurt feelings.

During the school years, representations come to be related in complex systems in which people can have several characteristics simultaneously. For example, in an angry exchange, two characters both can be simultaneously angry and affectionate. In a story script, one boy hits the other on the shoulder and says, "Hey, buddy, let's play ball and be friends." The second one responds, "I would like to be your friend, but I don't play with kids who hit" (Fischer and Pipp, 1984a). Similarly, people are perceived as being able to have two simultaneous emotions, even apparently contradictory ones, such as anger and joy (Harter, 1986).

These increasingly complex skills for understanding anger bring with them greater complexity in the action tendencies for anger. The examples have shown two such changes: Children become more proficient in their ability to restrain their anger, as in taking account of intentions; and they become more effective in acting upon that anger, as in using insults. The subordinate-category emotions, such as resentment and jealousy, require these sorts of complex symbolic scripts.

Starting at about age twelve, people begin to use abstractions about emotions, and by adulthood the abstractions can become complex and sophisticated. Adults may care about equality and justice. When these standards are violated, as in racial discrimination, an adult can become angry not only about the concrete injuries but also about the injuries done to the abstract standards. When a worker is required to stay late at work, his reaction will depend upon his appraisal of the justice of the request. If the request is seen as just and appropriate because, for example, it stems from an unanticipated emergency, the employee may be disappointed but probably will not be angry. Similarly, adults may care about capitalism and communism, espousing one and feeling threatened by the other.

With abstractions comes the ability to have conceptions of people's personalities (Fischer and Lamborn, forthcoming; Harter,

1986; Selman, 1980). With representations, children can describe a person only in concrete terms, such as nice or mean, tall or short, active or quiet. With abstractions, they can describe people with such concepts as conservative, introverted, conflicted, placid, or vindictive. These abstractions allow them to build complex models of their own and other people's personalities. Concepts like resentment and revenge seem to hinge on these abstractions.

Resentment: A Complex Form of Anger. Resentment is a complex form of anger, where the emotion script involves intricacies of personality and social situation. In feeling resentment, people perceive that they have been unjustly wronged but that to express their anger directly would lead to unwanted long-term consequences. As a result, the anger smolders. When an employee is repeatedly asked to work late, she can refuse the request and criticize her boss for poor planning. But in imagining carrying out those angry actions, she can also project her employer's response. The boss may not promote her next year or might even fire her. As a result of this emotion loop, the angry thoughts produce a feeling of fear about later negative consequences. The anger remains, but the angry actions are suppressed by fear. The outcome is resentment— smoldering anger about an offense that cannot safely be confronted.

By eight months, according to the skill theory of emotional development, an infant can experience simultaneous anger and fear. All that is required is the ability to relate the two sensorimotor actions of anger and fear (see Case, Hayward, Lewis, and Hurst, 1988). But resentment requires sustaining the feeling of anger at the affront. The infant can sustain that feeling only if the environment is constantly evoking the joint feelings of anger and fear.

By four or five years, according to the skill theory of emotional development, children can feel resentment on their own, without constant evocation from the environment. As soon as they can relate two representations, they can sustain their own thoughts, using one representation to evoke another. Consequently, at their optimal level they can think about the offense that makes them both angry and afraid. Later still, when they can build systems of multiple representations, they can even more easily sustain simultaneous anger and fear. And so their anger smolders.

Not until the development of abstractions, however, can

children readily understand the complex, subtle scripts that are usually involved when adults speak of resentment. The essence of resentment seems to be the discrepancy between the ability to act to overcome the short-term obstacle and the sense that taking this action would lead to even worse long-term consequences. Such a complex script becomes easy to control only during adolescence and adulthood, when a person can understand the subtleties of abstract social roles and motivations (Fischer, Hand, and Russell, 1984). At earlier ages, children must reduce the subtleties to a simpler concrete script.

The worker whose boss is constantly asking for unpaid overtime work will experience resentment, feeling legitimately angry but also feeling anxious about the repercussions of resisting the boss's demands. Likewise, competing businesspeople or suitors may feel resentment toward each other. The injured person may spend hours trying to understand the offender's motivations and predict what would happen if he or she expressed anger at the unjust demands. In one standard American script, the injured individual finds some fatal flaw in the injuring individual's personality and, as in many soap operas, uses that flaw to extract some revenge that finally acts out the long-suppressed anger.

This complex subordinate-category emotion is, of course, not the same across cultures. It epitomizes the sophisticated emotions described by scholars who emphasize the cultural relativity of emotions (Averill, 1982; Harre, 1986b).

Jealousy: An Organized Combination of Emotions. In resentment, fear is combined with anger, but the predominant emotion in the script is anger. In some subordinate-category emotions, such as jealousy, the combination of disparate basic-category emotions is more salient. The combination of emotions in jealousy makes an important point about the mixture of basic-category emotions in subordinate-category emotions. Contrary to some theories of basic emotions, the basic emotions are not simply blended the way two colors of paint can be mixed. Instead, they are organized in a specific script.

In jealousy, people simultaneously experience three basic-category emotions: (1) love for another person or attraction to some desired object or characteristic, (2) anger or resentment over not having the love returned or not possessing the desired object, and (3) especially in the case of love for a person, fear or anxiety that they may lose that person's love.

The ages of development for jealousy are predicted to be similar to those for resentment. Behaviors that adults categorize as jealousy will emerge by seven to eight months of age, when infants can simultaneously sustain actions or perceptions of love and anger. When a baby's parents are hugging each other, for example, he or she may want to be hugged, too, and may be angry about not being hugged. At four or five years, children can sustain simultaneous representations of both their own love for an object or person and some other person's possession of that object or that person's love.

Not until the development of abstractions in adolescence and adulthood, however, can people experience and understand subtle scripts for jealousy. For example, in the classic romantic triangle, one person is emotionally involved with two others, who are jealous of each other. Adults can spend many hours analyzing the motivations and personalities involved in such jealousy-producing situations.

The combination of anger, love, and anxiety in jealousy is not simply a blend of emotions, like a mixture of paint. It is an organization of these emotions, captured most straightforwardly by the script describing the total situation in which the combination occurs.

Conclusion

The skill approach to the development of emotions provides a general framework for understanding and predicting the many facets of emotional behavior. Based on an integration of recent emotion theories with skill theory, it resolves many of the controversies about the nature of emotions and predicts in detail how emotions and emotion-related skills develop.

The organization of emotions is characterized by a hierarchy of emotion categories, prototypes for each category, and processes that produce each emotion. Emotion categories fit into a hierarchy in which emotions are divided first into positive and negative, then into a set of basic categories, and finally into subordinate categories that constitute more differentiated forms of the basic categories.

Each of the basic categories can be defined in terms of a prototypic script that specifies the normal course of events for that emotion.

In the processing of information leading to emotions, people notice some change, appraise the change as positively or negatively related to their own concerns, and appraise how they can cope with it. From this process, the emotions arise as action tendencies that organize behavior according to the prototypic scripts. In complex emotions, the process recycles in an emotion loop, in which the appraisal process is applied to the person's own initial emotional reaction. The result is that people have emotions about their emotions.

Development moves generally from the basic emotions to the subordinate ones, but there is also much interweaving of their development. In the first few months of life, the basic emotions become organized as single sensorimotor actions. By about eight months, the subordinate emotions begin to appear in children's behavior. Gradually sensorimotor actions move through a series of developmental levels and tiers. Actions are coordinated in complex relations until at about two to three years they are transformed into representations of each basic emotion. Over the next several years, representations are coordinated in complex relations until at about ten to twelve years they are transformed into abstractions about each emotion. With each new level and tier, the basic- and subordinate-level emotions become more complex. Only with the attainment of abstract scripts for emotions in adulthood do people finally attain the subtle, sophisticated emotions described by some emotion theorists and captured in much literature and art.

Tomorrow

With the skill approach to emotional development, developmental scholars can move beyond oppositions between cognition and emotion, basic and subordinate emotions, infant and adult emotions, body and mind. The skill framework provides an integration of these numerous oppositions into a single, coherent analysis. Emotion, action, and thought can all be analyzed in one framework that shows how each type of behavior is an aspect of the functioning of a single, integrated organism. At the same time, each aspect can be differentiated as a component that makes its individual contributions to the person's functioning.

The next task is to fill in and test out the specifics of the framework, answering the multitude of questions that the framework poses. Here are a few of the most obvious questions that need to be pursued.

What are the action scripts for the basic emotions in infants, and how do they relate to the represented and abstract scripts of children and adults? What are the principles governing the development from basic- to subordinate-category emotions?

How do emotions facilitate some aspects of development while interfering with other aspects? More generally, how do emotions bias or influence the course of skill development (Fischer and Pipp, 1984a; Fischer and Lamborn, forthcoming; Malatesta and Fiore, 1985)?

What are the relations between major developmental transitions in emotions and in other skills? How do the functional mechanisms of development affect emotional behavior, and how do emotions contribute to these mechanisms?

References

Averill, J. R. "A Semantic Atlas of Emotional Concepts." *Journal Supplement Abstract Service: Catalogue of Selected Documents in Psychology*, 1975, 5, 330.

Averill, J. R. *Anger and Aggression: An Essay on Emotion.* New York: Springer-Verlag, 1982.

Bretherton, I., Fritz, J., Zahn-Waxler, C., and Ridgeway, D. "Learning to Talk About Emotions: A Functionalist Perspective." *Child Development*, 1986, 57, 529–548.

Bretherton, I., and Waters, E. (eds.). "Growing Points of Attachment Theory and Research." *Monographs of the Society for Research in Child Development*, 1985, 50 (1 and 2).

Campos, J. J., and others. "Socioemotional Development." In P. Mussen (ed.), *Handbook of Child Psychology.* (4th ed.) Vol. 2. New York: Wiley, 1983.

Case, R., Hayward, S., Lewis, M., and Hurst, P. "Toward a Neo-

Piagetian Theory of Affective and Cognitive Development." *Developmental Review*, 1988, *8*, 1-51.

Darwin, C. *The Expression of the Emotions in Man and Animals.* Chicago: University of Chicago Press, 1975. (Originally published 1872).

de Rivera, J. "The Structure of Anger." In J. de Rivera (ed.), *Conceptual Encounter: A Method for the Exploration of Human Experience.* Washington, D.C.: University Press of America, 1981.

Doi, T. *The Anatomy of Dependence.* Tokyo: Kodansha International, 1973.

Dunn, J., Bretherton, I., and Munn, P. "Conversations About Feeling States Between Mothers and Their Young Children." *Developmental Psychology*, 1987, *23*, 132-139.

Ekman, P. (ed.). *Darwin and Facial Expression.* Orlando, Fla.: Academic Press, 1973.

Ekman, P. "Expression and the Nature of Emotion." In K. R. Scherer and P. Ekman (eds.), *Approaches to Emotion.* Hillsdale, N.J.: Erlbaum, 1984.

Ekman, P., Friesen, W. V., and Ellsworth, P. C. "What Are the Similarities and Differences in Facial Behavior Across Cultures?" In P. Ekman (ed.), *Emotion in the Human Face.* (2nd ed.) Cambridge, England: Cambridge University Press, 1982.

Fischer, K. W. "A Theory of Cognitive Development: The Control and Construction of Hierarchies of Skills." *Psychological Review*, 1980, *87*, 477-531.

Fischer, K. W., and Elmendorf, D. "Becoming a Different Person: Transformations in Personality and Social Behavior." In M. Perlmutter (ed.), *Minnesota Symposium on Child Psychology.* Vol. 18. Hillsdale, N.J.: Erlbaum, 1986.

Fischer, K. W., and Farrar, M. J. "Generalizations About Generalization: How a Theory of Skill Development Explains Both Generality and Specificity." *International Journal of Psychology*, forthcoming.

Fischer, K. W., Hand, H. H., and Russell, S. L. "The Development of Abstractions in Adolescence and Adulthood." In M. Commons, F. A. Richards, and C. Armon (eds.), *Beyond Formal Operations.* New York: Praeger, 1984.

Fischer, K. W., and Hogan, A. "The Big Picture for Infant Development: Levels and Variations." In J. Lockman and N. Hazen
(eds.), *Action in Social Context: Perspectives on Early Development*. New York: Plenum, forthcoming.

Fischer, K. W., and Lamborn, S. "Mechanisms of Variation in
Developmental Levels: Cognitive and Emotional Transitions
During Adolescence." In A. de Ribaupierre (ed.), *Mechanisms of
Transition in Cognitive and Emotional Development*. New
York: Cambridge University Press, forthcoming.

Fischer, K. W., and Pipp, S. L. "Development of the Structures of
Unconscious Thought." In K. Bowers and D. Meichenbaum
(eds.), *The Unconscious Reconsidered*. New York: Wiley, 1984a.

Fischer, K. W., and Pipp, S. L. "Processes of Cognitive Development: Optimal Level and Skill Acquisition." In R. J. Sternberg
(ed.), *Mechanisms of Cognitive Development*. New York: W. H.
Freeman, 1984b.

Fischer, K. W., and others. "Putting the Child into Socialization:
The Development of Social Categories in Preschool Children."
In L. Katz (ed.), *Current Topics in Early Childhood Education*.
Vol. 5. Norwood, N.J.: Ablex, 1984.

Fox, N. A., and Davidson, R. J. "Hemispheric Substrates of Affect:
A Developmental Model." In N. A. Fox and R. J. Davidson (eds.),
The Psychobiology of Affective Development. Hillsdale, N.J.:
Erlbaum, 1984.

Frijda, N. H. *The Emotions*. Cambridge, England: Cambridge
University Press, 1986.

Haith, M. M., Bergman, T., and Moore, M. J. "Eye Contact and
Face Scanning in Early Infancy." *Science*, 1977, *198*, 853–855.

Harre, R. "Emotion Talk Across Times." In R. Harre (ed.), *The
Social Construction of Emotions*. Oxford, England: Basil
Blackwell, 1986a.

Harre, R. (ed.). *The Social Construction of Emotions*. Oxford,
England: Basil Blackwell, 1986b.

Harter, S. "Cognitive-Developmental Processes in the Integration
of Concepts About Emotions and the Self." *Social Cognition*,
1986, *4*, 119–151.

Izard, C. *Human Emotions*. New York: Plenum, 1977.

Izard, C. "On the Ontogenesis of Emotions and Emotion-Cognition

Relationships in Infancy." In M. Lewis and L. Rosenblum (eds.), *The Development of Affect*. New York: Plenum, 1978.

Lazarus, R. S. "On the Primacy of Cognition." *American Psychologist*, 1984, *39*, 124-129.

Leventhal, H., and Scherer, K. "The Relationship of Emotion to Cognition: A Functional Approach to a Semantic Controversy." *Cognition & Emotion*, 1987, *1*, 3-28.

Levy, R. I. *Tahitians: Mind and Experience in the Society Islands*. Chicago: University of Chicago Press, 1973.

Malatesta, C. Z., and Fiore, M. J. "Affect, Personality, and Facial Expressive Characteristics of Older People." Paper presented at international conference of the British Psychological Association on the Meaning of Faces, Cardiff, Wales, June 26-28, 1985.

Morsbach, H., and Tyler, W. J. "A Japanese Emotion: *Amae*." In R. Harre (ed.), *The Social Construction of Emotions*. Oxford, England: Basil Blackwell, 1986.

Plutchik, R. *Emotion: A Psychoevolutionary Synthesis*. New York: Harper & Row, 1980.

Rosch, E. "Principles of Categorization." In E. Rosch and B. B. Lloyd (eds.), *Cognition and Categorization*. Hillsdale, N.J.: Erlbaum, 1978.

Scherer, K. R. "Emotion as a Multicomponent Process: A Model and Some Cross-Cultural Data." In P. Shaver (ed.), *Review of Personality and Social Psychology*. Vol. 5. Beverly Hills, Calif.: Sage, 1984.

Scherer, K. R., Walbott, H. G., and Summerfield, A. B. (eds.). *Experiencing Emotions: A Cross-Cultural Study*. Cambridge, England: Cambridge University Press, 1986.

Schwartz, J. C., and Shaver, P. "Emotions and Emotion Knowledge in Interpersonal Relations." In W. Jones and D. Perlman (eds.), *Advances in Personal Relationships*. Vol. 1. Greenwich, Conn.: JAI Press, forthcoming.

Selman, R. L. *The Growth of Interpersonal Understanding: Developmental and Clinical Analyses*. Orlando, Fla.: Academic Press, 1980.

Shaver, P., Schwartz, J., Kirson, D., and O'Connor, C. "Emotion Knowledge: Further Exploration of a Prototype Approach."

Journal of Personality and Social Psychology, 1987, *52,* 1061–1086.

Shiffrin, R. M., and Schneider, W. "Controlled and Automatic Human Information Processing. Part Two: Perceptual Learning, Automatic Attending, and a General Theory." *Psychological Review,* 1977, *84,* 127–190.

Skinner, B. F. *Contingencies of Reinforcement: A Theoretical Analysis.* New York: Appleton-Century-Crofts, 1969.

Sroufe, L. A. "Socioemotional Development." In J. Osofsky (ed.), *Handbook of Infant Development.* New York: Wiley, 1979.

Stenberg, C., Campos, J., and Emde, R. "The Facial Expression of Anger in Seven-Month-Old Infants." *Child Development,* 1983, *54,* 178–184.

Zajonc, R. B. "On the Primacy of Emotion." *American Psychologist,* 1984, *39,* 117–123.

Chapter 7

Empathy and Sympathy

Nancy Eisenberg

Although philosophers (Blum, 1980) and psychologists (Feshbach, 1978; Hoffman, 1984) frequently have theorized about the role of sympathy and empathy in social behavior, our understanding of these emotional responses is relatively limited. For example, data concerning the developmental course of empathy and sympathy, determinants of their development, and their correlates are relatively few and somewhat inconsistent. Thus, although considerable progress has been made in the study of empathy and sympathy over the past two decades, many important questions remain unanswered or only partially addressed.

In this chapter, I briefly review some of the major issues that have been addressed by researchers, the empirical data that relate to these issues, and some of the most important questions that remain unanswered. This review is, of necessity, general, with the consequence that important complexities in the empirical research, conceptual subtleties, and relevant methodological issues sometimes are not discussed. However, when possible, references containing further discussion of relevant issues or problems are cited.

Note: Preparation of this chapter was supported by a grant from the National Science Foundation (BNS-8509223) and a Career Development Award from the National Institute of Child Health and Development (1 KO4 HD00717-01).

Definitional Issues

Over the years, empathy and sympathy have been defined in a variety of ways (see Eisenberg and Strayer, 1987). In some definitions, empathy has been viewed as a cognitive, inferential process (see, for example, Deutsch and Madle, 1975). Recently, however, many developmental and social psychologists have defined empathy and sympathy primarily in affective terms (for example, Batson, 1987; Hoffman, 1984; Staub, 1978).

Many researchers and theorists have not clearly differentiated between affective empathy and sympathy; however, this appears to be a useful distinction. Thus, in our recent work, empathy has been defined as an affective state that stems from the apprehension of another's emotional state or condition and is congruent with it (see Eisenberg and Strayer, 1987; Hoffman, 1984). Empathy includes emotional matching and the vicarious experiencing of emotions similar to those that the other is experiencing. Moreover, empathy requires at least a minimal awareness of the difference between self and other. In contrast, sympathy refers to an emotional response stemming from the apprehension of another's emotional state or condition, one that is not the same as the other's emotion but consists of feelings of sorrow or concern for the other's welfare. Sympathy often may stem from empathy, although it also may derive from role taking or other cognitive processes.

When individuals sympathize or empathize, their focus is not primarily on the self. Thus, sympathy and empathy (especially the former) differ from the vicariously induced emotional reaction of personal distress (Batson, 1987). Personal distress is defined as an aversive affective state (such as anxiety, discomfort, or apprehension) that leads to a self-focus and the egoistic motive to reduce one's own distress. It is likely that this type of reaction, like sympathy, frequently is a consequence of empathizing; however, sympathy and personal distress seem to result in different motivational sets (altruistic versus egoistic, respectively; Batson, 1987). I return to this issue shortly.

Theoretical Approaches

Space does not permit an extended discussion of theoretical approaches to the study of empathy and sympathy. Thus, only a few of the more influential or provocative theoretical perspectives are briefly discussed.

Most theorists have argued that there are affective and cognitive components to empathy (see, for example, Feshbach, 1978), although some precursors to empathy (such as reflexive crying; see Thompson, 1987) may be primarily noncognitive in nature. However, many psychologists have hypothesized that the function and role of cognition in empathy changes with age. For example, Hoffman (1984) has suggested that the child's increasing abilities to differentiate between self and other and to take the perspective of another affect the nature of the child's empathic responding. In brief, Hoffman argues that empathy is experienced in the first year of life as personal distress (empathic distress, in his words) or as purely vicarious contagion. This is because the child is unclear as to who is experiencing the distress. As the child learns both to differentiate between self and other and to take the other's perspective (in the toddler and preschool years), he or she increasingly understands the other's emotional state or condition and is better able to sympathize. Finally, when children come to understand (in middle to late childhood) that the self and others are individuals with separate and different histories and identities and that people have feelings beyond the immediate situation, they can imagine the other's emotional state or need even if there are no cues related to the other's state in the immediate context. They also may realize that others' distresses are chronic rather than merely transitory. At this highest level of empathy, a variety of types of information, including expressive cues from others, situational cues, and the knowledge of the other's life condition, are viewed as sufficient to elicit empathy (and sympathy).

Aspects of Hoffman's theory are difficult but not impossible to test. For example, Radke-Yarrow and Zahn-Waxler (Radke-Yarrow, Zahn-Waxler, and Chapman, 1983) have noted a sequence of apparent empathic responding in the first two years of life that generally is consistent with Hoffman's theorizing (discussed later in this chapter). However, although many of Hoffman's assertions are reasonable (especially from a cognitive-developmental perspective), most have not been empirically tested.

Hoffman's theory of empathy is highly developmental in its

approach. Other, less developmental theories also have been suggested. For example, a number of social scientists and biologists have suggested that empathy has evolved in humans because it facilitates the nurturant, cooperative, and prosocial behavior necessary for parenting (MacLean, 1982) or the survival of others who share one's own genes (Hoffman, 1981). In addition, some researchers have argued that individual differences in empathy and sympathy (as well as in prosocial behavior) are due to genetic factors (see Rushton and others, 1986). In support of this view, Rushton and others (1986) and Matthews, Batson, Horn, and Rosenman (1981) have found that identical twins are more similar than are dizygotic twins in self-report of empathy. However, self-report of socially desirable behavior may be influenced by a variety of factors, some of which may have a biological basis (for example, intelligence, desire for social contact, or temperament); consequently, convergent findings obtained with indexes that are not self-reported are needed before firm conclusions can be drawn regarding the role of genetic factors in empathy.

Another conceptual approach to the study of empathy is based on learning theory, especially on principles related to conditioning. For example, Aronfreed (1970) has suggested that children learn to empathize because their own affective states are paired with cues related to others' affective states. Similarly, Hoffman (1977) proposed that infants learn to respond empathically because of the association between the infant's distress or upset resulting from the quality of the mother's physical handling of the infant and maternal vocal and facial cues.

There is some support for the role of learning processes in empathy; researchers have demonstrated that others' facial expressions or behaviors that are indicative of pain can elicit similar reactions in observers and that these vicarious responses (for instance, increases in skin conductance) resemble the arousal responses elicited by the aversive stimulus itself (see Stotland, 1969). For example, Englis, Vaughan, and Lanzetta (1982) found that pairing another's facial distress with study participants' experiences of shock resulted in relatively strong empathic reactions (physiological and self-reported) to the other's facial distress even after shock was no longer administered. However, the other's smiles also elicited empathic responding (physiological responding) if such smiles had previously been paired with the receipt of shock. Thus, the observers' vicarious responses varied as a function of prior learning. Moreover, Aronfreed (1970) found that pairing another's expressions of pain or delight with children's receipt of negative or positive outcomes, respectively, was associated with enhanced positive responding among children. This finding may have been due to the conditioning of the children's own emotional reactions to cues related to others' reactions; however, Aronfreed did not directly assess the children's empathy, so his findings are only suggestive.

If conditioning processes play an important role in the development of empathy, this role is probably greatest in the early years. With age, cognitive interpretations of the other's situation may increasingly influence children's assessment of the other's situation and, consequently, their empathic and sympathetic responses. For example, Zillman and Cantor (1977) found that third and fourth graders reported feeling pleasure in response to another's pain (and distress in response to the other's pleasure) if the other had been depicted as malevolent. However, it is unclear at what age counterempathic reactions such as these (see Englis, Vaughan, and Lanzetta, 1982) first develop.

Developmental Changes

As mentioned previously, Hoffman (1984) has suggested that there are several stages in the development of empathy. In the first year of life, empathy is first experienced through very simple modes of empathic arousal (such as conditioning and mimicry), and it is voluntary and global in quality. Hoffman has suggested that this reaction may be a precursor of empathy. Later, when the child can differentiate between self and other, he or she begins to differentiate between another's and his or her own distress.

Empirical findings suggest that infants may experience others' distresses as their own. For example, infants tend to cry in response to crying by same-age conspecifics (see Thompson, 1987, for a review). Moreover, although six-month-olds do not react to peers' distresses with distress (Hay, Nash, and Pedersen, 1981), Radke-Yarrow and Zahn-Waxler (1984) found that ten- to fourteen-

month-olds tended to show signs of agitation and general disturbance in response to others' distresses. These young children
appeared to be experiencing either emotional contagion or personal
distress. Agitated responses tended to decrease in frequency with
age, whereas controlled, positive responses increased. At first,
children displayed tentative positive contacts, such as patting or
touching the victim. By the middle or end of the second year,
prosocial interventions and imitation of the other's emotion were
typical reactions to another's distresses. These prosocial interventions included physical contact, instrumental acts, and verbal
concern. Thus, the children appeared to experience sympathy in the
second year of life.

Radke-Yarrow and Zahn-Waxler (1984) also examined
individual differences in children's responding. Among one- and
two-year-olds, some children responded to others' distresses with
prosocial behavior accompanied by affective arousal. In contrast,
other children, who were equally effective in their prosocial
interventions, were cognitively prosocial: They approached others'
distresses by inspecting, exploring, and asking questions. Yet other
children either manifested an aggressive component (for example,
hit the person who caused the distress) or shut out and retreated
from others' signals of distress. These individual differences in
predominant mode of reaction were stable over a period of
approximately five years for two-thirds of the children.

There is very little research on age-related changes in
empathy and sympathy during the preschool years. However, there
have been numerous studies of changes in empathy in childhood.
The results of this research vary as a function of method of assessing
empathy. Responses to the commonly used picture-story measures
appear to increase with age into mid-elementary school and then
may level off (see Lennon and Eisenberg, 1987, for a review). With
these measures, children are told short stories (and/or view pictures)
about others in emotion-eliciting situations and then are asked how
they feel. If a child reports feeling the same emotion that the story
protagonist would be expected to feel, he or she is scored as
responding empathically. Similarly, empathy scores on question-
naire measures increase in the early school years, at least in response
to similar persons, whereas no consistent pattern of age-related

change is evident for persons older than approximately age eleven. In contrast, in experimental studies in which children were exposed to needy others, researchers have found both increases and no age-related change in reported empathy (Lennon and Eisenberg, 1987). However, in these studies, researchers did not attempt to differentiate between personal distress and empathy. In contrast, Eisenberg and others (1988) did differentiate between report of sympathy and personal distress and found an age-related increase in report of concern from ages four to five to second grade.

Findings with indexes that are not self-reported are the least clear. In the one relevant study involving physiological indexes, the findings were inconsistent (Wilson and Cantor, 1985). In another, heart rate markers of empathy did not differ for preschoolers and second graders (Eisenberg and others, 1988). Studies involving facial indexes of empathy also are inconsistent (see Lennon and Eisenberg, 1987).

In summary, the data regarding age differences in empathy are difficult to interpret. Sympathy appears to increase in the first two years of life. Moreover, self-report of empathy or sympathy generally increases with age in the school years, whereas facial indexes do not. Self-report of empathy or sympathy may increase due either to children's increasing awareness of the desirability of empathic/sympathetic responding or to real changes in emotional responsivity. Facial indexes of empathy may sometimes decrease with age due to the process of children learning to mask emotions during the early school years (see Cole, 1986; Shennum and Bugenthal, 1982).

As was suggested previously, some of the inconsistencies in the research findings no doubt are due to the failure of investigators to differentiate among various emotional reactions. It is possible that personal distress and sympathetic reactions have different developmental courses and are differentially socialized (for instance, parents may attempt to socialize empathy and sympathy but not personal distress in the early school years). Whether this is true cannot be determined until more differentiated measures of vicarious responding are used in developmental studies. Moreover, longitudinal research on empathy and related responses is sorely needed.

Gender Differences

Both laypeople and psychologists (for example, Block, 1973; Gilligan, 1987) frequently have assumed that females are more empathic or sympathetic than are males. Most often this reputed gender difference has been viewed as a consequence of the socialization of females into the nurturant, emotional, feminine role in contrast to the instrumental, dominant, masculine role. Moreover, a gender difference in empathy favoring females has been cited as resulting in more care-oriented moral reasoning and altruistic behavior among females than among males (Gilligan, 1987). However, it is not clear that such a gender difference actually exists or, if there is a real gender difference, what the exact nature of this difference is.

Specifically, in recent reviews, Eisenberg and Lennon (Eisenberg and Lennon, 1983; Lennon and Eisenberg, 1987) have found that the size of any gender difference in empathy varies dramatically as a function of the mode of assessing empathy (or sympathy). In studies in which people have reported their own general empathic/sympathetic tendencies or their own emotional reactions to another's distress in a specific situation, moderate to large gender differences generally have been obtained. However, virtually no gender difference has been obtained in most studies involving facial and physiological indexes of global empathic negative affect, although in very recent research there is some evidence of a gender difference favoring females in sympathetic facial expressions (Eisenberg and others, forthcoming).

This pattern of findings can be interpreted in at least two ways. First, it appears that gender differences in measures of empathy and sympathy are largest when it is relatively evident what is being assessed and respondents have control over their responses (for example, with self-report indexes, especially questionnaires). In contrast, there is little evidence of a gender difference when it is not clear what is being assessed and/or the individual is unlikely to control his or her responding. Thus, it is likely that the pattern of findings is due, in part, to the tendency for females both to present a feminine, emotionally responsive (gender-role consistent) image to others and to act in ways consistent with their own feminine self-image (derived in part from societal gender roles).

A second possible explanation for the pattern of findings is that different indexes of emotional responsiveness to others assess different things. Perhaps females really are more sympathetic and self-report indexes more frequently tap sympathetic responsiveness than do facial and physiological indexes. In general, researchers have not tried to differentiate sympathy from personal distress when using facial and physiological indexes; thus, in many studies these indexes may reflect personal distress as well as empathy or sympathy. However, it is not evident from examining the items on the commonly used empathy questionnaires that they actually tap sympathy rather than personal distress, role taking, or general emotionality.

To summarize, it currently is unclear whether there are real differences between the sexes in sympathetic or empathic responding. What is evident is that a multi-method approach to the study of gender differences in empathy is needed—one in which physiological and facial indexes as well as self-report indexes are used. Moreover, it is unlikely that consistent data will be obtained until researchers start to systematically differentiate between the various responses that have been labeled as empathy.

Socialization of Empathy

The body of empirical literature concerning the socialization of sympathy and personal distress is surprisingly small and uninformative. In most of the relevant research, various vicarious responses have not been differentiated; moreover, the indexes of socialization practices usually have consisted solely of self-report by parents or children. Given that people often may intentionally or unintentionally distort their self-report of socialization interactions, the results of findings from these studies must be considered to be merely suggestive until replicated with other procedures (such as observational studies).

Despite the aforementioned shortcomings in the available literature, there are some tentative conclusions that can be drawn from the research. First, there is some evidence that children who have secure attachments with their caretakers tend to be more empathic at three and one-half (Waters, Wippman, and Sroufe,

1979) and five years (Iannotti, Zahn-Waxler, Cummings, and Milano, 1987) than are children with insecure attachments. Second, empathic, supportive maternal care has been associated with six-month-old children's emotional responsivity towards others and with their helpful behavior. Moreover, undergraduates' and adolescents' empathy has been positively related to parental affection (see Barnett, 1987) and to mothers' (but not to fathers') empathy (Barnett, King, Howard, and Dino, 1980). The use of maternal inductions (reasoning) combined with a display of maternal emotion (such as anger or concern) also has been positively related to one- to two-year-olds' emotional responsivity and prosocial behavior (Zahn-Waxler, Radke-Yarrow, and King, 1979), whereas exposure to competitive values and goals has been negatively related to boys' (but not to girls') empathy (Barnett, Matthews, and Howard, 1979; see also Barnett, 1987).

There are other socialization practices that are likely to influence the development of empathy (for example, encourage-ment of a positive self-concept and encouragement of the perception of similarity to others); however, evidence regarding the relation of these practices to the development of empathy usually is indirect (see Barnett, 1987). Often conclusions regarding the socialization of empathy or sympathy have been drawn from data concerning prosocial behavior. Clearly, research focused primarily on the socialization of sympathy and empathy is needed.

Behavioral Consequences and Correlates

Empathy and sympathy frequently have been viewed as important determinants of a range of socially appropriate behav-iors, such as altruistic responding; cooperative, socially competent behavior; and the inhibition of aggression (see Eisenberg and Miller, 1987). In general, there is evidence to support these claims. With regard to altruism, people who experience sympathetic feelings are viewed as especially likely to assist others because of their other-oriented concern (Batson, 1987; Hoffman, 1984). Moreover, people who exhibit the trait or enduring tendency to empathize or sympathize are believed to be relatively altruistic because they are predisposed to respond sympathetically in many situations. Of course, sympathetic motivation alone is not sufficient for an individual to enact altruistic behavior; people must have the opportunity, necessary skills, and self-control to act on their sympathetic motivation, and their sympathetic motivation must be stronger than other personal goals and motives in the given situation (see Eisenberg, 1986).

Sympathetic feelings in a situation often may stem from the process of empathizing; however, personal distress is another likely outcome of empathizing (Batson, 1987; Piliavin, Dovidio, Gaertner, and Clark, 1981), especially for young children who have difficulty differentiating between their own and others' affective states (Hoffman, 1984). Feelings of personal distress can be expected to lead to egoistically motivated prosocial behaviors if assisting is the easiest way to reduce one's own distress. However, if escape from the aversive stimulus is relatively easy to achieve, feelings of personal distress might be expected to lead to escape from the aversive situation rather than to helping (Batson, 1987). Thus, although sympathy and personal distress both seem to lead to prosocial action in some situations, different patterns of behavior should result from these two emotional reactions when escape from the arousal-producing stimulus is easy.

Empirically, the relation of empathy to prosocial behavior appears to vary as a function of the method of assessing empathy. The relation of empathy to prosocial behaviors seems to be strongest in laboratory studies in which people report their emotional reactions to a needy other and have an opportunity to assist that needy other. This relation seems to be especially clear in studies with adults in which personal distress and sympathetic reactions have been differentiated (see Batson, 1987; Eisenberg and Miller, 1987). The positive relation between indexes of empathy and prosocial behavior also holds, however, in studies in which empathy has been measured using a variety of other methods (for example, questionnaires, facial reactions, physiological indexes, and experimental manipulations of empathy). The one instance in which there appears to be no relation between an index of empathy and prosocial behavior is when empathy has been assessed with the picture-story method (which involves children's self-report of empathic response in reaction to short hypothetical vignettes; Eisenberg and Miller, 1987).

In addition to the positive relations between most indexes of empathy and prosocial behavior, it appears that there is a low positive relation between empathy and indexes of children's social competence (Eisenberg and Miller, 1987). Similarly, there are negative associations between some indexes of empathy and aggressive and other externalizing behaviors (Achenbach and Edelbrock, 1984; Miller and Eisenberg, 1987). Thus, in general, empathy seems to be positively related to socially appropriate, desirable social behaviors and negatively related to harmful social behaviors.

Although the pattern of findings just described is consistent with theoretical predictions, it is not as strong as might be expected. This is probably due to a variety of factors. First, the same conceptual ambiguities and methodological problems that plague other research concerning empathy are endemic to this research. The failure of researchers to differentiate among various vicarious emotional reactions, such as sympathy and personal distress, is especially problematic in the work concerning the relation of empathy to prosocial behavior and aggression. This is because sympathy—but not personal distress—would be expected to facilitate other-oriented altruism in some situations (see Batson, 1987; Eisenberg and others, 1988). Moreover, sympathy and personal distress may both counteract aggressive tendencies in certain situations, but these situations may differ. Thus, the strength of the empirical relation between sympathy and altruism or aggression probably has been diluted.

Similar issues pertain to the conceptualization and operationalization of the indexes of social behavior that have been examined in relation to empathy. For example, not all prosocial behaviors are altruistically motivated (that is, performed without the motive of obtaining external rewards or avoiding externally produced aversive internal states); and sympathy should be expected to relate to altruistically motivated, not hedonistically motivated, prosocial behaviors. Consequently, in studies in which a given prosocial behavior could be performed for nonaltruistic reasons, one can expect an attenuated relation between that index of prosocial behavior and any index of sympathy (see Eisenberg, 1986, for further discussion of related issues).

In summary, it appears that sympathy and perhaps empathy do relate in important ways to some positive and negative social behaviors. Nonetheless, the roles of sympathy, empathy, and personal distress in the development of prosocial and antisocial behaviors have not been adequately delineated or investigated. Moreover, our understanding of the situational factors and moderating person variables that affect when sympathy and other vicarious emotional reactions influence social behavior is not adequate. Perhaps the next step in the research related to the roles of empathy and sympathy in social behavior should be the development of sophisticated conceptual models in which the interactions among personality variables, sociocognitive development, and environmental and emotional factors are considered. Initial attempts at such models have been published (see, for example, Eisenberg, 1986; Piliavin, Dovidio, Gaertner, and Clark, 1981); however, further refinement of these models is needed.

Conclusion

Initial studies and theory concerning empathy and sympathy suggest that vicarious emotional responding is an important factor in some modes of social interaction. However, our understanding regarding the development of empathy and sympathy, their socialization, and even their influence on behavior is rudimentary. Indeed, much less is known about sympathy and empathy than about the behaviors they are believed to influence (such as altruism and aggression). This is probably due in part to the difficulty of assessing internal affective states, as well as to the failure of most investigators to differentiate among various vicariously induced emotional reactions. In addition, another factor that may have impeded our understanding of empathy and sympathy is the limited amount of relevant theory available. However, due to the thoughtful contributions of contemporary psychologists such as Hoffman (1984) and Batson (1987), the study of sympathy and empathy is rapidly becoming more sophisticated and fruitful. Indeed, it is likely that future work in this area of study will result in important and exciting contributions to our understanding of emotional, social, and personality development.

Tomorrow

What is needed to reach the goal of understanding the development and consequences of empathy? First, a multi-method measurement approach involving self-report, facial, and physiological indexes of personal distress and sympathy is likely to prove fruitful for assessing different vicarious emotional reactions. Once better measures of vicarious emotional reactions are available and researchers differentiate among various types of vicarious emotional reactions, it will be possible to examine the relations of sympathy and personal distress to different types of social behaviors and to explore the socialization antecedents of empathy and related responses. Observational studies conducted in naturalistic and quasi-naturalistic settings are likely to prove especially useful for charting the role of sympathy in social interactions and for delineating situational factors that influence the expression of vicariously induced emotional reactions. In addition, intervention studies could be used both to learn about the effects of vicarious responding on subsequent behavior and to promote positive modes of interaction. In summary, by means of a conceptually differentiated, multi-method approach, it should be possible to learn much about vicarious emotional responding and its antecedents and consequences.

References

Achenbach, T. M., and Edelbrock, C. S. "Psychopathology in Childhood." *Annual Review of Psychology*, 1984, *35*, 227–256.

Aronfreed, J. "The Socialization of Altruistic and Sympathetic Behavior: Some Theoretical and Experimental Analyses." In J. Macaulay and L. Berkowitz (eds.), *Altruism and Helping Behavior*. Orlando, Fla.: Academic Press, 1970.

Barnett, M. A. "Effects of Competition and Relative Deservedness of the Other's Fate on Children's Generosity." *Developmental Psychology*, 1975, *11*, 665–666.

Barnett, M. A. "Empathy and Related Responses in Children." In
N. Eisenberg and J. Strayer (eds.), *Empathy and Its Development.*
Cambridge, England: Cambridge University Press, 1987.

Barnett, M. A., King, L. M., Howard, J. A., and Dino, G. A.,
"Empathy in Young Children: Relation to Parents' Empathy,
Affection, and Emphasis on the Feelings of Others." *Develop-
mental Psychology*, 1980, *16*, 243-244.

Barnett, M. A., Matthews, K. A., and Howard, J. A. "Relationship
Between Competitiveness and Empathy in Six- and Seven-Year
Olds." *Developmental Psychology*, 1979, *15*, 221-222.

Batson, C. D. "Prosocial Motivation: Is It Ever Truly Altruistic?" In
L. Berkowitz (ed.), *Advances in Experimental Social Psychology.*
Vol. 2. Orlando, Fla.: Academic Press, 1987.

Block, J. H. "Conceptions of Sex Role: Some Cross-Cultural and
Longitudinal Perspectives." *American Psychologist*, 1973, *28*,
512-526.

Blum, L. A. *Friendship, Altruism and Morality.* Boston: Routledge
& Kegan Paul, 1980.

Cole, P. M. "Children's Spontaneous Control of Facial Expression." *Child Development*, 1986, *57*, 1309-1321.

Deutsch, F., and Madle, R. A. "Empathy: Historic and Current
Conceptualizations, and a Cognitive Theoretical Perspective."
Human Development, 1975, *18*, 267-287.

Eisenberg, N. *Altruistic Emotion, Cognition and Behavior.*
Hillsdale, N.J.: Erlbaum, 1986.

Eisenberg, N., and Lennon, R. "Sex Differences in Empathy and
Related Capacities." *Psychological Bulletin*, 1983, *94*, 100-131.

Eisenberg, N., and Miller, P. A. "The Relation of Empathy to
Prosocial and Related Behaviors." *Psychological Bulletin*, 1987,
101, 91-119.

Eisenberg, N., and Strayer, J. "Critical Issues in the Study of
Empathy." In N. Eisenberg and J. Strayer (eds.), *Empathy and Its
Development.* Cambridge, England: Cambridge University
Press, 1987.

Eisenberg, N., and others. "Differentiation of Vicariously Induced
Emotional Reactions in Children." *Developmental Psychology*,
1988, *24*, 237-246.

Eisenberg, N., and others. "Sympathetic and Personal Distress in Children and Adults." *Developmental Psychology*, forthcoming.

Englis, B. G., Vaughan, K. B., and Lanzetta, J. T. "Conditioning of Counter-Empathetic Emotional Responses." *Journal of Experimental Social Psychology*, 1982, *18*, 375–391.

Feshbach, N. D. "Studies of Empathic Behavior in Children." In B. A. Maher (ed.), *Progress in Experimental Personality Research.* Orlando, Fla.: Academic Press, 1978.

Gilligan, C. "The Origins of Morality in Early Childhood Relationships." Paper presented at biennial meeting of the Society for Research in Child Development, Baltimore, Md., April 1987.

Hay, D. F., Nash, A., and Pedersen, J. "Responses of Six-Month-Olds to the Distress of Their Peers." *Child Development*, 1981, *52*, 1071–1075.

Hoffman, M. L. "Empathy, Its Development and Prosocial Implications." In C. B. Keasey (ed.), *Nebraska Symposium on Motivation.* Vol. 25. Lincoln: University of Nebraska Press, 1977.

Hoffman, M. L. "Is Altruism Part of Human Nature?" *Journal of Personality and Social Psychology*, 1981, *40*, 121–137.

Hoffman, M. L. "Interaction of Affect and Cognition on Empathy." In C. E. Izard, J. Kagan, and R. B. Zajonc (eds.), *Emotions, Cognition, and Behavior.* Cambridge, England: Cambridge University Press, 1984.

Iannotti, R., Zahn-Waxler, C., Cummings, E. M., and Milano, M. "The Development of Empathy and Prosocial Behavior in Early Childhood." Paper presented at annual meeting of the American Association for Research in Education, Washington, D.C., April 1987.

Lennon, R., and Eisenberg, N. "Gender and Age Differences in Empathy and Sympathy." In N. Eisenberg and J. Strayer (eds.), *Empathy and Its Development.* Cambridge, England: Cambridge University Press, 1987.

MacLean, P. D. "Evolutionary Brain Roots of Family, Play, and the Isolation Call. The Adolph Meyer Lecture." Paper presented at 135th annual meeting of the American Psychiatric Association, Toronto, Canada, May 1982.

Matthews, K. A., Batson, C. D., Horn, J., and Rosenman, R. H.

" 'Principles in His Nature Which Interest Him in the Fortune of Others . . .': The Heritability of Empathic Concern for Others." *Journal of Personality*, 1981, *49*, 237-247.

Miller, P. A., and Eisenberg, N. "The Relation of Empathy to Aggression and Psychopathology: A Meta-Analysis." *Psychological Bulletin*, 1987, *101*, 91-119.

Piliavin, J. A., Dovidio, J. F., Gaertner, S. L., and Clark, R. D., III. *Emergency Intervention*. Orlando, Fla.: Academic Press, 1981.

Radke-Yarrow, M., and Zahn-Waxler, C. "Roots, Motives, and Patterns in Children's Prosocial Behavior." In E. Staub, D. Bar-Tal, J. Karylowski, and J. Reykowski (eds.), *Development and Maintenance of Prosocial Behavior: International Perspectives on Positive Behavior*. New York: Plenum, 1984.

Radke-Yarrow, M., Zahn-Waxler, C., and Chapman, M. "Prosocial Dispositions and Behavior." In P. Mussen (ed.), *Handbook of Child Psychology*. (4th ed.) Vol. 4. New York: Wiley, 1983.

Rushton, J. P., and others. "Altruism and Aggression: The Heritability of Individual Differences." *Journal of Personality and Social Psychology*, 1986, *50*, 1192-1198.

Shennum, W. A., and Bugenthal, D. B. "The Development of Control over Affective Expression in Nonverbal Behavior." In R. S. Feldman (ed.), *Development of Nonverbal Behavior in Children*. New York: Springer-Verlag, 1982.

Staub, E. *Positive Social Behavior and Morality: Social and Personal Influences*. Vol. 1. Orlando, Fla.: Academic Press, 1978.

Stotland, E. "Exploratory Studies in Empathy." In L. Berkowitz (ed.), *Advances in Experimental Social Psychology*. Vol. 4. Orlando, Fla.: Academic Press, 1969.

Thompson, R. A. "Empathy and Emotional Understanding: The Early Development of Empathy." In N. Eisenberg and J. Strayer (eds.), *Empathy and Its Development*. Cambridge, England: Cambridge University Press, 1987.

Waters, E., Wippman, J., and Sroufe, L. A. "Attachment, Positive Affect, and Competence in the Peer Group: Two Studies in Construct Validation." *Child Development*, 1979, *50*, 821-829.

Wilson, B. J., and Cantor, J. "Developmental Differences in Empathy with a Television Protagonist's Fear." *Journal of Experimental Child Psychology*, 1985, *39*, 284-299.

Zahn-Waxler, C., Radke-Yarrow, M., and King, R. "Child-Rearing and Children's Prosocial Initiations Towards Victims of Distress." *Child Development*, 1979, *50*, 319–330.

Zillman, D., and Cantor, J. R. "Affective Responses to the Emotions of a Protagonist." *Journal of Experimental Social Psychology*, 1977, *13*, 155–165.

Chapter 8

Pubertal Processes and the Early Adolescent Transition

J. Brooks-Gunn

Early adolescence is a life phase during which several important life events occur that seem to elicit or encourage changes in self-definitions, relationships, emotional expression, and risk-taking behaviors. Both biological and social events have been the object of study, although more focus has been given to puberty than to other events—such as the move to middle school and increased academic demands—given theoretical speculations on the meaning of pubertal changes to the child, significant others, and society. The overarching theme of this chapter is the role of pubertal processes (as well as a comparison of different biological and social events) in the behavioral, relational, and emotional changes seen during the early adolescent transition. To clarify puberty's salience as an organizing feature of much of this decade's research, a brief history of the original issues chosen for study, as well as their subsequent refinements and offshoots, will be presented. Then five current research issues will be considered, which represent, in my opinion, the most promising and exciting courses being pursued. Finally, since the enthusiasm with which a relatively new field goes about its

Note: The preparation of this chapter was supported by grants from the National Institute of Child Health and Human Development and the William T. Grant Foundation; their help is greatly appreciated.

155

business sometimes obscures underlying assumptions, some of the major beliefs about changes in early adolescence will be highlighted in an attempt to make explicit the premises that influence the design and interpretation of today's work (Brooks-Gunn, 1988a).

The Study of Puberty

Before considering the role of pubertal processes in early adolescent transitions, a few comments about puberty are in order. First, the study of pubertal processes must be sensitive to individual differences in the timing and sequencing of events. Puberty is itself a series of events with great interindividual onset, rate, duration, and offset. For example, breast development may be initiated anywhere between eight and thirteen years of age and completed as early as age twelve or as late as age eighteen and still be within normal ranges. Similarly, intraindividual variability also is common; for example, while breast buds supposedly appear before pubic hair, the opposite is seen in one-quarter of all girls (Marshall and Tanner, 1969). The same is true for deviations from the so-called norm in timing and sequencing of other pubertal events—including menarche, rises in gonadotropin levels, penile growth, spermarche, voice changes, and growth spurt.

Variations such as these may enhance or limit research. The fact that pubertal processes are not strictly ordered allows for a partial disentanglement of their possible associations with behavior. For example, breast growth is associated with positive peer relationships, greater salience of reproductively linked sex roles, and a positive body image, while the development of pubic hair is not; possible explanations include the culturally mediated reproductive meaning attached to breast growth and its salience to others, given that breast growth is easily seen while pubic hair growth is not (Brooks-Gunn and Warren, forthcoming). An inherent danger exists as well. Many studies do not measure specific pubertal processes but use, for example, global ratings of clothed teens by adult observers. Results of these studies are sometimes interpreted as being due to processes that have not been measured and are assumed to be due to puberty per se rather than to specific pubertal changes. Such studies need to be circumspect in their inferences, limited to discussing the social salience or stimulus value of biological change rather than direct biological effects on behavior.

Second, few behavioral studies have been mounted that measure both hormones and physical characteristics; this is due in part to expense, intrusiveness, and the difficulty of putting together interdisciplinary teams. Often, the implicit premise is offered that measuring physical changes is an "accurate enough" reflection of hormonal changes. The social stimulus value of a child's developing body is so great that no associated behavior changes may be attributed to biological processes alone unless hormonal measures are gathered and their effects are compared with those of physical changes with stimulus value. Several groups of investigators have initiated such research (this will be discussed later). However, the proclivity to make inferences about direct biological effects in the absence of appropriate designs is great, and appropriate caution has not been taken in some of the pubertal research (just as it has not been in the menstrual and pregnancy literature; see Parlee, 1973; Ruble and Brooks-Gunn, 1979). The specification of models testing direct and indirect biological effects would be extremely helpful here.

Third, the relative roles of biological and social events are not addressed adequately. Often, studies examine biological or social factors or do not present relative effect sizes when including both types of factors. Being sensitive to the context in which pubertal change takes place, which is characteristic of most research today, is not enough: Interactions between biological and social factors need to be tested. In the few studies in which such an approach is taken, interactions are quite common (Brooks-Gunn, Petersen, and Eichorn, 1985).

A Brief History of Pubertal Research

The study of the early adolescent life phase seems to be in a state similar to that of infancy research fifteen to twenty years ago. Then a graduate student, I found working in the field of infancy a heady experience. The number of investigators was manageable, informal networks of information sharing existed, and methodologies for studying infants were being defined, debated, and refined.

Perhaps best of all, the complexity and depth of infants' cognitive and social abilities were just being realized. In just one decade, we had gone from the neonate's world described by James as "a blooming, buzzing confusion" to a discussion of visual acuity, perceptual tracking, and information processing. Socially, infants were no longer characterized as passive recipients of information but were described as actively constructing their world, recognizing facial and auditory features of persons, integrating social dimension information, and responding to and eliciting different reactions from familiar and unfamiliar adults.

Today, the same excitement permeates the study of early adolescence. While the physical changes of this life phase have been extensively documented by physical anthropologists, physicians, and, increasingly, endocrinologists (Grumbach and Sizonenko, 1986; Tanner, 1962), much less developmentally oriented research is under way on the possible behavioral effects of physical changes (and their interaction), the influence of different biological events or sequences on adolescent behavior, and the vast array of social events and role changes that also occur during early adolescence. The roots of this research extend back into the past two decades. Two seminal works that appeared in the 1970s highlighted both the lack of systematic study and the importance of this life phase for healthy development (Hamburg, 1974; Lipsitz, 1977). At the same time, the question of whether "storm and stress" was an appropriate appellation for young adolescents, or for some subset of adolescents who were particularly vulnerable to the social and biological events with which they were confronted, came under research scrutiny (Offer, 1987). A related theme involved whether changes in self-images during adolescence were best characterized as continuous or discontinuous (Nesselroade and Baltes, 1974). Generally, early studies did not confirm beliefs in either intense "storm and stress" as a feature of all young adolescents or of major discontinuities in self-images. These studies implicitly assumed that emotionality and self-image alterations were predicated, at least in part, on the physical tranformation from child to adult. Somewhat surprisingly, pubertal processes were not the object of study; therefore, possible links between emotionality or self-image and pubertal change were never made, nor were models proposed to demonstrate how pubertal change might either influence or interact with behavior.

It is difficult, perhaps even impossible, to reconstruct the events that led to the current focus on pubertal processes and the early adolescent transition. With the advantage of hindsight, I suggest that the *Zeitgeist* was favorable for many reasons, including: the acceptance of a broader definition of child development (or more accurately, human development), interest in continuity across life phases, concerns about the development of pathology and the pathology of development, and the portrayal of development as an interaction between the organism and the environment (Brim and Kagan, 1980; Cicchetti, 1984; Lerner, 1985; Scarr, 1985). Perhaps even more relevant was the coming together of a small group of developmentalists who were interested in reproductive processes more generally.

Different research perspectives converged at a conference on girls at puberty held at the Salk Institute in 1981 (see Brooks-Gunn and Petersen, 1983). Issues generating interest and debate included (1) the psychological meaning of reproductive events to women—in this case the salience of menarche using cross-cultural, social-cognitive, biological, and socialization perspectives; (2) the biological and environmental antecedents of delayed maturation in girls; and (3) the possible gender-role intensification occurring at the time of early adolescence. Cutting across these themes was a realization that current models for each were either too biological or too environmental and that biobehavioral interactions were not being studied. Indeed, while the research reported at this conference considered the context in which physical maturation took place, none of the investigators, with the exception of Simmons and her colleagues, were proposing interactional models, testing alternative models, or explicitly considering how the co-occurrence of biological and social changes may affect an individual's behavior. Also, the processes by which pubertal change might influence behavior were not well specified. Finally, possible effects of pubertal change on others' behavior or on the adolescent's interactions with others were only alluded to (Steinberg and Hill [1978] conducted an early relevant study; since it focused on boys' interactions with their parents, this work was not included in *Girls at Puberty*).

Several years later, investigators took a dramatic turn toward more contextually based research, as well as more direct testing of possible pathways by which pubertal change might influence behavior. At a 1983 Society for Research in Child Development study group, developmentalists studying possible effects of variations in maturational timing met. Almost all were examining timing effects as a function of contextual factors or testing interactional models. Also, underlying processes to account for pubertal effects were being proposed. Finally, work on the psychological salience of pubertal change to significant others, and on its effect on interactions, was beginning (see Brooks-Gunn, Petersen, and Eichorn, 1985).

However, the research was still limited by its focus on a few behavioral domains and a few biological processes and by a lack of alternative model testing. Refinements and additions continued at a rapid pace, as evidenced by work presented at five conferences in 1986 and 1987 (see Brooks-Gunn and Petersen, forthcoming; Gunnar, 1988; Irwin, 1987; Lerner and Foch, 1987; McAnarney and Levine, 1987). Missing until recently were studies of antecedent events that may influence how adolescents and their parents manage the early adolescent transition (Block and Gjerde, 1988; Baumrind, 1987). Also, little work has addressed the consequences of success in negotiating early adolescent transition, although several longitudinal studies are currently addressing this issue. Additionally, work on social-cognitive and self-definitional processes underlying the response to biological and social change is just beginning. Finally, the emergence of certain forms of problem behavior and severe disorders in early adolescence, and their links to gender, are fast becoming topics of interest (Attie and Brooks-Gunn, forthcoming; Brooks-Gunn and Petersen, forthcoming; Rutter, Izard, and Read, 1986).

Perhaps most encouraging are current efforts to construct more sophisticated models. Direct and indirect biological influences on behavior are being compared, as discussed earlier. The relative effects of biological and social events and chronological and maturational age are being explored in order to embed pubertal effects in historical, age-graded, and cultural contexts.

Current Issues

As the field of early adolescence has become more diverse, more focused research issues are being addressed. Five particularly exciting ones are: (1) the emergence or increase in emotionality and in problem behaviors during early adolescence; (2) biological, as well as social-cognitive, personality, and psychodynamic, processes underlying emotional and relational changes seen in early adolescence; (3) changes in parent-child relationships and possible consequences of the way in which such changes are negotiated; (4) the intensification of gender roles; and (5) the possibility that adolescents may be more sensitive to the occurrence of social events during the time of rapid physical change than at other points in the life course.

Emotionality and Problem Behaviors. Early characterizations of early adolescence as a stormy period have not been substantiated. Emotionality and moodiness of the young adolescent is not an indicator of clinical dysfunction, and large interindividual variation exists (Offer, 1987). However, increases in negative emotions do seem to occur between late childhood and early to middle adolescence. Biological, social cognitive, and psychodynamic perspectives have been offered to account for increased emotionality.

Hormonal factors are postulated to account in part for the rise in negative emotions, either through activation effects of changes in hormone levels at puberty or through organizational effects occurring prenatally (Beach, 1975; Coe, 1988). Hormonal activation may influence behavior indirectly or directly. Hormonal activation is thought to influence emotional states such as excitability, arousal, or emotionality; these in turn may influence how individuals behave. Increased excitability and arousability may result in more rapid and/or more intense mood fluctuations; or they may render a girl more sensitive to environmental conditions, resulting in her experiencing more negative emotions following interchanges with peers or parents or other events that could be interpreted as discomforting.

Typically, physical changes with social stimulus value are

hypothesized not to influence emotionality per se, but instead to interact with behaviors carried out in and shaped by the social world (for example, leadership, school functioning, peer and parent relationships, dating, experimentation with adult behaviors). The sparse literature to date supports this premise: Hormones, but not secondary sexual characteristic development, are associated with emotionality—specifically, with aggressive affect in boys and depressive and aggressive affect in girls (Brooks-Gunn and Warren, forthcoming; Olweus, Block, and Radke-Yarrow, 1986; Susman and others, 1987). These effects may be greatest when the endocrine system is being turned on; in my study of 100 early adolescent girls, negative affect increased as the endocrine system was undergoing its greatest change, leveling off or dropping after the endocrine had reached its apex in change.

Many issues remain to be tested with biological models, over and above replications of findings to date. First, direct and mediated effects need to be tested. For example, levels of testosterone are related to sexual activity in boys, independent of secondary sexual development (Udry and others, 1985). However, whether engagement in sexual intercourse increases androgen levels or androgen levels influence sexuality is not known. Additionally, contextual effects, if entered into the equation, might account for more of the variation in sexual activity than do hormonal levels. Initiation of sexuality is highly associated with what is normative in one's peer group (Furstenberg, Moore, and Peterson, 1986), so it is likely that while very early sexual initiations may in part be hormonally influenced, by the time the behavior is normative, social factors may account for sexual initiation (see Gargiulo, Attie, Brooks-Gunn, and Warren, 1987, for a similar argument about dating behavior). Thus, even if hormonal effects are demonstrated, they must be evaluated relative to contextual effects and relative to interactive effects before assuming a direct relation between hormones and behavior.

Second, the actual effect sizes of hormonal associations must be taken into account, as well as the relative size in relation to social factors. In one study, social factors and interactions of social and pubertal factors accounted for more variance in emotionality than did pubertal factors. Specifically, the combination of negative life events and the interaction of negative life events with pubertal status measures accounted for 17 percent of the variance in depressive affect, while estradiol accounted for only 4 percent of the variance. Many studies find stronger effects of pubertal status on behavior when interactions between biological and social factors are considered or combinations of both types of factors are taken into account, although these studies have not examined hormonal functioning (Brooks-Gunn and Warren, forthcoming).

Third, not only may hormonal activation effects be overshadowed by environmental events, but effects may be bidirectional. We know that the hypothalamic-pituitary-gonadal system is exquisitely sensitive to environmental conditions. For example, when weight loss is large (as in the case of anorexia nervosa), levels of gonadotropin secretions are suppressed in women, with the most obvious manifestations being amenorrhea and anovulatory cycles (Warren, 1985). In some adolescents with anorexia nervosa or exercise-induced weight loss, a reversion to the prepubertal pattern of low luteinizing hormone (LH) secretion, lowered amplitude secretion, and noctural LH spiking occurs. These changes are reversible with weight gain. Also, the genetic program for the timing of puberty may be partially overridden through such environmental factors as nutritional intake, weight, and intensity and extensivity of exercise (Brooks-Gunn, 1988a; Malina, 1983).

Fourth, we know very little about lability of mood, even though this construct is part and parcel of the notion of "storm and stress." Eccles and her colleagues (1988) are currently collecting weekly blood and mood-state profiles from a sample of young adolescents in order to see whether large hormonal fluctuations are associated with lability.

The other postulated mechanisms, the social-cognitive, personality, and psychodynamic perspectives, have not been systematically studied with regard to emotionality, and models that include such mechanisms would be welcome additions to the field. They have been theoretically linked to parent-child relational changes, the issue to be considered next.

Parent-Child Relationships. The "storm and stress" construct probably arose from adults' efforts to raise and interact with young adolescents (Blos, 1979; Hall, 1904). I have no doubt that such experiences lend face validity to the construct. However, face validity may sometimes hamper research. Several beliefs underlie the notion of stormy parent-child relationships: (1) changes are a direct consequence of pubertal growth; (2) change is of necessity conflictual, given the child's demands for more autonomy; and (3) the changes are initiated in large part by the adolescent. The literature to date does not confirm all of these beliefs; explicit testing of these beliefs would be extremely valuable.

Presently, parent-child relationships are being portrayed in more subtle ways. Attention is being given to those particular situations that may be conflictual, the intensity of conflicts, the meanings of such conflicts to the parents and to the child, and the timing of these particular conflicts. Conflict and disagreement seem to be almost universal, even though they may not be intense (Smetana, 1988). Such conflict is typically seen as temporary, as Hill's (1988) use of the word *perturbation* implies. Generally, parent-child relationships are thought to be transformed, as both parents and young adolescents renegotiate their relationship, moving toward more individuation from one another and more mutuality with one another (Grotevant and Cooper, 1986). While research has documented the nature of early adolescent relationships, discussion is sparse on actual developmental changes (from late childhood through late adolescence) and on the processes underlying such changes.

Changes in parent and child expectations for one another may be as important as changes in actual interaction patterns, although much less research has focused on the former. Germane to our focus on early adolescence is the fact that physical characteristics, independent of developmental age, influence parental expectations. Same-age children who are tall for their age groups are expected by adults to perform more difficult and more socially mature tasks (Brackbill and Nevill, 1981). Leadership and school achievement have been associated with children's and adolescents' height to a small degree (Duke, Jennings, Dornbusch, and Siegel-Gorelick, 1982; Tanner, 1966), suggesting the social stimulus value of physical characteristics (the role parents may play in the acquisition of such values has not been specified, however). As children enter puberty, parents may expect their more developed children to exhibit more socially adult behavior. For example, more physically mature girls may elicit greater freedom from parents, thus making it more likely that they will engage in dating. These expectations may result in changes in interactions, although the process by which this occurs has not been studied.

A corresponding change in the expectations of the young adolescent may occur, at least in some domains. In terms of autonomy, pubertal children seem to expect to be granted increased freedom in curfews, dress, and choice of friends (Simmons and Blyth, 1987). When such expectations occur in the early-maturing child, they may be met with parental resistance because the age norms for certain behaviors may be at odds with the "pubertal" age norms and parents may be less prepared to acknowledge the child's expectations (and demands) for more adult treatment. One might expect a press for relational change on the adolescent's part as a function of maturational timing and status, as well as age.

With regard to relational changes, the renegotiation and transformation conceptual models most often discussed have not been applied to the pubertal child. Instead, the focus has primarily been on the distancing of the parent and child from one another and on increases in conflict and assertiveness (Hill, 1988; Smetana, 1988; Steinberg, 1987).

Intensification of Gender Roles. An intriguing and increasingly asked question has to do with the emergence of gender differences or larger gender differences at the time of early adolescence. Hill and Lynch (1983) coined the phrase *intensification of gender roles.* They proposed that pressures to act in sex-stereotypic ways increased as the mature body emerged, probably in response to others' expectations and behaviors and as a result of changes in self-definition. That salience of adult reproductive roles occurs after the onset of breast development and menarche are cases in point (Brooks-Gunn, 1984), as are the expectations for more "adult" behavior placed on pubertal children and the increased vigilance of parents of pubertal girls.

Surprisingly, few studies have directly tested Hill and Lynch's thesis. Part of the problem may lie in what we would consider proof of their premise. Four different procedures for testing their premise are enumerated here as examples of possible directives for future research. The first of these procedures is across-age comparisons. One could envision comparisons of late childhood, early adolescent, and middle adolescent life phases. Problems surface, however. First, few measures exist that are appropriate for eight- to fifteen-year-olds. Even for those that do exist, construct comparability across this age range has not been demonstrated (Brooks-Gunn, Rock, and Warren, forthcoming). Second, the behaviors for which a process such as gender intensification may be relevant may only surface in early adolescence. That is, while parents continually monitor their children's activities and friends, their focus may be much different before than after puberty has taken place. Vigilance may be triggered by a daughter's mature body as well as by the interest of pubertal boys, so that measuring parental vigilance, or the daughter's response to it, would be meaningless in late childhood. Another illustration may be taken from the parent-child conflict literature: Disagreements about choice of friends do not seem to emerge prior to puberty (Smetana, 1988; Brooks-Gunn and Zahaykevich, forthcoming).

Another way of testing Hill and Lynch's premise is to compare same-age early adolescents who differ in regard to their pubertal status. Indeed, the sparse literature might be read as supportive, in that early-maturing boys are more likely to be characterized by stereotypic masculine attributes (for example, leadership and independence) than are on-time or later-maturing boys. Such differences may persist into adulthood. However, maintenance of such sex-stereotypic behaviors may not be functional after adolescence; early-maturing boys with sex-stereotyped attributes may be less flexible and adaptable as adults.

What about girls, toward whom much of the gender-role intensification debate is directed? Early-maturing girls seem to engage in a variety of "adult" behaviors sooner than do their later-maturing peers, although a "catch-up" phenomenon seems to exist (Magnusson, Strattin, and Allen, 1985). Early-maturing girls also are more likely to have older friends, presumably with whom they are engaging in sex, smoking, and drinking. Thus, parents may increase vigilance and protectiveness because the daughter simultaneously wishes to move and is enticed into moving toward friendships with mature peers. Whether such patterns have any effects on the acquisition of stereotypic feminine behaviors and the decline of more independent, achievement-oriented behaviors has not been studied extensively (Brooks-Gunn, 1988).

Rather than focusing on the so-called sex-stereotyped attributes, another approach is to examine identity issues for which girls and boys may be more vulnerable. Borrowing from Erikson, it is my premise that girls are more vulnerable to problems with autonomy and achievement, boys to problems with intimacy. Examples from ongoing work follow.

With respect to autonomy, psychodynamic and personality theorists have argued that the process of individuation may be quite different for girls than for boys. Girls are believed to be more emotionally focused with and less individuated from their mothers than are boys (Chodorow, 1978; Josselson, 1980). Such differences may explain, in part, why girls speak "in a different voice"—more interpersonally, intimately, and relationally focused than boys (Gilligan, 1982). Perhaps parent-child interactions occurring at early adolescence are reflective (and perhaps causal) of a more facilitative discontinuous experience for boys than for girls. For example, observational studies suggest that girls are interrupted more often and ignored more, while boys assert themselves more as puberty progresses (Hill, 1988). Mothers seem to exert more covert power over their daughters postmenarcheally than premenarcheally, and maternal projection and use of covert power are associated with daughters' compliance postmenarcheally, suggesting a partial explanation for the nonassertive behavior seen by girls in family interaction studies (Zahaykevich, Sirey, and Brooks-Gunn, under review). Clearly, more work on the process of individuation for girls and boys, as well as on the antecedents and consequences of parental behavior, is necessary.

At the same time, boys may be more vulnerable than are girls to problems of intimacy. While friendship patterns are being studied (Berndt, 1982), intimacy is not always the focus. Gilligan's (1982) work underscores the importance of intimacy for females; it is left to literary writers and popular psychologists to decry men's inability to form close relationships. Boys may be more vulnerable than girls to intimacy problems that emerge or become more salient at the time of puberty. The fact that in our culture it is unacceptable to talk about male pubertal changes and the feelings they engender may play a pivotal role in the way males structure their friendships. For example, in a small study of pubertal boys, almost none had received direct information from adults or peers about ejaculation, and almost none had discussed its occurrence (Gaddis and Brooks-Gunn, 1985). In contrast, almost all girls today talk over pubertal changes with their mothers and their close girlfriends. However, whether and how such differences influence disclosure and intimacy are not known.

Finally, one might borrow from developmental psychopathology to investigate gender divergence. Several well-documented findings are relevant. Three of the most well-studied and most prevalent psychiatric problems (and their less severe forms) are depression (depressive affect), conduct disorders (aggressive behavior and affect), and eating disorders (compulsive eating). All three are linked to gender, become more prevalent after puberty, and are associated with personality factors and contextual events (Attie and Brooks-Gunn, forthcoming; Rutter, Izard, and Read, 1986; Robins, 1966). Prospective studies are necessary in order to understand the antecedents of these disorders and, in a more normative sense, the less severe problems, as well as how the antecedents may differ for males and females. Additionally, comparative studies of different problems may be critical in order to see whether similar or a different set of factors predispose a boy to be vulnerable to aggression and a girl to depression, for example. Almost no such studies exist.

Sensitivity to Occurrence of Social Events. A particularly intriguing but virtually unexplored issue is whether early adolescents, by virtue of either pubertal changes or just the number of social and biological changes occurring, are more sensitive to environmental events or contextual factors than are individuals in other life phases. While few studies directly address this issue, several promising approaches exist. For example, Elder, in his ground-breaking study, *Children of the Great Depression* (1974), demonstrated that the experience of a major life crisis had very different long-lasting effects on children as a function of their age at the time of the event. Another example is the study of alterations in families as a function of divorce and remarriage (Hetherington,

Cox, and Cox, 1985). Changes in family composition have profound effects on some children; these effects are most likely to show themselves at early adolescence (Furstenberg, Brooks-Gunn, and Morgan, 1987). In general, such longitudinal studies may address whether developmental trajectories are more likely to be altered by environmental events in early adolescence than at other times or whether earlier environmental events are more likely to have effects during early adolescence than in other life phases subsequent to the event being studied.

A related notion involves the possibility that early adolescence is marked by more discontinuity than are other life phases, again because of the multiplicity of events taking place as well as qualitative differences in the events occurring during puberty that may necessitate novel coping strategies or alterations in self-understanding (Damon and Hart, 1982). However, little research is directly addressing the possibility of organizational changes as they might be associated with pubertal change.

Tomorrow

While by no means exhaustive, the preceding issues illustrate both current approaches to the study of puberty and future directions. At the same time, many other concerns remain. In the biological realm, we still do not understand fully either the physiological mechanisms responsible for initiating and regulating neuroendocrine maturation and somatic growth or how environmental factors may interact with biological factors to enhance or impede maturation. From a clinical perspective, the biological and social markers for such severe problems as depression, conduct disorders, and eating disorders are not well understood, nor are the reasons for their emergence or increase following the early adolescent transition. Cognitively, few investigators are examining the possible role of pubertal processes in cognitive change or in the role of cognition in the emergence of negative emotions.

Social cognition perspectives are just beginning to be applied to the early adolescent transition, with this work being directed toward attributions and rule setting in the conventional, social, and moral realm. Other processes (self-definitions, social comparisons, and so on) also await investigation. Psychodynamic perspectives are regrettably rare in our research, even though clinical theorizing has been the basis for much of the current thinking on parent-child relationships, "storm and stress," identity formation, and gender-role intensification—all topics of current interest and debate. Sociologically, too few cross-cultural and multi-ethnic studies have been conducted. Finally, not enough attention is being given to the progression from pubertal growth to sexuality (Brooks-Gunn and Furstenberg, 1989). However, on balance, the acceptance of new methods to study puberty, the adoption of interactional and contextual models, the inclusion of biological and social factors in most studies, and the eagerness for transdisciplinary research all bode well for the next decade of research.

References

Attie, I., and Brooks-Gunn, J. "The Emergence of Eating Disorders and Eating Problems in Adolescence: A Developmental Perspective." *Journal of Child Psychology and Child Psychiatry*, forthcoming.

Baumrind, D. "A Developmental Perspective on Adolescent Risk Taking in America." In C. E. Irwin (ed.), *Adolescent Social Behavior and Health*. New Directions for Child Development, no. 37. San Francisco: Jossey-Bass, 1987.

Beach, F. A. "Behavioral Endocrinology: An Emerging Discipline." *American Scientist*, 1975, *63*, 178–187.

Berndt, T. J. "The Features and Effects of Friendship in Early Adolescence." *Child Development*, 1982, *53*, 1447–1460.

Block, J., and Gjerde, P. F. "Depressive Symptomatology in Late Adolescence: A Longitudinal Perspective on Personality Antecedents." In J. E. Rolf and others (eds.), *Risk and Protective Factors in the Development of Psychopathology*. New York: Cambridge University Press, 1988.

Blos, P. "The Second Individuation Process." In P. Blos (ed.), *The Adolescent Passage: Developmental Issues at Adolescence*. New York: International Universities Press, 1979.

Brackbill, Y., and Nevill, D. "Parental Expectations of Achievement as Affected by Children's Height." *Merrill-Palmer Quarterly,* 1981, *27* (4), 429–441.

Brim, O. G., Jr., and Kagan, J. *Constancy and Change in Human Development.* Cambridge, Mass.: Harvard University Press, 1980.

Brooks-Gunn, J. "The Psychological Significance of Different Pubertal Events to Young Girls." *Journal of Early Adolescence,* 1984, *4* (4), 315–327.

Brooks-Gunn, J. "Transition to Early Adolescence." In M. R. Gunnar (ed.), *Minnesota Symposia on Child Psychology.* Vol. 21. Hillsdale, N.J.: Erlbaum, 1988a.

Brooks-Gunn, J. "Antecedents and Consequences of Variations in Girls' Maturational Timing." *Journal of Adolescent Health Care,* 1988b, *9* (5), 1–9.

Brooks-Gunn, J., and Furstenberg, F. F. "Adolescent Sexual Behavior." *American Psychologist,* 1989, *44* (2).

Brooks-Gunn, J., and Petersen, A. C. *Girls at Puberty: Biological and Psychosocial Perspectives.* New York: Plenum, 1983.

Brooks-Gunn, J., and Petersen, A. C. "The Emergence of Depression in Adolescence: Biopsychosocial Perspectives." Special issue, *Journal of Youth and Adolescence,* forthcoming.

Brooks-Gunn, J., Petersen, A. C., and Eichorn, D. "The Timing of Maturation and Psychosocial Functioning in Adolescence." *Journal of Youth and Adolescence,* 1985, *14* (3 and 4).

Brooks-Gunn, J., Rock, D., and Warren, M. P. "Comparability of Constructs Across the Adolescent Years." *Developmental Psychology,* forthcoming.

Brooks-Gunn, J., and Warren, M. P. "The Psychological Significance of Secondary Sexual Characteristics in Nine- to Eleven-Year-Old Girls." *Child Development,* 1988, *59.*

Brooks-Gunn, J., and Warren, M. P. "Biological Contributions to Affective Expression in Young Adolescent Girls." *Child Development,* forthcoming.

Brooks-Gunn, J., and Zahaykevich, M. "Parent-Child Relationships in Early Adolescence: A Developmental Perspective." In

K. Kreppner and R. M. Lerner (eds.), *Family Systems in Life-Span Development.* Hillsdale, N.J.: Erlbaum, forthcoming.

Chodorow, N. *The Reproduction of Mothering: Psychoanalysis and Sociology of Gender.* Berkeley: University of California Press, 1978.

Cicchetti, D. "The Emergence of Developmental Psychopathology." *Child Development,* 1984, *55,* 1–7.

Coe, C. "The Role of Gonadal Hormones in the Pubertal Transition: Activation or Concatenation?" In M. R. Gunnar (ed.), *Minnesota Symposia on Child Psychology.* Vol. 21. Hillsdale, N.J.: Erlbaum, 1988.

Damon, W., and Hart, D. "The Development of Self-Understanding from Infancy Through Adolescence." *Child Development,* 1982, *53,* 841–864.

Duke, P. M., Jennings, D. J., Dornbusch, S. M., and Siegel-Gorelick, B. "Educational Correlates of Early and Late Sexual Maturation in Adolescence." *Journal of Pediatrics,* 1982, *100* (4), 633–637.

Eccles, J. S., and others. "Hormones and Affect at Early Adolescence." Paper presented at symposium on the hormonal contributions to adolescent behavior, Society for Research in Adolescence, Alexandria, Va., March 1988.

Elder, G. H. *Children of the Great Depression.* Chicago: University of Chicago Press, 1974.

Furstenberg, F. F., Jr., Brooks-Gunn, J., and Morgan, P. *Adolescent Mothers in Later Life.* New York: Cambridge University Press, 1987.

Furstenberg, F. F., Jr., Moore, K. A., and Peterson, J. L. "Sex Education and Sexual Experience Among Adolescents." *American Journal of Public Health,* 1986, *75* (11), 221–222.

Gaddis, A., and Brooks-Gunn, J. "The Male Experience of Pubertal Change." *Journal of Youth and Adolescence,* 1985, *14* (1), 61–69.

Gargiulo, J., Attie, I., Brooks-Gunn, J., and Warren, M. P. "Dating in Middle School Girls: Effects of Social Context, Maturation, and Grade." *Developmental Psychology,* 1987, *23* (5), 730–737.

Gilligan, C. *In a Different Voice: Psychological Theory and*

Women's Development. Cambridge, Mass.: Harvard University Press, 1982.

Grotevant, H. D., and Cooper, C. R. "Individuation in Family Relationships: A Perspective on Individual Differences in the Development of Identity and Role-Taking Skill in Adolescence." *Human Development,* 1986, *29,* 82–100.

Grumbach, M. M., and Sizonenko, P. C. *The Control of the Onset of Puberty: II.* Orlando, Fla.: Academic Press, 1986.

Gunnar, M. R. (ed.). *Minnesota Symposia on Child Psychology.* Vol. 21. Hillsdale, N.J.: Erlbaum, 1988.

Hall, G. S. *Adolescence: Its Psychology and Its Relations to Physiology, Anthropology, Sociology, Sex, Crime, Religion, and Education.* 2 vols. East Norwalk, Conn.: Appleton-Century-Crofts, 1904.

Hamburg, B. A. "Early Adolescence: A Specific and Stressful Stage of the Life Cycle." In G. V. Coelho, B. A. Hamburg, and J. E. Adams (eds.), *Coping and Adaptation.* New York: Basic Books, 1974.

Hetherington, E. M., Cox, M., and Cox, R. "Long-Term Effects of Divorce and Remarriage on the Adjustment of Children." *Journal of the American Academy of Child Psychiatry,* 1985, *24* (5), 518–530.

Hill, J. P. "The Role of Conflict in Familial Adaptation to Biological Change." In M. R. Gunnar (ed.), *Minnesota Symposia on Child Psychology.* Vol. 21. Hillsdale, N.J.: Erlbaum, 1988.

Hill, J. P., and Lynch, M. E. "The Intensification of Gender-Related Role Expectations During Early Adolescence." In J. Brooks-Gunn and A. C. Petersen (eds.), *Girls at Puberty: Biological and Psychosocial Perspectives.* New York: Plenum, 1983.

Irwin, C. E. (ed.). *Adolescent Social Behavior and Health.* New Directions for Child Development, no. 37. San Francisco: Jossey-Bass, 1987.

Josselson, R. L. "Psychodynamic Aspects of Identity Formation in College Women." *Journal of Youth and Adolescence,* 1980, *2,* 3–52.

Lerner, R. M. "Adolescent Maturational Changes and Psychosocial

Development: A Dynamic Interactional Perspective." *Journal of Youth and Adolescence,* 1985, *14* (4), 355–372.

Lerner, R. M., and Foch, T. T. (eds.). *Biological-Psychosocial Interactions in Early Adolescence: A Life Span Perspective.* Hillsdale, N.J.: Erlbaum, 1987.

Lipsitz, J. *Growing Up Forgotten: A Review of Research and Programs Concerning Young Adolescents.* Lexington, Mass.: Heath, 1977.

McAnarney, E. R., and Levine, M. *Early Adolescent Transitions.* Lexington, Mass.: Heath, 1987.

Magnusson, D., Strattin, H., and Allen, V. L. "A Longitudinal Study of Some Adjustment Processes from Mid-Adolescence to Adulthood." *Journal of Youth and Adolescence,* 1985, *14* (4), 267–283.

Malina, R. M. "Menarche in Athletes: A Synthesis and Hypothesis." *Annals of Human Biology,* 1983, *10* (1), 1–24.

Marshall, W. A., and Tanner, J. M. "Variations in Pattern of Pubertal Changes in Girls." *Archives of Diseases in Childhood,* 1969, *44,* 291–303.

Mussen, P. H., and Jones, M. C. "Self-Conceptions, Motivations, and Interpersonal Attitudes of Late- and Early-Maturing Boys." *Child Development,* 1957, *28,* 243–256.

Nesselroade, J. R., and Baltes, P. B. "Adolescent Personality Development and Historical Change: 1970-1972." *Monographs of the Society for Research in Child Development,* 1974, *39* (entire issue 1).

Offer, D. "In Defense of Adolescence." *Journal of the American Medical Association,* 1987, *257* (24), 3407–3408.

Olweus, D., Block, J., and Radke-Yarrow, M. *Development of Antisocial and Prosocial Behavior: Research, Theories, and Issues.* Orlando, Fla.: Academic Press, 1986.

Parlee, M. B. "The Premenstrual Syndrome." *Psychology Bulletin,* 1973, *80* (6), 454–465.

Peskin, H. "Influence of the Developmental Schedule of Puberty on Learning and Ego Functioning." *Journal of Youth and Adolescence,* 1973, *2,* 273–290.

Robins, L. *Deviant Children Grown Up*. Baltimore, Md.: Williams & Wilkins, 1966.

Ruble, D. N., and Brooks-Gunn, J. "Menstrual Symptoms: A Social Cognitive Analysis." *Journal of Behavioral Medicine*, 1979, *2*, 171–194.

Rutter, M., Izard, C. E., and Read, P. B. *Depression in Young People: Developmental and Clinical Perspectives*. New York: Guilford Press, 1986.

Scarr, S. "Constructing Psychology: Making Facts and Fables for Our Times." *American Psychologist*, 1985, *40* (5), 499–512.

Simmons, R. G., and Blyth, D. A. *Moving into Adolescence: The Impact of Pubertal Change and School Context*. New York: Aldine Press, 1987.

Smetana, J. G. "Concepts of Self and Social Convention: Adolescents' and Parents' Reasoning About Hypothetical and Actual Family Conflicts." In M. R. Gunnar (ed.), *Minnesota Symposia on Child Psychology*. Vol. 21. Hillsdale, N.J.: Erlbaum, 1988.

Steinberg, L. "The Impact of Puberty on Family Relations: Effects of Pubertal Status and Pubertal Timing." *Developmental Psychology*, 1987, *23*, 451–460.

Steinberg, L. D., and Hill, J. P. "Patterns of Family Interaction as a Function of Age, the Onset of Puberty, and Formal Thinking." *Developmental Psychology*, 1978, *14*, 683–684.

Susman, E. J., and others. "Hormones, Emotional Dispositions, and Aggressive Attributes in Young Adolescents." *Child Development*, 1987, *58* (4), 1114–1134.

Tanner, J. M. *Growth at Adolescence*. Springfield, Ill.: Thomas, 1962.

Tanner, J. M. "Galtonian Eugenics and the Study of Growth: The Relation of Body Size, Intelligence Test Score, and Social Circumstances in Children and Adults." *Eugenics Review*, 1966, *58*, 122–135.

Udry, J. R., and others. "Serum Androgenic Hormones Motivate Sexual Behavior in Boys." *Fertility and Sterility*, 1985, *43* (1), 90–94.

Warren, M. P. "When Weight Loss Accompanies Amenorrhea."

Contemporary Obstetrics and Gynecology, 1985, *28* (3), 588–597.
Zahaykevich, M., Sirey, J. A., and Brooks-Gunn, J. "Mother-
Daughter Individuation During Early Adolescence." Unpub-
lished manuscript under review.

Chapter 9

Emotional Development and the Affective Disorders

Dante Cicchetti
Jennifer White

 The effort to relate the study of emotional development to the study of the affective disorders is an extremely worthwhile endeavor for several important reasons. First, knowledge gained regarding the processes that underlie normal emotional development can serve as a map to direct attempts to understand the abnormal aspects of emotional behavior in the affective disorders at different developmental points across the life span. Second, by studying infants, children, and adolescents who either are "at risk" for or have an affective disorder, we can enhance our knowledge of the processes and mechanisms underlying normal affective development. However, until only recently, little research had been conducted at the interface between emotional development and the affective disorders (see, for example, Cicchetti and Schneider-Rosen, 1986, and Trad, 1987). Due to the paucity of research in the study of normal emotional development, the controversy surrounding the existence of the affective disorders in infancy and childhood, and the absence of an appropriate theoretical perspective, there was virtu-

Note: The writing of this chapter was supported by grants to Dante Cicchetti from the John D. and Catherine T. MacArthur Foundation Network on Early Childhood, the National Center on Child Abuse and Neglect, and the National Institute of Mental Health (R01-MH7960). We would like to thank Victoria Gill for typing this manuscript.

177

ally no research before the last decade that sought to elucidate the ways whereby the study of emotional development and the affective disorders could mutually inform each other. It is the aim of this chapter to outline the progress that has been made in this enterprise during recent times, to chart the developments that have made this growth possible, and to set forth some guidelines for future theory and research.

At the outset, it should be stated that the term *emotion* will be used interchangeably with the term *affect*. Although there has been very little agreement in contemporary psychology concerning the definition of emotion, the aspects that comprise it, and the interrelation among these various elements, here emotion will be understood generally as having the following four components: nonverbal expressive, verbal expressive, experiential, and biological.

Historical Perspective

Although it is not entirely clear why the study of the emotions has been neglected by developmental psychologists, several reasons seem likely. Briefly, the conceptualization within traditional psychoanalytic thought of the emotions as exerting a disorganizing effect upon development, as well as the difficulty in generating testable hypotheses from psychoanalytic theory in order to conduct empirical research, limited the systematic examination of psychoanalytic hypotheses about the nature of affect. Partly in response to the problems associated with psychoanalytic theory, the behaviorist movement that reached ascendancy during the middle of the twentieth century advocated that the discipline of psychology be restricted to the study of observable behaviors. Due to the imprecision in the definition and assessment of emotions, a reduction in the systematic investigation of the emotions resulted (see Cicchetti and Pogge-Hesse, 1981, for an elaboration).

In addition, the focus of Piagetian theory on cognitive development led to a proliferation of research and theorizing about the developing cognitive capacities of the infant and child with a corresponding neglect of the emotional domain. Nonetheless, it is interesting to note that although Piaget's theory of cognitive development was responsible, in part, for the focus in developmental psychology on the study of the cognitive realm at the expense of the emotional, Piaget ([1954] 1981) was one of the few theorists to formulate a theory of the ontogenesis of the emotions (see Cicchetti and Hesse, 1983). However, in Piaget's conceptualization of affect as the driving energy underlying the cognitive structures, the role assigned to affect was clearly a secondary one. Furthermore, although the study of the emotions has had a long history of research within the fields of psychophysiology, psychobiology, and the neurosciences, the vast majority of the work conducted has been adevelopmental. It was not until quite recently that researchers studying the neural and psychophysiological substrates of emotion began to employ a developmental perspective.

Beginning in the 1970s, a dramatic increase in interest in the study of emotional development spawned a wealth of research efforts directed at investigating the processes underlying the verbal expressive, nonverbal expressive, biological, and experiential aspects of emotion development. For example, recent methodological advances in the measurement of facial expression and in the investigation of the psychophysiological correlates of emotions have made significant contributions to our understanding of emotional development in infancy (Davidson, 1984; Izard, 1977). Likewise, research on the development of emotion language, children's understanding and awareness of their emotions, and the ontogenesis of social and personal display rules and mechanisms of defense have enhanced our knowledge of emotion during childhood (Hesse and Cicchetti, 1982).

Though it is indisputable that important theoretical and empirical advances have been made, controversy continues to surround a number of major issues, including the way in which discrete emotions evolve (Campos and others, 1983). Moreover, there also has been an absence of agreement concerning the appropriate taxonomy for classifying emotions, as well as a failure to learn the correspondence between overt emotional expression and internal felt emotional experience.

In addition to the lack of knowledge about normal emotional development, the controversy surrounding the existence of depression in infancy and childhood has prohibited interest in ascertaining the connection between affective development and the affective disorders. Although there has been a burgeoning of interest in childhood depression, and while impressive theoretical and empirical advances have been made, there has continued to be a great deal of disagreement over many issues of critical importance to the formulation of a comprehensive theory of childhood depression. For example, disagreement has characterized attempts to establish diagnositc criteria and classification schemes for the childhood affective disorders. Likewise, considerable debate has been generated concerning the role of biological versus psychological/environmental causation and the relation between childhood affective disorder and subsequent adult depression (Cicchetti and Schneider-Rosen, 1984; Sroufe and Rutter, 1984). Furthermore, in recent years a number of researchers have proposed the application of adult criteria for the diagnosis of depression in children. Such thinking has characterized the formation of the childhood depression diagnostic category in both the Diagnostic and Statistical Manuals III and III-R (American Psychiatric Association, 1980, 1987). Much debate has ensued about the appropriateness of applying an adevelopmental nosology to the study of childhood affective disorders. Consequently, it is unclear whether existing epidemiological incidence and prevalence rates represent veridical claims, underestimates, or overestimates of this group of disorders.

Because the developmental perspective has only recently begun to be applied to the affective disorders, it is hardly surprising that so little work exists that focuses on the relation between emotional development and the affective disorders. It is possible, however, to find a few examples of researchers and theorists who have examined the implications of various components of affective development for childhood depression.

Early attempts to view childhood depression from a developmental perspective primarily involved targeting a particular psychological or psychobiological mechanism known to occur in adult depression in order to discern the possible operation of this process in children. Even within the limits of these earlier efforts to consider the implications of the study of the affective disorders and the domain of affective development for each other, it became apparent that there were many domains of development, besides the affective arena, that needed to be taken into account within a developmental approach to depression (most notably, cognitive, socioemotional, biological, linguistic, and moral development). It will be argued here that the most useful developmental approach to the study of the affective disorders, and the one that can elucidate its relationship with the domain of emotional development most meaningfully, is the organizational perspective.

Organizational-Developmental Psychopathology Perspective

Throughout this chapter, it has been emphasized that while an understanding of normal affective development can contribute to our knowledge of the affective disorders, it is equally true that the study of the affective disorders throughout the life span can help elucidate our understanding of affective development. Such a position is reflective of a "developmental psychopathology approach" (Cicchetti, 1984), according to which any form of psychopathology can be conceptualized as a distortion in the normal ontogenetic process. By examining the nature of these distortions as they are manifested in various forms of psychopathology, one can acquire an understanding of normal developmental processes. By studying the differences between distortions that occur within the same form of psychopathology at different points in the life span, one can gain an understanding of the way in which the structures involved in that particular psychopathology change over time.

It also has become increasingly clear that an effort to highlight the role of one developmental system for the study of the affective disorders, even one as important to it as the emotional, requires attention to other developmental domains (Cicchetti and Schneider-Rosen, 1986). Moreover, as we noted earlier, affects or emotions themselves are comprised of a variety of components (verbal expressive, nonverbal expressive, biological, and experiential) that necessitate reference to a diversity of disciplines, including clinical and developmental psychology, biochemistry, neurophysiology, linguistics, and ethology. Therefore, research efforts to examine the relationship between affective development, on the one hand, and the affective disorders, on the other, require a developmental perspective that is in accordance with the "organizational" perspective on development.

Within an organizational approach to development, "normal" or "healthy" development is not defined in terms of the mean. Rather, it is defined in terms of a series of interlocking social, emotional, and cognitive competences. Competence at one period of development, which tends to make the individual broadly adapted to his or her environment, prepares the way for the formation of competence at the next (Sroufe and Rutter, 1984). Pathological development, in contrast, is viewed as a lack of integration of the social, emotional, and cognitive/linguistic competencies that are important to achieving adaptation at a particular developmental level. Because early structures often are incorporated into later structures, an early deviation or disturbance in functioning may ultimately cause more profound disturbances to emerge later on.

However, the organizational approach to development allows that, just as early competence may lead to later adaptation and incompetence to later maladaptation, this isomorphism in functioning may not be the only expected outcome. It is argued that it is necessary to engage in a comprehensive evaluation of those factors that may influence the nature of individual differences, the continuity of adaptive or maladaptive behavioral patterns, and the different pathways by which the same developmental outcomes may be achieved. Consequently, it is important to map out the processes whereby the normal course of development in the social, emotional, cognitive, and/or linguistic domains, in dynamic transaction with the "inner" (that is, biological) constitutional and "outer" (that is, familial conditions, stresses, support systems, peer groups) environmental influences on the child, may lead to outcomes that either inhibit or exacerbate early deviations or maintain or disrupt early adaptation. Therefore, it is essential to look for prototypes and precursors of psychopathology by considering the continuity or discontinuity of adaptive or maladaptive behavioral patterns, the individual's level of functioning in relation to age- and stage-appropriate expectations, the quality and stability of the caregiving environment, and the nature of the experiences to which the child is exposed. In our opinion, the application of the organizational-developmental psychopathology perspective to the study of the relationship between affective development and the affective disorders will yield the most meaningful, productive program of research.

Guidelines for Future Theoretical and Empirical Work on the Interface Between Emotional Development and the Affective Disorders

In this section, we focus on four promising areas in which the relation between emotional development/regulation and the affective disorders of childhood can be elucidated.

Neuropsychological Approach to Emotional Development and the Affective Disorders. Evidence from a variety of lines of research has contributed to a growing understanding of the role of the cerebral hemispheres in emotional functioning in adults (see Tucker, 1981, for a review of this literature). Although controversy has surrounded their interpretation, the results from these studies have provided a foundation of knowledge regarding the hemispheric substrates of emotion. It is proposed here that similar efforts need to be directed toward understanding the neuropsychological correlates of affective development in infancy and childhood. The acquisition of this knowledge can help inform our understanding of depression in infancy and childhood. Moreover, in that the emotional dysfunctions of infants and children can be understood as distortions of normal emotional processes, a neuropsychological perspective of depression across the life span could teach us about the development of these hemispheric substrates of emotion.

One important source of information about the neural bases of emotion in adults derives from neuropsychological assessments of patients in whom there is evidence of emotional dysfunction as a result of brain damage, epilepsy, or psychopathology. Other information has come from studies using the electroencephalogram (EEG) to assess the patterns of brain activation associated with normal emotional functioning. Together, the results from these studies suggest that various key aspects of emotional perception and production are lateralized. For example, patients with left frontal brain damage consistently have been found to show a catastrophic depressive reaction, whereas patients with right frontal brain damage demonstrate euphoria and indifference to their condition. Several EEG studies of subjects engaged in normal emotional functioning have identified different patterns of frontal hemispheric activation asymmetries associated with positive versus negative emotions. For the most part, it appears that there is relatively less left frontal activation and/or greater right frontal activation during negative emotional states, such as sadness, disgust, and fear. This asymmetry is reversed for positive emotions, such as happiness and interest.

Because information regarding the underlying brain mechanisms is still lacking, the results of these studies have led researchers to different conclusions about how affect is lateralized. While some researchers have attributed a greater role to the left hemisphere in the production of negative affect, others have argued that it has a positive affective bias and that it is the deactivation of this positive bias that results in negative affect. It has also been argued that, depending on the level of activation associated with the frontal region of the right hemisphere, affect will shift from negative to positive.

Although there appears to be a consistent pattern of hemispheric specialization for emotion emerging from the adult literature, it was not until very recently that systematic investigations of such patterns were conducted beyond adulthood. In the first attempt to investigate the existence of EEG activation frontal asymmetry in infants, Davidson and Fox (1982) recorded the EEG of ten-month-old infants in response to negative and positive videotapes. The infants showed greater relative left-sided frontal activation in response to the happy video segment and greater relative right-sided activation in response to the sad segment.

Studies of adults have indicated that resting EEG differences among subjects are related to differences in emotional style. A similar finding has been reported for infants (Davidson and Fox, forthcoming). Ten-month-old infants with resting right frontal activation were more likely to cry in response to brief maternal separation than were those with left frontal activation during rest. Such a finding suggests that there are important individual differences in hemispheric asymmetries that may effect a predisposition toward a particular affective style—either positive or negative.

It is conceivable that there may be certain individuals who are constitutionally vulnerable to depression, as evidenced by long-term hemispheric activation asymmetries. One plausible explanation is that the overactivation of the right hemisphere may have a genetic basis. It is equally likely that certain experiences can affect the developing brain structures and prime them for chronic activation asymmetry (Tucker, 1981). In that hemispheric asymmetries may be mediated by both genetic factors and socialization, the offspring of depressives may be especially at risk for a negative affective bias.

Experiences encountered during postnatal ontogenesis may likewise either exacerbate a preexisting frontal asymmetry constitutional diathesis and/or contribute to its formation. To provide a compelling example, Main and Solomon (forthcoming) have recently discovered a new attachment classification entitled the disorganized/disoriented (Type D) category. Main has suggested that it is the interjection of *fear* into the caregiving experience that is essential to developing a disorganized/disoriented attachment. Fear must certainly be a common experience for physically and emotionally abused children. It also is probable that there are frightening aspects to emotional and physical neglect. Research in our laboratory has documented that nearly 80 percent of maltreated babies develop Type D attachments with their caregivers. Many of the mothers of these infants have been found to have a clinically diagnosed depressive disorder. Likewise, infants of "psychologically unavailable" caregivers (many of whom also are depressed women) demonstrate high incidences of disorganized/disoriented relationships (see discussion in Carlson, Cicchetti, Barnett, and Braunwald, forthcoming). We believe that longitudinal follow-up investigations of disorganized/disoriented infant attachments may reveal a high occurrence of chronic hemispheric activation asymmetry. Babies who possess the combination of a genetic diathesis for an affective disorder and an abusive environment are likely to be at greatest risk.

In light of this observation, it is interesting to note that Fox and Davidson (1984) have hypothesized that sadness is a complex emotion whose expression is mediated bilaterally and which, therefore, requires maturation of the cerebral commissures. In support of this hypothesis, Fox and Davidson cite evidence for a close link between the onset of locomotion and the concomitant development of the expression of fear and sadness. In their view, both developments have their neural substrates in the maturation of certain cerebral commissural pathways. Consequently, they believe that a clear expression of sadness is not possible until the first half of the second year of life. From this perspective, it would appear that if a depressive episode can occur during infancy, it might not be accompanied by feelings of sad affect until the second year of life.

The suggestion by Fox and Davidson (1984) that the ability to inhibit negative affect during the middle of the second year of life may have a neural basis in the increased inhibition by the left hemisphere of the right hemisphere, made possible by the development of transcallosal pathways, is also of interest to understanding the affective disorders in childhood. Fox and Davidson argue that, in addition to the more advanced differentiation that occurs in the functional development of the commissural pathways, the increased functional activity of the left hemisphere associated with language development may be the underlying change in brain function responsible for the increased affective regulation that is observable in the middle of the second year. Based on these suggestions, it is possible to hypothesize that infants who are old enough to express fully developed sadness, but who have not yet developed the neural substrates for the inhibition of negative affect, may be at particular risk for the development of depression. This is especially likely to be the case if the infant is the offspring of a parent with an affective disorder.

A further line of inquiry stems from the way in which a neuropsychological approach to the study of emotion has helped reveal the tight links between emotion and cognition. Tucker (1981) has argued that certain types of cognitions and cognitive skills are facilitated or hampered by particular mood states. For example, neuropsychological assessments of adult depressives have revealed a deficit in visuospatial and perceptual skills associated with right posterior cerebral dysfunction that improves with the remission of the depression. Interestingly, EEG studies have shown that depressives who show right frontal activation demonstrate a corresponding right posterior inhibition of activity. It has been argued that the pattern of frontal activation asymmetries associated with depression may exhibit an inhibiting effect on the right posterior regions, thereby providing the neural mechanism for the observed cognitive deficits in depression. Clearly, it is important to consider the implications of the interconnectivity of the developing substrates of emotional and cognitive functioning for our understanding of depression in infancy and in childhood. In fact, when Brumback, Staton, and Wilson (1980) administered neuropsychological tests to endogenously depressed children ranging in age from six to thirteen years, before and after antidepressant medication, they found that antidepressant drug treatment resulted in greater improvement in right- than in left-hemisphere functioning. Because these children are capable of experiencing a cognitive dysfunction similar to that found in adult depressives, it would appear that they might be at risk for particular types of learning problems. Furthermore, it is likely that the inability to perform certain tasks may perpetuate a depressive episode. Given the possible contributions that developmental neuropsychological assessment could make to the diagnosis, course, and sequelae of the affective disorders, we believe that additional research in this area needs to be conducted.

A developmental neuropsychological approach also can be used to elucidate the relationship between affective comprehension and the affective disorders. Studies have shown that patients with right posterior damage are unable to pick up on the social and affective cues involved in interpersonal relationships. It may be that the depression associated with a subgroup of children may be mediated through a neuropsychological deficit involving the right posterior regions. Due to their inability to rely on social cues to negotiate increasingly complex social situations throughout their development, these children may become more and more isolated and alienated, leading to depression. Such an example highlights the possibility that there are multiple neuropsychological pathways to the common outcome of a depressive episode.

Another extremely important area to investigate in the hemispheric lateralization of emotion pertains to the realm of developmental neurochemistry and the relation between affective and cognitive development in the affective disorders. Tucker (1981) has pointed to the role of neurotransmitter systems in hemispheric activation and to their implications for elucidating the relationship between affect and cognition. Studies need to be conducted with infants and children to assess the relation among the development of neurotransmitter systems, hemispheric patterns of activation, and the affective disorders. As Puig-Antich (1986) has noted, there is much clinical and animal evidence to suggest that during development in infancy and childhood the balance between different neuroregulatory systems is not equivalent to that in adulthood. Differences in such a balance between children and adults could have important implications for the assessment, diagnosis, and treatment of the affective disorders.

Socialization of Affect. During the neonatal period, the affective expression of the infant is immediate and unmodulated. At this point, the infant's affect is sensorimotor affect that is controlled by subcortical programs. Although socialization has played no role yet in the expression of affect, the young infant has been neurally primed to be aware of and responsible to the emotional signals of its caretakers. In other words, infants are prepared to be affectively influenced by others. As Malatesta and Izard (1984) have argued, it is these underlying neural programs that ensure that the basic components of emotional expression occur during normal development; however, it is only with the input from a social partner that there is continuity in affective expression, as well as increased modulation and affective regulation.

Given the important role accorded to socialization during affective development, it is hardly surprising that, in addition to being genetically at risk, children with depressed parents have been shown to be environmentally at risk for developing a future affective disorder. Information pertaining to the homeostatic regulation of infants of affectively disordered parents stems from several sources. In an important study, Cohn and Tronick (1983) concluded that even simulated depression could result in negative infant affectivity, subsequently impairing the infant's capacity to engage in self-regulation. These findings revealed that the flexibility of rhythms evidenced during sequences of normal interaction were significantly impaired during phases of simulated depression. Subsequently, Field (1984) compared dyadic interactions between a sample of mothers suffering from postpartum depression and a sample of normal mothers simulating depression. A difference in coping strategy emerged, with infants in the postpartum group evidencing resigned, passive, and mimicking behavior, while infants in the simulated depression group were active in their protests. These studies indicate that differences in homeostatic regulation can emerge very early in the lives of infants exposed to a depressed parent.

A related, potentially very important area of study concerns the examination of the growing literature on the role of maternal imitation in the socialization of infant emotional development and its implications for the development of the affective disorders. Although there has been much investigation into the role of infant imitation in emotional ontogenesis, systematic efforts to study the ways in which mothers imitate their infants' facial expressions have been a recent occurrence.

It has been suggested that maternal imitation of infant facial expressions and gestures serves a number of different functions, including increasing infants' gazing at their mothers, facilitating the infants' sense of control over the environment, encouraging infant imitation, and enhancing the attachment relationship between the infant and the mother. Mothers who are depressed may lack the ability to imitate their infants' facial expressions and gestures. It is possible that either a lack of maternal imitation or a deviancy within this system may increase the risks for depression among the offspring of affectively disordered parents through a number of possible mechanisms: by serving to decrease their sense of self-efficacy, by bringing about an insecure attachment relationship, or by instilling a negative emotional set in the offspring. More in-depth study of the role of maternal imitation in normal emotional development needs to be done before this issue can be addressed definitively in the study of the affective disorders.

Research suggests that there appear to be patterns of maternal imitation that correspond to different periods in infants' development. For example, while mothers tend to imitate primarily the positive affective expressions of their infants at three months of age, by the time their infants are six months old, mothers tend to make more imitations of their infants' negative facial expressions

(Malatesta and Izard, 1984). This work has clear implications for the study of risk factors associated with the development of an affective disorder. Depressed mothers may engage less frequently in imitation, or they may have a tendency to imitate negative facial expressions more readily than positive ones. Although emotionally healthy mothers do imitate their infants' negative expressions, this occurs later than the imitation of positive affect and is conducted in a mock fashion. It is likely that depressed mothers may not be capable of mock negative affect, thereby placing their infants at risk for emotion regulation difficulties.

A burgeoning area of inquiry on the interface between linguistic and emotional development, and one that we believe holds great promise for augmenting our understanding of normal and abnormal emotional development, is that of internal states language usage (Bretherton and Beeghly, 1982). It has been suggested that the use of emotional language actually facilitates control over nonverbal emotional expressions, which in turn enhances control over the emotions themselves (Hesse and Cicchetti, 1982). Within this view, parents who frequently use emotional language to interpret their own and others' (nonverbal) emotional expressions in effect provide their children with mechanisms to help control their nonverbal emotional expressions. In contrast, parents who use emotional language in an effort to intellectualize or defend against emotional experience may be exhibiting an overcontrolled coping style. In this way, it can be argued, parents transfer their coping skills to their children via their use of emotional language. It could be hypothesized, then, that depressed parents may transmit depression to their offspring via the nature of the emotional language these parents employ. Therefore, we think it is important to study parents' emotional speech and their socialization of emotional language in their children as potential protective or vulnerability factors in childhood depression. It also is important to examine the parents' inappropriate or maladaptive labelings of emotion in this regard.

Attachment, Working Models, Affective Development, and the Affective Disorders. A growing number of investigators have emphasized the central role that attachment relationships play in the regulation of affect. In view of the cyclicity and the less stable caregiving environments frequently associated with the affective disorders, it is reasonable to expect attachment patterns to be adversely affected in the offspring of parents with an affective disorder. Despite the heterogeneity of depressive illness, researchers are beginning to find that depressive symptomatology does interfere with caregiver functioning and with the establishment of a positive affective relationship with the child.

In the largest investigation conducted to date, Radke-Yarrow, Cummings, Kuczynski, and Chapman (1985) found that insecure attachments were infrequent in children of normal parents or of parents having a minor depression. However, the children of parents with an affective disorder did evidence disturbances in attachment, which were primarily insecure avoidant (Type A), or insecure avoidant/resistant (Type A/C). In addition, children of bipolar mothers evidenced the highest percentage (79 percent) of insecure attachments.

Further evidence for the role of attachment in affective development and of its potential importance to the affective disorders can be found in the proposed subtypes for the newly discovered disorganized/disoriented (Type D) category of attachment. Main and Solomon (forthcoming) have tentatively set forth three different subtypes within the D attachment category: depressed, apprehensive, and avoidant/resistant (A/C). The depressed subtype infant has been identified on the basis of showing depressed affect, although it is unclear, given our poor understanding of the relationship between affective expression and feeling in infancy, to what extent the infant who is manifesting depressed affect is actually feeling depressed. Given the proposed relationship between alcoholism and depression, it is interesting to note that, in one sample, 35 percent of the offspring of alcoholic parents were found to meet criteria for the Type D attachment category (O'Connor, Sigman, and Brill, 1987).

Results such as these suggest that maternal depression may interfere with the capacity to relate in a way that promotes the development of a secure attachment. Depressed mothers may be perceived as inconsistent and unpredictable. An inability to respond to affect and associated physical and emotional unavailability are likely to compound the child's difficulties in establishing a secure relationship. By utilizing the construct of "working models" to describe the development of the schemata that children use to understand themselves, it is possible to show the interrelationships among attachment, depression, and self-understanding.

Bowlby (1973, p. 203) describes working models as an individual's conscious or unconscious mental representations "of the world and of himself in it, with the aid of which he perceives events, forecasts the future, and constructs his plans." Two of the most important parts of these working models are: (1) childrens' conceptions of their attachment figures, their whereabouts, and likely response to their behavior; and (2) children's conceptions of how acceptable or unacceptable they are in the eyes of their attachment figures (that is, their self-image).

Because these working models are constructed out of children's own actions, the feedback they receive from these actions, and the actions of caregivers, they consist of something closer to an "event schemata" than a static "picture." They include affective, "appraising" components, as well as cognitive components. As such, there will be wide variations across individuals in working models, and individuals' working models will fairly accurately reflect their own experience, as well as their cognitive, affective, and behavioral skills. Once organized, these internal working models tend to operate outside conscious awareness and resist dramatic change.

Recent evidence gathered in our laboratory provides strong support for a close correspondence between a positive working model of relationship to the major attachment figure and a positive working model of the self. This research has been conducted with maltreated and demographically matched nonmaltreated youngsters drawn from the lower socioeconomic strata. Nearly half of the maltreating mothers we have studied have been clinically depressed, as have approximately 20 percent of the comparison mothers.

Low-felt security derived from insecure attachments to primary figures can be seen as a potential basis for the development of working models of the self and others that are depressogenic (for example, "I'm not worth loving," "others won't love me"). The development of negative self-schemata is thought to play an extremely important role in the etiology and perpetuation of depressive bouts (Beck, 1967). Of particular interest to the developmentalist is the relationship between earlier and later negative self-schemata. Clearly, longitudinal work on the development of working models would help illuminate the role they play in the etiology and/or sequelae of depression.

Affective Development and Bipolar Disorder. In DSM-III-R (American Psychiatric Association, 1987) it is stated that a depressive episode can begin at any age, including infancy. The essential feature of bipolar disorder is the presence of one or more manic episodes, generally accompanied by one or more major depressive episodes. Unlike the diagnostic criteria for depression, which provide a specific age of onset as early as infancy, the diagnostic criteria for bipolar disorder do not specify any particular age of onset. This information gap in the DSM-III-R reflects the virtual absence of knowledge in contemporary psychology and psychiatry regarding the developmental correlates of bipolar disorder. Although it is commonly believed that bipolar disease does not occur before puberty, in fact, with few exceptions, very little research has been conducted on the etiology, course, and sequelae of bipolar disorder in childhood.

We believe that longitudinal studies investigating the development of the offspring of a parent with bipolar illness need to be conducted. Such children appear to be at particularly high risk of developing a bipolar disorder. Recent evidence suggests that there is a strong genetic component to bipolar illness. The occurrence of bipolar disorder has clearly been shown to be greater among first-degree biological relatives of individuals with bipolar disorder than among the general population. Moreover, these longitudinal high-risk studies are needed to identify possible precursor expressions of bipolar disorder in children because manic-depressive illness may be manifested differently in children than in adults, due to developmental differences within the structures or systems underlying bipolar disorder.

For example, a number of researchers have stressed the important role played by two different neurotransmitter systems within bipolar disorder. It has been proposed that the balance between the cholinergic and adrenergic systems in the central nervous system, as well as the serotonergic system, may dictate the affective changes associated with bipolar illness. Puig-Antich (1986) has hypothesized that the slower development of the catecholamine systems, which do not fully mature until adulthood, may be responsible for the rarity of mania and elation seen in childhood. Puig-Antich (1986) also cites evidence suggesting that low catecholamine activity may be the precipitating factor for depression in bipolar adults. Therefore, it may be that the exact type of affective disorder an individual is at risk for developing may not be discovered before the full catecholamine neurotransmitter system has fully differentiated. Hence, prospective longitudinal studies of the offspring of bipolar parents in which developmentally appropriate neurobiological, biochemical, socioemotional, and cognitive-linguistic measures are collected and their relation examined concurrently could enhance our understanding of the precursors, course, and correlates of bipolar disease.

Furthermore, research conducted on children at risk for bipolar disorder may help illuminate inquiry into the study of the role of biochemical factors, affective regulation, and socialization in normal emotional development. Using the example just given, it is possible to see how issues related to the biochemical contributions to bipolar disorder in childhood raise important questions about the normal development of neurotransmitter systems in children and point to areas within the field of normal affective development, as well as developmental neurobiochemistry, that need to be addressed.

The few studies that have investigated the socioemotional functioning of the offspring of bipolar parents suggest that there are indeed disturbances that begin early in their development (Cicchetti and Aber, 1986). For example, toddlers with a bipolar parent evidence difficulty in maintaining friendly social interactions, in helping their playmates, and in sharing. They also have problems regulating and modulating hostile impulses, demonstrating more maladaptive patterns of aggression toward both adults and peers. Most noteworthy are the striking similarities between the behavior of these toddlers and the clinical reports of manic-depressive adult patients in the literature. The results of these studies indicate that the offspring of parents with manic-depressive disorder appear to be at heightened risk for difficulties in affect regulation. At this point, it is not known how early affect dysregulation relates to the etiology of bipolar disorder. Future research needs to be focused in this direction.

Tomorrow

In this chapter, we have introduced and discussed several issues we believe are critical for enhancing our knowledge of the relation between emotional development and the affective disorders. All of these themes—the developmental neuropsychology of emotion, the socialization of affect, internal "working models" of relationships and of the "self," and bipolar disorder—share important components. All necessitate a multi-domain approach to the study of developmental processes. Additionally, research on these topics holds great promise for elucidating the organization of normal and pathological affective systems. Moreover, guided by the tenets of an organizational developmental psychopathology perspective, each focal issue is best examined through a multidisciplinary approach. Because descriptive and theoretical formulations of depressive and manic-depressive disease must take into account the biological reorganizations and the changing integration of development in the social, emotional, cognitive/linguistic, and social-cognitive domains, we believe that the introduction of an overarching developmental perspective will result in profound advances in the understanding of the affective disorders in childhood. Furthermore, the implications of this approach for the diagnosis of childhood affective disorders and subsequent treatment planning also are vast. All too often, failure to assess adequately the presence of an affective disorder may result in an exacerbation of associated difficulties. By expanding the breadth of knowledge on emotional development and associated symptomatic indicators, previously undetected or misdiagnosed conditions may be more effectively addressed.

References

American Psychiatric Association. *Diagnostic and Statistical Manual of Mental Disorders.* Vol. 3. Washington, D.C.: American Psychiatric Association, 1980.

American Psychiatric Association. *Diagnostic and Statistical*

Manual of Mental Disorders. Vol. 3. (Rev. ed.) Washington, D.C.: American Psychiatric Association, 1987.

Beck, A. *Depression: Causes and Treatment.* Philadelphia: University of Pennsylvania Press, 1967.

Bowlby, J. *Atachment and Loss.* Vol. 2: *Separation.* New York: Basic Books, 1973.

Bretherton, I., and Beeghly, M. "Talking About Internal States: The Acquisition of an Explicit Theory of Mind." *Developmental Psychology,* 1982, *18,* 906–921.

Brumback, R., Staton, R., and Wilson, H. "Neuropsychological Study of Children During and After Remission of Endogenous Depressive Episodes." *Perceptual and Motor Skills,* 1980, *50,* 1163–1167.

Campos, J., and others. "Socioemotional Development." In P. Mussen (ed.), *Handbook of Child Psychology.* (4th ed.) Vol. 2. New York: Wiley, 1983.

Carlson, V., Cicchetti, D., Barnett, D., and Braunwald, K. "Finding Order in Disorganization: Lessons from Research in Maltreated Infants' Attachments to Their Caregivers." In D. Cicchetti and V. Carlson (eds.), *Child Maltreatment: Theory and Research on the Causes and Consequences of Child Abuse and Neglect.* New York: Cambridge University Press, forthcoming.

Cicchetti, D. "The Emergence of Developmental Psychopathology." *Child Development,* 1984, *55,* 1–7.

Cicchetti, D., and Aber, J. L. "Early Precursors to Later Depression: An Organizational Perspective." In L. Lipsitt and C. Rovee-Collier (eds.), *Advances in Infancy.* Vol. 4. Norwood, N.J.: Ablex, 1986.

Cicchetti, D., and Hesse, P. "Affect and Intellect: Piaget's Contributions to the Study of Infant Emotional Development." In R. Plutchik and H. Kellerman (eds.), *Emotion: Theory, Research and Experience.* Vol. 2. Orlando, Fla.: Academic Press, 1983.

Cicchetti, D., and Pogge-Hesse, P. "The Relation Between Emotion and Cognition in Infant Development: Past, Present, and Future Perspectives." In M. Lamb and L. Sherrod (eds.), *Infant Social Cognition: Empirical and Theoretical Considerations.* Hillsdale, N.J.: Erlbaum, 1981.

Cicchetti, D., and Schneider-Rosen, K. "Toward a Developmental

Model of the Depressive Disorders." In D. Cicchetti and K. Schneider-Rosen (eds.), *Childhood Depression*. New Directions for Child Development, no. 26. San Francisco: Jossey-Bass, 1984.

Cicchetti, D., and Schneider-Rosen, K. "An Organizational Approach to Childhood Depression." In M. Rutter, C. C. Izard, and P. B. Read, *Depression in Young People: Developmental and Clinical Perspectives*. New York: Guilford Press, 1986.

Cohn, J. F., and Tronick, E. "Three-Month-Old Infants' Reactions to Simulated Maternal Depression." *Child Development*, 1983, *54*, 185–193.

Davidson, R. "Affect, Cognition, and Hemispheric Specialization." In C. Izard, J. Kagan, and R. Zajonc (eds.), *Emotions, Cognition, and Behavior*. New York: Cambridge University Press, 1984.

Davidson, R., and Fox, N. "Asymmetrical Brain Activity Discriminates Between Positive Versus Negative Affective Stimuli in Human Infants." *Science*, 1982, *218*, 1235–1237.

Davidson, R. J., and Fox, N. A. *Resting Patterns of Brain Electrical Asymmetry Predict Infants' Response to Maternal Separation*, forthcoming.

Field, T. M. "Early Interactions Between Infants and Their Postpartum Depressed Mothers." *Infant Behavior and Development*, 1984, 7, 517–522.

Fox, N. A., and Davidson, R. J. "Hemispheric Substrates of Affect: A Developmental Model." In N. A. Fox and R. J. Davidson (eds.), *The Psychobiology of Affective Development*. Hillsdale, N.J.: Erlbaum, 1984.

Hesse, P., and Cicchetti, D. "Toward an Integrative Theory of Emotional Development." In D. Cicchetti and P. Hesse (eds.), *Emotional Development*. New Directions for Child Development, no. 16. San Francisco: Jossey-Bass, 1982.

Izard, C. *Human Emotions*. New York: Plenum, 1977.

Kinsbourne, M. "The Neuropsychological Analysis of Cognitive Deficit." In R. Grenell and S. Gabay (eds.), *Biological Foundations of Psychiatry*. New York: Raven Press, 1976.

Main, M., and Solomon, J. "Procedures for Identifying Infants as Disorganized/Disoriented During the Ainsworth Strange Situation." In M. Greenberg, D. Cicchetti, and E. M. Cummings (eds.), *Attachment During the Preschool Years*. Chicago: University of Chicago Press, forthcoming.

Malatesta, C., and Izard, C. "The Ontogenesis of Human Social Signals: From Biological Imperatives to Symbol Utilization." In N. Fox and R. Davidson (eds.), *The Psychobiology of Affective Development*. Hillsdale, N.J.: Erlbaum, 1984.

O'Connor, M. J., Sigman, M., and Brill, N. "Disorganization of Attachment in Relation to Maternal Alcohol Consumption." *Journal of Consulting and Clinical Psychology*, 1987, *55*, 831–836.

Piaget, J. *Intelligence and Affectivity: Their Relationship During Child Development*. Palo Alto, Calif.: Annual Reviews, 1981. (Originally published 1954.)

Puig-Antich, J. "Psychobiological Markers: Effects of Age and Puberty." In M. Rutter, C. C. Izard, and P. B. Read, *Depression in Young People: Developmental and Clinical Perspectives*. New York: Guilford Press, 1986.

Radke-Yarrow, M., Cummings, E. M., Kuczynski, L., and Chapman, M. "Patterns of Attachment in Two- and Three-Year-Olds in Normal Families and Families with Parental Depression." *Child Development*, 1985, *56*, 884–893.

Rourke, B. "Syndrome of Non-Verbal Learning Disability: The Final Common Pathway of White-Matter Disease/Dysfunction?" *The Clinical Neuropsychologist*, 1987, *1*, 209–234.

Sroufe, L. A., and Rutter, M. "The Domain of Developmental Psychopathology." *Child Development*, 1984, *55*, 1184–1199.

Trad, P. V. *Infant and Childhood Depression: Developmental Factors*. New York: Wiley, 1987.

Tucker, D. "Lateral Brain Function, Emotion and Conceptualization." *Psychological Bulletin*, 1981, *89*, 19–46.

Chapter 10

Development
in the Visual Arts

Ellen Winner

Our current views of children's drawings have been formed by a very specific group of individuals: Western-trained psychologists living in the late nineteenth and twentieth centuries. This historical-cultural grounding has profoundly shaped what has been seen. Implicit in the descriptions and interpretations of children's drawings are two deeply rooted and potentially contradictory assumptions about the purposes of art. One assumption is that what develops is the ability to represent the visual world and to do so in increasingly realistic ways. Thus children's drawings are studied because of what they reveal about children's ability to *represent* and because of the strategies they use to represent in a graphic medium (Freeman, 1980; Goodnow, 1977). This assumption is usually accompanied by the belief that a striving toward realism is natural and universal. This "realist" view of what develops in the individual mirrors art historians' accounts of what developed in Europe between the Renaissance and the nineteenth century, when the ideal of illusionistic (that is, realistic) representation predominated (Gombrich, 1960). When children's drawings are viewed as windows on the child's representational skill, the young child's drawings are seen as less developed than those of the older child, just as a seventeenth-century Dutch painting would be seen as more developed than a medieval one.

The assumed value of realistic rendering is sometimes in conflict with the second assumption—the view that what matters in the domain of drawing is not only representational skill but also some kind of aesthetic skill. Children not only are learning how to represent on paper, but they are also acquiring the ability to play with form and color so that the resulting composition is aesthetically appealing and expressive. When children's drawings are viewed as windows on the child's aesthetic sensitivity, the simple, playful drawings of very young children may look more advanced than those of school-aged children who have sacrificed invention for convention—just as a painting by Paul Klee might appear to be an advance over a nineteenth-century academic still life. This latter view of what develops (or declines) in the individual has been shaped by more recent trends in art history, in which artists have rejected realism or even representation altogether in favor of abstraction. This assumption is usually accompanied by the belief that a striving toward aesthetic form is natural but that this tendency may be permanently or temporarily arrested by the media or by schooling (since the value of realism still permeates the mass culture).

It is generally agreed that children's drawings change lawfully with age, and considerable consensus has been reached in working out a description of the sequences of drawing development. However, this description, which will be summarized later in this chapter, has been derived primarily from drawings by Western children, usually selected at random and not for any exceptional ability in the visual arts (Arnheim, 1974; Gardner, 1980; Kellogg, 1969). The order, the timing, and even the nature of the sequences may differ for other groups, such as non-Western children or impaired or gifted children.

In this chapter, I examine the potential universality of some aspects of this "stage" sequence, turning for evidence to what is known about the development of drawing in non-Western cultures and to what is known about drawing skills in exceptionally gifted children. Three issues guide the discussion of cross-cultural evidence: (1) All children in our culture begin to draw representationally (but not realistically) in the preschool years. Is this development a natural and universal one, or is it to be found only in cultures that value representation rather than abstraction in the visual arts? (2) All children in our culture show an interest in mastering the rules of realistic representation during the late elementary school years. Is this development natural, or is it due to exposure to realistic pictures and hence culture-specific? (3) By and large, preschool-aged children in our culture today are allowed (sometimes even encouraged) to invent their own, often odd, graphic equivalents for objects (for example, people look like tadpoles; the four legs of a table are drawn radiating out of the table like a fold-out). Only after an initial period of play and invention are children taught the culture's rules for graphic representation. To what extent does the adult artist's ability to go beyond established procedures draw upon this early period of play and invention, before the imposition of convention?

Two questions guide the discussion of children with exceptional ability in the visual arts: (1) How does the trajectory of drawing development in the gifted child compare with that of "normal" drawing development? (2) What cognitive, perceptual, and motivational factors characterize the visually gifted child and thus help "explain" his or her gift?

Taken together, the evidence from non-Western cultures and from exceptionally skilled children should help fix what is universal about artistic development, what is plastic and shaped by the culture, and which aspects are specific to children with precocious ability in drawing.

Trajectory of Drawing Development

Symbolizing Through Scribbles. Sometime between the ages of one and two, children begin to scribble with whatever tools they can get their hands on. Contrary to early accounts (for example, Kellogg, 1969), scribbles are rarely just nonsymbolic designs. One- and two-year-olds are already symbolic creatures, and they show some understanding that marks on a page can stand for things in the world. Even very early scribbles have been shown to be experiments in representation, although scribblers initially rely on gestural rather than pictorial representation. The symbolic status of early scribbles cannot be discovered through inspection of the marks left on the page, but it is revealed if one observes or overhears the child in the *action* of drawing. For example, a two-year-old studied by Matthews (1984) moved his brush all around in a rotating motion and said he was making an airplane. This child was symbolizing the airplane's motion by moving the brush in the same way as he imagined the airplane moved. But nothing about the final static marks on the page indicated an airplane. (See also Wolf, 1983, 1985, for similar examples.)

Usually by the age of three, but sometimes earlier, scribbles symbolize pictorially: Children often begin to make a gestural scribble and then notice that it looks like something. The scribble is then named and further elaborated. The same child studied by Matthews drew a cross-like shape and called it an airplane. In this case, the shape of the marks on the page actually captured the shape of an airplane. Hence, this scribble symbolized through the form of its line rather than through the child's gestures as he drew.

Early Pictorial Representation: Invention and Flavor. Children's early representational drawings (which begin to proliferate around age four) are schematic and generic. Children invent simple visual equivalents for objects and do not attempt to show much of an object's actual visual qualities, such as its color, its texture, or details of its contour (Arnheim, 1974; Smith, 1985). Typically, children select the most salient features of the generic form of an object and depict these features using simple geometric forms—circles, stick lines, squares, dots, and so on. These basic units are joined together where the features of the depicted object join (Smith, 1985). Thus forms are built up out of units rather than depicted with a single fluid contour line. Moreover, these figures are general; for instance, the same tadpole form is used to depict any person the child chooses to draw.

Drawings produced during the preschool years are rich in flavorfulness because they are both playful and inventive. In this sense, they resemble works by contemporary Western artists. By playful, I mean that not everything is in the service of representation. Children at this age are unconcerned with realism and appear to play with form and color simply for the visual effects yielded: They are not governed by the goal of visual realism. The sun may be painted purple because the child likes purple or because the brush with purple paint on it was the one most easily grasped. Each object or part of an object is accorded its own separate bounded space, even at the cost of realism (Goodnow, 1977). And even though they know that arms do not grow from the head, children persist in drawing tadpole humans in this way, perhaps because they like the radial symmetry yielded. (See Gardner, 1980, p. 73, for a quote from a child insisting on her desire to draw this way even though the resulting depiction does not look accurate.)

By inventive, I mean that children *invent* visual equivalents for objects rather than simply attempting to mimic adult schemas— hence the often surprising forms found in children's drawings, which adults (at least Western twentieth-century adults imbued with contemporary aesthetic standards) find charming. (See, for example, the child described by Arnheim [1980] who drew a complete circle around a person's head in order to show that the person was wearing a necklace.)

It is because of the above-described qualities of playfulness and inventiveness that the years from four to seven have been viewed as a period of flowering (Gardner, 1980; Rosenblatt and Winner, 1988a; Winner, 1982). To add to this picture of the child as burgeoning artist, children of this age become deeply involved in drawing: They draw often, and they may draw for extended periods in intense concentration, seemingly oblivious to the rest of the world. Many, if not most, educators in the West today—at least those influenced by the tradition of Dewey and Rousseau—firmly believe that at this age children should be left alone to explore the graphic medium and to invent their own visual equivalents for what they try to represent.

Late Childhood and Adolescent Drawings: Convention and Realism. During the middle elementary school years, children enter a "conventional" or "literal" stage, and they become governed by the efforts to draw realistically or to mimic adult conventions of drawing, such as those of cartoons and caricatures (Gardner, 1980; Lowenfeld and Brittain, 1970; Luquet, 1927). At this age, children show a heightened interest in mastering adult techniques (for example, perspective, shading, foreshortening; see Willats, 1977), and educators begin to step in and correct the child's drawings and model adult schemas for representing the world as it appears.

Some have noted that the child's new interest in mastering the rules of realistic representation is accompanied, at least at first, by a decline in inventiveness, playfulness, and flavorfulness (Gardner, 1980; Ives, Silverman, Kelly, and Gardner, 1979; Winner and Gardner, 1981). Thus the child comes to look less like an artist, even though he or she is in the process of mastering skills and techniques that most artists would agree are necessary. Artists who violate canons of realism do so with the full knowledge of the canons they are breaking. The preschooler who draws in a playful, nonrealistic fashion does so with less knowledge of how to draw otherwise. Nonetheless, in their willingness to explore and invent rather than follow prescribed rules, preschoolers look more like artists than do elementary school children. In addition, children in middle childhood become less interested in drawing, and draw less and with less intensity, than do preschool children. To the extent that children do continue to draw with interest, this activity usually occurs at home, outside of school art classes (Wilson and Wilson, 1977).

Drawing ability and drawing activity level off in the preadolescent years for most children. It is only the child with exceptional interest and ability who continues to draw and develop in drawing during adolescence and beyond.

The two assumptions stated at the outset of this chapter lead to competing interpretations of the preceding sketch of drawing development. To the extent that techniques of realistic depiction are held up as the ideal endstate, then children's drawings must be seen to improve linearly with age. But to the extent that inventiveness and play with form are held up as the ideal, then children's drawings may be seen to decline in quality after the onset of the school years.

Cross-Cultural Evidence

The Drive Toward Representation. In almost all cultures, graphic art has been used for purposes of representation. However, objects are often decorated in nonrepresentational motifs (see Gombrich, 1979), and some cultures have rejected representation in art: The fundamentalist Islamic religion forbids it, for instance, and some twentieth-century Western artists have rejected representation in favor of abstraction for a variety of conceptual and art-historical reasons. Nonetheless, as far as can be determined, cultures have either had some form of representational art or they have had actively to reject or prohibit it.

The near universality of representation in art strongly suggests that the drive to represent in a graphic medium is natural rather than a cultural invention. This assumption permeates Western psychologists' studies of children's drawings. The strongest evidence against this assumption has been offered by Alland (1983), an anthropologist who studied children drawing in non-Western cultures. But even Alland's evidence does not succeed in forcing us to reject the universality of representation.

Alland asked children in a range of cultures to make a single picture of their choice. One of the cultures studied was that of Ponape—a culture in which little emphasis is given to the visual arts and in which art is not even taught in elementary school. In Ponape, no child under five made a representational drawing. In contrast, representational pictures were commonly made by Japanese children of the same age. Alland explains the lack of early representational drawing in Ponape as a result of the sparsity of models of graphic representation in the culture. That is, children simply may not get the idea that art can be used to represent. This would suggest that representation occurs only with modeling and is culture-specific.

However, this conclusion cannot be drawn, because older children in Ponape *did* draw representationally, even though their drawings were relatively impoverished. Moreover, the preschool children might well have arrived at representation had they been asked to make more than one picture. And finally, it is also likely that some of the preschool "designs" were actually representations, but the representational meaning may have been carried by the movements made in marking rather than in the lines left behind. As stated previously, this kind of gestural representation in scribbling has been found to be the precursor to pictorial symbolization, in which recognizable representational forms are created.

Given that Alland found representational drawings by children in all of the cultures he studied—even in one with few representational models—and given the universality of representation in adult art, I think it fair to conclude that the urge to represent the visual world on paper is a natural one. Given paper, markers, and time to explore how markers can be used to make forms, children automatically arrive at representation as a goal, even if representation is gestural before it is pictorial. Just as children universally use speech sounds to represent linguistically and objects and gestures to represent in symbolic play, they are also predisposed to use marks on paper not just to decorate but to symbolize.

The Drive Toward Realism. Faithful representation of the visual world has been but one among many valued goals throughout the history of art. The ideal of realistic representation is one that dominated the artistic world in Europe primarily between the Renaissance and the nineteenth century (Gombrich, 1960). At other times and in other cultures, artists have sought to capture "the spirit of the thing" rather than its likeness (for example, Chinese landscape painting) or have developed a symbolic rather than a realistic style of representation (for example, Egyptian art and the art of preliterate societies). Westerners assume—in my view, correctly—that the canons of realism developed by artists from the Renaissance and later (such as the rules of linear and atmospheric perspective) are in fact realistic, while other styles of representation look less true to life. This assumption has been challenged by philosopher Nelson Goodman (1976), who has argued that there is no privileged form of representation that is more realistic than other forms. In his view, all forms of representation are simply conventions and we learn to see our culture's form as more realistic than that of another culture. But I find this relativistic argument unconvincing. While the Western rules of realism (perspective, foreshortening, and so forth) are learned conventions that can only *approximate* our experience of the three-dimensional world (Gombrich, 1960; Kennedy, 1974), these nonetheless yield forms that approximate our visual experience more closely than do the rules used, for example, by traditional Chinese or Egyptian artists.

I have argued that realism is not universal and that even realistic representation relies on conventions. There is therefore little reason to expect that the urge to draw realistically is a natural one, growing automatically out of the child's experience with seeing and drawing. In the West, children during the middle elementary school years begin to try to master techniques of realistic representation developed in the Renaissance—techniques such as perspective, foreshortening, and shading. But the drive to master these comes not from any natural and universal urge to depict the world faithfully but from the urge to master the pictorial conventions of one's culture. Evidence for this claim is that children of this age are equally interested in drawing cartoons and caricatures— forms of representation that are not at all illusionistic but that are highly conventional (Wilson and Wilson, 1977). While techniques of realistic representation are likely to be learned in school, cartoons and caricatures are more likely to be mastered outside of school as children derive their inspiration from the images produced by older children or seen on posters, in magazines, on television, and so on (Wilson and Wilson, 1977).

Further evidence for the claim that what children master at this age are pictorial conventions, whether or not these are realistic, comes from the study of children in China today (Winner, forthcoming). Chinese children are taught to paint in two different styles: a traditional style that eschews realism in favor of schemas that capture the essence of the object depicted (for instance, schemas for goldfish, bamboo, or monkeys); and a Western pseudo-childlike cartoon style featuring smiling figures in bright colors and in varieties of positions. Both styles are highly schematic and rule governed, and children come to master the rules of each system through imitation of the teachers' drawings. Rarely are children encouraged to make observational drawings from life. And rarely do children show any spontaneous desire to draw things as they appear in the world rather than as they appear in pictures. Hence, unlike American children of late elementary school age, Chinese children are less likely to try to draw realistically. Their paintings look either like traditional Chinese brush paintings or like cartoon figures.

The evidence from art produced by children in China, and by American children outside of the culture of school, points to the clear conclusion that there is nothing natural about the goal of realism. What is natural and inevitable, I believe, is the drive to master the pictorial conventions that are valued in one's culture or subculture. This drive to master the rules of a domain arises in other areas as well. It is during the elementary school years that children come to learn the rules of spelling, grammar, music notation, mathematics, and so on. Whatever the culture values in art—realistic representation or some other style—is what the child will struggle to master during the middle childhood years.

Mastering Rules and Inventing Rules: Which Should Come First? In the West, children do not begin to acquire adult conventions of realism until age nine or ten. It is often assumed that children are not able to draw realistically until this time, and hence we do not try to teach children realistic techniques until this age.

Methods of teaching drawing in China are radically different from methods in use today in the West (though not so different from nineteenth-century Western methods), and the drawings that result from this method of teaching are surprisingly precocious in their mastery of adult techniques (Winner, forthcoming). The heart of the Chinese teaching method is to teach complex adult representational schemas to children in step-by-step incremental fashion through imitation. The teacher models the schema over and over for the children, showing them not only how it should look in the end but also how each line should be made en route to the final product. This method is begun in kindergarten classes with children as young as three.

The Chinese method dramatically reveals that children as young as four and five can draw in an adult idiom that is different from, but just as complex as, a Western adult idiom. By the age of eight or nine, their traditional Chinese paintings may be nearly indistinguishable from those of an adult artist, at least to an untrained eye. Thus there is nothing natural about the age at which children can master adult pictorial techniques. If the task is broken down into incremental parts, and if children learn by copying adult pictorial schemas modeled for them in step-by-step fashion, then even preschool children can produce remarkably skilled, adult-like drawings.

But what are the consequences of such early imposition of adult conventions for later creativity? Deeply rooted in contemporary Western views of development and education is the Rousseauian belief that the preschool years should be devoted to self-directed exploration and play. Only after such a period should children be taught adult rules and conventions. Such an early exploratory phase of learning has been held up as necessary if the child is to be able to go beyond the conventional rules and demonstrate creativity and individuality (see Dewey, 1909; Hall, 1965; and Whitehead, 1929, for expositions of this notion). Whitehead argued, for instance, that without an initial stage, which he called the period of "romance," all later systematic learning would remain barren.

Western art educators follow this model. Children are usually not taught adult conventions of picturing before the school years. This practice fundamentally affects the kinds of drawings that preschoolers produce and accounts for the vast difference between Western preschool drawings (free, simple, full of odd, invented schemas) and Chinese preschool drawings (controlled, complex, conforming to adult schemas).

As the Chinese model makes abundantly clear, children can be taught to draw in an adult idiom even at the age of three, four, or five. What we know little about are the consequences of such early adult intervention. Western psychologists assume that a period of creativity and exploration must precede one in which basic skills are taught. Chinese educators believe the opposite: Basic skills must precede creativity, and, indeed, there is no possibility of creativity without basic skills. You must walk before you can run, goes an old Chinese saying.

The Chinese method is undoubtedly more typical than the contemporary Western "Rousseauian" method. In nineteenth-century America, and in some parts of the country even today, children are given step-by-step drawing lessons at an early age. Thus it seems clear that encouraging children to invent their own way before teaching them the adult way is only one means of producing adult artists who are inventive. The Chinese method must also work, since there has been no lack of innovation in Chinese art history. But what we do not know is whether an initial period of invention is *particularly* facilitative of later adult creativity and whether such an early period is more *likely* to yield artists who make sharp breaks with tradition rather than those who build upon tradition.

Evidence from Exceptional Populations

The study of drawing development in children gifted in drawing can help reveal which aspects are universal and in which aspects the gifted child diverges from the rest of the population. The search for the underpinnings of drawing giftedness can help explain how it is possible for gifted children to draw the way they do. In what follows, I define a gifted child either as one who will, as an adult, become a recognized artist (for example, Picasso as a child) or as one who, while still a child, is considered by his or her teachers to be gifted because his or her representational skill is at least several years ahead of that of his or her peers.

Development of Drawing in the Artistically Gifted Child. If we define a prodigy as a child under ten years old who performs at an adult level in a domain (see Feldman and Goldsmith, 1986), then we must conclude that such prodigies are very rare in the visual arts—much rarer than in the more formalized, rule-governed domains of chess, music, and mathematics. Whether the dearth of prodigies in the visual domain is in any way related to the fact that this domain is less formalized than are domains such as mathematics is simply not known. The two most famous living exceptions are Nadia, an autistic child whose drawings at age four resembled sketches by Renaissance masters (Selfe, 1977), and Yani, a Chinese child who at ages four and five was painting complex traditional Chinese brush paintings far more complex than those produced by the average well-trained Chinese child (Li and Jiang, 1984).

While prodigies are rare in the visual arts, there are many cases of children who display considerable precocity in drawing. By the time they reach the age of four or five, there is no problem in identifying such children (Gordon, 1987; Winner and Pariser, 1985). These children are precocious in their ability to draw realistically (Gardner, 1980; Gordon, 1987; Hurwitz, 1983; Pariser, 1985; Wilson and Wilson, 1981). The first sign of precocious realism in gifted children's drawings is that, in place of static schematic figures built up out of geometric units, forms are captured by a confident, fluid contour line that seems to capture the movement of the figure (Clark and Winner, 1985; Gordon, 1987; Pariser, 1985). Drawings by

Klee between the ages of four and seven, and by Toulouse-Lautrec at age six, display this characteristic clearly (Pariser, 1985).

There is thus considerable consensus that (at least in the West), the earliest sign of precocity in drawing, once children have begun to draw, is the ability to capture the contour and the movement of forms. Early drawings by the gifted also tend to be richer in decorative detail than those of nongifted children (Clark and Winner, 1985; Gordon, 1987). In one very important respect, however, early drawings by the gifted are similar to those by ordinary children: They are free, imaginative, inventive, and expressive. Hence, although precocious realism and an interest in decorative detail are signs of giftedness in drawing, early drawings by the gifted have the same quality of flavorfulness as do drawings by ordinary children of the same age.

Gifted children draw more than do average children. In Bloom's (1985) retrospective study of talented sculptors, he reports that as children these sculptors drew constantly. In a case study of two children who drew with precocious ability in realism, Clark and Winner (1985) noted that by the time the children reached the age of five, the drawings they produced were programmatic. That is, each child had developed a thematic focus, and the drawings produced thereafter were explorations of this focus. For one child, the theme was linearity; for the other, the theme was the human figure. Each drawing seemed to build on what came before, as the children produced a series of explorations of their chosen theme— for instance, exploring angular line, flowing line, spriraling line, and so on. Bloom (1985) made the same observation: Children who would become successful sculptors as adults drew in a goal-oriented manner as children. And, almost always, the goal for which they were striving was realism.

During the middle childhood years, Western children who are going to become artists become intensely involved in mastering Western conventions of realism. For example, the sculptors studied by Bloom (1985) reported that during their elementary school years they strove to acquire skill in realistic rendering, even if this meant copying or tracing works by adult artists. Thus gifted children enter a "conventional" stage much like ordinary children.

During this "conventional" stage, these children seem to

pass through the same decline in inventiveness and flavorfulness as do ordinary children (Clark and Winner, 1985; Pariser, 1985). In a study of the juvenilia of Picasso, Klee, and Toulouse-Lautrec, Pariser (1985) reports that both Klee and Toulouse-Lautrec looked back as adults with displeasure at their adolescent work. When Klee compiled a catalogue of his works, he left out most of what he had drawn between the ages of thirteen and seventeen but included some drawings from early childhood. Werckmeister (1977) notes that Klee's drawings as a ten-year-old show "a painful concern for accuracy and no trace of effort to be inventive or expressive" (p. 139; cited in Pariser, 1985). Two gifted children studied by Clark and Winner (1985) did their most free and inventive work before they were seven; their high school work was more constrained. And Gordon (1987) reports that the childhood art of artists becomes more faltering and less spontaneous and self-assured during the middle childhood years.

The difference between gifted children and others is that the gifted children arrive at the conventional stage earlier, achieve much greater levels of skill, and usually do not lose interest in drawing during adolescence (in fact, they begin to identify themselves as artists at this time [Bloom, 1985; Gordon, 1987]). Moreover, inventiveness and playfulness return in full force in the adolescent and adult years.

Paradoxically, Western twentieth-century artists often feel that their adult work is closer in spirit to their work as very young children than to their later childhood work. Whether this sentiment is a reflection of the kind of art valued in the twentieth century or whether artists in any aesthetic tradition would value the freshness and simplicity of the art of the young child is not known.

Cognitive-Perceptual and Personality-Motivational Characteristics of Children with Exceptional Drawing Ability. A few studies have attempted to pinpoint cognitive-perceptual and personality-motivational factors that differentiate gifted child artists from those who lack exceptional drawing ability. Researchers have looked at idiot savants as well as nonimpaired children who draw with unusual skill. There have been a number of reported cases of autistic and/or severely retarded children who nevertheless are able to draw extremely realistically (Henley, forthcoming; Park,

1978; Sacks, 1985; Selfe, 1977, 1983). The fact that such children exist is conclusive evidence that exceptional drawing ability can exist independently of IQ and makes it reasonable to suppose that drawing ability is independent of IQ in the normal brain as well. Attempts to use drawing as an index of IQ have relied on the number of features children include when asked to draw a person (Goodenough, 1926; Harris, 1963). While this measure correlates modestly with IQ, it may have little to do with drawing ability.

O'Connor and Hermelin (n.d.) studied five idiot savant "artists" (young adults) and compared them with controls matched for IQ and diagnosis. The artists outperformed the nonartists in their ability to copy abstract and representational drawings from memory; to recall abstract, unfamiliar, nonverbalizable shapes in the form of Persian letters; and to identify incomplete line drawings. Thus these artists seemed to have at least two abilities that underlie or are associated with their drawing skill: above-average visual memory and a richer or more easily accessible internal lexicon of images, which allows them to identify quickly incomplete drawings.

Studies of the nonimpaired gifted yield the same kinds of results. Hermelin and O'Connor (1986) compared twelve- to fourteen-year-olds gifted in drawing with controls matched on IQ. Like the impaired artists, these "normal" artists outperformed the controls in their ability to recall nonverbalizable forms and identify incomplete pictures. This study also included children gifted in mathematics, along with a math control group matched in IQ. Interestingly, on the task of identifying incomplete pictures, the art-gifted group performed better than did the math-gifted group, even though the latter had higher IQs—which provides one more piece of evidence for the IQ independence of drawing skill and its cognitive-perceptual underpinnings. The math-gifted performed as well as did the art-gifted in the recall of nonverbalizable forms, suggesting that at least some of the cognitive-perceptual underpinnings of drawing ability may be useful for mathematics as well (see also O'Connor and Hermelin, 1983).

In studies in our laboratory, we have found results compatible with those of Hermelin and O'Connor. Our data show that elementary school children selected by their teachers as gifted in drawing have superior memories for pictorial displays but not for verbal material (Rosenblatt and Winner, 1986, 1988a). Just the opposite pattern was found for children gifted in writing (Rosenblatt and Winner, 1986). We also found that the "artist" group had a higher than normal frequency of left-handers, a finding also reported by Mebert and Michel (1980) for adult artists. Left-handedness proved unrelated to skill level, however: right-handed children in our artist group produced drawings judged to be as good as those by left-handers. Thus giftedness in drawing appears to be associated with—but not made possible by—left-handedness, which may indicate superior right-hemisphere ability (Geschwind and Galaburda, 1987).

Much more fine-grained research is needed if we are to obtain a full description of the nature of the cognitive and perceptual abilities of children gifted in drawing. For example, we do not know whether gifted children encode *all* visual information at a superior level or whether they do so only for pictures they encode as "aesthetic" objects (see Goodman, 1976, for a discussion of this distinction). In a small set of intensive case studies, we have found that children gifted in drawing encode both kinds of pictures equally well, while for children not gifted in drawing, the aesthetic pictures have an advantage. This suggests that artistically gifted children read all visual displays as aesthetic stimuli and hence grant them the kind of "thick" attention normally accorded only to objects treated as art. Research is also needed to determine other kinds of visual-spatial and perhaps even motor abilities that distinguish the budding artist (for example, mental rotation, sense of direction, fine motor control) and to determine whether the underpinnings of drawing skill are the same as those that underlie skill in other forms of visual art, such as sculpture or painting. (For a preliminary investigation of some of these questions, see Casey, Winner, Brabeck, and Sullivan, 1988.)

Giftedness in drawing may well manifest itself before the child has begun to draw representationally, perhaps when the child is as young as two or three. But we do not yet have measures to tap this. A reasonable hypothesis is that children who are going to draw at a level above that of their peers display early on an unusual interest in visual patterns. These children may be drawn to visual exploration of accidental forms, blots, shadows, and so on. And they may be more likely than other children to note visual similarities between objects. There is a need for research to discover whether children who, for instance, utter frequent visual metaphors (see Winner, 1979) turn out to be children with exceptional graphic skill. An early proclivity to notice visual qualities may manifest itself in drawing, but it may also reveal itself in some genotypically similar but phenotypically dissimilar form, such as an ability to write using rich visual imagery or an interest in scientific fields in which pattern recognition and visual discrimination are important. In brief, one must distinguish between visual gifts, which may take the child in a variety of directions, and skill as a visual artist, which may build upon some of the same abilities that lead to an interest in science, engineering, architecture, or even writing (see Gardner, 1983).

The research clearly suggests that children skilled in drawing have some unusual visual abilities that differentiate them both from the nongifted and from children gifted in other domains. However, when personality characteristics are investigated, certain traits describe children gifted in drawing as well as in writing (and thus perhaps in other domains too). Rosenblatt and Winner (1986) found that gifted drawers and writers both achieved superior scores on paper-and-pencil measures of, among other things, sensitivity, self-discipline, and self-sufficiency. Perhaps children gifted in any domain have certain personality characteristics irrespective of the domain of gift. These characteristics may either follow from or lead to excellence in drawing and writing. Whether these traits are shared by children gifted in other artistic domains or in nonartistic domains is not known.

Tomorrow

Evidence from non-Western cultures leads to several conclusions that I believe will endure. The drive toward representation in drawing is natural and universal: It need not be imposed by the culture. There is nothing natural about the drive toward realism, however. Instead, there seems to be a push, in middle childhood, toward mastery of the culture's graphic conventions, whether these be conventions of realism or of some other style. With imitative and incremental training, children can master adult conventions in early childhood. Often, in the West, we assume that such early imposition of adult rules will stifle later creativity. This belief grows out of the assumption that the creative adult draws upon the inventions made in early childhood—in the period before he or she learned adult conventions. What remains unexamined today is whether such early freedom is most likely to produce adult artists who invent new ways of drawing or whether innovation can just as easily grow out of mastery of a tradition from an early age.

A small population of children are precocious at realistic rendering. This precocity is found among healthy as well as autistic or retarded children and appears to be independent of other nonvisual cognitive skills. As do nongifted children, these precocious children pass through a "conventional" stage in which the struggle to master rules interferes with the fluidity and expressiveness found in the early drawings. It is striking that, although artists often denigrate their conventional period, they all seem to go through it. Perhaps this stage is developmentally necessary, even though artists may not recognize this. Unlike ordinary children, these gifted children do not stop drawing at this point but instead find their identity as artists. While these children demonstrate superior skills on visual tasks (thus differentiating themselves from children gifted in other domains), they also display certain personality characteristics shared by children gifted in other domains. The notion that the cognitive-perceptual skills of gifted draftsmen are specific to this population but the personality and motivational characteristics are more general, though specific to individuals gifted in *some* domain, remains to be substantiated by further study. In addition, the existence of exceptional drawing ability in impaired populations raises the question, as yet unanswered, of whether there is some causal connection between the impairment and the gift or the two are independent of one another.

There are, then, some universals: the drive to represent on paper; the creation of flavorful, inventive drawings in early childhood, provided that children are left alone; the drive, in middle childhood, to master the conventions of the culture; and the interference of conventional mastery with the flavorfulness found in preschool drawings. But there are also aspects of development that are not universal: There is no natural drive toward realism; inventiveness can precede (and later follow) mastery of conventions (as in the West), or it can occur only after such mastery (as in China); occasionally, children can skip the schematic stage and draw with precocious realism in the preschool years; and such children do not lose interest in drawing in late childhood but instead deepen their interest and commitment at this time. The evidence from other cultures and from exceptional populations forces us to conclude that there is not just one developmental trajectory in drawing, but there are at least several.

In my view, one of the most interesting directions that future research might take is to attempt to determine the sufficient, necessary, or simply facilitating conditions for creative achievement in the visual arts. One such condition might be a period in early childhood of unfettered exploration prior to the acquisition of the culture's graphic conventions. Whether such a period fosters later innovation is a question that can be answered only through cross-cultural comparisons. Careful study of the evolution of creativity in adolescents and young adults educated in a society where skill-oriented training is imposed in the preschool years (as it is in China) can help to resolve this question.

A second condition is the cluster of skills that may underpin and perhaps allow artistic ability. For instance, exceptional abilities to notice and recall visual information, and to manipulate visual images, may be among the skills needed to create in the visual arts. There is already some preliminary evidence that such skills underlie artistic ability (Hermelin and O'Connor, 1986; Rosenblatt and Winner, 1988a; Winner, 1988), but much more research is needed to delineate precisely which skills are or are not components of talent in the visual arts.

Underlying the cluster of abilities that co-occur with artistic talent may be a neurological tendency toward visual-spatial abilities. That such a proclivity might predispose a child to develop and excel in the visual arts is suggested by the higher than average frequency of left-handedness among artistic populations. While we know that left-handers often have a different kind of brain organization from right-handers (see Annett, 1985), the *role* that left- or right-handedness plays in artistic giftedness remains a mystery.

Answers to these questions will help determine the role of early experience to the shaping of artistic creativity, and the role of cognitive-perceptual predisposition and neurological biases in exceptional artistic ability.

References

Alland, A. *Playing with Form: Children Draw in Six Cultures.* New York: Columbia University Press, 1983.

Annett, M. *Left, Right, Hand and Brain: The Right-Shift Theory.* Hillsdale, N.J.: Erlbaum, 1985.

Arnheim, R. *Art and Visual Perception.* Berkeley: University of California Press, 1974.

Arnheim, R. "Problems of Space in Early Forms of Art." Paper presented at the National Symposium for Research in Art, University of Illinois, Urbana-Champaign, October 1980.

Bloom, B. (ed.). *Developing Talent in Young People.* New York: Ballantine, 1985.

Casey, M., Winner, E., Brabeck, M., and Sullivan, K. "Visual-Spatial Abilities in Art, Math, and Science Majors: Effects of Sex, Handedness, and Spatial Experience." Paper presented at the International Conference on Thinking, Aberdeen, Scotland, 1988.

Clark, M., and Winner, E. Unpublished research, Project Zero, Harvard Graduate School of Education, 1985.

Dewey, J. *How We Think.* Lexington, Mass.: Heath, 1909.

Feldman, D., and Goldsmith, L. *Nature's Gambit: Child Prodigies and the Development of Human Potential.* New York: Basic Books, 1986.

Freeman, N. *Strategies of Representation in Young Children.* Orlando, Fla.: Academic Press, 1980.

Gardner, H. *Artful Scribbles: The Significance of Children's Drawings.* New York: Basic Books, 1980.

Gardner, H. *Frames of Mind: The Theory of Multiple Intelligences.* New York: Basic Books, 1983.

Geschwind, N., and Galaburda, A. *Cerebral Lateralization: Biological Mechanisms, Associations, and Pathology.* Cambridge, Mass.: Bradford Books, 1987.

Gombrich, E. *Art and Illusion: A Study in the Psychology of Pictorial Representation.* Princeton, N.J.: Princeton University Press, 1960.

Gombrich, E. *The Sense of Order: A Study in the Psychology of Decorative Art.* Oxford, England: Phaidon, 1979.

Goodenough, F. *Measurement of Intelligence by Drawings.* San Diego, Calif.: Harcourt Brace Jovanovich, 1926.

Goodman, N. *Languages of Art.* Indianapolis, Ind.: Hackett, 1976.

Goodnow, J. *Children Drawing.* Cambridge, Mass.: Harvard University Press, 1977.

Gordon, A. "Childhood Works of Artists." *The Israel Museum Journal,* 1987, *4*, 75-82.

Hall, G. "The Ideal School as Based on Child Study." In C. Strickland and C. Burgess (eds.), *Health, Growth, and Heredity.* New York: Teachers College Press, 1965.

Harris, D. *Children's Drawings as Measures of Intellectual Maturity.* San Diego, Calif.: Harcourt Brace Jovanovich, 1963.

Henley, D. "Incidence of Artistic Giftedness in the Multiply Handicapped." In H. Wadeson (ed.), *Advances in Art Therapy.* New York: Wiley, forthcoming.

Hermelin, B., and O'Connor, N. "Spatial Representation in Mathematically and in Artistically Gifted Children." *British Journal of Educational Psychology,* 1986, *56*, 150-157.

Hurwitz, A. *The Gifted and Talented in Art: A Guide to Program Planning.* Worcester, Mass.: Davis Publications, 1983.

Ives, S., Silverman, J., Kelly, H., and Gardner, H. *Artistic Development in the Early School Years: A Cross-Media Study of Storytelling, Drawing, and Clay Modelling.* Harvard Project Zero Technical Report No. 8. Cambridge, Mass.: Harvard University, 1979.

Kellogg, R. *Analyzing Children's Art.* Palo Alto, Calif.: National Press Books, 1969.

Kennedy, J. M. *A Psychology of Picture Perception: Images and Information.* San Francisco: Jossey-Bass, 1974.

Li, S., and Jiang, C. *Yani's Monkeys.* Beijing, China: Foreign Languages Press, 1984.

Lowenfeld, V., and Brittain, W. *Creative and Mental Growth.* (5th ed.) New York: Macmillan, 1970.

Luquet, G. *Le dessin enfantin.* Paris: Alcan, 1927.

Matthews, J. "Children Drawing: Are Young Children Really

Scribbling?" In R. Evans (ed.), *Early Child Development and Care.* Vol. 17. New York: Gordon and Breach, 1984.

Mebert, C., and Michel, G. "Handedness in Artists." In J. Herron (ed.), *Neuropsychology of Left-Handedness.* Orlando, Fla.: Academic Press, 1980.

O'Connor, N., and Hermelin, B. "Visual and Graphic Abilities of the Idiot-Savant Artist." Unpublished manuscript, MRC Developmental Psychology Project, Institute of Education, London, n.d.

O'Connor, N., and Hermelin, B. "The Role of General Ability and Specific Talents in Information Processing." *British Journal of Developmental Psychology,* 1983, *1,* 389–403.

Pariser, D. "The Juvenilia of Klee, Toulouse-Lautrec, and Picasso: A Report on the Initial Stages of Research into the Development of Exceptional Graphic Artistry." Paper presented at conference: "The History of Art Education." Pennsylvania State University, November 1985.

Park, C. "Review of L. Selfe, *Nadia: A Case of Extraordinary Drawing Ability in an Autistic Child.*" *Journal of Autism and Childhood Schizophrenia,* 1978, *8* (4), 457–472.

Rosenblatt, E., and Winner, E. "Cognitive and Personality Profiles of Children Gifted in Either Drawing or Writing." Unpublished manuscript, Harvard Project Zero, Harvard University, 1986.

Rosenblatt, E., and Winner, E. "Is Superior Visual Memory a Component of Superior Drawing Ability?" In L. Obler and D. Fein (eds.), *The Exceptional Brain.* New York: Guilford, 1988a.

Rosenblatt, E., and Winner, E. "The Art of Children's Drawings." *Journal of Aesthetic Education,* 1988b, *22* (1), 3–15.

Sacks, O. "The Autist Artist." *New York Review of Books,* 1985, *25,* 17–21.

Selfe, L. *Nadia: A Case of Extraordinary Drawing Ability in an Autistic Child.* Orlando, Fla.: Academic Press, 1977.

Selfe, L. *Normal and Anomalous Representational Drawing Ability in Children.* Orlando, Fla.: Academic Press, 1983.

Smith, N. "Observation Drawing: Changes in Children's Intention and Translation Methods Grades K-Six." *Arts and Learning Special Interest Group Proceedings,* 1985, *3,* 47–62.

Werckmeister, O. "The Issue of Childhood in the Art of Paul Klee." *Arts Magazine,* 1977, *52* (1), 138–151.

Whitehead, A. *The Aims of Education.* New York: Free Press, 1929.

Willats, J. "How Children Learn to Represent Three-Dimensional Space in Drawings." In G. Butterworth (ed.), *The Child's Representation of the World.* New York: Plenum, 1977.

Wilson, B., and Wilson, M. "An Iconoclastic View of the Imagery Sources in the Drawings of Young People." *Art Education,* 1977, *30,* 5–11.

Wilson, B., and Wilson, M. "Instruments for the Identification of Artistic Giftedness." Unpublished manuscript, Department of Art Education, Pennsylvania State University, 1981.

Wilson, B., and Wilson, M. "How We Learn to Draw." In A. Hurwitz (ed), *Drawing for the Schools: A Conference.* Baltimore: College of Art, Maryland Institute, 1983.

Winner, E. "New Names for Old Things: The Emergence of Metaphoric Language." *Journal of Child Language,* 1979, *6,* 469–491.

Winner, E. *Invented Worlds: The Psychology of the Arts.* Cambridge, Mass.: Harvard University Press, 1982.

Winner, E. "Visual-Spatial Abilities in Young Artists." Paper presented at the conference "Art and the Brain," Chicago, May 1988.

Winner, E. "How Can Chinese Children Draw So Well?" *Journal of Aesthetic Education,* forthcoming.

Winner, E., and Gardner, H. "The Art in Children's Drawings." *Review of Research in Visual Arts Education,* 1981, *14,* 18–31.

Winner, E., and Pariser, D. "Giftedness in the Visual Arts." *Items,* 1985, *39* (4), 65–69.

Wolf, D. "Representation Before Picturing." Paper presented at the annual meetings of the British Psychological Association, Cardiff, Wales, September 1983.

Wolf, D. "Drawing Conclusions: Insights into the Nature of Art from Children's Drawings." Paper presented at symposium: "From Scribbling to Art." Ichenhausen, West Germany, September 1985.

Chapter 11

Beyond a Modular
View of Mind

Howard Gardner

Not too many years ago, a chapter on modularity would have made little sense to psychologists. The temper of the time was distinctly nonmodular. While different sensory systems were of course recognized, all important mental processes were assumed to be general. There existed laws of perception, laws of memory, and, above all, laws of learning; and these laws were assumed to obtain across all kinds of content and to proceed in similar ways across all species.

Today, however, discussions of modularity are rampant. Interest in the existence of different cognitive modules and/or different neural modules is widespread. In general, this focus on modularity is a reaction to overly ambitious accounts of cognition—especially those put forth by learning theorists and behaviorists. These accounts purported to obtain across all contents and organisms and did not adequately take into account various constraints or specificities. Taking a more modular perspective, it has proved possible to make far more precise descriptions of mechanisms in areas such as language (Chomsky, 1980) and visual

Note: Portions of this chapter were presented at the meeting of the American Psychological Association, New York City, August 29, 1987. The research described herein was supported in part by the Spencer Foundation, the Carnegie Corporation, the National Institute of Neurological Diseases, Communication Disorders and Stroke (NS 11408 and 06209) and the Veterans Administration.

perception (Marr, 1982). These accounts are persuasive in their respective domains even as they emerge as surprisingly distinct from one another. Thus modularity triumphs on important dimensions: It has advanced both theory and empirical description.

Perhaps indicating a significant *Zeitgeist* dimension, modularity has reared its head across different cognitively oriented disciplines. Most manifest in the area of cognitive science (Fodor, 1983), it is also reflected in artificial intelligence in the shift from a search for general problem-solving algorithms (Newell and Simon, 1972) to an interest in expert systems (Feigenbaum, Buchanan, and Lederberg, 1971). Intelligence theory has also taken a modular turn (Gardner, 1983; Sternberg and Detterman, 1986), and even developmental psychology has recently proved sympathetic to a more domain-specific or modular perspective (Carey, 1985; Keil, 1979).

Different Senses of Modularity

In my own case, I began with a distinct bias against modularity but have found myself increasingly attracted to a modular perspective. Trained as a Piagetian—and it is relevant that Piaget himself was trained in the laboratory of Binet's associate, Simon—I was initially sympathetic to "generalist" accounts of cognition and intelligence. Yet, as I will detail in this chapter, my work in developmental psychology and in neuropsychology gradually converted me into a modularist—though one with reservations.

It must be stressed that, whether one examines cognitive science or neuroscience, modularity does not speak with one voice. In the case of cognitive science, the "modal" position on modularity posits quite discrete, encapsulated, and "reflex-like" processing mechanisms. Favorite examples of modular processes include the perception of illusions, syntactic parsing, and face recognition (Fodor, 1983). Those capacities that are not modular are consigned to a "central system"—a completely penetrable storehouse of information and processing mechanisms whose mode of operation proves so unconstrained that it falls outside the realm of scientific explanation, at least in the foreseeable future.

My own cognitivist view of modularity is less encapsulated and more encompassing (Gardner, 1983, 1985a, 1985b). I posit the existence of separate "intelligences": information-processing systems that have evolved to analyze specific kinds of content. The seven intelligences I have identified are geared toward the analysis of, respectively, linguistic information, logical-mathematical information, spatial information, bodily-kinesthetic information, musical information, information about other individuals, and information about oneself (Gardner, 1983). At the core of these intelligences there may exist dedicated modules of the Fodor sort; but the intelligences themselves consist of loosely coupled sets of modules, at least some of which are penetrable and which combine regularly among themselves to carry out meaningful human tasks. While the "modal module" account is acontextual and acultural, my account of intelligence is predicated on the assumption that human capacities are exercised in a meaningful human context and that the intelligences are channeled and exploited to carry out significant human functions. Only in freaks do modules operate in relative or complete isolation.

There is a similar gamut of positions in a neuroscientific approach to modularity. Modules can be identified at a microscopic level of analysis, as when a particular set or column of cells responds only to a line of a certain angle or to a particular phoneme or phoneme cluster (Mountcastle, 1978). There are also modules that can be identified at a much more macroscopic level; these modules, associated with significant regions of cortex, may carry out face recognition, syntactic analysis, melodic detection, or even broader categories, such as spatial or linguistic analysis (Gardner, 1983; Gazzaniga, 1985; Luria, 1966). There is less sympathy within neuroscience for a central system: Where would it be located? How would it work? Yet even within neuroscience, certain brain regions, such as the frontal lobes and the cross-sensory association areas, are often considered to be involved in the broadest human functions, such as planning or synthesis.

One could describe current accounts of human cognition as attempts to steer between the Scylla of rigid modularity and the Charybdis of unregulated central systems. I think it desirable to put forth an account that builds on the demonstrations of modularity and yet avoids the despair of a central systems account. Such an intermediate position needs to provide an account of constrained as well as broader human capacities. In the remainder of this chapter, I will seek to provide such an account. I begin by delineating some of the reasons why it may be necessary to go beyond a strictly modular account. I then review two lines of my own work that point to the need for supramodular mechanisms or processes. I conclude by suggesting some mechanisms that, while building on a modular perspective, may enable us to explain some phenomena that appear to be supramodular.

The Need to Transcend Modularity

In modeling cognition, it is useful for many reasons to attempt to tease apart various systems and to see whether one can provide an account of how each one operates. This is the appeal of positing seven, or seventy, or seven thousand different modules. Yet in various ways human beings do not appear to be organisms that are simply a bundle of seven or seven thousand mechanisms. Let me list three classes of observations that give at least this modularist pause:

1. From a phenomenal perspective, we individuals do not feel like a number of different systems; there is the perception of a unified entity with a sense of self and with a single consciousness.

2. Again, from an observational perspective, other human beings also do not appear to be a collection of disparate systems, each proceeding in its own unorchestrated way. There is at least the appearance of organization and integration, if not unity, in the behavior of other persons as well.

Indeed, in considering individuals who are exhibiting complex skills, it appears that various capacities work well together. For example, from the perspective of multiple intelligences theory, the conductor may have a high degree of musical intelligence. Yet it is apparent that a skilled conductor is not only making use of a number of intelligences—for example, bodily, interpersonal, and linguistic—but is yoking these intelligences in an often seamless way.

3. Finally, and perhaps most persuasively, human beings seem to exhibit certain capacities that by their very nature span the modules. I refer here to analogical thinking, synthesizing capacity,

and wisdom. These most vaunted of human capacities are precisely the ones that most clearly elude a modular account.

Those who would attempt a scientific account of human cognition and behavior are challenged to explain these various human phenomena. How do we yoke various modules or intelligences? Is there some kind of a supramodular intelligence or executive whose function it is to orchestrate among these intelligences? And, if so, is this executive better thought of as "intelligent"— consciously selecting and combining modules for different ends—or as a "dumb" traffic cop, which simply makes certain that no two modules attempt to operate at the same time? Is the executive present at birth, or does it emerge slowly and perhaps imperfectly during the course of development? Or, to take another approach, might it be that human beings are most accurately described as *lacking* an executive, with the tendency to posit an executive simply reflecting our need to tell a coherent story to (or about) ourselves?

These questions now permeate cognitive science. They are difficult questions, and I make no pretense that I can answer them. Le me therefore now suspend the grandiose tone for a time and move instead to research from my own laboratory—research that brought me face-to-face with issues of modularity and ultimately with the need to go beyond modularity.

Evidence from Developmental Psychology

Over a decade ago, Dennie Wolf and I decided to carry out a longitudinal study of the development of symbol-using skills in young children. For seven years, we and our collaborators observed nine firstborn children as they became symbolic creatures in seven different domains: language (particularly story telling), symbolic play, music, two-dimensional depiction, three-dimensional depiction, bodily expression, and numerical symbolization. We established that, within these domains, there is a regular sequence of development that can be accounted for adequately in terms of ordinal scales. We also identified consistent differences in the styles of symbolization evinced by certain youngsters (Gardner and Wolf, 1983; Shotwell, Wolf, and Gardner, 1979; Wolf and Gardner, 1981, 1987). Although our major results were obtained on this small sample of youngsters, we were able to confirm most of our major findings with a larger cross-sectional population of seventy children.

The central issue of the study, and the one that brought us directly into contact with issues of modularity, concerned the generality of the symbolic capacity. According to Piaget ([1945] 1962) and other theorists of development, there exists a general "semiotic function" that develops rapidly in the years before school and that expresses itself at the same time in essentially similar form across different symbolic systems. This default position of course runs completely counter to a modular account, in which each symbolic system is assumed to have its own developmental mechanisms and where each develops at its own rate, with little identifiable association to milestones in other symbolic spheres.

Our study placed us in a favorable position to resolve this issue. We could identify the major milestones of development in each symbol system—essentially establishing ordinal scales. We could then examine these symbolic trajectories in order to determine the extent to which each symbol system was yoked to the others. To the extent that milestones occurred regularly across symbol systems, evidence would be gained for a classical "semiotic position." If, however, a developmental breakthrough in one domain had little or no predictive value for an advance in another domain, then evidence for a more modular position would be obtained.

To our surprise, the resulting picture turned out to be more complex than had been anticipated on prior analysis. We found, on the one hand, clear evidence for module-like mechanisms, which we termed *streams of development*. Within each symbolic domain, there were certain progressions that were quite predictable within that domain but that had essentially no predictive power for the nature and time of emergence of events occurring within other domains. In the case of language, there is syntactic growth; in music, there is mastery of the pitch and scalar systems; in drawing there is the perfection of contours; while in three-dimensional depiction, there is the handling of space, including vacant or negative space. Children exhibit predictable developmental courses in each of these stream-like areas; but except for a general advance associated with increasing age, a child's position in one symbolic domain cannot predict his or her level of performance in another, randomly selected domain.

Here, then, is evidence for a modular form of development—one that might even come close to fulfilling Fodor's lengthy list of criteria. It is important to note that these stream-like capacities have a syntactic or formal flavor to them. Rather than being directly involved in reference or semantics, they seem to be skills or capacities that can be mobilized *in the service* of meaning. They are the *forms of symbolization,* so to speak, and their development seems to entail the working out of the formal constraints of a domain or medium.

Were this the only part of our story, we would have dealt a strong blow to the classical semiotic account. Another part of our findings, however, cannot be readily explicated in terms of a modular account. We discovered that, at approximately yearly intervals during early childhood, a set of capacities emerge that are ultimately expressed much more generally (see Bruner, 1964). We have termed these capacities the *waves of symbolization.* Each wave commences, like a stream-like property, within the confines of a particular symbolic system. Unlike a well-behaved stream, however, these capacities soon spill over into other symbolic domains, sometimes even inappropriately so. They can be analogized to emerging new muscles that, once they have begun to develop, seek to express themselves in as many contexts as possible.

Let me take a concrete example. The first wave of symbolization, which occurs between eighteen and twenty-four months, is the emergence of event-structuring capacity. At this age, children exhibit awareness that there are events or actions in the world that are carried out by agents and that have consequences. More to the point, these toddlers become able to realize this awareness in symbolic forms. In language and in symbolic play, they express the conceptions "Daddy eat," "baby go bed," "get ball," and dozens of other enactments of simple agent-event scenarios.

What is striking is that this event-structuring knowledge is not restricted to the realms of language and symbolic play, where it is appropriate. Rather, as one looks across other domains, one also sees evidence of event structuring—even when it is not ordinarily considered an appropriate form of expression within that domain.

Take, for example, a request for a two-year-old to draw a truck. Rather than seizing the marker and attempting to make a form that bears a topological relation to a truck, the child frequently will seize the marker and run it back and forth across the page, uttering "vroom vroom" as an accompaniment to this truck-like motion. So far as we can tell, the child has converted the drawing task into a symbolic play task, where the marker itself becomes the agent—the truck moving back and forth across some kind of imaginary terrain. The wave of event structuring has broken through the borders of its "proper" media and invaded the domain of representational drawing.

The same kind of wave-like seepage is repeated at least three more times during early childhood. At age three, a capacity that we term *topological mapping* emerges; the child is able to express in symbolic form the relative sizes, strengths, or extents of a reference. This capacity emerges initially in drawing and in three-dimensional depiction but is then evidenced as well across a wider range of domains. At age four, a capacity called *digital mapping* emerges. This capacity reflects an appreciation of the fundamental aspects of number, such as one-to-one correspondence. At first evident in counting and creating equivalent arrays, it soon is found, even inappropriately so, in other symbolic realms ranging from drawing to dancing.

Finally, between the ages of five and seven, there emerges a powerful new form of symbolization, called *notational* or *second-order symbolization*. This ability allows the child to capture in a compact symbol or notation the contents of a first-order symbol. Thus written language captures spoken language, written musical notation captures heard or sung patterns, and so forth. Once again, this newly emerging "wave" is manifested broadly and sometimes inappropriately across a range of domains. And it recurs at ever higher levels of abstraction (third- and fourth-order notations) over the course of development.

Can we think of these processes in terms of modular or supramodular criteria? My own view is that the waves represent four ways—and perhaps *the* four principal ways—in which human beings can express meanings: through narrative, through relations of topological similarity, through enumeration, and through notations which themselves stand for the aforementioned first-order forms of symbolization (see Gardner, Howard, and Perkins, 1974; Goodman, 1976; Langer, 1942). Each of these forms of symbolization has its natural home in one or two domains of knowing, but each can be stretched far more widely. The fact that these aspects of symbolization are involved in reference gives them license to be utilized whenever some form of reference or denotation becomes a possibility. (In this way, they differ from the streams, which have far less referential potential.)

In mature symbolization, these extensions are infrequent, so the operation of these forms of symbolization may *seem* to be modular. Yet it seems patent that in the course of development certain capacities or skills are attracted to (or at least exercised in) alien domains of experience and are expressed there, at least for a while. Thus, in the above instance, the young scribbling artist draws on event-structuring skills to execute drawings until he or she comes to appreciate that drawing is actually a symbolic domain in which topological mapping is the symbolic option of choice. It may be in the nature of early experience that these capacities are "up for grabs"—and are not nearly so encapsulated or impermeable as classical modular theory would have one believe. Development may entail an exploration to discover the most applicable place for an emerging ability, the places to which it can be comfortably stretched, and the loci in which it is manifestly inappropriate.

Evidence from Neuropsychology

My initial work in neuropsychology focused on the aphasias. Whatever inclination I might have had to favor an organismic or holistic account of brain functioning (Goldstein, 1948) was soon dashed. Aphasia turned out to be the arena par excellence for modularity. Not only is the language function quite separate from other functions, so that distinct lesions can either devastate or wholly spare language competence, but even within the linguistic area there is ample opportunity for invoking a modular account. Syntactic, phonological, and, to a certain extent, semantic capacities appear to be subserved by different cortical regions and can often be spared or impaired in relative distinction from other linguistic (and nonlinguistic) capacities.

Because I was interested as well in the fate of artistic capacities after damage to the brain, I began to administer artistic tasks to aphasic individuals. In neuropsychology, it is important to determine whether a deficit is due to the locus of brain damage or to the mere fact of brain damage. Accordingly, I included right-hemisphere-damaged patients (whose language is ostensibly intact but who have lesions of comparable size) as a control group. To my considerable surprise, the aphasic patients often did quite well on the artistic tasks, even including those that involved language. In contrast, the right-hemisphere-damaged patients not only exhibited significant difficulties in handling such tasks but often approached them in ways that were qualitatively different from those of both the aphasic patients and the normal controls (Gardner, Brownell, Wapner, and Michelow, 1983).

This surprising set of discoveries has led in the last decade to a sustained program of research on the linguistic (and particularly the narrative) capacities of right-hemisphere-injured patients. Working with various colleagues, Hiram Brownell and I have documented a long list of impairments associated with right-hemisphere disease. Such patients have unexpected difficulties in comprehending metaphors, indirect speech acts, and sarcastic remarks and in drawing inferences, comprehending and completing jokes, and following a narrative of any complexity (Weylman, Brownell, and Gardner, 1988). We have ruled out significant difficulties in understanding words or utterances of sentence length. Moreover we have shown that these patients are often perfectly adequate at a formal level: They know what a joke or a story *should* be like, they have generally preserved script knowledge, and they can give literally correct paraphrases of stories or utterances.

Where, then, does their problem lie? In my view, these patients have great difficulty in "getting the point" of utterances. The words are accurately comprehended and some proper associations are made, but the patients cannot combine the various parts of a message in order to infer what the speaker was driving at, how he or she was feeling, or what the point of a joke or a narrative was meant to be. It seems as if the various specific computations are carried out adequately enough but the patient lacks a mechanism for deciding *when* to draw upon a certain computation and *how* to combine computations in order to secure the larger picture of what is intended. In terms of my own terminology, the particular "frames of mind" may not be greatly impaired, but the injured right hemisphere of the brain cannot keep various frames *in* mind.

This "frame assessor" or "frame combiner" seems an excellent candidate for a supramodular capacity. A certain capacity in normal and aphasic patients allows the individual to piece together fragments of a narrative or an utterance (even from fragmentary evidence) in order to figure out what was intended. This capacity is for some reason impaired or inoperative in right-hemisphere-damaged patients, so the modules, left to operate in isolation, are not properly orchestrated or oriented.

Though our own observations of the narrative problems displayed by right-hemisphere-injured patients had not been anticipated, a number of commentators have noted the synthetic or organizing potential of the right hemisphere (Bever, 1975; Ornstein, 1986). There has been a tendency among researchers to assume that these difficulties are secondary to the well-known deficiency in spatial processing associated with right-hemisphere disease (Moya, Benowitz, Levine, and Finkelstein, 1986). It is possible that some patients do spatialize narratives and that impaired spatial ability may render our tasks more difficult. However, it seems to be stretching unreasonably the notion of spatial processing to attempt to account for difficulties in understanding metaphors, indirect requests, or sarcastic remarks in terms of such a deficit.

My own view is that narrative comprehension is a complex activity that may require the interaction of a number of modules. I propose that narrative comprehension involves at least: linguistic competence (to understand the propositional content), logical-mathematical intelligence (to figure out causal relations), spatial ability (to monitor locations), and personal intelligences (to comprehend personality, motivation, interaction, and the like). These modules must ultimately work together in order for comprehension or production of narrative to occur competently. To the extent that the modules themselves are impaired or, while separately intact, are cut off from one another, narrative comprehension may be undercut.

There is another possibility. Perhaps in the right-hemisphere-damaged patient, various "stream-like" analytic or modular capacities remain relatively preserved but the "wave-like" semantic capacities have been compromised. Thus the right-hemisphere-damaged patient is unable to put together fragments into the narrative mode of event structuring or into the spatial-temporal framework of topological mapping. Bereft of these integrative mechanisms, he or she is reduced to dealing with fragments that are unorganized or even unorganizable.

How, then, might we account for the contrasting performance profiles of left- and right-hemisphere-damaged patients on the narrative tasks? I suggest the following, perhaps overlapping, possibilities:

1. Perhaps in left-hemisphere-damaged patients, the modules besides language are relatively preserved. Taken together, even in the absence of a well-functioning language module, they allow the patient to garner the major points of the utterance. In contrast, because of difficulties in spatial and personal forms of thought and (possibly) some aspects of language and logic, the right-hemisphere-damaged patient has meager strategic options to aid him or her in making sense of complex discourse. This possibility could be investigated by examining the status of the aforementioned range of nonlinguistic modules in patients with difficulties in narrative competence and relating these deficits to the kinds of problems displayed in narrative comprehension.

2. Over the course of development, various modules have come to be joined together to work efficiently in such tasks as narrative comprehension. The orchestration and monitoring of this combination take place routinely in the right hemisphere, perhaps especially in its frontal regions (Lezak, 1976). Because the disease disturbs the monitoring process, the right-hemisphere-damaged patient is reduced to separate analyses, while the left-hemisphere-damaged patient can still combine modules (even if these are somewhat impaired) for the purpose of "getting the point." This possibility could be investigated by determining whether other

processes that require complex orchestration are also impaired by right-hemisphere disease.

3. The right hemisphere might be dedicated, from birth or from early infancy, to an executive or unifying role. Whenever it is injured, the patient will evince special difficulty in synthesizing or organizing. The left-hemisphere-injured patient can continue to attempt to organize or synthesize, though he or she will not always be totally successful in doing so. This possibility could be investigated by examining processes of synthesis or "amodal perception" in normal infants and in infants with different kinds of pathology.

4. The right hemisphere may become the locus for those "wave-like" modes of processing that develop over the course of childhood. Thus while some modules are primarily "housed" in the left hemisphere (though others are in the right), the semantic, sense-making computations tend to be lateralized in the nondominant hemisphere. Studies with brain-injured infants and young children could help indicate the developmental course of capacities such as event structuring, topological mapping, and digital or notational symbolization.

The Need for a Developmental Perspective on Modularity

To summarize my discussion thus far, the current interest in modularity stems from a realization that prior accounts of cognition paid insufficient attention to the detailed mechanisms of different forms of information processing. Instead, these accounts assumed, prematurely, that such key processes as memory and learning occurred in the same fashion across all contents, contexts, and species.

My own work in developmental psychology and in neuro-psychology has lent some support to a modular perspective. In the case of early symbolization, there are clear instances of stream-like properties that unfold exclusively within a single domain and show little affiliation with events in other domains. In the case of neuropsychological studies, there is mounting evidence that linguistic capacities at and below the sentence level are mediated by a set of dedicated mechanisms and that there may well be similarly encapsulated modules for dealing with specific aspects of language, such as syntax or phonology.

Yet these same lines of research point to phenomena that cannot readily be accounted for in terms of a strict modular perspective. We need to be able to account not only for stream-like aspects of symbolization but also for those wave-like mechanisms that sweep, even inappropriately, across diverse symbolic domains. By the same token, we need to account not only for the modules of language and other content-linked systems but also for the the orchestration and combination of these modules in the service of larger tasks, such as the comprehension of narrative.

It is appropriate to suggest mechanisms for these processes, and I have proposed in this chapter a number of candidate mechanisms. For instance, in the case of development, there may be a phase—linked either to age or to degree of expertise—in which a seemingly modular mechanism comes to be used quite widely—perhaps as a means of determining just where it is, or is not, appropriate. Possibly those processes that are referential or denotative lend themselves particularly well to "wave-type" exploitation. In the case of neuropsychology, there may be a combining, orchestrating, or executive process that is (or comes to be) localized primarily in the right hemisphere. This mechanism may be present at birth, it may evolve slowly during development, it may be related to wave-like processing, and/or it may appear to be permanent and largely automatized during maturity; yet a lesion in a crucial spot will compromise it, leaving the individual to fend with isolated or insufficiently linked modules.

Tomorrow

What is striking to a developmentalist is the extent to which discussions of modularity have been carried out thus far in a largely nondevelopmental context. The major spokesmen in cognitive science—Jerry Fodor and Noam Chomsky in favor of modularity, Herbert Simon and John Anderson against it—are united in their relative disregard for developmental phenomena or processes. Yet in my view, the key to determining what is modular in either sense and to explaining processes that go beyond modularity is inextricably linked to an adequate account of cognitive development.

Given a developmental "set," researchers in cognitive science may well be able to enhance our understanding of these modular issues. In the case of artificial intelligence, it should be possible to model different kinds of modular systems and see how they can combine and whether their mere combination can lead to the appearance of supramodular mechanisms. Recent work with massive parallel distributed systems may hold special promise for elucidating the ways in which certain stages or phases are realized and passed through and the ways in which certain activities come to be combined or dissociated (Rumelhart and McClelland, 1986). By the same token, in the area of neuroscience, studies of the effects of combinations of brain lesions (in human and in nonhuman subjects) and investigations of the effects of similar lesions at different ages or phases of development can also help illuminate the place and the limits of modularity.

Within the field of developmental psychology proper, I feel it is timely for researchers to sort out the relationship between those processes that seem to be most distinctly modular and those that lay the greatest claims to being supramodular or general. Part of this task must be undertaken on the theoretical level and will involve some of the considerations that I have raised here. But of equal importance will be the design of experimental studies, training studies, and other empirical investigations that can be seen, by adherents of both perspectives, as testing crucial claims and controversies.

It is important for those of a neo-Piagetian or information-processing perspective to look at a wide range of tasks and skills in terms of claims about working memory or putatively common operations—and to do so through the probing of capacities that clearly are central to their respective domains. By the same token, it is important for those of a modular or domain-constraint perspective to document that those capacities that they consider modular are indeed as restricted in mode and scope of operation as has been claimed in their theoretical pronouncements.

Ultimately, I have some confidence that issues of modularity versus generality can be better understood if we revisit the funda-

mental insights of Piaget, Werner, Luria, and Vygotsky in the light
of recent work in the cognitive and neural sciences. We may be able
to understand how we can go beyond modularity even as we may
come to discover that we can never completely escape the limits of
modular mechanisms. The British novelist E. M. Forster, in what is
possibly his most famous utterance, remarked, "Only connect." As
human beings, it is our lot to attempt to effect connections among
our various modular capacities, even though, in my view, we will
never completely succeed in doing so.

References

Bever, T. G. "Cerebral Asymmetries in Humans Are Due to the
    Differentiation of Two Incompatible Processes: Holistic and
    Analytic." In D. Aaronson and R. Rieber (eds.), *Developmental
    Psycholinguistics and Communication*. New York: The New
    York Academy of Sciences, 1975.
Bruner, J. S. "The Course of Cognitive Growth." *American
    Psychologist*, 1964, *19*, 1–15.
Carey, S. *Conceptual Change in Childhood*. Cambridge, Mass.:
    MIT Press, 1985.
Chomsky, N. *Rules and Representations*. New York: Columbia
    University Press, 1980.
Feigenbaum, E. A., Buchanan, B. G., and Lederberg, J. "On
    Generality and Problem Solving: A Case Study Using the
    DENDRAL Program." In B. Meltzer and D. Michie (eds.),
    Machine Intelligence. Vol. 6. Edinburgh, Scotland: Edinburgh
    University Press, 1971.
Fodor, J. A. *The Modularity of Mind*. Cambridge, Mass.: MIT
    Press, 1983.
Gardner, H. *Frames of Mind: The Theory of Multiple Intelligences*.
    New York: Basic Books, 1983.
Gardner, H. "The Centrality of Modules: A Comment on J. A.
    Fodor, *The Modularity of Mind*." *Behavioral and Brain Sciences*,
    1985a, *8*, 12–14.
Gardner, H. *The Mind's New Science: A History of the Cognitive
    Revolution*. New York: Basic Books, 1985b.
Gardner, H., Brownell, H., Wapner, W., and Michelow, D. "Miss-

ing the Point: The Role of the Right Hemisphere in the Processing of Complex Linguistic Materials." In E. Perecman (ed.), *Cognitive Processing in the Right Hemisphere*. Orlando, Fla.: Academic Press, 1983.

Gardner, H., Howard, V., and Perkins, D. "Symbol Systems: A Philosophical, Psychological, and Educational Investigation." In D. Olson (ed.), *Media and Symbols*. Chicago: University of Chicago Press, 1974.

Gardner, H., and Wolf, D. "Waves and Streams of Symbolization." In D. R. Rogers and J. A. Sloboda (eds.), *The Acquisition of Symbolic Skills*. New York: Plenum, 1983.

Gazzaniga, M. *The Social Brain*. New York: Basic Books, 1985.

Goldstein, K. *Language and Language Disturbances*. Orlando, Fla.: Grune & Stratton, 1948.

Goodman, N. *Languages of Art*. Indianapolis, Ind.: Hackett, 1976.

Keil, F. *Semantic and Conceptual Development: An Ontological Perspective*. Cambridge, Mass.: Harvard University Press, 1979.

Langer, S. K. *Philosophy in a New Key*. Cambridge, Mass.: Harvard University Press, 1942.

Lezak, M. *Neuropsychological Assessment*. New York: Oxford University Press, 1976.

Luria, A. R. *Higher Cortical Functions in Man*. New York: Basic Books, 1966.

Marr, D. *Vision*. New York: W. H. Freeman, 1982.

Mountcastle, V. "An Organizing Principle for Cerebral Function: The Unit Module and the Distributed System." In G. M. Edelman and V. B. Mountcastle (eds.), *The Mindful Brain*. Cambridge, Mass.: MIT Press, 1978.

Moya, K. L., Benowitz, L. I., Levine, D. N., and Finkelstein, S. "Covariance Deficits in Visual-Spatial Abilities and Recall of Verbal Narratives After Right-Hemisphere Stroke." *Cortex*, 1986, 22, 381–398.

Newell, A., and Simon, H. A. *Human Problem Solving*. Englewood Cliffs, N.J.: Prentice-Hall, 1972.

Ornstein, R. *Multimind*. Boston: Houghton Mifflin, 1986.

Piaget, J. *Play, Dreams, and Imitation in Childhood*. New York: Norton, 1962. (Originally published 1945.)

Rumelhart, D., and McClelland, J. *Parallel Distributed Processing.* Vol. 1. Cambridge, Mass.: MIT Press, 1986.

Shotwell, J., Wolf, D., and Gardner, H. "Styles of Achievement in Early Symbolization." In M. Foster and S. Brandes (eds.), *Symbol as Sense: New Approaches to the Analysis of Meaning.* Orlando, Fla.: Academic Press, 1979.

Sternberg, R., and Detterman, D. *What Is Intelligence?* Hillsdale, N.J.: Erlbaum, 1986.

Weylman, S., Brownell, H., and Gardner, H. " 'It's What You Mean, Not What You Say': Pragmatic Language Use in Brain-Damaged Patients." In F. Plum (ed.), *Language, Communication, and the Brain.* New York: Raven Press, 1988.

Wolf, D., and Gardner, H. "On the Structure of Early Symbolization." In R. Schiefelbusch and D. Bricker (eds.), *Early Language: Acquisition and Intervention.* Baltimore, Md.: University Park Press, 1981.

Wolf, D., and Gardner, H. (eds.). "The Making of Meanings." Unpublished manuscript, Project Zero, Harvard University, 1987.

Chapter 12

Creativity:
Proof That Development Occurs

David Henry Feldman

We appear to be in the midst of a resurgence of radical nativism, a viewpoint that attributes much of human experience and activity to innate factors. This resurgence has gone so far as to raise questions about the viability of the concept of development itself (Chomsky, 1980; Fodor, 1980, 1983; Liben, 1987). Although there are now strong counterresponses in the literature to the claim that development is yet another human illusion, like self or God or progress, the need still remains to put the antidevelopmental claims to rest once and for all (Bickhard, 1979, 1980; Campbell and Bickhard, 1986, 1987; Feldman and Benjamin, 1986; Liben, 1987). The purpose of this chapter is to provide another argument against the radical nativist position by showing that, because it is impossible to ignore the reality of human creativity, development must perforce exist.

There are, however, a number of preliminaries to be attended to before tackling the main points in the argument. First, it must be acknowledged that an argument for development does not require a denial that biological factors play a significant part in the process. As we shall see, natural human qualities are vital aspects of the

Note: The work reported here was supported by grants from the Andrew W. Mellon Foundation, the Jesse Smith Noyes Foundation, and the Spencer Foundation. Grateful acknowledgment is also given to those who read and responded to earlier drafts of this chapter, especially Robert Campbell, William Damon, Howard Gardner, Lynn T. Goldsmith, and the members of the Developmental Science Group at Tufts University.

overall account. Second, it is essential to be explicit about what is meant by creativity and development in the context of the present discussion. Finally, it must be recognized that the argument put forward here is substantially conceptual and theoretical in nature and, by virtue of this, must be taken as preliminary to the establishment of a firmer empirical base on which to make (and test) its claims.

Definitional Issues

For the past thirty years, creativity has most often been taken to mean the ability to generate infrequent or unusual ideas, and it typically has been assessed by standardized tests (Guilford, 1950; Torrance, 1962). Unfortunately, there has been little evidence that these tests actually assess anything resembling the ability to make truly creative contributions, such as establishing a new theorem, producing a remarkable work of art, or discovering a new sub-atomic particle (Feldman, 1970; Gardner, 1988; Wallach, 1971, 1985).

I use the term *creativity* here to mean the purposeful transformation of a body of knowledge, where that transformation is so significant that the body of knowledge is irrevocably changed from the way it was before. This kind of transformation can be accomplished conceptually, as in the case of proposing a new theory, or by making new products or representations, developing new technologies, or proposing innovative practical techniques. This notion of creativity emphasizes high-level functioning brought to bear on specialized problems, in contrast to notions of creativity that argue for a generic life force (Maslow, 1972) or quality of mind (Guilford, 1950). There is a place for such notions in an overall account of creativity, but that is not the best place to start. As Gruber (1981) has argued, it is best to begin with unambiguous cases of creativity, such as Darwin's theory of biological evolution, Einstein's ideas about the physical universe, or Mozart's great operatic works. From there we can move, if we wish, toward establishing common qualities among more widespread transformational uses of mind.

Obviously, the definition proposed here assumes a quality of human purposefulness, an unusual set of talents, and probably optimal circumstances for developing those talents in a distinctive direction. This point will be discussed further later in this chapter. For now, it is sufficient to note that, as used here, creativity refers to relatively rare events that are marked by their transforming effect on existing bodies of knowledge. When domains are reorganized in ways that can reasonably be described as qualitative and irreversible, then creativity of the sort defined here has occurred. It is itself a formidable problem to judge when a change is sufficiently powerful to be considered qualitative and irreversible, but criteria do exist and have been tested empirically with some success (Feldman, Marrinan, and Hartfeldt, 1972; Jackson and Messick, 1965).

The relationship between creativity and development, then, is based on the importance of transformations to both of these processes. The concept of development is of course the broader of the two, referring to any internal transformation of a body of knowledge that yields a qualitatively advanced (for that person) reorganization of knowledge. Developmental changes may be as common as the periodic systemwide reorganizations of each individual's intellectual structure, as described by Jean Piaget, or as idiosyncratic as the achievement of a more advanced level of mastery of an esoteric body of knowledge, such as chess or juggling (Feldman, 1980; Walton, Adams, Goldsmith, and Feldman, 1987). Creativity is a particularly strong and powerful instance of development, in which a personal, internal reorganization also leads to a significant change in the external form of a domain. A given instance of development may or may not contain the possibility for creative reorganization, but it always sets the stage for such a possibility (see Feldman, 1980, 1982, and Feldman and Benjamin, 1986, for discussions of the relation between creativity and development).

By emphasizing purposefulness in the creative process, I do not mean to deny the importance of natural biological factors, for they are vital in at least two senses. Some people are more naturally gifted and/or inclined toward representing experience through various domains than are others. Individuals also differ naturally in the personal, emotional, and social qualities that co-occur with their cognitive strengths and weaknesses (Gardner, 1982, 1988; Chapter Eleven of this volume; Wexler-Sherman, Gardner, and

Feldman, 1988). The sources of such individual variations are numerous to be sure, but at least some of that variation is undoubtedly a direct function of biological processes.

The second sense in which biology is central to the account proposed here is Piagetian. Development is assumed to be a universal human process, which means that it must be strongly supported by a biological substrate (Bringuier, 1980; Piaget, 1971a). Creativity, being a special case of development, must also be based on biological processes, but less directly so. Understanding creativity therefore requires understanding development, including the biological aspects of development (Feldman, 1974, 1980, 1982; Gardner, 1982).

However, biological processes alone are not a sufficient source of explanation for creativity, let alone development. To argue that innate capabilities determine in every important detail all that an individual will ever accomplish is to legislate against the existence of a problem, but it fails to provide any better an explanation for the phenomenon than any other radically reductionist scheme. To "explain" that a fire attributable to arson started because of a reaction between flammable material and a heat source is to miss the point, even if (and this is closer to the mark) the nature of the material can be specified and the heat source can be identified.

That there are biologically programmed processes that are common across individuals is no reason to assume that such processes adequately explain why individuals differ from one another in what they accomplish, and it is certainly no warrant for denying the existence of such phenomena as development or creativity. Turning away from complex issues like creativity in favor of explaining other phenomena at other levels—even if those explanations turn out to be an important part of the story—is not a satisfactory response to the issue of development and the implications of assuming a nondeterministic view of human development and change.

The main purpose of this discussion is to begin to glimpse the form that an explanation of development and creativity must take. The best place to start is with what we already know about the process, and what we already know about development comes largely from the work of Piaget and his collaborators.

Development as Construction: The Influence of Piaget

The most important advance of this century for understanding development and, by virtue of this, for understanding creativity was Piaget's constructivist theory (Feldman, 1985; Piaget, 1971a, 1971b, 1975, 1979, [1972] 1982). Piaget knew that it was vital to the achievement of his epistemological goals to be able to account for creativity, although he was never able to do so to his own satisfaction (Bringuier, 1980; Feldman, 1982, 1988; Feldman and Benjamin, 1986; Piaget, 1971b). What he was able to do was to provide the fundamental breakthrough in epistemology upon which an adequate explanation of creativity might be built.

The central problem in understanding creativity is understanding change—how it is experienced and how it is controlled: How much change is there in the real world of experience? How do changes occur? Can there be changes in knowledge or experience that go beyond what already exists? What is the relationship between the individual's experience of change and a decision to create changes that alter aspects of the world?

Piaget argued that, while change is inevitable, it has order and can be comprehended. He saw individuals during their life spans going through a series of lawful changes both large (the four stages of thought) and small (local accommodations). Bodies of knowledge also change, and even the physical world changes, although the principles upon which it does so change slowly, if at all. For Piaget, the goal of epistemology was to describe the various systems that people construct for describing and explaining changes in their world. This way of thinking about change places the human mind (Piaget's "epistemic subject") at the center of the process, in control of the mental structures developed to bring stability and order to systems for understanding the world. In this respect, Piaget's developmental psychology was the first distinctly psychological theory of intellectual change.

Instead of being driven to explaining development on the basis of the external world alone, as behaviorist approaches had done, or to supporting nativist explanations of innate biological unfolding, Piaget held to a "constructivist" position. He argued that changes in experience and in the interpretation of experience are inevitable but that the source of such interpretation lies in individuals' building and revising theories based on their experiences with the world rather than in the individual alone or in the environment alone. Piaget posited that there were laws to be discovered and revised regarding how such cognitive changes take place, and establishing such laws was the central goal of his epistemology.

Piaget attempted to provide an explanation of change in knowledge structures through a process termed *equilibration*. His formulation was revolutionary in at least two respects. First, his change mechanism led to transformations not only in the individual's store of knowledge but in the very mental structures that are the sources of knowledge. Thus not only does knowledge change, but knowledge-gathering capabilities also change. Second, Piaget proposed that changes in knowledge come about not just from mental reflection but also from action, which he defined as the desire to understand the world through activity, exploration, and interpretation (Feldman, 1985; Flavell, 1963; Piaget, 1975, 1979). What makes Piaget's epistemology so much more powerful than its predecessors' is this distinctly constructivist character.

Finally, since the principles of knowledge formation change as a function of the individual's own epistemological purposes, Piaget gave new substance and status to the self: "Free will" can exist as biological adaptation and psychological epistemic reality. The most remarkable examples of individually rendered changes in thought processes are often called "creative" because they not only change a person's understanding of a domain but lead to changes in the codified structures of knowledge in that domain as well—that is, they change existing bodies of knowledge (Feldman, 1974, 1980, 1988; Feldman and Benjamin, 1986).

Despite these extraordinary advances, Piaget was unable to account for how creative changes come about. He did understand that his theory would be incomplete until he was able to explain adequately how truly new, qualitative changes can be achieved through the conscious, directed efforts of individuals. Near the end of his life, he reiterated a point he had made many times before: "The central problem of constructivist epistemology is the problem of the construction or creation of something that did not exist before" (Piaget and Voyat, 1979, p. 65). It was his failure to fully recognize the importance of differences between universal and nonuniversal domains that left him unable to posit a satisfying account of novel, creative thought (Piaget, [1972] 1982).

Limitations of Piaget's Theory

As concerned as Piaget was about the systems people create for understanding the world, he failed to see any theoretical importance in differences between universal reorganizations of knowing systems (the famous four "stages" of development) and nonuniversal reorganizations such as we are considering here (Feldman, 1980). Nonuniversal reorganizations are those transformations in knowing systems that apply to a particular domain of knowledge but are not universally attained. Such changes are not guaranteed to occur in all individuals or for mastery of all bodies of knowledge, but they nonetheless are developmental in all other essential senses of the term (Feldman, 1980; Vygotsky, [1934] 1962).

In both universal and nonuniversal development, the individual struggles to interpret the world. But because development in nonuniversal domains is not guaranteed, there is more of a role for individual talent or inclination, on the one hand, and for specific, domain-related influences, on the other. While Piaget frequently used examples from mathematics and other nonuniversal domains to illustrate what he meant by qualitative shifts in knowing, he failed to exploit important differences between universal and nonuniversal shifts in knowing systems (Feldman, 1980).

The key problem with Piaget's account of individual change, then, is that it does not deal systematically with the humanly crafted aspects of a changing world. The world that Piaget's system deals with best is a stable, natural, physical world, with durable underlying logical principles governing its functioning. The child's challenge is to discover these immutable principles. These discoveries lead to mental changes that are more than quantitative, as, for example, when a child "solves" the integration of number and order in a seriation problem. What does not change either qualitatively or quantitatively in such a situation is the domain, the body of knowledge itself. Even the term that Piaget uses to describe individual changes—*accommodation*—signifies that change is in the child's mind, not in the external world as represented by the body of knowledge. Creative changes that require the domain to "accommodate" along with the individual are simply not well integrated into Piaget's universalist framework.

Piaget believed that the same principles of change that account for universal knowledge development could also account for change in bodies of knowledge (Bringuier, 1980). This idea offered a productive point of departure, and it has led to efforts to describe creativity as a cognitive-developmental phenomenon governed by equilibration processes (Feldman, 1974, 1980, 1982; Gruber, 1981). But it eventually led to an impasse, since it is not obvious where to look within the Piagetian framework for the reasons why some individuals and some reorganizations lead to changes in the domain while others do not. The universalist assumption virtually prevents serious consideration of other processes that might be called into play to help explain unique reorganizations as distinguished from universal ones (Feldman, 1980).

It seems clear, despite these criticisms, that Piaget was moving toward considering nonuniversal bodies of knowledge and their role in development. Indeed, as early as around 1970, he began to wonder if his most mature stage of Formal Operations was truly as universal as he had originally thought (Piaget, 1972). He mused that perhaps individuals did not display Formal Operational thinking in all domains but rather manifested the tendency toward this form of thought only through a particular domain, with different domains accessible to different individuals. While never giving up his belief in the underlying unity of the development of mind, he began to consider the possibility that identifying universal processes in different minds might require accessing them through different, specific knowledge domains. This line of thought brought Piaget as close as he was to get to the crucial distinction between universal and nonuniversal bodies of knowledge (Feldman, 1974, 1980, 1982, 1988; Feldman and Goldsmith, 1986).

What is of central importance for understanding creativity is that the processes that govern such changes, while sharing much in common with the universals of Piaget's theory, are also different in certain important respects. For Piaget, the creation of Boolean algebra was a novelty in need of an explanation. For deep epistemological reasons, Piaget was tied to the centrality of universal qualities of mind, the application of which might lead to both universal and nonuniversal reorganizations of thought. When applied to particular bodies of knowledge, universal cognitive achievements might indeed lead to specific changes in nonuniversal domains such as Boolean algebra, but just *how* they might do so cannot be explained within Piaget's universalist framework. The phenomenology of change in the two situations—trying to better comprehend an existing body of knowledge versus trying to transform its deep structure—is a different sort of activity and requires a different epistemology.

Although Piaget's own epistemology prevented him from accounting for truly creative accomplishments, he was still extremely close to the mark. Piaget wrote that: "The whole of human history is a history of *inventions* and creations which do not stem simply from the potentialities of the human race as a whole" (Piaget, 1971b, p. 212, emphasis original). Having come this close, Piaget characteristically fell back on biology, saying that the answer to how such inventions could arise would come from studies of the evolution of the nervous system. Yet he was very close to a plausible psychological explanation of novelties, including nonuniversal ones.

In spite of Piaget's monumental contributions to our understanding of mental development, and in spite of the truly revolutionary nature of his theory, he was unable to propose a plausible explanation for major examples of human creativity. This was no small piece of unfinished business. And Piaget was aware that he had failed to resolve a central issue: "[The] crux of my problem is to try to explain how novelties are possible and how they are formed" (Piaget, 1971b, p. 194).

The Crafted World: Source of a Different Epistemology

Piaget assumed that the same epistemological purposes that accounted for universal changes in thought would account for nonuniversal ones. It is no doubt true that the child's inherent curiosity about the world and efforts to comprehend it through equilibration processes are key factors in the desire to know. These qualities are necessary, to be sure, but are they sufficient? Beyond an inherent curiosity, individuals must come to believe that bodies of knowledge, disciplines, and fields of endeavor are not immutable but in fact can be changed. The distinctive feeling necessary for creativity in the larger sense is the belief that the knowledge structures existing in the world—its disciplines and technologies—have been changed by consciously directed human efforts and can continue to be changed when necessary. This is a vastly different epistemological position from the one Piaget explored, and it is essential to creativity (Bruner, Olver, and Greenfield, 1966).

Piaget's framework requires individual accommodation to an existing system for comprehending the world, a powerful but ultimately limiting source of new knowledge. Creativity, in the form of major new transformations of knowledge, occurs when a different stance is taken—a stance that questions the adequacy of existing domains for comprehending the world and that requires the world itself to accommodate. Although subtle, this shift in expectation and orientation is essential if creativity is to occur. Where does the feeling come from that the world must accommodate? It comes at least in part from the world itself—from clear evidence that other people have already made significant changes in the world and have forced it to accommodate. This kind of evidence, which is virtually everywhere, may not be obvious to the growing mind without assistance from those who have gone before. It also comes from culturally held beliefs that intentional changes are, at least some of the time, desirable and that those people who can facilitate valuable changes are given special recognition (Csikszentmihalyi and Robinson, 1986).

The world is therefore made up of fundamentally different sorts of things, those that are "natural" and those that are "humanly made." There is increasing evidence that children are inherently aware of certain distinctions among properties of objects, such as alive/not alive (Carey, 1985; Keil, 1986). These ontological distinctions are natural divisions of the young mind. Although the matter has not been empirically tested, it seems plausible to propose that children might also make a distinction at an early age between natural and humanly crafted aspects of the world: things that have "always been there or were put there by God" and things that are there because other people made them. Although it may take some time for children to refine this distinction, it is vital to the process of creative transformation that such a distinction be deeply appreciated by the developing mind.

When creativity occurs, it occurs in part because a person is motivated by the belief that, through his or her individual efforts, the world can be changed. Certain features of the world seem less changeable, and it is the understanding of these features that Piaget sought to capture in his universal stages: the logic underlying knowledge about space, time, causality, and morality. Most of the environment, however, particularly in urban, industrialized cultures, is in fact of human construction and human design. Awareness of this distinction is one of the most powerful sources for understanding that it is possible to transform the world—to make it a different place. The perception of this possibility is essential to all major forms of creativity.

This last point touches upon the crux of the nativist/ constructivist debate (Piattelli-Palmarini, 1980): Is it possible to create something genuinely new with a mind that does not inherently already contain that new thing? Antidevelopmentalists argue that in principle it is impossible to create a more powerful mind from a less powerful one (Chomsky, 1980; Fodor, 1980, 1983). Yet recognizing the importance of the crafted world allows us to show that the mind can indeed create something new without already possessing a preformed version of the new idea. The crafted world offers myriad examples of new ideas and products, as well as cultural prosthetics that encode the techniques and provide the tools for making other new things (Bruner, Olver, and Greenfield, 1966; Olson 1970). The crafted world provides the opportunity for a developing mind to access the accumulated knowledge of a culture, perceive selected and preserved examples of human efforts at transformation, and learn about the techniques for bringing about such changes. It is upon the crafted world that the possibility of creativity depends, not the preexistence of new ideas in the mind.

The error of earlier analyses, including Piaget's, was the

assumption that every new idea and product of importance had to be invented in its entirety by an individual. In fact, this is not true. Know-how, tradition, and example after example of the fruits of earlier creative activity are available to the growing mind. From these sources, in conjunction with the individual's own disposition toward novel activity, will emerge the makings of genuinely new things. Without accepting the strong form of the behaviorist argument, I would argue that new possibilities can be catalyzed in the developing mind from the outside, interacting with and influencing the individual's future course of understanding.

It is indeed possible for there to be something new under the sun. One need only consider how much of what is now under the sun would not be there if the humanly crafted world were to suddenly disappear (Csikszentmihalyi and Robinson, 1986; Feldman, 1988; Gardner, 1988). The implications of this argument are that development and creativity do occur—indeed they must occur—since the evidence for their occurrence is all around us in the form of the crafted world of human cultures.

The antidevelopmentalist argument is false because its assumptions are false; development is from the outside in as well as from the inside out. The potential for using outside information must be inherent in the human mind, of course, but a more powerful nonuniversal mental structure can be constructed from a less powerful mental structure through the use of externally available information, prosthetics, and instruction (Bruner, Olver, and Greenfield, 1966; Olson, 1970). All that must be assumed is the potential to use such information, not its presence in some preformed state.

The Transformational Imperative: A Mechanism for Change

Having just proposed that creativity (and, in fact, most nonuniversal development) depends upon the existence and availability of both humanly crafted environments and techniques for changing them, the question remains as to where the principles of change themselves come from. The crafted world provides numerous examples of significant, radical transformations in bodies of knowledge, as well as an appreciation for the fact that what is now "the state of the art" can be changed again. The actual capabilities for effecting such changes, however, must come from individual minds. I have called this tendency of mind to produce novel constructions "the transformational imperative" (Feldman, 1988).

The transformational imperative differs quite substantially from the equilibration mechanism proposed by Piaget, because it is intended to account for the tendency to transform away from stable knowledge states—in direct contrast to the Piagetian emphasis on transformation toward more logically mature structures and greater stability. In my own reflections on and speculations about transformation, I have found it helpful to distinguish between knowledge processes that seek to preserve reality and those that seek to change it. For the most part, the study of cognitive development has dealt with processes whose primary function is to construct a stable, coherent, internally consistent view of reality. The processes traditionally studied represent conscious, rational, logical, and categorical efforts to establish and preserve a stable and unchanging interpretation of experience. Piaget was of course a preeminent contributor to this line of thought.

Yet anecdotal accounts and self-reports from individuals who have made creative contributions strongly suggest that such rational thought processes are complimented by nonrational, noncategorical, fluid, and transformational thinking that often goes on outside of conscious awareness (Feldman, 1988; Freud, 1958; Gedo, 1983; Ghiselin, 1952). Creators themselves maintain that this sort of transformational thinking contributed in critical ways to the eventual form of their work—be it poems, mathematical equations, musical compositions, or scientific theories. When asked to reflect on the process of inspiration, Jean Cocteau wrote: "We indulge ourselves like invalids who try to prolong dream[ing] and dread resuming contact with reality; in short, when the work that makes itself in us and in spite of us demands to be born, we can believe that the work comes to us from beyond and is offered us by the gods" (Ghiselin, 1952, p. 82).

Piaget's preoccupation with the consciously directed aspects of transformation may have kept him from explicitly including within his system these more primitive tendencies to transform. Yet it is precisely these processes that are necessary to the appearance of the "novelties" that Piaget so earnestly wanted to explain. This has of course been clear to the psychoanalytic community for many years (Arieti, 1976; Freud, 1958; Gedo, 1983; Kris, 1952). Any explanation of creativity that does not include some kind of inherent nonrational tendency to take outrageous liberties with reality is likely to fall short of the mark (Feldman, 1988).

Granting, then, that a powerful tendency to change reality occurs naturally in human mental functioning, there remains the formidable challenge of specifying the principles upon which such a tendency might operate. Kurt Fischer (Fischer and Pipp, 1984) has proposed a set of transformation rules for rational thought; a complementary set for nonrational thought could prove useful to the further understanding of creative thought. Perhaps further studying transformations in a variety of other states of consciousness, such as dreaming, daydreaming, drug states, or meditation, will make it possible to build a plausible set of such principles (Hartmann, 1984; Wilber, Engler, and Brown, 1986).

At the very least, it makes sense to consider the very real tension between the competing tendencies to preserve a constructed reality and to change it (Arieti, 1976). It is almost certain that such tendencies vary in intensity from person to person and within persons across domains. So far as we know, Einstein lived a quiet and conservative life; it was only in his thoughts about the forces governing the physical universe that his ideas were radically transformational. It is virtually certain that individuals also vary in how readily or in what domains they are inclined to transform knowledge; understanding these differences should help account for why some individuals seem more prepared to change things in various realms than do others.

Essentials for Creativity

Based on the previous discussion, an adequate explanation of creativity would seem to require a tripartite set of processes: (1) something like Piaget's equilibration process, which is a rational, conscious, intentional tendency to construct systems of order; (2) the perception of the external world of crafted objects and ideas as a changeable reality; and (3) a powerful innate tendency to change reality outside the bounds of stable, ordered experience. All three seem to be critical ingredients for an adequate account of change, particularly for changes that substantially transform the world.

The third ingredient, the transformational imperative, is intended to contrast with the conscious, rational preference for assimilation to an already known reality. Accommodation has always seemed awkward within Piaget's system, performed only reluctantly and grudgingly by the epistemic subject. I suspect that this is because accommodation runs counter to the purposes of a system dedicated to preserving itself, whereas the opposite is true of a system whose purpose is to transform itself. It would seem that a framework invoking assimilation, accommodation, *and* transformation as equal components in a balanced system would yield a better rendering of the equilibration process, all operating within the context of a world of both cultural and natural objects (Feldman, forthcoming). Were such an expanded version of Piaget's change process adopted as a heuristic to guide inquiry, it would be better suited to the purpose of building a satisfying explanation of major reorganizations in thought.

Antidevelopmentalism Reconsidered

This chapter began with the observation that radical nativism has challenged the viability of the concept of development. I hope it is clear by this point that, while this challenge needs to be met head on, it need not discourage developmentalists interested in articulating major qualitative transformations in thinking. The basic premise of the nativist charge is false: It *is* possible for something more developed to emerge from something less developed without resorting to preformist explanations. The existence of the crafted world in all its manifestations, including techniques and technologies for making qualitatively different things from other things, ensures that development can and does occur.

The clearest examples of development are those changes in the crafted world that we identify as "creative." By so labeling the fruits of certain human efforts to transform, we give objective credibility to the existence of qualitative, irreversible transformations, both in various objects in the world and in our understanding of them (Jackson and Messick, 1965). In other words, we have demonstrated that development, in the sense that the term is usually meant, exists. By interacting with domains that are available in the world of humanly created culture, individuals are able to transcend constraints and extend systems. When such interactions lead to significant changes in the domains themselves, then the individuals who created these external reorganizations have concurrently created internal changes in their own systems for understanding and interpretation.

Not all significant reorganizations in thought can be considered creative in the sense of leading to transformations in a body of codified knowledge. Strictly speaking, we have only proven that development occurs in those instances in which the label "creative" can be conferred on the outcome of an effort to transform. It is much more difficult to support a claim that qualitative reorganization has taken place in a person's mind when that person is only able to do what others have done before. This is why Piaget's theory was so vulnerable to the nativist attack, a vulnerability that is avoided in the present discussion.

Tomorrow

To have shown—at least in the extreme situation of creative accomplishment—that development exists is surely a step forward. But it leaves a great deal to be done. If development *only* occurs in extreme situations such as those we have called creative, then the argument for development still lacks sufficient force to refute the nativist logic entirely; the strong form of the present argument rests on an unproven assumption that all qualitative reorganizations in thought—creative and noncreative alike—rest on similar principles. What must be done is to show in what senses more common forms of reorganizations in thought also transcend constraints and establish qualitative advances in thought. But note how far we have come toward constructing a positive framework for guiding efforts to comprehend developmental change and how little this framework depends on innate structures.

That events occur that are genuinely developmental should

now be clear; that they can be achieved by processes that do not require preexisting structures or innate knowledge should also be clear. The question now is to understand *how* development works and, in particular, how development works when it changes the world in ways that become part of the crafted human culture (Feldman, 1988). However sufficient or insufficient the processes proposed in the present account turn out to be for explaining development, they do not describe *how* such processes might be used in the construction of a qualitatively new thought or idea. This seems to be the next step in understanding development, and a giant step it will be.

References

Arieti, S. *Creativity: The Magic Synthesis*. New York: Basic Books, 1976.

Bickhard, M. "On Necesary and Specific Capabilities in Evolution and Development." *Human Development*, 1979, *22*, 217–224.

Bickhard, M. "A Model of Developmental and Psychological Processes." *Genetic Psychology Monographs*, 1980, *102*, 61–116.

Bringuier, J. C. *Conversations with Jean Piaget*. Chicago: University of Chicago Press, 1980.

Bruner, J., Olver, R., and Greenfield, P. *Studies in Cognitive Growth*. New York: Wiley, 1966.

Campbell, R. L., and Bickhard, M. *Knowing Levels and Developmental Stages*. Basel, Switzerland: Karger, 1986.

Campbell, R. L., and Bickhard, M. "A Deconstruction of Fodor's Anticonstructivism." *Human Development*, 1987, *30*, 48–59.

Carey, S. *Conceptual Change in Childhood*. Cambridge, Mass.: MIT Press, 1985.

Chomsky, N. "On Cognitive Structures and Their Development." In M. Piattelli-Palmarini (ed.), *Language and Learning: The Debate Between Jean Piaget and Noam Chomsky*. Cambridge, Mass.: Harvard University Press, 1980.

Csikszentmihalyi, M., and Robinson, R. E. "Culture, Time and the Development of Talent." In R. Sternberg and J. E. Davidson (eds.), *Conceptions of Giftedness*. New York: Cambridge University Press, 1986.

Feldman, D. H. "Faulty Construct-ion: A Review of Michael Wallach and Cliff Wing's *The Talented Student." Contemporary Psychology*, 1970, *15*, 3-4.

Feldman, D. H. "Universal to Unique: A Developmental View of Creativity and Education." In S. Rosner and L. Abt (eds.), *Essays in Creativity*. Croton-on-Hudson, N.Y.: North River Press, 1974.

Feldman, D. H. *Beyond Universals in Cognitive Development.* Norwood, N.J.: Ablex, 1980.

Feldman, D. H. (ed.). *Developmental Approaches to Giftedness and Creativity*. New Directions for Child Development, no. 17. San Franciscc: Jossey-Bass, 1982.

Feldman, D. H. "The End of a Revolution or the Beginning? A Review of Christine Atkinson's *Making Sense of Piaget: The Philosophical Roots." Contemporary Psychology*, 1985, *30*, 604-605.

Feldman, D. H. "How Development Works." In I. Levin (ed.), *Stage and Structure: Reopening the Debate*. Norwood, N.J.: Ablex, 1986.

Feldman, D. H. "Creativity: Dreams, Insights and Transformations." In R. Sternberg (ed.), *The Nature of Creativity*. New York: Cambridge University Press, 1988.

Feldman, D. H. "Universal to Unique: Toward a Cultural Genetic Epistemology." *Archives de Psychologie*, forthcoming.

Feldman, D. H., and Benjamin, A. C. "Giftedness as a Developmentalist Sees It." In R. Sternberg and J. Davidson (eds.), *Conceptions of Giftedness*. New York: Cambridge University Press, 1986.

Feldman, D. H., and Goldsmith, L. T. *Nature's Gambit: Child Prodigies and the Development of Human Potential*. New York: Basic Books, 1986.

Feldman, D. H., Marrinan, B., and Hartfeldt, S. "Transformational Power as a Possible Index of Creativity." *Psychological Reports*, 1972, *30*, 491-492.

Feynman, R. "The Pleasure of Finding Things Out." *NOVA* episode on Public Television (WGBH, Boston), January 25, 1983.

Fischer, K., and Pipp, S. "Processes of Cognitive Development: Optimal Level and Skill Acquisition." In R. J. Sternberg (ed.), *Mechanisms of Cognitive Development*. New York: W. H. Freeman, 1984.

Flavell, J. H. *The Developmental Psychology of Jean Piaget.* New York: D. Van Nostrand, 1963.

Fodor, J. "Fixation of Belief and Concept Acquisition." In M. Piattelli-Palmarini (ed.), *Language and Learning: The Debate Between Jean Piaget and Noam Chomsky.* Cambridge, Mass.: Harvard University Press, 1980.

Fodor, J. *The Modularity of Mind.* Cambridge, Mass.: MIT Press, 1983.

Freud, S. "The Relation of the Poet to Day-Dreaming." In B. Nelson (ed.), *On Creativity and the Unconscious.* New York: Harper & Row, 1958.

Gardner, H. "Giftedness: Speculations from a Biological Perspective." In D. H. Feldman (ed.), *Developmental Approaches to Giftedness and Creativity.* New Directions for Child Development, no. 17. San Francisco: Jossey-Bass, 1982.

Gardner, H. "The Fruits of Asynchrony: A Psychological Examination of Creativity." In R. Sternberg (ed.), *The Nature of Creativity.* New York: Cambridge University Press, 1988.

Gedo, J. E. *Portraits of the Artist: Psychoanalysis of Creativity and Its Vicissitudes.* New York: Guilford Press, 1983.

Ghiselin, B. (ed.). *The Creative Process.* New York: Mentor, 1952.

Gruber, H. *Darwin on Man: A Psychological Study of Scientific Creativity.* (2nd ed.) Chicago: University of Chicago Press, 1981.

Guilford, J. P. "Creativity." *American Psychologist,* 1950, *5,* 444–454.

Hartmann, E. *The Nightmare: The Psychology and Biology of Terrifying Dreams.* New York: Basic Books, 1984.

Jackson, P., and Messick, S. "The Person, the Product, and the Response: Conceptual Problems in the Assessment of Creativity." *Journal of Personality,* 1965, *33,* 309–329.

Keil, F. "On the Structure-Dependent Nature of Stages of Cognitive Development." In I. Levin (ed.), *Stage and Structure: Reopening the Debate.* Norwood, N.J.: Ablex, 1986.

Kris, E. *Psychoanalytic Explorations in Art.* New York: International Universities Press, 1952.

Liben, L. (ed.). *Development and Learning: Conflict or Congruence?* Hillsdale, N.J.: Erlbaum, 1987.

Maslow, A. "A Holistic Approach to Creativity." In C. W. Taylor (ed.), *Climate for Creativity*. Elmsford, N.Y.: Pergamon Press, 1972.

Olson, D. *Cognitive Development: The Child's Acquisition of Diagonality*. Orlando, Fla.: Academic Press, 1970.

Piaget, J. *Biology and Knowledge*. Chicago: University of Chicago Press, 1971a.

Piaget, J. "The Theory of Stages in Cognitive Development." In D. R. Green, M. P. Ford, and G. B. Flamer (eds.), *Measurement and Piaget*. New York: McGraw-Hill, 1971b.

Piaget, J. "Intellectual Evolution from Adolescence to Adulthood." *Human Development*, 1972, *15*, 1–12.

Piaget, J. *The Development of Thought: Equilibration of Cognitive Structures*. New York: Viking Penguin, 1975.

Piaget, J. "Correspondences and Transformations." In F. Murray (ed.), *The Impact of Piagetian Theory on Education, Philosophy, Psychiatry, and Psychology*. Baltimore, Md.: University Park Press, 1979.

Piaget, J. "Creativity." In J. M. Gallagher and D. K. Reid (eds.), *The Learning Theory of Piaget and Inhelder*. Monterey, Calif.: Brooks/Cole, 1982. (Originally published 1972.)

Piaget, J., and Voyat, G. "The Possible, the Impossible, and the Necessary." In F. Murray (ed.), *The Impact of Piagetian Theory on Education, Philosophy, Psychiatry, and Psychology*. Baltimore, Md.: University Park Press, 1979.

Piattelli-Palmarini, M. (ed). *Language and Learning: The Debate Between Jean Piaget and Noam Chomsky*. Cambridge, Mass.: Harvard University Press, 1980.

Torrance, E. P. *Guiding Creative Talent*. Englewood Cliffs, N.J.: Prentice-Hall, 1962.

Vygotsky, L. S. *Thought and Language*. Cambridge, Mass.: MIT Press, 1962. (Originally published 1934.)

Wallach, M. *The Creativity-Intelligence Distinction*. New York: General Learning Press, 1971.

Wallach, M. A. "Creativity Testing and Giftedness." In F. D. Horowitz and M. O'Brien (eds.), *The Gifted and Talented: Developmental Perspectives*. Washington, D.C.: American Psychological Association, 1985.

Walton, R. E., Adams, M. L., Goldsmith, L. T., and Feldman, D. H.

"A Study of the Relation Between Thought and Emotion in the Development of Expertise." Paper presented at the biennial meeting of the Society for Research in Child Development, Baltimore, Md., April 1987.

Wexler-Sherman, C., Gardner, H., and Feldman, D. H. "Early Assessment: The Spectrum Approach." *Theory into Practice,* 1988, *27,* 77–83.

Wilber, K., Engler, J., and Brown, D. P. *Transformations of Consciousness.* Boston: New Science Library, 1986.

Chapter 13

Making Cognitive Development Research Relevant to Education

Deanna Kuhn

It was not that long ago that relevant research was strictly second class. Research that related directly to real world issues and problems was labeled "applied," and strongly implied by that label was lack of rigor. Today, in contrast, we are concerned that our research be relevant. Competently designed and executed research programs are vulnerable to criticism and dismissal on the grounds of irrelevance, and the priority of our concerns regarding internal versus external validity has largely been reversed. What are the manifestations of this desire for relevance within the field of cognitive development? Is relevance a realized or realizable goal, and what are the obstacles to its attainment?

Cognitive development research occupies a distinctive position with respect to the issue of relevance. No other area of social science research is as directly relevant to a social enterprise of such massive proportions as education—an enterprise that influences the lives of virtually every member of society. All industrialized societies are committed to educating their young and have allocated substantial resources and organized complex institutions to accomplish the task. Moreover, indications are that educational institutions presently accomplish this task far from perfectly. What richer opportunity could exist for a research field to offer its expertise and make itself relevant? In this chapter, I will argue that this potential has been only partially realized and suggest some reasons why.

Cognitive Development Research and Education

Despite the globality of the educational enterprise, not all societies, or all elements within a society, have been of a single mind regarding what efforts to educate ought to consist of or what they should achieve. Therefore, cognitive development research might contribute to education in two quite different ways. On the one hand, it might assist in devising the most effective means to implement the educational goals a society has adopted. On the other, it might assist a society in defining its educational goals.

It is only in the first respect that cognitive development research has undertaken to contribute to education. Many psychologists, as well as many educators, would claim that this is as it should be. Educational objectives reflect the fundamental values of a society, and in formulating those values and objectives, social scientists have a rightful role to play as citizens, but not as scientists. A different point of view is possible, however—one that maintains that an enhanced understanding of the nature and directions of cognitive development can help clarify the goals of education and, moreover, that it is this contribution to education by cognitive development research that ultimately is the most significant one. In the following pages, I will take this view, and also I will suggest a number of aspects of the recent history of cognitive development research that may have worked against the realization of such a contribution.

It is important to observe first of all that cognitive development research is now making contributions to education in the first of the two ways indicated above more actively and more successfully than ever before. In the late 1970s and 1980s, it became much more common to find cognitive development researchers involved in investigations of the learning that actually goes on in schools. This research has yielded significant insight into acquisition of basic skills in text decoding and comprehension and in simple mathematics, and, moreover, much of it has been of a form directly utilizable by educators. The impetus for a good portion of this research was the "back to basics" movement that pervaded education only a decade or two ago, in the context of which educators turned to psychologists for help in understanding the factors involved in acquisition of the basic verbal and quantitative skills so many students appeared to lack.

But now the problem is a new one. Strikingly, for such a traditionally pluralistic field, education and educators have in recent years increasingly become of a single voice. The flurry of commissions and reports and books on the state of American education all reflect the same basic message: By the middle elementary grades, most students have acquired basic skills in decoding and comprehending text and in simple computational procedures, and we have improved methods for teaching those skills to the minority who have not acquired them. But most students of this age and older exhibit disturbingly little in the way of higher-order thinking skills: mathematical reasoning and problem solving in the quantitative domain and, in the verbal domain, the ability to reflect on what is read and make reasoned judgments supported by evidence. To best equip them to confront tomorrow's world, we clearly should be teaching students how (not what) to think; yet all the indications are that we are failing to do so.

We might expect that cognitive development researchers would be able and eager to conduct research that would address this educational crisis, just as their research on the acquisition of basic skills addressed an earlier one. In this case, however, matters are more complex. The definition, rather than only the implementation, of goals is implicated, for despite the unanimity of the current belief that the fostering of higher-order thinking abilities should be a central aim of education, the clarity of this aim drops markedly as soon as one moves to an even slightly reduced level of generality. What *are* the specific higher-order thinking skills that we would like students to attain?

It is educators rather than psychologists who have taken the lead in addressing this question. The variety of experimental programs that have been developed for teaching thinking skills represent practical attempts to address a practical objective, but they also reflect a theoretical effort to define thinking skills. The serious limitation of such efforts in the latter respect, however, is that they are largely uninformed by either theory or empirical data on the nature of thinking. Hence, no matter how rich or intuitively compelling they might be, such taxonomies of thinking skills cannot escape their status as merely one person's notion versus another's of what constitutes sound thinking. Why have researchers in cognitive development not jumped in to produce empirical research that would fill this void? In the widely cited volumes by Chipman, Segal, and Glaser (1985), intended to bring psychology researchers and practitioners into a dialogue on the topic of thinking skills, researchers displayed a willingness to comment on practitioners' programs and to reflect on broad conceptual issues, such as the generality versus specificity of thinking skills, but very few psychology researchers have entered into the effort to define higher-order thinking skills.

The work of psychologists who have endeavored to develop new, more satisfactory concepts of intelligence addresses this objective in a broad, general way. These psychologists have all taken the position that conceptions of intelligence must be broadened beyond the traditional ones associated with the psychometric approach and, in particular, they must encompass the competencies people display in everyday, practical (nonacademic) contexts. Cole (Laboratory of Comparative Human Cognition, 1983), Gardner (1983; Chapter Eleven of this volume) and Sternberg (1985; Sternberg and Wagner, 1986) are examples. As soon as one turns to the matter of empirical research to support such a view, however, a paradox arises. The first question to be raised about a new measure of "practical" intelligence that has been devised is its relation to established measures of intelligence. This concern about anchoring new measures to existing ones must be seen as paradoxical, given the original aim to break out of and go beyond traditional, arguably narrow conceptions of what constitutes intelligence. Yet we must appreciate the dilemma of those who have undertaken the development of these new conceptions and measures. If they did not assess and report such correlations (with traditional measures of intelligence), their efforts would be left in a curious limbo. "This is a type of cognitive competence that I consider important," the researcher would in effect say, "and here is a way I have devised to measure it." As psychologists, we have been trained to regard such efforts as incomplete at best. And so we dutifully anchor new constructs to existing ones, hoping to attain the only acceptable outcome of such anchoring research—a modest correlation between new constructs and old ones. If new measures of practical intelligence correlate extremely highly with traditional measures of intelligence, they are subject to dismissal as *nothing but* alternative measures of traditional psychometric intelligence. Conversely, if they show no correlation, they are subject to dismissal as unvalidated, or , in other words, as not measures of intelligence at all.

The situation is very similar for those who have devised curricula to teach thinking skills. Psychologists who have commented on these efforts have tended to be skeptical on the grounds of lack of validation (Chipman, Segal, and Glaser, 1985). But what would and should such validation consist of? Those programs that have been subjected to systematic assessment (see Baron and Sternberg, 1987, or Nickerson, Perkins, and Smith, 1985, for reviews of programs) have tended to rely on traditional tests of critical thinking, of intelligence, or, especially, of school achievement, whether or not these measures assess the thinking competencies that were the object of the instructional program. Use of school achievement measures reflects the paradox particularly well, implying that improvement in school performance is an objective of the experimental program. But might not the direction of this relationship more profitably be the reverse—that the nature of the thinking skills believed to be important to effective thinking shape the content of the school curriculum? Despite its appeal, this stance leaves the designer of thinking curricula in the same "unanchored" position described previously: "Here are some forms of cognitive competence I believe to be important, and here are some ways I have devised to assess (and to teach) them."

What, then, should be concluded regarding the researcher's role? Is there some legitimate role for empirical research in the effort to identify the thinking skills that it is widely agreed should be a major aim of education? Or should researchers properly wait until someone makes the value judgment that a particular conceptually defined set of skills is worthy of attention, at which point they can embark on those tasks within their domain of expertise: operationalizing these skills, submitting them to precise measurement, identifying the component skills that comprise them, and anchoring them to existing constructs?

To the contrary, I would claim that the role of cognitive development researchers in defining thinking skills should be a fundamental one and that it is their essential contribution that has been missing from the thinking skills movement. There are two important ways in which cognitive development researchers can and should ground curriculum developers' efforts in appropriate empirical evidence. First, they can do research that would help define thinking skills explicitly, through careful empirical observation of the thinking strategies people actually use (whether sound or faulty), conducted across the range of contexts that make up people's lives. Second, they can examine the directions in which such thinking skills develop naturally, with age and with practice. It is the latter kind of data that developmental researchers are of course ideally suited to provide.

Through both kinds of research, researchers can help educators define more precisely what education for thinking might mean. In the absence of such research, how can the educator make informed decisions about the thinking skills people should have and justify allocation of educational resources to foster them? Yet, developmental researchers have not readily embarked on the kinds of research programs that would provide an essential knowledge base to support the burgeoning thinking skills movement in education. In the next section, I will suggest some reasons for this that have to do with the recent history of the field.

Factors That Have Inhibited Study of the Development of Higher-Order Thinking Skills

In the last half century of research in psychology, perhaps the broadest impediment to progress in our understanding of human thinking has been the hesitation psychologists have exhibited toward studying behavior as it occurs in natural contexts, preferring instead to study cognitive (as well as social) behavior in artificial tasks and contexts. As a result, we know little about the thinking strategies people use in their everyday lives. More recently, however,

research practices have begun to change, with compelling demonstrations of the influence of context and meaning on the competencies people exhibit. Yet until such a data base is better established, it
is difficult to say what kinds of thinking skills people do or ought to
possess to function effectively.

The Reductionist Influence. Historically aligned with the
preference for artificial assessment contexts and tasks has been a
preference for studying behavior in its simplest possible forms. The
latter preference is associated with the reductionist research strategy
that dominated psychology in the 1950s and 1960s, as reflected, for
example, in the paired-associate learning paradigm. If we are able
to achieve a thorough understanding of a phenomenon (in the
paired-associate case, the phenomenon of learning) in its simplest
possible form, so the claim goes, it will be possible to generalize this
understanding to the much more complex manifestations of the
phenomenon that are the real object of interest. This promise, of
course, has largely failed to be realized, and researchers today are
much more cautious about investing a great deal of research effort
in the study of forms of behavior that are not of interest in their own
right. In the 1980s, as we noted earlier, we are much more likely to
see cognitive development researchers involved in investigations of
the learning that actually goes on in schools. Yet the belief has
lingered that efforts should be concentrated on such learning in its
simplest forms, until we are sure that we understand it well. Thus
studies of verbal achievement have focused on acquisition of basic
reading skills and studies of mathematical achievement on very
simple computational skills. As we already have noted, we
understand much less about the sorts of competencies we would like
schools to foster in the more advanced years of schooling.

Focus on Developmental Origins of Skills. We turn now to
several more specific factors in the recent history of cognitive
development research that may have had an inhibiting influence on
investigation of the development of higher-order thinking skills.
One of these is preoccupation with the developmental origins of
skills. If tasks are presented in familiar, facilitative contexts,
stripped of extraneous demand, or if minimal training is provided,
how early in life can particular cognitive competencies (notably
those associated with Piaget's stage of concrete operations) be

identified (Gelman and Baillargeon, 1983)? Enthusiasm for this line of research has led to a focus on cognitive competencies in their most implicit, rather than explicit, forms. The attainment of a cognitive strategy in explicit form implies conscious awareness and control—the individual knows what the strategy is, that he or she has the capacity to apply it, and the contexts in which it is appropriate or useful to do so. Attainment of a strategy in implicit form, in contrast, may be meaningful only from the objective perspective of the researcher; it may have no psychological reality from the perspective of the subject. To use an example that figures prominently in my own research, to be described shortly, researchers in several studies have traced acquisition of a covariation strategy to an early age (Shultz and Mendelson, 1975; Siegler, 1975): Quite young children will attribute an outcome to an antecedent that covaries with the outcome over one that does not. While it may be appropriate and useful to regard this evidence as indicating emergence of a covariation principle, or strategy, the strategy clearly is, at best, of a rudimentary form. Our research has documented that considerable development must occur before an individual exhibits conscious awareness and control of the use of covariation as a principle for inferring relations among variables.

Despite rapid growth of interest in the topic of metacognition, at present we know much less about cognitive strategies in their explicit forms than in their implicit forms (Gelman, 1985; Karmiloff-Smith, 1986). Yet, the qualities of conscious awareness and control are presumed in the case of higher-order thinking skills, and the development of explicit, consciously controlled cognitive skills (in contrast to implicit, unconscious forms of knowing) has always been assumed by educators to be primary in importance. In stark contrast, a number of psychologists in recent years have regarded such skills as epiphenomena—irrelevant to, and not particularly revealing of, the "real" mental processes that produce a judgment, with the implication that only the latter are worthy of investigation.

Focus on Domain-Specific Knowledge. A second factor in the recent history of cognitive development research that has inhibited the study of higher-order thinking skills is the focus on the role of domain-specific knowledge in conceptual development—an emphasis that has drawn attention away from the forms of thought. Theorists and researchers disposed toward broad structural or strategy explanations of developmental change have been justly criticized for ignoring the contribution to developmental change likely to be played by the child's growing knowledge base (Chi and Ceci, 1987). To the extent that a changing knowledge base co-occurs with developmental change, changes in strategy need not be invoked as explanatory factors.

The enthusiasm that has been displayed in recent years both for the investigation of developmental origins of skills and for the investigation of the role of domain-specific knowledge has led to research programs that have been very productive but that may have had similar inhibitive effects on the field. In both cases, the research has tended to be taken as having provided an answer, or an explanation, for developmental change when in fact what it has done is introduce questions, or complicating factors, in understanding the developmental process. In the case of developmental origins, the researcher who produces evidence that an ability is present in a more limited or rudimentary form at an earlier age than previously realized rarely means to suggest that there are no differences between the ability in this rudimentary form and in later, more fully developed forms. Were this the implication, little of importance would have been learned about *development* of the ability. Rather, evidence of precursors, or rudimentary forms, of an ability that will develop more fully indicate that the course of development of the ability is longer or more complex than was previously known. That course of development remains to be understood.

Similarly, evidence that growth in the knowledge base co-occurs with other developmental change creates a complicating factor: It does not furnish an explanation for that change. If we claimed that it did so, we would then be in a position to say no more than that cognitive development consists of the development of a knowledge base, leaving unanswered all the interesting questions: How is this knowledge base organized? How does the organization change with development? What are the mechanisms of development? Few, if any, of the researchers who have investigated the role of domain-specific knowledge would express enthusiasm for the return to a simple accumulative growth model of developmental change. Thus the questions just posed are the ones that remain to be answered. That this is so becomes especially clear when a very broad definition of domain-specific knowledge is adopted. Carey (1985a), for example, suggests that changes in a child's understanding of causality can be attributed to increases in domain-specific knowledge regarding the concept of "cause," and Chi and Ceci (1987) similarly classify a very broad range of phenomena in the category of domain-specific knowledge.

The most likely outcome, of course, will be that strategy change interacts with change in the knowledge base. An implication is that strategy change must always be examined within the context of a particular knowledge base. We cannot assume that the content to which the strategy is applied is irrelevant, or, put differently, that the strategy is a general one that operates in a comparable way across different kinds of content (though that may turn out to be the case). The approach adopted by knowledge-base enthusiasts has been to not rule out in principle the possibility that strategy change may occur (while maintaining that there exists no firm evidence for it) and to focus on the objective of seeing how much of development can be accounted for by acquisition of domain-specific knowledge.

As we shall see in the next section, however, that picture has begun to change as researchers have begun to produce strong evidence of strategy change in such fundamental areas as problem solving and inference. Thus, inferences may be constrained by the knowledge base, as knowledge-base proponents would emphasize, but the reverse constraint may operate as well: Strategies may constrain the growth of knowledge bases.

Focus on the Products Rather Than on the Process of Change. A final way in which the field of cognitive development has been less than ideally disposed to investigations of the nature of higher-order thinking skills is that until recently its focus has been on the products rather than on the process of change. In education there exists a long and distinguished literature, dating back to the beginning of the century, reflecting the view that the only effective way to teach students to think is to engage them in thinking. Dewey's classic *How We Think* (1909) certainly reflected this view, as did the writing of other respected educational theorists of his time, such as Symonds (1936), who wrote: "In order to learn to think one must practice thinking in the situation in which it is to be used and on material on which it is to be exercised. . . . In short, practice in thinking itself is necessary for the improvement of thinking" (pp. 235–236). This view remained prominent several decades later. In the early 1960s, a report by the Educational Policies Commission of the National Education Association entitled *The Central Purpose of American Education* claimed: "The rational powers of any person are developed gradually and continuously as and when he uses them successfully. There is no evidence that they can be developed in any other way. They do not emerge quickly or without effort. . . . Thus the learner must be encouraged in his early efforts to grapple with problems that engage his rational abilities at their current level of development, and he must experience success in these efforts" (1961, p. 17).

Given the consistency of this view in educational circles over seven or eight decades, it is striking how little empirical research exists that pertains to it. The relevant research would be essentially observational in character, focusing on the manner in which thinking strategies evolve in the course of their exercise. However, aligned with the domination of stimulus-response theoretical models, treatment-outcome models have to a great extent governed the design of research in psychology and education. Observational studies of behavior change initiated by subjects themselves in the course of ongoing activities are not readily assimilable to such models. More recently, however, interest has grown in microgenetic studies of the process of change, and I will describe some of this research having to do with thinking skills in the next section. If cognitive development research is to be relevant to the concerns of educators who wish to foster the development of higher-order thinking skills, it is essential that it address the nature of the change process.

Empirical Studies of the Development of Thinking Skills

The line of research that has received the greatest attention in the last decade as a new direction for cognitive development research is probably the research on scientific concepts and conceptual change pioneered by Carey (1985b, 1986) and several others, and one might regard this work as providing a potentially fruitful framework within which to conceptualize higher-order thinking. Both children and adults, this research indicates, hold a variety of naive, intuitive conceptions—usually misconceptions—about how the world works. The development of scientific understanding thus consists of a succession of incorrect theories within individual conceptual domains. Such conceptual change, it is stressed, is likely to involve not only changes in the relations among terms in the domain but also changes in the very meaning of the core terms themselves, a process likened to Thomas Kuhn's (1962) characterization of the history of science as a progression of paradigms that replace one another. This line of research has been closely associated with the domain-specific approach discussed in the previous section, as developmental change is conceived of in terms of reorganizations of knowledge within specific content domains rather than reflections of broader cognitive strategy changes that cut across content domains.

As we noted in the previous section, however, that picture has begun to change; and in most of the remainder of this section I describe research from both my own and several others' laboratories indicating that strategies for exploring and coming to understand the world differ significantly and in characterizable ways across development (Dunbar and Klahr, forthcoming; Klahr and Dunbar, forthcoming; Kuhn and Phelps, 1982; Kuhn, Amsel, and O'Loughlin, 1988; Schauble and Kuhn, in preparation; Shute, Glaser, and Raghavan, forthcoming; Voss and others, 1986). It is this work suggesting differences and development in ways of thinking that is most salient to educators interested in teaching people to think more effectively (though the conceptual change research also has important educational implications, the most general and notable being that the educator must make contact with students' existing naive theories rather than attempt simply to superimpose new, formal theories). A likely reason the conceptual change literature has tended to discount strategic change is that, thus far at least, it has focused on identifying and describing conceptual structures themselves and concerned itself to a much lesser extent with the mechanisms in terms of which conceptual change occurs. If the revision of theories underlies cognitive development, we need to know more about how it occurs. It is in this respect that we are most likely to find strategy change.

The pioneering work in identifying such changes by Inhelder and Piaget (1958) has three significant drawbacks, each of which has led to a diminishment of its influence. The first is the central role that propositional logic plays in their model of formal operational reasoning, and the second is the dominating role played by the concept of stage. Cheng, Holyoak, and Nisbett and their colleagues have made a convincing case against the utility of formal logic as a model of thinking (Cheng and Holyoak, 1985; Cheng, Holyoak, Nisbett, and Oliver, 1986; Holland, Holyoak, Nisbett, and Thagard, 1986), one that applies to propositional logic approaches to understanding higher-order thinking (Braine and Rumain, 1983; O'Brien, 1987), as well as to Inhelder and Piaget's logical model of the stage of formal operations. People, they claim, base their thinking on pragmatic schemas common to everyday life (which may be very general—for instance, permission, obligation, cause) rather than on formal logical rules. The concept of stage has proven equally problematic. Little evidence exists to support the existence of global stages in the strong sense that Piaget and Inhelder portrayed them, though, unfortunately, this fact has led many developmentalists to swing to the opposite, and equally implausible, extreme reflected in the claim that developmental change is entirely localized. The third drawback to Inhelder and Piaget's work is an increasing awareness that thinking occurs in a context that significantly shapes its form and expression and that these contextual factors are not ones that formal structural theories of development readily accommodate.

Despite the drawbacks of their theoretical model, an evolution in thought during adolescence along the lines that Inhelder and Piaget attempted to characterize is of crucial theoretical and practical importance, especially given the indications that, unlike earlier Piagetian stages, the stage of formal operations may not develop in all individuals. Despite the sharp decline in popularity of stage models, and the resulting decline in interest in formal operations, quite a few authors (see Fischer, 1984; Pascual-Leone, 1984; Sternberg, 1984) have suggested that the most fruitful way to conceptualize higher-order thinking is as third-order operations building on the second-order "operations on operations" (or formal operations). Commons, Richards, and Kuhn (1982) developed an instrument to assess such forms of thought. The limitation of this approach, however, is that it maintains the same abstract formalism that characterizes Piaget's stage models. In other words, cognitive operations are assumed to function in a uniform way irrespective of the content about which a subject is reasoning. With the exception of some later work by Inhelder and her colleagues (Karmiloff-Smith and Inhelder, 1974), Inhelder and Piaget in their work on formal operations never regarded their subjects' particular theories about the phenomena they were exploring as directing or even influencing the experimentation process.

In subsequent work (Kuhn, Amsel, and O'Loughlin, 1988), my co-workers and I have taken the subject's own theories as a starting point (in this respect aligning our work with that of the conceptual change researchers). We have framed our research in the context of what we argue is the heart of scientific thinking—the coordination of theory and evidence: How do children or adults differ from scientists in the processes by which they evaluate new evidence and reconcile it with their existing theories? In a series of studies, the theories of children and adults were assessed within a particular domain (for example, the relation of various foods to health); they were then asked both to generate and to evaluate various forms of evidence, sometimes consonant and sometimes conflicting with their own theories.

Subjects' skills in generating evidence that would support a theory (that two variables were causally related) or contradict it and their skills in evaluating evidence that was insufficient, indeterminate, or contradictory to a theory showed developmental change but were notably weak even among adults. Inferences of a causal relation, for example, were often made when the evidence was not present to support them, and inferences of noncausality were not made when evidence was present to support them. But even more notable than the lax criteria subjects employed for making inferences was the nature of the interaction between subjects' own theories and evidence, an interaction we interpreted as reflecting limitations in both differentiation and coordination of theories and evidence. Subjects had difficulty in generating, as well as in evaluating, evidence if they did not have a theory in place that accorded with that evidence, and they often exhibited exclusively theory-based reasoning when asked to interpret evidence. They displayed a need to maintain theories and evidence in alignment with one another, either by "adjusting" the evidence to fit the theory or by adjusting the theory to fit the evidence (the latter typically without realization that they had done so). In evaluating evidence, identical evidence was interpreted one way in relation to a favored theory and another way in relation to a theory not favored, suggesting that the evidence is not sufficiently differentiated from the theory itself; it does not retain its own identity—its constancy of meaning—across the range of theories to which it might be related. At the extreme, pieces of evidence are regarded not as standing apart from the theory and bearing on it but as *instances* of the theory that serve to illustrate it.

Based on this research, we concluded that a major development in scientific reasoning skill is the differentiation and coordination of theory and evidence, and hence attainment of control over the process by means of which theory and evidence interact in one's own thinking, and we hypothesized three key skills critical to this achievement. First is encoding and representation of evidence separate from representation of the theory. If new evidence is merely assimilated to the theory, as an instance of it, the possibility of constructing relations between the two, as separate entities, is lost. Second, the individual must be able to represent the theory itself as an object of cognition in order to relate evidence to it. Third, the ability to coordinate theory and evidence requires temporarily bracketing, or setting aside, one's acceptance (or rejection) of the theory in order to assess what the evidence by itself would mean for the theory were it the only basis for making a judgment. Individuals who possess and apply these skills will have attained a considerable measure of (though probably never total) control of the processes of interaction between theory and evidence as they occur in their own thinking. They might choose to regulate these processes in such a way as to reflect Bayesian principles of inference, in which interpretations of evidence are adjusted as a function of prior theories, but, if so, they know that such adjustments are being made and they are in control of their application. If these individuals chose to disregard the probabilities attached to prior theoretical beliefs and evaluate the evidence independent of them, they would be able to do so.

Our results indicated some development in these skills from middle childhood to adulthood (though performance of adults was far from optimum). Most likely, we proposed, two kinds of skills codevelop and mutually reinforce one another, one dealing with interpretation of evidence itself and the other with the coordination of evidence with theories. To the extent that the individual has acquired explicit and well-developed criteria or rules for interpreting evidence, these criteria are less likely to be compromised by the biasing effects of theoretical preference. Conversely, to the extent that the individual is able to dissociate evidence from the context of his or her own theoretical beliefs and regard that evidence as an independent entity in its own right, a concern for consistent and explicit criteria for interpreting evidence will be enhanced.

Other recent research on scientific reasoning portrays a similar picture of limited competence even among adults. Studies by Voss and others (1986) and by Shute, Glaser, and Raghavan (forthcoming) are not developmental and confined to adults, but they both suggest limited competence in the various phases of scientific activity: generating hypotheses, designing experiments to test them (generating data), and evaluating evidence. In research by Klahr and Dunbar (forthcoming; Dunbar and Klahr, forthcoming), the performance of a group of elementary school children was compared with that of college adults. Klahr and Dunbar cast their work in an explicit information processing framework in which (following Simon and Lea, 1974) the scientific reasoning process is regarded as a search in two problem spaces—that of hypotheses and that of experiments. In their studies, they observe subjects in self-directed exploratory activity as they engage the goal of discovering the function of a particular key (the REPEAT key) on a computerized toy. Adult subjects they could readily classify as "theorists" or "experimenters": Theorists conceived of the correct function and then designed an experiment to test their hypothesis, while experimenters induced the correct function based on data they had already generated. This dichotomy did not serve well for the children, however, as only two of twenty-two discovered the function. Klahr and Dunbar noted several major differences in process between the children and the adults. Consistent with the findings of Kuhn, Amsel, and O'Loughlin (1988), children accepted a hypothesis as true on the basis of minimal evidence. Their criteria for causal inference are clearly quite different from those of adults. The children generated as much data as did the adults; however, they were less able to make use of their data in discovering the correct function. Instead, the children appeared content with local interpretation—that is, making an inference consistent with the last result generated (ignoring earlier discrepant evidence).

Our own most recent work (Schauble and Kuhn, in preparation) suggests a way to interpret the deficiencies of Klahr and Dunbar's child subjects. In this work, we likewise observed elementary school children in self-directed exploratory activity, but in our case each subject participated in weekly sessions extended over a period of several months (enabling us to observe how strategies change over time with practice). The major purpose of this research was to examine the extent to which the specific skills in generating and evaluating evidence assessed by Kuhn, Amsel, and O'Loughlin in a structured task setting (and also assessed in the Schauble and Kuhn study) could be identified in subjects' self-directed scientific activity—that is, when they were free to generate and evaluate evidence as they chose in the service of a goal of understanding a particular microworld. The microworld in this case was a microcomputer-presented racetrack containing cars that had different features (for example, color, engine size, presence/absence of a tail fin) and that traveled at different speeds in test runs the subject could construct. The subject's task over the series of sessions was to determine what made a difference in how fast the cars traveled.

The results revealed the anticipated weaknesses in both designing and interpreting experiments, consonant with our earlier research of this type (Kuhn and Phelps, 1982). The current study, however, afforded us the opportunity to observe how subjects' theories about the effects of the cars' features (which had been assessed at the outset) influenced the discovery process as subjects' understanding of the microworld increased over the period of weeks. While the extent to which the subject's theoretical beliefs biased interpretation of data declined over time, this progression could not accurately be characterized as one in which subjects gradually set aside their own theories in order to attend to and interpret the evidence. Instead, we found a close interlocking of theory and evidence, one that again suggested insufficient differentiation between the two. Rather than setting aside theories, which were often wrong, and simply interpreting the evidence before them, subjects most often replaced their original theories with new theories of the causal mechanism involved (or absent)—usually before acknowledging the corresponding pattern in the evidence. As Kuhn, Amsel, and O'Loughlin (1988) had found in the more structured assessment situation, what subjects were not willing to do was interpret evidence of the effectiveness or ineffectiveness of a feature unless or until they had a compatible theory in place that made sense of that evidence.

Those subjects who made the least progress fell into two major categories, both of which reflect failures in the coordination of theory and evidence: We can refer to the two types as theory driven and data driven, similar to Klahr and Dunbar's characterization of theorists and experimenters; but in our case we are describing unsuccessful, rather then successful, procedures. Theory-driven subjects in our case were so bound to their original theories that they had difficulty attending to evidence at all, had difficulty generating evidence that would provide useful information, and, when they did interpret evidence, typically distorted it to fit their theories. Data-driven subjects, in contrast, were overly bound to the evidence. They likewise had difficulty in generating informative experiments, but each piece of evidence they did generate they felt obliged to explain. Like Klahr and Dunbar's child subjects, however, they confined themselves to local interpretation of isolated results rather than searching for a broader pattern of results over many instances (some of which might appear discrepant, due to the simultaneous operation of several variables), as more successful subjects did. Stated differently, their evidence generation was insufficiently guided by a theoretical representation that would have enabled them to make better sense of their results. Theoretical interpretation was of a local, "make-do" nature only. Many of these subjects ended their activity with the conclusion that a particular feature "sometimes makes a difference."

While space does not permit us to discuss all the implications of this study here, two are worth brief mention, as they converge with results of other studies. One, suggested by the performance of the data-driven subjects just described, is the importance of a mental representation, or model, that directs activity. Like Voss and others (1986) and Shute, Glaser, and Raghavan (forthcoming), who examined adults' reasoning about causal relations in the domain of economics, we see the subjects' evolving representation of the microworld being explored as critical. Our subjects frequently based their experiments on variations of a canonical car that embodied the feature levels they regarded as producing optimal speed—a car that clearly served this representative function. A second construct our results point to as critical is explicit, or metacognitive, knowledge of strategies. Kuhn and Phelps (1982) suggested that the reason their preadolescent subjects exhibited many weeks of variable strategy usage and took so long to attain consolidated usage of more advanced strategies is that during this period they not only were perfecting use of the advanced strategies through practice but were developing metacognitive knowledge about the strategies—that is, that they were the necessary or best strategies to use and why. The Schauble and Kuhn study provides a test of the hypothesis that their subjects' weaknesses were metacognitive as well as strategic. Each subject was provided a notebook for the course of the study and asked to use it to keep records to help him or her discover how the cars' features affected their speed. Though these fifth and sixth graders were well past the age at which researchers have inferred presence of a "covariation strategy," as discussed earlier, not one subject recorded covariation data (that is, feature combinations and corresponding speed outcomes), the data that were essential to the causal inferences to be made. Some recorded only the cars' features without outcomes, and others recorded outcomes without noting the cars' features, and some recorded neither. Clearly, these subjects did not know what they needed to know to master this problem.

Another direction we have taken our work is out of the arena of scientific reasoning per se and into the broader domain of informal, or everyday, reasoning (Perkins, 1985; Voss and others, 1986). Thinking in scientific contexts represents only a minute portion of all the thinking human beings engage in. In what ways might the limitations in thinking skills that we have described manifest themselves in everyday thought? We have explored this question by asking subjects from four age groups from early adolescence to old age to describe their own causal theories regarding several familiar phenomena and then to relate evidence to them. The topics—for example, the reason prisoners return to crime after they are released—were chosen as topics that people are likely to have occasion to think and talk about and about which people are able and willing to make causal inferences without a large base of technical knowledge. They nevertheless involve phenomena the true causal structure of which is complex and uncertain. The weaknesses in coordinating theory and evidence we have observed in many subjects' responses parallel those described earlier. Subjects often relate a story, or script (for example, in the case of the prisoner topic, a prisoner being released from prison, returning to his community, and being tempted back into crime). Our request for supporting evidence typically produces merely an elaboration of the script. Our attempt to elicit alternative theories or counterevidence is often unsuccessful. Theory and evidence are fused into a script of "how it happens." One of our adolescent subjects put it best. When we asked her for evidence that would support her theory, she replied, "Do you mean can I give you an example?"

We would argue that the key elements in a subject like the girl just quoted developing skills in differentiating and coordinating theory and evidence are (1) recognition of the possibility of alternative theories and (2) recognition of the possibility of evidence that does not fit a theory. The first achievement is likely to facilitate the second, as the presence of multiple, contrasting theories makes it difficult to assimilate the same evidence to both of them. In the case of each of these achievements, awareness that things could be otherwise is the key element. A script becomes a theory when its possible falsehood and the existence of alternative theories are recognized. Instances become evidence when the possibility of their lack of concordance with a theory is recognized.

Conclusion

In this chapter, I have portrayed recent research on scientific reasoning skills as consonant with two theses: (1) that cognitive development is characterized by significant strategic change not restricted to a particular content domain, and (2) that a major feature of this strategic change can be conceptualized as the development of skills in the differentiation and coordination of theory and evidence. Though Perkins (1985) did not find education effects in his research, both my own research described in this chapter and that of Voss and others (1986) show dominant effects of education level (college versus noncollege) on the reasoning skills examined, over other variables such as age, sex, and expertise. Research evidence regarding these skills thus begins to make a contribution to defining more precisely what it means to be educated. In so doing, it addresses the concerns of educators seeking to define what develops in the domain of higher-order thinking skills and in what directions and in what ways such development might be encouraged.

Yet we cannot leave the topic of higher-order thinking skills without acknowledging the incompleteness of the preceding portrayal. The picture we have portrayed thus far is one of development progressing toward an endpoint of perfect objectivity in which theory and evidence are treated as entirely independent entities, each preserving its own identity and boundaries while being evaluated against the other. In fact, however, virtually all modern philosophies of science reject such a model, emphasizing the complex interdependence of theory and evidence (Feyerabend, 1975; Kuhn, 1962; Lakatos, 1970; Popper, 1965; Toulmin, 1953). That which is chosen for observation, the tools of examination, and the interpretation of what is observed are all framed and influenced by theory of both the cosmic and local types. A stream of research beginning with Perry (1970) points to a developmental course of increasing recognition of the extent to which all knowledge is relative to a frame of reference, rather than absolute (Basseches, 1980; Kitchener and King, 1981; Leadbeater, 1986; Leadbeater and Kuhn, 1988; Sinnott, 1981). Though space is insufficient to describe any of this work here or to note commonalities and differences in the various approaches, all of it is addressed to a crucial aspect of the development of higher-order thinking, one that has received little attention within the thinking skills movement. The individual who melds theory and evidence into a single representation of "the way things are" fails to recognize the possibility of more than a single reality. How does such a person react to the discovery that conflicting assertions about reality are made by reasonable people, each of whom offers "scientific" evidence in support of his or her assertions? Must such a realization lead to unbounded, unreasoned relativism, in which criteria for meaningful scientific inquiry vanish, or to the limited conception of science in which the inquiring activity of the scientist is dismissed as mere subjectivity intruding into the world of hard, objective fact (both stances that have been observed in the above-cited research)? Alternatively, can an understanding of science develop in which the interconnection of theory and evidence, of fact and interpretation, is appreciated, with neither sacrificed to the other? The research cited in this chapter converges in the finding that such an understanding is not attained by most individuals. Without some such understanding, their interest in and appreciation of the process of scientific inquiry must be, at best, vulnerable. And hence their thinking is less fully developed than it might be.

Tomorrow

In this chapter, I have referred to two distinct historical evolutions occurring over the last several decades. One, within the field of education, is an evolution from a dominating concern with basic skills mastery to a concern with higher-order thinking skills of the sort that will best equip students to confront tomorrow's world. The other evolution, within the field of psychology, is an evolution away from artificial research problems and contexts and toward a concern for context, meaning, and relevance to real-world phenomena.

These two evolutions may turn out to have been in synchrony with one another, enabling us to predict their increasingly fruitful intersection. Educators are perhaps more of one mind about what education's mission is than ever before. Psychologists, in turn, have developed both the research approaches and the interests to make them willing and able to address educators' present concerns. It is possible, then, that we can look forward to a richer alliance between psychology and education, one in which the psychologist does more than devise ways to implement the educator's goals. Psychologists and educators increasingly may find themselves participating in a shared effort to define what it means to be educated and the forms that education for thinking should take.

References

Baron, J. B., and Sternberg, R. (eds.). *Teaching Thinking Skills: Theory and Practice.* New York: W. H. Freeman, 1987.

Basseches, M. "Dialectical Schemata: A Framework for the Empirical Study of the Development of Dialectical Thinking." *Human Development,* 1980, *23,* 400–421.

Braine, M., and Rumain, B. "Logical Reasoning." In P. Mussen (ed.), *Handbook of Child Psychology.* (4th ed.) Vol. 3. New York: Wiley, 1983.

Carey, S. "Are Children Fundamentally Different Kinds of Thinkers and Learners than Adults?" In S. Chipman, J. Segal, and R. Glaser (eds.), *Thinking and Learning Skills.* Vol. 2. Hillsdale, N.J.: Erlbaum, 1985a.

Carey, S. *Conceptual Change in Childhood.* Cambridge, Mass.: MIT Press, 1985b.

Carey, S. "Cognitive Science and Science Education." *American Psychologist,* 1986, *41,* 1123–1130.

Cheng, P., and Holyoak, K. "Pragmatic Reasoning Schemas." *Cognitive Psychology,* 1985, *17,* 391–416.

Cheng, P., Holyoak, K., Nisbett, R., and Oliver, L. "Pragmatic Versus Syntactic Approaches to Training Deductive Reasoning." *Cognitive Psychology,* 1986, *18,* 293–328.

Chi, M., and Ceci, S. "Content Knowledge: Its Representation and Restructuring in Memory Development." In H. W. Reese and L. Lipsitt (eds.), *Advances in Child Development Behavior.* Orlando, Fla.: Academic Press, 1987.

Chipman, S., Segal, J., and Glaser, R. (eds.). *Thinking and Learning Skills.* Vols. 1 and 2. Hillsdale, N.J.: Erlbaum, 1985.

Commons, M., Richards, F., and Kuhn, D. "Systematic and Metasystematic Reasoning: A Case for Levels of Reasoning Beyond Piaget's Stage of Formal Operations." *Child Development*, 1982, *53*, 1058–1068.

Dewey, J. *How We Think.* Lexington, Mass.: Heath, 1909.

Dunbar, K., and Klahr, D. "Developmental Differences in Scientific Discovery Strategies." In D. Klahr and K. Kotovsky (eds.), *Simon and Cognition: Proceedings of the 21st Carnegie-Mellon Symposium on Cognition.* Hillsdale, N.J.: forthcoming.

Educational Policies Commission, National Education Association. *The Central Purpose of American Education.* Washington, D.C.: National Education Association, 1961.

Feyerabend, P. *Against Method.* London: National Labor Board, 1975.

Fischer, K. "The Development of Abstractions in Adolescence and Adulthood." In M. Commons, F. Richards, and C. Armon (eds.), *Beyond Formal Operations: Late Adolescent and Adult Cognitive Development.* New York: Praeger, 1984.

Gardner, H. *Frames of Mind: The Theory of Multiple Intelligences.* New York: Basic Books, 1983.

Gelman, R. "The Developmental Perspective on the Problem of Knowledge Acquisition." In S. Chipman, J. Segal, and R. Glaser (eds.), *Thinking and Learning Skills.* Vol. 2. Hillsdale, N.J.: Erlbaum, 1985.

Gelman, R., and Baillargeon, R. "A Review of Some Piagetian Concepts." In P. Mussen (ed.), *Handbook of Child Psychology.* (4th ed.) Vol. 3. New York: Wiley, 1983.

Holland, J., Holyoak, K., Nisbett, R., and Thagard, P. *Induction: Processes of Inference, Learning, and Discovery.* Cambridge, Mass.: MIT Press, 1986.

Inhelder, B., and Piaget, J. *The Growth of Logical Thinking from Childhood to Adolescence.* New York: Basic Books, 1958.

Karmiloff-Smith, A. "From Meta-Processes to Conscious Access: Evidence from Children's Metalinguistic and Repair Data." *Cognition*, 1986, *23*, 95–147.

Karmiloff-Smith, A., and Inhelder, B. "If You Want to Get Ahead, Get a Theory." *Cognition*, 1974, *3*, 195–212.

Kitchener, K., and King, P. "Reflective Judgment: Concepts of Justification and Their Relationship to Age and Education." *Journal of Applied Developmental Psychology*, 1981, *2*, 89–116.

Klahr, D., and Dunbar, K. "Dual Space Search During Scientific Reasoning." *Cognitive Science*, forthcoming.

Kuhn, D., Amsel, E., and O'Loughlin, M. *The Development of Scientific Thinking Skills*. Orlando, Fla.: Academic Press, 1988.

Kuhn, D., and Phelps, E. "The Development of Problem-Solving Strategies." In H. W. Reese (ed.), *Advances in Child Development and Behavior*. Vol. 17. Orlando, Fla.: Academic Press, 1982.

Kuhn, T. *The Structure of Scientific Revolutions*. Chicago: University of Chicago Press, 1962.

Laboratory of Comparative Human Cognition. "Culture and Cognitive Development." In P. Mussen (ed.), *Handbook of Child Psychology*. (4th ed.) Vol. 1. New York: Wiley, 1983.

Lakatos, I. "Falsificationism and the Methodology of Scientific Research Programmes." In I. Lakatos and A. Musgrave (eds.), *Criticism and the Growth of Knowledge*. Cambridge, England: Cambridge University Press, 1970.

Leadbeater, B. "The Resolution of Relativism in Adult Thinking: Subjective, Objective, or Conceptual?" *Human Development*, 1986, *29*, 291–300.

Leadbeater, B., and Kuhn, D. "Interpreting Discrepant Narratives: Hermeneutics and Adult Cognition." In J. Sinnott (ed.), *Everyday Problem Solving: Theory and Applications*. New York: Praeger, 1988.

Nickerson, R., Perkins, D., and Smith, E. *The Teaching of Thinking*. Hillsdale, N.J.: Erlbaum, 1985.

O'Brien, D. "The Development of Conditional Reasoning: An Iffy Proposition." In H. W. Reese (ed.), *Advances in Child Development and Behavior*. Vol. 20. Orlando, Fla.: Academic Press, 1987.

Pascual-Leone, J. "Attentional, Dialectic, and Mental Effort: Toward an Organismic Theory of Life Stages." In M. Commons, F. Richards, and C. Armon (eds.), *Beyond Formal Operations: Late Adolescent and Adult Cognitive Development*. New York: Praeger, 1984.

Perkins, D. "Postprimary Education Has Little Impact on Informal Reasoning." *Journal of Educational Psychology*, 1985, *77*, 562–571.

Perry, W. *Forms of Intellectual and Ethical Development in the College Years.* New York: Holt, Rinehart & Winston, 1970.

Popper, K. *The Logic of Scientific Discovery.* (2nd ed.) New York: Harper & Row, 1965.

Schauble, L., and Kuhn, D. "Applying Scientific Thinking Skills in Exploration of a Microworld." In preparation, Teachers College, Columbia University.

Shultz, T., and Mendelson, R. "The Use of Covariation as a Principle of Causal Analysis." *Child Development*, 1975, *46*, 394–399.

Shute, V., Glaser, R., and Raghavan, K. "Discovery and Inference in an Exploratory Laboratory." In P. L. Ackerman, R. J. Sternberg, and R. Glaser (eds.), *Learning and Individual Differences.* New York: W. H. Freeman, forthcoming.

Siegler, R. "Defining the Locus of Developmental Differences in Children's Causal Reasoning." *Journal of Experimental Child Psychology*, 1975, *20*, 512–525.

Simon, H., and Lea, G. "Problem Solving and Rule Induction: A Unified View." In L. Gregg (ed.), *Knowledge and Cognition.* Hillsdale, N.J.: Erlbaum, 1974.

Sinnott, J. "The Theory of Relativity: A Metatheory for Development?" *Human Development*, 1981, *24*, 293–311.

Sternberg, R. "Higher-Order Reasoning in Postformal Operational Thought." In M. Commons, F. Richards, and C. Armon (eds.), *Beyond Formal Operations: Late Adolescent and Adult Cognitive Development.* New York: Praeger, 1984.

Sternberg, R. *Beyond IQ: A Triarchic Theory of Human Intelligence.* Cambridge, England: Cambridge University Press, 1985.

Sternberg, R., and Wagner, R. *Practical Intelligence: Nature and Origins of Competence in the Everyday World.* New York: Cambridge University Press, 1986.

Symonds, P. *Education and the Psychology of Thinking.* New York: McGraw-Hill, 1936.

Toulmin, S. *Philosophy of Science*. New York: Harper & Row, 1953.

Voss, J., and others. "Informal Reasoning and Subject Matter Knowledge in the Solving of Economics Problems by Naive and Novice Individuals." *Cognition and Instruction*, 1986, *3*, 269–302.

Chapter 14

Infants in Relation: Performers, Pupils, and Partners

Ina Č. Užgiris

 In the past decade, researchers have become increasingly interested in the social experience of infants and young children. Both infant skills for interpersonal engagement and parental activities with infants have been scrutinized, producing new conceptions of infant-parent interaction. My title for this chapter echoes Macmurray's (1961) title for his philosophical treatment of mutual relatedness, considered by him to be fundamental to the human condition. The title alludes to the new importance accorded to interpersonal experience in current discussions of infant development. A focus on the social experiences of infants, however, not only highlights new questions for study but also requires new methodologies for their appropriate investigation. In this chapter, several themes central to an interactive approach to infant development are presented, and their implications for future work are discussed.

Note: The research on imitative interactions has been supported by the Spencer Foundation. Janette B. Benson, Maria Fafouti-Milenkovic, Jan C. Kruper, and Marie Vasek have contributed to the research work and to my thinking about infant-parent interactions. My thanks go to them and to the many graduate students who have struggled with me to understand the functions of imitation in development.

Changing Perspectives on Infant Development

Although the topic of parent-child relations suggests an interest in the effects of the child on the parent as well as those of the parent on the child, this bidirectionality of influence has not been explicitly recognized in research studies until quite recently. In earlier major studies, maternal attitudes and care practices were evaluated for their effects without a direct consideration of the characteristics of the child involved (see Sears, Maccoby, and Levin, 1957). Dimensions of parental behavior, such as acceptance-rejection or permissiveness-control, were delineated and studied, but without consideration of the contribution made by the child to those parental attitudes and practices (for a review, see Martin, 1975). The dimensions describing parent-child interaction were considered to be characteristics of the parent. Similarly, when ensuing child behavioral characteristics, such as aggressiveness or dependence, were assessed, they were treated as tendencies belonging to the child. The socialization concept of parent-child relations fostered a unidirectional understanding of parent-child interaction: It was the parent who actively shaped the child through love and discipline toward behavior patterns acceptable to society, while the child responded more or less pliably to parental treatment, in keeping with his or her inherent dispositions. The prevalent image was of two separate entities participating in an action-reaction chain, with the process open to a cause-effect interpretation.

Eventually, the minimal predictability of child characteristics from parental practices, as well as evidence of variability in one parent's practices toward different children, led to an explicit acceptance of the child's influence on parent-child relations (see Bell, 1968; Rheingold, 1969; Yarrow, 1963). The roles of the child's sex, constitutional characteristics, and responsiveness to parental actions in modifying parental practices were acknowledged first. There was a call for a more reciprocal view of parent-child relations, reflected in studies of child effects on parents (see Leach and Costello, 1972; Moss, 1967; Osofsky and O'Connell, 1972) and even in book titles on this topic (Bell and Harper, 1977; Lewis and Rosenblum, 1974). This shift toward a more reciprocal conception of parent-child relations was bolstered by a simultaneous reevaluation of the perceptual, cognitive, and social abilities of young infants, which showed them to be much more capable than previously thought (Stone, Smith, and Murphy, 1973). Nevertheless, the conception of parent and child as two separate entities influencing each other over time in an action-reaction pattern was implicitly maintained, even though studies of child rearing came to be called studies of parent-child interaction.

More recently, in work on mother-infant interaction, it became evident that the pattern of relations between a mother and her infant evolves not only as a result of their individual characteristics but also as a result of their social exchanges with each other, which are continuously mutually constructed (Sameroff, 1975). A search for a new image to represent the mutuality of mother-infant interaction ensued. The terms *transaction, dialogue,* and *negotiation* have been used in an attempt to convey the understanding that a mother and her infant form a system characterized by mutual regulation and mutual evolution (Schaffer, 1977; Tronick, 1982; Užgiris, 1979). At present, this conception extends to infant interactions with all significant others in the infant's social world. However, the changed conception of infant-adult relations has not yet produced a commensurate change in the methodological aspects of infant-parent interaction studies (Užgiris and Fafouti-Milenkovic, 1985).

Research on Infant-Parent Interaction. What kind of evidence has contributed the most to the reconceptualization of infant-parent interaction? Of greatest importance in this respect have been very detailed observations of mothers and infants in face-to-face engagements or other play activities, as well as more traditional studies of infant skills, indicating that infants may have the wherewithal to be partners in interaction. Descriptions of even young infants showing different configurations of activity in regard to persons and to objects have been viewed as an indication that infants begin their lives among others with at least an incipient capacity to communicate with them (Bateson, 1975; Brazelton, Koslowski, and Main, 1974; Trevarthen, 1974). Such a communicative mode of interaction has been taken to epitomize the social relatedness of infants.

Several features of infant-adult interaction sustain the interpretation that it is a mutually regulated interpersonal exchange. First, the turn-taking pattern in the actions of the two participants has been described repeatedly (see Bateson, 1975; Kaye, 1977; Stern, 1974; Trevarthen, 1977). Although instances of simultaneous action and particularly simultaneous vocalization have been noted (Bakeman and Brown, 1977; Papoušek and others, 1986; Stern, Jaffe, Beebe, and Bennett, 1975), the overall pattern seems to be one of complementary responsiveness to the other. Orientation and gaze are used by both partners to structure the flow of the interaction.

Second, the apparent meaningfulness of their actions to both partners suggests that the actions of one serve to inform the other. Not only are the facial expressions, movements, and vocalizations of the infant interpreted by the adult as meaningful and expressive of the infant's state, but the infant also seems to have expectations regarding the analogous behaviors of the adult. The most dramatic evidence on this count comes from studies in which the mother is requested to hold still and become unresponsive to the overtures of her infant. In this situation, infants typically make several attempts to engage the mother but then become concerned or distressed (see Fogel, Diamond, Langhorst, and Demos, 1982; Tronick and others, 1978). In addition, Cohn and Tronick (1983) have shown that if the mother is asked to simulate a depressed state and interact with her infant in an unexpressive manner, the infant's mood becomes negative and the flow of the interaction is disrupted. It has been shown that the dynamics of interaction also become different if the infant is given an unfamiliar partner (see Dixon and others, 1981; Fafouti-Milenkovic and Užgiris, 1979; Fogel, 1980).

Finally, evidence that the probability of onset, offset, or duration of particular actions varies with the ongoing or preceding actions of the partner indicates that the course of early infant-adult interactions is mutually regulated. Stern (1977; Stern and Gibbon, 1979) has particularly emphasized the factor of timing in such regulation. Other studies (Anderson, Vietze, and Dokecki, 1977; Kaye and Fogel, 1980; Freedle and Lewis, 1977) have shown that specific categories of action, such as vocalization, are highly sensitive to the relevant actions of the partner from the first weeks of life.

Whether these observed features of infant-adult interaction are considered indicative of communication between the partners depends on how communication is defined and how the evidence of smooth intermeshing is interpreted. Although communication is generally construed more broadly than an exchange of information by linguistic means, infants' capacity to engage in genuine communication has been questioned on the grounds that infants have limited knowledge of themselves and others and make little distinction between means and goals in their activities. Arguments have been made that early infant-parent exchanges only appear to involve communication because the adult—usually the mother— skillfully manages to insert her own actions into the infant's flow of activity and to sensitively interpret the expressive behaviors of her infant (Schaffer, 1984). Such arguments, however, carry a trace of earlier views of interaction, in which the activities of the two participants were regarded independently of each other. Studies mentioned previously indicate that infants actively contribute to the shaping of interactions in which they participate. If communication is conceived as joint activity, then the contribution of each partner need not be equivalent, as long as the goal of shared understanding is attained.

It seems to me that the minimal constituents of communicative activity are a directedness toward sharing with another, a content to be shared, and a means for conveying and grasping that content. The process of communication requires access to these constituents by both participants. Infants have a repertoire of actions for participating in exchanges in which affect and involvement with the other are shared. This sharing is not achieved through the use of a conventional code of gestures or vocalizations but through a similar interpretation of certain expressions, intonations, and the tempo of actions by both adult and infant. Thus the beginnings of communication are found in those exchanges that create a shared understanding of each other's involvement in the ongoing interaction by both participants.

Unquestionably, the very early communicative exchanges are limited in a number of respects. For instance, the content that can be shared is quite restricted and the means used for communication are not distanced from the content. Nevertheless, the recognition that shared understanding is grounded in exchanges forming a part of early interactions suggests the important possibility that full-fledged communication evolves as a result of participation in the early protocommunicative exchanges (Fafouti-Milenkovic and Užgiris, 1979; Kaye, 1982). Much of the understanding about communication that is presumed in more advanced forms of communication may be constructed during these early infant-adult interactions.

Perspectives on Joint Activity. An interactive approach to infant development, by emphasizing the activities constructed while in relation to a partner, subordinates an analysis of the contributions of each partner to an analysis of the forms of activity carried out jointly. The joint activities are taken not as the outcome of the efforts of one or the other partner but as the products of their joint efforts while engaged with each other. With another partner, or in another context, each might make different contributions and appear to have different skills.

The special status of joint activity between a child and an adult was recognized many years ago by Vygotsky ([1934] 1962, 1978), whose views are currently gaining increasing prominence (Rogoff and Wertsch, 1984; Wertsch, 1985). Vygotsky's claims about the social construction of human knowledge and the primacy of the interpsychological over the intrapsychological plane have become well known. They fit with the view of achievement as the product of action in context and suggest that there may be important effects of performance with another that carry over to individual competence. Interaction with a partner whose actions reflect the views, knowledge, and skills of a culture holds special importance not because of any direct instruction but because of the activities that are jointly constructed.

The importance of joint activity for the development of human competence also has been highlighted in Bruner's (1978) work. His concept of "scaffolding" refers to supportive adult actions that make it possible for an infant or a child to participate in some activity or to achieve a goal that would be impossible otherwise. Scaffolding basically consists of adult actions that fill in gaps or narrow the available options, thereby enabling a child to practice and master various constituent parts of an activity. Occurrence of scaffolding has been observed during such mother-child interactions as playing various games (Bruner and Sherwood, 1976; Ratner and Bruner, 1978) or labeling pictures in books (Ninio and Bruner, 1978). Although the notion of scaffolding does not emphasize quite the same aspects of interaction as does Vygotsky's idea of construction on the interpsychological plane, both suggest that interaction is to be studied not only for what it reveals about the current status of the partners but also for what it may contribute to their development in the future.

The existing literature on infant-adult interactions shows that these interactions exhibit several potentially important characteristics. First, parents and other adults treat infants as persons capable of feelings, desires, and individual preferences that can be expressed during interactions (Kruper and Užgiris, 1987). Sometimes these interpretations seem to be made on the basis of infant facial expressions, vocalizations, or body movements, and sometimes they appear to be imputed without any clear foundation in observable acts. The important point is that adults do treat infants as partners sharing essential attributes with themselves and fashion their interactions in accord with such interpretation. Thus, although the quantity and the specific content of interpretations may vary in different cultures, infants from the very beginning participate in social relations of mutuality, reciprocity, and potential symmetry.

Second, early infant-parent interactions exhibit a structure similar to social interactions generally; that is, they are coherent, sequentially organized, with turns allocated between the partners and with marked beginnings and endings. The genesis of the turn-taking structure may lie in adult sensitivity to infant rhythms, which permits them to insert their own actions into the pauses between infant acts. However, the very rare occurrence of overlaps and the fraction-of-a-second duration of many acts suggest that some mutual regulation takes place. Moreover, once infants begin to participate not only in interactions based on activities having a biological rhythm (for example, burst-pause sucking or vocalizing) but also in interactions in which such rhythms are less clear (such as visual co-orientation), the reciprocity of infant-parent interaction becomes undeniable. Again, even if initially supported by adult sensitivity, a mutually regulated structure for interaction emerges during the infant's first year of life.

Third, infant-parent interactions appear to be grounded in a shared experience of the acts exchanged. There is a convergence of attention, first on each other and then on surrounding objects. Affect is shared, actions are reciprocated, and directions of activity are negotiated. Again, initially, the adult may be more often responsible for creating the common ground for interaction; nevertheless, infants from early on participate in interactions having shared meaning and contribute to the delineation of that meaning. Stern (1985) has captured in the notion of attunement the convergence that is sought in infant-parent interactions.

These three characteristics are important, because they indicate that during interactions with adults infants experience the mutual relations fundamental to human sociality. At first, the participation of the infant may not be commensurate with that of the adult, but over the course of the first year, infant and adult roles become more symmetrical. And, as has been suggested, the very participation in interactions may generate the changes that are observed.

Methodology of Interaction Studies. The focus on infant-parent interaction has also produced a shift in the typical methods of investigation. Less direct approaches relying on parental reports or observer ratings have been replaced by direct observation and videorecording of more or less structured interactions. Nevertheless, not all studies using the newer direct approaches have dealt with the process of interaction. It is important to distinguish studies that are concerned with interpersonal interaction from those that deal with some aspect of the actions of one member of a dyad in an interactive setting. For example, studies of the rate of vocalization by infants varying in birth status or by mothers from different socioeconomic groups may be carried out in an interactive setting, but they may reveal little about the interaction if only rates of vocalization for each partner separately are determined. Unless the observations are treated in a manner that allows the recovery of dependencies between the actions of the two partners, no statements about the interaction can be made.

The study of young infants' interactions requires the adoption of appropriate categories and methods of analysis. Even if the actions of the members of a dyad are coded with respect to a time line, so that dependencies between their actions can be examined, the choice of coding categories may be such that the data have relatively little to say about interaction. If discrete, elemental acts are coded for each partner, their additive combination is not likely to recover meaningful events within the interaction. A focus on interaction requires a different level of analysis.

For example, if smiles, vocalizations, and looks are coded for an infant and touches, looks, and vocalizations are coded for a mother, it is doubtful that some combination of these acts in time could uniquely define such meaningful interactive activities as greeting, soothing, or play. A look with a vocalization embedded in a greeting routine does not carry the same interpersonal meaning as a look and a vocalization expressing discomfort; less elemental coding categories are needed if the more complex process of interaction is to be characterized. Because states of interaction describe the dyad and not the members individually, they are not adequately captured by action categories directed to each individual member. More holistic categories referring to the meaning of the exchanges are required. Such categories may be more or less global, but they must encompass the contribution of both participants.

The objection may be raised that categories at this level are likely to reflect the cultural understanding of the researcher. One response to this objection is that human interactions are culturally bound and make sense within a given cultural context; if different observers can agree on their application, these categories are not likely to be more culturally limited than are most categories in psychological research. Another response is to admit that the study of cultural differences in the construal of basic patterns of interaction might be an interesting line of research. Taking refuge in elemental categories is not a solution if the interest is in understanding interactions.

An investigator's implicit conception of the interaction process is reflected also in the methods of analysis. The recording of specific behaviors and their subsequent additive combination into more global categories suggests a rather mechanistic view of interaction. A specific act of one partner (for example, vocalization plus looking) is treated as setting off some response by the other, which, in turn, is responded to by the first partner. When interaction is conceptualized as a chain of actions and reactions alternating between the two partners, it may be appropriate to examine which specific act of one partner precedes or follows which of the other with greater than chance probability. When, however, the interacting partners are viewed as a single system, different approaches become more appropriate.

Various types of sequential analyses and pattern analyses are more likely to reveal the dynamics of interaction than are more familiar procedures comparing the relative incidences of acts in various categories (Bakeman and Gottman, 1986). Although lag analyses (Sackett, 1979) and Markov analyses (van Hooff, 1982) have become better known in recent years, they are not the complete answer. Approaches based on goodness of fit procedures (Duncan and Fiske, 1985) or semi-Markov processes (Howard, 1971) may be more suitable for analyzing sequential dependencies of interest in interaction data, but there is a great need for advances in this area.

It is argued here that interaction is best studied as a dynamic system. For a meaningful coordination of actions to take place in real time, both partners must monitor each other and anticipate the subsequent acts of the other in order to adjust their own acts and to influence those of the partner. They must share an understanding of the interaction. At any one time, the acts of partner A cannot be taken as the stimuli for the subsequent acts of partner B because there is continuous anticipation on the part of both, continuous adjustment on the part of both, and continuous integration of the many aspects of both of their activities. A set of categories that considers the meaning of each partner's actions while referring to their joint activity comes closer to depicting the process of interaction as a self-regulating system. Similarly, methods of analysis that describe the dynamics of the system as a whole and consider the components in relation to the whole are better suited for informing about the process of interaction.

Mutual regulation of interaction places an emphasis on

shared understanding and on communication of such shared understanding. Although the means of communication may be restricted in early infancy, more mutual and more conventional understanding may actually arise as a result of participation in interactions in which shared meaning is enacted. The facilitated performance of meaningful activities may provide the experiential base upon which to build the schemas for those activities that make engagement in them possible. To illustrate the increasing mutuality, reciprocity, and symmetry of early infant-parent interactions, our research on imitative interactions between infants and their mothers is described in the next section.

Imitative Interactions

Imitation as a phenomenon has continuously attracted the interest of psychologists (see Baldwin, 1895; Bandura, 1986; Guillaume, [1926] 1971; Miller and Dollard, 1941; Piaget, [1945] 1962; Vinter, 1985). It has been given many theoretical interpretations, and many attempts have been made to pin it down empirically (for a review, see Uzgiris, 1981). The highlighting of different facets of imitation (such as the learning of new behaviors, facilitation of social conformity, and mimicry) has led to different evaluations of its role in development. It is not my intent here to review either the theoretical views or the methodological controversies concerning imitation. My interest in imitation stems from its interpersonal aspects and pertains to its occurrence during the early years of life (Uzgiris, 1984). Imitative interactions have a number of characteristics that permit them to be viewed as a microcosm of early interaction in general.

An Interpersonal Perspective on Imitation. An imitative interaction refers to the production of similar acts in close temporal sequence by two partners engaged with each other. Because in such a case the acts need not be novel for either partner and no acquisition of acts by either partner need be implied, the term *matching* may be preferable to *imitation.* Nonetheless, imitation is the more familiar term, and even matching, through enactment, may contribute to new understanding or skill. Therefore, in this chapter, the term *imitation* is retained.

When imitation is viewed as part of interpersonal interaction, several characteristics become apparent. Imitation involves a social encounter; the model is usually present to observe and to react to the imitation of his or her acts. Even in delayed imitation, the model is often part of the situation in which the actual imitation takes place. Interpersonal imitation also has a sequential pattern and extends over time: The model's act is followed by the observer's act; and the sequence of modeling and imitation need not end with one repetition but may continue over several rounds. In that case, the one who first imitated becomes the model and the roles are exchanged. As in most reciprocal exchanges, the determination of who is matching whom becomes less interesting than is a characterization of the exchange itself. In such a modeling and imitation sequence, modifications of the acts may be introduced by either partner.

In interpersonal situations, imitative exchanges are also related to the ongoing interaction. The acts modeled and imitated are not arbitrary but are related to the current interests and goals of the partners. Both modeling and imitation can be selective, thereby giving a certain emphasis or direction to the exchange. Imitative interactions in infancy often have this theme-and-variations quality.

Clearly, imitative exchanges are only one type of complementary exchange seen during interaction. In fact, they form a relatively small proportion of the exchanges between infants and adults during the early months of life. In other types of complementary exchanges, the partners also reciprocate with each other, but the acts of one partner do not match those of the other. For example, during mother-infant interactions, a vocalization by one partner may more often be followed by a different vocalization than by a matched vocalization, or a hand bang may more often be followed by vocalization than by hand banging. However, the importance of matching does not lie in its frequency.

Matching is one means through which to share an experience with a preverbal infant and to overtly indicate that an experience in common has been attained, for an imitative exchange creates a behavioral similarity that is open to be perceived and grasped by both partners. Moreover, even in other complementary exchanges, on close inspection one can find aspects that are being matched. For example, many of the attunements described by Stern (1985) seem to contain a matching of tempo or affective tone, although the content of the acts differs. Thus, in the examples given above, a vocalization differing in sound may be matched in pitch and a vocal response to banging may match the rhythm of the motor acts. Nevertheless, there are also exchanges that are clearly antagonistic, manipulative, or irrelevant; matching exchanges do not epitomize the nature of early interactions, but they exhibit many characteristics that make early interactions important for development.

Mother-Infant Imitation. In recent years, there have been numerous studies of infant imitation, but their goals have differed from those stated in this chapter. They generally have aimed either to assess infant abilities to process information in particular ways or to determine the adequacy of theoretical accounts of infant imitation; therefore, they have involved highly controlled or experimental situations (Meltzoff and Moore, 1983). There have been very few studies of imitation in infancy during relatively unconstrained interactions (see Pawlby, 1977).

The data to be presented here are derived from a study of mother-infant interactions during the first year of life (Užgiris, 1984). The interactions took place in a laboratory and were videorecorded. Only the mother and her infant were in the room during the recording. The mothers were instructed to play with their infants as they normally did; the only restriction was that mother and child were to try to stay seated, facing each other. The face-to-face interactions lasted an average of about eleven minutes. Only some aspects of the obtained results are pertinent to the present discussion and thus are reported here.

Periods of interpersonal involvement accounted for about 64 percent of interaction time. Imitation or matching episodes were coded within periods of interpersonal involvement and were defined as those exchanges in which one partner repeated the act of the other partner exactly or approximately within a two-second interval and without other intervening activity. Both vocal and motoric actions were counted. One act was considered to be a turn; an act by one partner and a matching act by the other were considered a round. Thus a matching episode consisted of at least one round, but it also could contain a greater number of rounds or additional turns by one of the partners. Matching of vocalizations, motoric acts, and their combinations were counted. There were four age groups in the study, consisting of twenty mother-infant dyads in each group. The ages of the infants averaged two and one-half months, five and one-half months, eight and one-half months, and eleven and one-half months in each group, respectively, with an equal number of boys and girls per group. The social and economic status of the families was above average.

The first finding of note was that imitative episodes were observed for all age groups, but their frequency did increase with infant age. Although mothers matched the acts of their infants in all groups, older infants matched the acts of their mothers more often than did younger ones. However, matching by the mothers of older infants also was more frequent, so that both partners were responsible for the overall increase in matching activity (see Table 14.1). The changes in imitation during the first year of life thus reflect the mutuality existing between mother and infant. A more detailed examination of imitative exchanges also reveals an increasing reciprocity and symmetry between the partners during this period.

The increasing reciprocity between the partners is shown by the increased length of imitative episodes with age. The performance of the same act once by each partner was considered to be one round and was the minimal exchange for a matching episode. If a mother matched her infant's act and the infant did not reciprocate, the episode was counted as one round in length. For an episode to be counted as two rounds in length, each partner had to perform the

**Table 14.1. Mean Number of Matching Episodes
During Interpersonal Interaction.**

Age of infants by group (months)	Infant's act matched by mother	Mother's act matched by infant	All episodes
2½	4.8	0.9	5.7
5½	5.2	0.6	5.8
8½	8.2	2.4	10.6
11½	11.7	3.5	15.2

act at least twice. Thus if an infant matched the mother's act, the mother reciprocated, and the infant matched a second time, the episode was counted as two rounds in length. Most of the observed episodes were one round in length for all age groups; however, two- and three-round episodes constituted about 25 percent of all imitative episodes in the two older groups.

It may be argued that a one-round episode in which the infant's act is matched by the mother is fundamentally different from a one-round episode in which the mother's act is matched by the infant or from a two-round episode in terms of the infant's contribution to the matching activity. An episode in which the mother matches her infant's act may be less compelling as evidence of mutuality than would be an episode in which the infant in turn matches the mother. Therefore, the greater frequency of one-round episodes in which the mother's act is matched by the infant and of two-round and longer episodes among the two older groups supports the claim of increasing mutuality in mother-infant interaction.

The essential symmetry of imitative exchanges is indicated by the similar number of turns taken by the two partners during a matching episode. In all groups, about 50 percent of the turns were taken by each partner (see Table 14.2). There were two types of additional turns that were observed: ending turns and repeated turns. That is, after completing a round, one partner could take another turn that, if not reciprocated, ended the episode but gave that partner an additional turn; or the partner could repeat the act once more, taking two turns in a row, and, if the partner then reciprocated, have a repeated turn. Table 14.2 shows that additional turns were more frequent for the mothers, especially among the groups with younger infants. However, in the two older-infant groups, the infants also took some additional turns, which largely consisted of repeated turns. This demonstrates that the older infants reciprocated more not only by being the first to match their mothers' acts and by extending episodes started by their mothers but also by more actively regulating such imitative exchanges through the repetition of turns when their partners did not respond immediately.

Taken together, these findings show that matching activity becomes more extensive and more reciprocal as the infant's first year

Table 14.2. Mean Number of Turns During Matching Episodes.

Age of infants by group (months)	Total turns		Additional turns	
	Mother	Infant	Mother	Infant
2½	6.8	6.6	0.5	0.2
5½	8.7	8.3	1.3	0.3
8½	15.6	14.9	2.4	1.0
11½	23.2	21.7	3.6	1.6

of life progresses. In the context of interpersonal interaction, matching serves as a means for communicating with the partner. The basic meaning that matching conveys is mutuality or sharing of a feeling, understanding, or goal. It serves to affirm the act of the partner in the context of the ongoing engagement and to increase the symmetry of the relationship. During the infant-adult interaction, matching may serve as a stepping-stone in the child's achievement of more conventional means of communication by helping to establish, first, that some states and interests can be shared by others and, second, that specific acts can be mutually understood to express those shared states or interests.

In my view, a fruitful direction for gaining knowledge about human development lies in the study of interaction between children and others present in their world. For it is through interaction with others that even the impersonal aspects of the world are recognized and given meaning and status for the child. However, the study of interactions requires both a theoretical and a methodological reorientation. Some of the implications of focusing on interactions in the study of development are sketched in the concluding section.

An Interactive Approach to Development

An interactive approach to understanding human development necessitates both conceptual and methodological shifts (see Rogoff and Gauvain, 1986). In this approach, attributions concerning individuals become subordinated to characterizations of interpersonal relations, and analyses of individual attainments become embedded in analyses of the dynamics of functioning. Above all, if this approach is to be productive, the treatment of empirical observations must become commensurate with conceptualization.

Studies of infant development from the standpoint of interpersonal interaction have become more prevalent only within the last decade. Our research on imitative exchanges between mothers and infants described in this chapter merely illustrates one aspect of this type of study. As a whole, these studies highlight three characteristics of development during infancy.

First, above all, the interactions between infants and adults are grounded in mutuality. Although the exchanges between infants and adults may involve only protocommunication during the early months, they still involve an exchange of shared affect and activity. Without the assumption on the part of parents that their expressions and actions have a meaning for their child and that the child's acts can be interpreted in the usual fashion, an interpersonal relationship could not begin. During matching exchanges in our study, the overt display of similar acts could be apprehended by both partners. With age, the production of matching exchanges became more evenly shared by both partners, but they were available for the expression of accord in the relationship from the first months of life.

Second, although the early interactions may be asymmetrical in the sense that the mother adjusts her actions more to the limited understanding and skill of the infant in order to maintain the flow of the interaction, development is characterized by the progression toward greater symmetry. Whether in the choice of interest, the direction of the interaction, or the contribution to its flow, infants become increasingly equal partners during the first months of life. This was evident in the matching exchanges. In the second part of the first year, infants were more often the first to match their mother's acts, and they were more likely to continue the matching activity started by their mothers. Moreover, the higher frequency of matching activity between infants and adults might be taken as an indication of greater symmetry in their relationship as well, because a matching exchange may be viewed as the epitome of a symmetrical relation.

Third, the course of development in infancy is marked by transitions from interactions that appear to embody a particular understanding or skill, but in which the contribution of the infant to its manifestation is not completely certain, to interactions in which the contribution of both partners cannot be doubted. These transitions are sometimes viewed as indications that the infant's capacities for certain kinds of actions must mature or must be attained—with due warning against their illusory attribution at too young an age. In contrast, those who emphasize the achievement of competence in the course of interaction with others see the early manifestations of capacities during interaction not as illusory but as basic evidence that the support and guidance of more competent others is the frame for human development. This position has been argued by Kaye (1982) with respect to the development of representation. It is also the perspective argued by Vygotsky (1978).

My point in underlining this characteristic is to stress that in emphasizing the supporting and guiding role of adults we run the risk of overlooking the role of the child's actual performance of the actions involved. By being guided through an activity, the child experiences the performance of that activity and can learn from that performance. The essential part of what is learned may not be the specific acts of one or the other partner but the schema for the activity as a whole, which can then be used by the child to regulate participation in similar activities in the future. It is the achievement of a clearer understanding of the whole that may underlie the appearance of a more certain possession of some understanding or skill.

In terms of such enactment, matching exchanges can be very important. The model can help the observer perform a particular act, and, having performed it, the observer may have a better grasp of it. Extended matching episodes in which the performance of specific acts can be adjusted and perfected may be particularly important in helping the child bridge transitions from understanding acts to understanding the schemas of activities.

Interactive competence possessed by human beings may be no less basic than linguistic competence or communicative competence. In child development, we might set for ourselves the task of reconstructing the rules for interaction implicitly known by infants, children, and adults. As Chomsky (1965) has gone about delineating grammatical rules fundamental to linguistic ability and Habermas

(1979) is proposing to delineate the rules fundamental to the ability to communicate, it may be no less important to delineate the rules fundamental to human ability to interact interpersonally from the earliest days of life. Infants do not function interpersonally as well as adults, but they are active participants and learners, becoming more competent as they perform in interactions.

Tomorrow

Studies of children in interaction with others are becoming more prominent on the research horizon and are likely to remain important as the social and cultural lineaments of human activities continue to be investigated. It is important, however, to distinguish the study of interpersonal interaction as a basic form of human activity from the study of contextual effects on various activities in a social setting. The latter requires a less radical change in conception and methods, but the study of the dynamics of interaction is likely to yield greater returns in terms of understanding human competencies and their development.

Sensitivity to the pervasive influence of social and cultural conditions promises new understanding of the plasticity and the limits of human competencies. The reality grasped by the human mind is seen to be sculpted by the cultural context (Lakoff, 1987). In the pursuit of contextual effects, however, there is the possibility of forgetting the developmental perspective. It seems easier to adopt static definitions of competencies in order to study their realization in different contexts. But human competencies are not static. They have the potential for development—and not only during child-hood. A focus on how incipient competencies are practiced, particularized, and perfected may best reveal the subtleties of the workings of the human mind.

References

Anderson, B. J., Vietze, P., and Dokecki, P. R. "Reciprocity in Vocal Interactions of Mothers and Infants." *Child Development,* 1977, *48,* 1676–1681.

Bakeman, R., and Brown, J. V. "Behavioral Dialogues: An

Approach to the Assessment of Mother-Infant Interaction." *Child Development,* 1977, *48,* 195–203.

Bakeman, R., and Gottman, J. M. *Observing Interactions: An Introduction to Sequential Analysis.* Cambridge, England: Cambridge University Press, 1986.

Baldwin, J. M. *Mental Development in the Child and the Race.* New York: Macmillan, 1895.

Bandura, A. *Social Foundations of Thought and Action.* Englewood Cliffs, N.J.: Prentice-Hall, 1986.

Bateson, M. C. "Mother-Infant Exchanges: The Epigenesis of Conversational Interaction." *Annals of the New York Academy of Sciences,* 1975, *263,* 101–113.

Bell, R. Q. "A Reinterpretation of the Direction of Effects in Studies of Socialization." *Psychological Review,* 1968, *75,* 81–95.

Bell, R. Q., and Harper, L. V. *Child Effects on Adults.* New York: Wiley, 1977.

Brazelton, T. B., Koslowski, B., and Main, M. "The Origins of Reciprocity." In M. Lewis and L. A. Rosenblum, *Origins of Behavior.* Vol. 1: *The Effect of the Infant on Its Caregiver.* New York: Wiley, 1974.

Bruner, J. S. "Learning How to Do Things with Words." In J. S. Bruner and A. Garton (eds.), *Human Growth and Development.* Oxford, England: Clarendon Press, 1978.

Bruner, J. S., and Sherwood, V. "Peek-a-Boo and the Learning of Rule Structures." In J. Bruner, A. Jolly, and K. Sylva (eds.), *Play—Its Role in Development and Evolution.* New York: Basic Books, 1976.

Chomsky, N. *Aspects of the Theory of Syntax.* Cambridge, Mass.: MIT Press, 1965.

Cohn, J. F., and Tronick, E. "Three-Month-Old Infants' Reaction to Simulated Maternal Depression." *Child Development,* 1983, *54,* 185–193.

Dixon, S. D., and others. "Early Infant Social Interaction with Parents and Strangers." *Journal of the American Academy of Child Psychiatry,* 1981, *20,* 32–52.

Duncan, S., and Fiske, D. W. *Interaction Structure and Strategy.* Cambridge, Mass.: Cambridge University Press, 1985.

Fafouti-Milenkovic, M., and Užgiris, I. Č. "The Mother-Infant

Communication System." In I. Č. Užgiris (ed.), *Social Interaction and Communication During Infancy*. New Directions for Child Development, no. 4. San Francisco: Jossey-Bass, 1979.

Fogel, A. "The Effect of Brief Separations on Two-Month-Old Infants." *Infant Behavior and Development*, 1980, *3*, 315–330.

Fogel, A., Diamond, G. R., Langhorst, B. H., and Demos, V. "Affective and Cognitive Aspects of Two-Month-Olds' Participation in Face-to-Face Interaction with the Mother." In E. Z. Tronick (ed.), *Social Interchange in Infancy*. Baltimore, Md.: University Park Press, 1982.

Freedle, R., and Lewis, M. "Prelinguistic Conversations." In M. Lewis and L. A. Rosenblum (eds.), *Interaction, Conversation, and the Development of Language*. New York: Wiley, 1977.

Guillaume, P. *Imitation in Children*. Chicago: University of Chicago Press, 1971. (Originally published 1926.)

Habermas, J. *Communication and the Evolution of Society*. Boston: Beacon Press, 1979.

Howard, R. A. *Dynamic Probabilistic Systems*. Vol. 2: *Semi-Markov and Decision Processes*. New York: Wiley, 1971.

Kaye, K. "Toward the Origins of Dialogue." In H. R. Schaffer (ed.), *Studies in Mother-Infant Interaction*. Orlando, Fla.: Academic Press, 1977.

Kaye, K. *The Mental and Social Life of Babies*. Chicago: University of Chicago Press, 1982.

Kaye, K., and Fogel, A. "The Temporal Structure of Face-to-Face Communication Between Mothers and Infants." *Developmental Psychology*, 1980, *16*, 454–464.

Kruper, J. C., and Užgiris, I. Č. "Fathers' and Mothers' Speech to Young Infants." *Journal of Psycholinguistic Research*, 1987, *16*, 597–614.

Lakoff, G. *Women, Fire, and Dangerous Things: What Categories Reveal About the Mind*. Chicago: University of Chicago Press, 1987.

Leach, P. J., and Costello, A. J. "A Twin Study of Infant-Mother Interaction." In F. J. Mönks, W. W. Hartup, and J. de Wit (eds.), *Determinants of Behavioral Development*. Orlando, Fla.: Academic Press, 1972.

Lewis, M., and Rosenblum, L. A. *Origins of Behavior.* Vol. 1: *The Effect of the Infant on Its Caregiver.* New York: Wiley, 1974.

Macmurray, J. *Persons in Relation.* London: Faber and Faber, 1961.

Martin, B. "Parent-Child Relations." In F. D. Horowitz (ed.), *Review of Child Development Research.* Vol. 4. Chicago: University of Chicago Press, 1975.

Meltzoff, A. N., and Moore, M. K. "The Origins of Imitation in Infancy: Paradigm, Phenomena, and Theories." In L. P. Lipsitt (ed.), *Advances in Infancy Research.* Vol. 2. Norwood, N.J.: Ablex, 1983.

Miller, N. E., and Dollard, J. *Social Learning and Imitation.* New Haven, Conn.: Yale University Press, 1941.

Moss, H. A. "Sex, Age, and State as Determinants of Mother-Infant Interaction." *Merrill-Palmer Quarterly,* 1967, *13,* 19-36.

Ninio, A., and Bruner, J. S. "The Achievement and Antecedents of Labelling." *Journal of Child Language,* 1978, *5,* 1-15.

Osofsky, J. D., and O'Connell, E. J. "Parent-Child Interaction: Daughters' Effects upon Mothers' and Fathers' Behaviors." *Developmental Psychology,* 1972, *7,* 157-168.

Papoušek, M., and others. "Vocal Matching in Turns and in Unison in Dialogues Between Mothers and Infants of Presyllabic Age and Its Significance for the Development of Speech." Poster presented at the Fifth Biennial International Conference on Infant Studies, Los Angeles, April 1986.

Pawlby, S. J. "Imitative Interaction." In H. R. Schaffer (ed.), *Studies in Mother-Infant Interaction.* Orlando, Fla.: Academic Press, 1977.

Piaget, J. *Play, Dreams and Imitation in Childhood.* New York: Norton, 1962. (Originally published 1945.)

Ratner, N., and Bruner, J. S. "Games, Social Exchange, and the Acquisition of Language." *Journal of Child Language,* 1978, *5,* 391-401.

Rheingold, H. L. "The Social and Socializing Infant." In D. A. Goslin (ed.), *Handbook of Socialization Theory and Research.* Skokie, Ill.: Rand McNally, 1969.

Rogoff, B., and Gauvain, M. "A Method for the Analysis of Patterns, Illustrated with Data on Mother-Child Instructional

Interaction." In J. Valsiner (ed.), *The Individual Subject and Scientific Psychology.* New York: Plenum, 1986.

Rogoff, B., and Wertsch, J. V. (eds.). *Children's Learning in the "Zone of Proximal Development."* New Directions for Child Development, no. 23. San Francisco: Jossey-Bass, 1984.

Sackett, G. P. "The Lag Sequential Analysis of Contingency and Cyclicity in Behavioral Interaction Research." In J. D. Osofsky (ed.), *Handbook of Infant Development.* New York: Wiley, 1979.

Sameroff, A. G. "Early Influences on Development: Fact or Fancy?" *Merrill-Palmer Quarterly,* 1975, *21,* 267–294.

Schaffer, H. R. (ed.). *Studies in Mother-Infant Interaction.* Orlando, Fla.: Academic Press, 1977.

Schaffer, H. R. *The Child's Entry into a Social World.* Orlando, Fla.: Academic Press, 1984.

Sears, R. R., Maccoby, E. E., and Levin, H. *Patterns of Child Rearing.* New York: Harper & Row, 1957.

Stern, D. N. "Mother and Infant at Play: The Dyadic Interaction Involving Facial, Vocal, and Gaze Behaviors." In M. Lewis and L. A. Rosenblum, *Origins of Behavior.* Vol. 1: *The Effect of the Infant on Its Caregiver.* New York: Wiley, 1974.

Stern, D. N. *The First Relationship: Infant and Mother.* Cambridge, Mass.: Harvard University Press, 1977.

Stern, D. N. *The Interpersonal World of the Infant.* New York: Basic Books, 1985.

Stern, D. N., and Gibbon, J. "Temporal Expectancies of Social Behaviors in Mother-Infant Play." In E. B. Thoman (ed.), *Origins of the Infant's Social Responsiveness.* Hillsdale, N.J.: Erlbaum, 1979.

Stern, D. N., Jaffe, J., Beebe, B., and Bennett, S. L. "Vocalizing in Unison and in Alternation." *Annals of the New York Academy of Sciences,* 1975, *263,* 89–100.

Stone, L. J., Smith, H. T., and Murphy, L. B. (eds.). *The Competent Infant.* New York: Basic Books, 1973.

Trevarthen, C. "Conversation with a Two-Month-Old." *New Scientist,* 1974, *62,* 230–235.

Trevarthen, C. "Descriptive Analyses of Infant Communicative Behavior." In H. R. Schaffer (ed.), *Studies in Mother-Infant Interaction.* Orlando, Fla.: Academic Press, 1977.

Tronick, E. (ed.). *Social Interchange in Infancy.* Baltimore, Md.: University Park Press, 1982.

Tronick, E., and others. "The Infant's Response to Entrapment Between Contradictory Messages in Face-to-Face Interaction." *Journal of the American Academy of Child Psychiatry,* 1978, *17,* 1–13.

Užgiris, I. Č. (ed.). *Social Interaction and Communication During Infancy.* New Directions for Child Development, no. 4. San Francisco: Jossey-Bass, 1979.

Užgiris, I. Č. "Two Functions of Imitation During Infancy." *International Journal of Behavioral Development,* 1981, *4,* 1–12.

Užgiris, I. Č. "Imitation in Infancy: Its Interpersonal Aspects." In M. Perlmutter (ed.), *The Minnesota Symposia on Child Psychology.* Vol. 17: *Parent-Child Interactions and Parent-Child Relations in Child Development.* Hillsdale, N.J.: Erlbaum, 1984.

Užgiris, I. Č., and Fafouti-Milenkovic, M. "Over het Verband Tussen Methode en Theorie bij Onderzoek naar Ouderkind Interaktie" [The Tie Between Methodology and Theory in the Study of Parent-Infant Interaction]. In J. de Wit, H. J. Groenendaal, and J. M. van Meel (eds.), *Psychologen Over het Kind* [Psychologists Discuss Children]. Vol. 8. Lisse, The Netherlands: Swets & Zeitlinger, 1985.

van Hooff, J.A.R. "Categories and Sequences of Behavior: Methods of Description and Analysis." In K. R. Scherer and P. Ekman (eds.), *Handbook of Methods in Nonverbal Behavior Research.* Cambridge, England: Cambridge University Press, 1982.

Vinter, A. *L'Imitation chez le nouveau-né* [Newborn imitation]. Neuchâtel, Switzerland: Delachaux and Niestlé, 1985.

Vygotsky, L. S. *Thought and Language.* Cambridge, Mass.: MIT Press, 1962. (Originally published 1934.)

Vygotsky, L. S. *Mind in Society: The Development of Higher Psychological Processes.* (M. Cole, V. John-Steiner, S. Scribner, and E. Souberman, eds.) Cambridge, Mass.: Harvard University Press, 1978.

Wertsch, J. V. *Vygotsky and the Social Formation of Mind.* Cambridge, Mass.: Harvard University Press, 1985.

Yarrow, L. J. "Research in Dimensions of Early Maternal Care." *Merrill-Palmer Quarterly,* 1963, *9,* 101–114.

Chapter 15

Toddlers' Peer Relations: Shared Meaning and Semantics

Edward Mueller

 The beginnings of peer relations in babies and toddlers have been studied for over ten years. A general review of what we have learned has been presented by Hartup (1983). Specific reviews concerning the underlying cognitive changes implied in early peer interactions (Brownell, 1986) and the developmental status of peer relations compared with parent-child relations (Hay, 1985) have also appeared. Clearly much has been learned, and this is not the place to review this knowledge.

My goal in this chapter is more critical: I will challenge some of the conclusions of these prior reviews and suggest that a redirection of peer research is needed. The direction I find promising involves the intensive study of toddler meaning, or semantics. I will show that this approach may clarify some central problem areas in our understanding of peers—specifically how

Note: This chapter was written while I was a visiting professor at the University of Rome. Support for this visit from the Departimento di Psicologia dei Processi di Sviluppo e Socializzazione is gratefully acknowledged. Support from the MacArthur Foundation and from Boston University for the presentation in Tokyo for an earlier version of this paper is also acknowledged with thanks. I would also like to thank Professor Luigia Camaioni, University of Rome, for discussing her research with me in such helpful detail.

children become friends and how early peer relations relate to early parent-child relations.

I have organized this discussion into three substantive problem areas, each stated in the form of a question. I see these questions as the central issues of interest to developmental researchers today.

Problem 1: Have the Cognitive Changes Underlying Developments in Early Peer Relations Been Demonstrated Conclusively?

General Combinatorial Capacity. Writing in *Child Development,* Celia Brownell (1986) recently summarized attempts to uncover the cognitive bases of early peer relations. She reports that two general cognitive correlates of changes in peer skills have been established. One is the increasing ability to integrate previously established actions into smooth sequences or combinations. For example, our own research has often pointed to the relative increase in coordinated, socially directed behaviors among toddler peers over time (see Mueller and Brenner, 1977). Brownell points out that such combinations have been demonstrated in many domains of toddler functioning, leading to the notion that the second year of life is a period marked by the emergence of a general combinatorial capacity (Fenson and Ramsay, 1981).

I wish to call into question both the uniqueness and the generality of this general combinatorial capacity. Regarding uniqueness, it must be demonstrated that more change in combinatorial abilities occurs at the toddler age than at some other developmental period. Such demonstrations are lacking in the existing studies. They are needed because from Piaget's research we know that there is great development in combinatorial ability at an even earlier age—infancy—leaving in doubt whether the changes observed in toddlers reflect any fundamental cognitive change. In other words, it seems possible to hold the view that the increase in combinatorial abilities exhibited in toddlerhood simply illustrates the Wernerian principle that development moves in the direction of increasing differentiation and integration. Perhaps combinatorial abilities develop during infancy and simply attain gradual expression in ever more diversified social relationships during toddlerhood.

Regarding generality, it must be demonstrated that the supposed underlying "new cognitive ability" expresses itself across different functional domains (for instance, peer play versus toy play) at the same developmental time for a given child, with significant interchild variation in time of the general emergence. Existing studies do not seem to satisfy either the uniqueness or the generality criteria, leaving the general combinatorial hypothesis for toddlerhood in doubt.

Decentration. The second general cognitive hypothesis discussed by Brownell is the decentration hypothesis. Decentration is defined as "the child's ability to conceive of objects and actions as independent of herself and her own action schemes or the ability to represent self as one sort of object among, but distinct from, all other objects" (Brownell, 1986, p. 278).

Even when one allows for some inherent vagueness in this Piagetian definition, Brownell's treatment of decentration seems obscure. For example, she suggests that the well-documented decrease in object-mediated peer play across the second year supports the idea of decentration. Yet it seems just as plausible to maintain that object-mediated peer play, involving as it does the coordination of the toy with the peer, must itself represent the product of major decentration at an earlier time. Or, to approach the matter from the other side of development, what if one maintains that the real decentration occurs only when the child accommodates his or her social behavior to the social needs of others as frequently as his or her social action emanates from personal needs of the self? In this case, the Shugar and Bokus (1986) data would suggest that one-year-olds have not yet begun to decenter their peer activity. This research implies that toddlers only join with peers when it suits what is of interest to them at the moment.

In short, the hypothesis of decentration change seems to suffer from the same vagueness and lack of specificity to the toddler period as does the hypothesis of a special combinatorial advance at this age. There is no conclusive evidence from the peer literature that the child can decenter his or her action in major new ways just because he or she can now interact with peers. My own position is that we do better to reserve the term *decentration* for describing the relatively clear changes in the transition from primary to secondary circular reactions, which, of course, occurs well before the second year.

In summary, the combinatorial and decentration hypotheses emerging on the basis of Piaget's research have surely received some support in the peer research of the last two decades, but definitive demonstrations of their exact functioning in the peer relations of toddlers is lacking. Brownell's useful summary surely demonstrates the promise of this approach, but, for some reason, the crucial demonstrations needed have not appeared.

Semantic Primacy. Given the productivity of the Piagetian hypotheses in advancing our knowlege of early peer relations in the 1970s, one may ask whether any similar cognitive-linguistic hypotheses have emerged more recently that might do the same thing again. Perhaps this question may be answered in the affirmative by considering the "semantic primacy hypothesis" from philosophy and psycholinguistics.

As early as 1972, Macnamara (quoted in Snow, 1977, p. 41) proposed that "children are able to learn to talk because they can work out the meaning of the sentences they hear independent of the sentences themselves." Within psycholinguistics, then, semantic primacy is simply the view that the understanding of meaning develops earlier than do other linguistic structures, such as syntax and phonetics.

In one sense, the semantic primacy hypothesis is but a restatement of the still-valid principle that "comprehension precedes production." But this old formulation was too restricted to the linguistic system: It begged the question of where comprehension came from in the first place. It was still possible to believe that understanding meaning was simply a matter of hearing words spoken; language remained, as it were, a self-sufficient or "closed" system.

Semantic primacy rejects such a view and forces us to look to the child's prior knowledge of the world for the basis of his or her initial comprehension of meaning. The hypothesis is receiving empirical support, including van der Geest's (1977) demonstration that children's language is more semantically complex than is that which their mothers direct back to them and Shatz and Gelman's (1977) evidence that older children's speech modifications to young children are based more on semantic considerations than on grammatical ones. Snow (1977) suggested that mothers can facilitate language learning by picking up on and developing the topics that their children introduce. It appears that the topic or meaning of an interaction must be present in the child first before the mother can effectively scaffold onto it.

In short, semantic primacy suggests that there is a system of meaning that precedes verbal communication and that this system may be crucial in understanding the emergence of language. Perhaps toddler peer communication, where two preverbal children are both at approximately the same level in their understanding of meaning, is a good place to study the nature and development of early semantics in general.

When such study is conducted (Brenner and Mueller, 1982), a rather curious result emerges: Meaning seems to be more easily identifiable in social interaction than in social action. In other words, when one watches one-year-olds in a play group, one frequently sees them directing behaviors (looks, smiles, hits, object takes) to others toddlers. Yet one is hard pressed to say what these behaviors mean to the toddler producing them. For example, when a child takes a toy from a peer, does he or she mean to assert possession rights in a social gesture, or does he or she merely wish to have the toy for his or her own purposes?

It is only in social interaction itself that social meaning becomes clear, and it becomes clear precisely when it is shared. That is, when two toddlers agree on the topic of an interaction between them (such as peek-a-boo or run-chase; for the complete list of shared meanings observed, see Table 15.1, p. 321), the interaction becomes meaningful to the observer in the sense that the observer could take the place of one of the interactants and the topic could be continued unchanged.

Thus social meanings turn out to be the abstract, representational topics that underlie meaningful social interactions. They may be *the* natural cognitive units of social development. They are "cognitive" both in the Piagetian sense of being more general or representational than is action and in the Miller, Galanter, and

Pribram (1960) sense of being relatively enduring plans or goals guiding action. The notion that "meaning" is very close to the concept of "purpose" or "goal" is a view I have defended elsewhere (see Mueller, 1986).

There are several reasons why social meanings differ from social actions. In the first place, the specific behaviors performed in the service of a given meaning become flexible. For example, in a peek-a-boo game, it hardly matters whether the child hides by running behind a curtain or by pulling a towel over his or her face. It hardly matters whether the other child laughs at the child's sudden appearance or merely smiles and jumps excitedly. The specifics of action, while constrained, become freed, and this is why attempts to predict human interaction as Markovian sequences of particular behaviors must, I believe, inevitably be found to be inadequate.

In the second place, social meaning is always more abstract than are individual social acts. No single action can communicate the meaning of a social encounter between toddlers. The meaning of a social encounter can be signaled, but it cannot yet be symbol-ized, because toddler communication is presymbolic. For example, suppose that a child wishes to play "run-chase" with a peer. The child can make a dash at his or her partner with exaggerated facial gestures, or he or she can suddenly run away from the partner with looks and smiles over the shoulder. The child has thus signaled the meaning by enactment of the two complementary roles that make up run-chase. But he or she cannot communicate the entire game because he or she lacks the symbolic phrase "run-chase." Language, of course, proves to be a much more efficient means of communicat-ing meanings than the enactment of roles ever could be.

The basic point is that social meaning proves to be something very different from social action—necessarily more representational and goal-like and seemingly very closely tied to social interaction, at least in the sense that it is most readily identified in this context in our research on toddler peer behavior. (At the same time, I should stress that I do not wish to restrict the concept of "meaning" to its social context for reasons discussed in Mueller, 1986.)

In summary, the general hypothesis developed here is that the greatest advances in our knowledge of the cognitive organization of peer processes will emerge not by conceiving of cognition only in structural units, such as "coordination" and "decentration," but rather by reconceiving it in meaningful functional units, such as "object possession struggle" and "point and name." The structure of an interaction will be found to follow from its meaning, not the reverse. For example, object exchange must have a complementary organization (where receiving complements offering), because two toddlers cannot successfully offer things to each other at once. Motor copy, in contrast, involves no behavioral complementarity and includes simultaneity in place of turn taking.

There are many pitfalls in this semantic approach. One is to assume that social interaction is the source of all social meaning. My guess is that this is wrong because it ignores the fact that babies are not neutral machines with no goals of their own: They are biological systems with intrinsic goals or drives. Thus it is the concordance of goals between toddlers that generates shared meanings from individual meanings, rather than the reverse. Take, for example, the shared meaning of "peek-a-boo." In this game, one partner, say the mother, hides and then reappears suddenly. The infant partner seems to obtain delight and joy at the reappearance. Perhaps we can hypothesize that this game relates to the fundamental need of the infant to remain in visual contact with the mother (attachment), on the emotional side, and to understand the mother's—and indeed all objects'—permanent existence (object permanence), on the cognitive side. It is *not* that the child develops attachment goals or object permanence goals because of peek-a-boo. To the contrary, peek-a-boo becomes one of the primary peer games because the meanings underlying it are so primary in the infant's goal hierarchy. Elsewhere I have made the same argument for the shared meaning of "object possession struggle," suggesting that it relates to the growing motive to possess objects in the second year (Mueller, 1986).

In summary, meaning is coherence of purpose in the child (Mueller, 1986), a coherence that always reflects the child's developmental goals and interests more than it reflects any actual need to accommodate to peer activity (see Shugar and Bokus, 1986; Ladd and Emerson, 1984). Nevertheless, the shared meanings present in the early social relations may give us insight into the emerging organization of infant goals.

Problem 2: What Is the Relationship Between Parent-Child Relations and the Early Emergence of Peer Relations?

In recent years, the social development literature has seen a debate between those who see peer relations as a largely separate system in early social development (see Lewis and Schaeffer, 1981) and those who adhere to the Freudian hypothesis, seeing an adequate attachment to a primary caregiver as crucial in all subsequent social relations (see Sroufe, 1983). Recently peer researcher Dale Hay (1985) joined the debate on the side of those who see early peer relations as a parallel and equal system in early social development. She concludes that "children's attainments in forming attachments to parents parallel the steps they take in relating to their peers" (Hay, 1985, p. 122).

I think the early peer research has been subject to strident and unjust criticism at times from certain attachment theorists. As Hay pointed out, early peer researchers never seem to be able to get beyond trying to convince people that relations between young peers exist. Yet with her remark that attainments in attachment are paralleled by peer attainments, I think Hay has gone too far in the direction of counterattack. I do not think that such a conclusion is warranted either empirically or theoretically. While there is no question that, as Hay (1985, p. 137) maintains, peer relations change and grow across early development, there has been no demonstration that such changes parallel what is occurring in parent-child relations with respect either to the development of security or to the development of coherent sense of self (Bretherton, forthcoming).

To the contrary, one can be struck by the functional differences between parent-child and peer relations at every point in development through mid-adolescence (Mueller and Silverman, forthcoming). Throughout this period, parent-child relations have as core functions construction of the child's self-concept and senses of effectance motivation and felt security. Peer relations, in contrast, relate more closely to the development of perceived equality, cooperation, and tension management play.

I think it is possible for Hay to maintain the parallelism model partly because the attachment researchers have had too narrow a view of the functions of the parent-child relationship, focusing on the security function, and, as a consequence, they have been content to measure the relationship in too narrow a way— namely, the strange situation. The strange situation tells one too little about the child's emerging self-concept (his or her tendency to attribute positive feelings to the self and to perceive others as valuing the self) and about the typical quality of the mother and child's play. Thus, given the functional separation of parent-child and peer relations, and given the focus of parent-child research on only one particular function of the parent-child relationship, other important relations between the two social systems might have been missed in the existing research.

Take, for example, the important communicative function: the ability of two persons to share meaning. This may be the same sort of function that the attachment theorists call "goal-corrected partnerships" (Bowlby, 1982, p. 267); as such, it is usually treated as one of the later stages of attachment, whereas I will show that shared meaning appears to be part of the very origins of the mother-child relationship in the first year of life.

Among very young children, shared meaning was first studied in peer relations (Brenner and Mueller, 1982). From the time that article was published, I have been trying without success to understand shared meaning in early mother-child relations. However, recent studies by Luigia Camaioni, University of Rome, suggest that my own attempts may have failed because my subjects were always over twelve months old. Camaioni and Laicardi (1985) reported that, in their study, the major emergence of shared meanings between mother and child occurred in the second half of the first year, with no significant growth thereafter.

Camaioni and Laicardi did not derive their meaning categories from the ones in the Brenner and Mueller study; indeed, their research was conducted "blind" with respect to the Brenner and Mueller meaning types. Instead, it was their purpose to study "social games" characterized by the repetition of specific behaviors or by the presence of invariant conventional roles. The titles of seventeen types of games located in their study are presented as

Table 15.1, alongside the thirteen shared meanings identified by Brenner and Mueller. From the game titles alone, it is possible to see the striking similarity in the meanings shared between mother and child and between peers across these two wholly independent studies.

Specifically, nine of the thirteen shared meanings in the peer study were found to be present in the mother-child relation in recognizable form, and often labeled in the same way. Furthermore,

**Table 15.1. A Comparison of Early Shared Meanings
in Mother-Child and Peer-Peer Interaction.**

Mother-Child		*Peer-Peer*	
(Camaioni and Laicardi, 1985)		(Brenner and Mueller, 1982)	
1.	Tactile stimulation (tickling)	11.	Rough and tumble
2.	Perceptual stimulation (visual/acoustic)	1.	Vocal prosocial
3.	Vocal imitation	3.	Vocal copy
4.	Gestural imitation	4.	Motor copy *and*
		5.	Curtain running
5.	Give and take	8.	Object exchange
6.	Peek-a-Boo	7.	Peek-a-Boo
7.	Horsie		[absent]
8.	Pat-a-Cake		[absent]
9.	Bye-Bye		[absent]
10.	Ball	13.	Ball (Musatti and Mueller, 1985, same sample)
11.	Build–Knock down		[absent]
12.	No		[absent, but pretense games in toddler girls reported by Bragg, 1983]
13.	Point and name	12.	Shared reference
14.	Put on–take off, slip on–slip off, open-shut		[motor copy, in part]
15.	Joint book reading		[absent]
16.	Question-answer		[absent]
17.	Linguistic imitation		[vocal copy, in part]
			Peer only
		2.	Positive affect as a meaning sharer
		6.	Run-Chase
		9.	Object possession struggle
		10.	Aggression

of the shared meanings found only among peers, two would not be considered games at all, since they involve struggle or aggression, nor would mother and child be likely to engage in them in the presence of an observer. In addition, "positive affect as a meaning sharer" may well be similar to certain stimulation games (see Camaioni and Laicardi numbers 1 and 2) and should thus not be considered as missing. Thus, run-chase appears to be the only shared meaning in early peer relations that is absent from mother-child games, suggesting remarkable overlap in the meanings present in the two social systems. (I had the opportunity to study the unpublished full definitions of the meanings in the Camaioni study, and it confirms the impression of similarity observable from the game titles.)

The apparent universality or robustness of these game topics across relationships is supported by the following facts: (1) The result appeared in spite of the small sample sizes in both studies. (2) The subjects derived from different cultures: Italy and the United States. (3) Both sets of researchers were totally blind as to the categories of meaning observed by the other.

In addition, while the mother-child system included many games not found in early peer interaction (horsie, pat-a-cake, bye-bye, build–knock down, no! [playful copying of the mother's prohibitory act], joint book reading, and question-answer), all these games appear to require some physical or intellectual skill simply not present between toddler peers. For example, the game of horsie was defined as the mother bouncing her child on her knee. Obviously, it is impossible for two toddlers to engage in such a game together.

Table 15.1 also suggests that the mother-child game repertoire is better developed and at an earlier age than is the peer-peer repertoire. First, there simply were more kinds of meaningful games observed between mother and child than between peers. Second, Camaioni (1986) reports more games that were unique to specific mother-child pairs; indeed, for two of the three pairs studied, first baby words emerged during games that were unique to the pair. In contrast, no games specific to single dyads were observed by Brenner and Mueller.

Given the extreme similarity of the shared meanings identified in the two studies, it is interesting to note *when* they emerged in the two types of relationships. The results appear to support earlier emergence in mother-child relations. Specifically, Camaioni (personal communication, July 6, 1987) found that her three babies all adopted active roles (defined as playing an active role in more than 50 percent of the games at a given age) at ages ranging from eight and one-half to ten months. In contrast, Brenner and Mueller found the major increase in peer shared meaning occurring between fifteen and eighteen months.

Such results oppose the view that shared meanings are developed with equal rapidity in both parent-child and peer relations, that the two systems develop in parallel fashion with respect to meaning. These data support the contrary view that social meanings emerge first in mother-child relations, with later expression among peers only of that subset of meanings that can feasibly be extended to peers—with almost no new meanings added.

It is interesting to note that only Camaioni's conventional games (numbers 5 through 17 in Table 15.1) showed longitudinal growth. Nonconventional games (numbers 1 through 4) showed no changes either in frequency or in level of child participation. Yet it was just these nonconventional games, especially the imitative ones, that appeared with such frequency in the Brenner and Mueller peer data. Just such a difference is confirmed in a more recent peer study by Camaioni, Baumgartner, and Pascucci (forthcoming). In short, while peer and parent-child relations appear to utilize the same meaning set, peer relations retain a more highly imitative, less complementary quality well into the second year. In contrast, parent-child relations were found to be more complementary from the start.

In summary, the two studies under consideration support the view that the mother-child and peer relationships are closely related in terms of their constituent meanings. Also, because the meanings emerge earlier in the mother-child relation, at least in the cross-sectional evidence available so far, it can still be maintained that Freud was correct—that the mother-child relationship is the birthplace of social meaning itself.

More generally, I suggest that we peer researchers have failed to see this continuity in social development previously because we approached the matter with too much emphasis on cognitive-structural variables (based on Piaget) and too little regard for the functional content or semantics of actual peer interaction.

It could be that the semantic study of parent-child relations will prove to be more important than the study of attachment in uncovering the central continuities of early social development. This study of meaning is crucial, because it must somehow form the basis of the child's self-concept, as well as of the child's comprehension of the idea of meaning itself—an idea that seems critical if the child is to learn to speak. In the last analysis, it is shared meaning that is necessary if two children are truly to communicate. This corpus of sharable meanings appears to develop first between mother and child, and it may form the basis of what we call "quality of attachment" as well.

Problem 3: How Does the Sharing of Meaning Relate to Children's Friendship Formation?

The study of play and friendship is surely among the most subtle of topics approached by students of peer relations. The concept "friendship" is used in different ways in popular culture, and its very nature appears to change across development (Howes, forthcoming; Mueller and Silverman, forthcoming).

Let us begin with a straightforward proposition about the relation of friendship to shared meaning and go on to reject it later on. The proposition is this: There exists a linear relation between the number of shared meanings between two persons and the closeness of their friendship. In other words, the more shared meanings between two persons, the higher is the probability that they will nominate each other as primary friendship choice in a sociometric assessment. Space does not permit a full review of studies supporting this linear hypothesis, but let me cite two such studies.

Lederberg, Rosenblatt, and Vandell (forthcoming) studied actual outdoor play episodes in both hearing and deaf preschoolers. At least for the hearing subjects, both temporary and long-term friends matched each other's positive behaviors in play more often than did nonfriends. This study did not examine the nature of behavioral matching in detail, but it would appear reasonable to presume that shared meanings underlie the matching of behavior. Thus, speaking quantitatively, there were more shared meanings among friends than among nonfriends in a preschool sample.

Ladd and Emerson (1984) used a picture-sort procedure of personal-social characteristics to study shared knowledge among mutually preferred versus unilaterally chosen friends. (Perhaps I should clarify that the latter case did not involve friendship at all, since there was no reciprocity of preference.) In this study, first and fourth grade children were asked to select characteristics that were "descriptive of themselves and their friend" and other characteristics that were "descriptive of their friend but not of themselves."

A first interesting finding was that first graders' knowledge of their friends was essentially limited to knowledge of themselves. They seldom knew things about others that were not also present in their self-descriptions. In contrast, fourth graders also had a shared knowledge of others' unique characteristics—that is, characteristics that were not part of their self-perceptions. These findings are compatible with the view of young children as limited in peer understanding, with possible friendships corresponding to what is of interest to the self.

At both grade levels, Ladd and Emerson found—and this is the crucial finding for our purpose—that friends were more alike in their self-attributions and more accurate at predicting characteristics common to both partners than were nonfriends. The authors conclude that "shared knowledge appears to be associated with intimate or close relations in children" (1984, p. 938). Because shared knowledge and shared meanings are such similar concepts, it would appear that shared meanings increase with friendship formation. Thus the linear hypothesis receives support for children of both preschool and school ages, the latter support appearing to be more direct.

Why, given this support, do I have reservations about the linear hypothesis? Basically, I do not think it is incorrect; rather, it is incomplete, ignoring other key features of friendship formation processes, specifically the biophysical and socioemotional features. By biophysical features, I mean the fact that people do not base friendship decisions only on sharable activities and knowledge but also on personal physical features, such as gender, race, and physical appearance (Epstein, 1986). Acquainted persons with many shared interests and values may never become friends because these surface variables intervene, preventing their ever discovering their commonalities.

Just as these variables are somehow "superficial," so socioemotional variables in friendship process are somehow "deep"—sometimes even outside awareness and not usually reportable on a self-attribution scale such as the one used by Ladd and Emerson. These are the kinds of variables that give individuals their stable interpersonal styles but that also lock them into certain patterns of joining across relationships: We are all familiar with the passive-aggressive character or the schizoid personality (Shapiro, 1965). But it is not just in pathology that character is evident. We all have styles of relating to others, and we all seek out certain kinds of friendship partners and avoid others.

What I am reaching for in these concluding speculations is the idea that the linear hypothesis fails to account for the different salience of particular shared meanings to the individual in forming friendships. Duck, Miell and Gaebler (1980) have speculated that friendship is motivated by the need for self-confirmation. I take this to mean that older children and adults are attracted not merely to those with whom they can do a lot of things but, more importantly, to those who acknowledge and somehow join them with respect to their innermost needs for continuing personal growth at whatever stage they may be (Mueller and Silverman, forthcoming) in their peer relations.

Because the linear hypothesis treats all shared meanings as equal, it will never be adequate for understanding how adults form intimate friendships. For this we have to find methods for undercovering the core strivings of the self for interpersonal joining. In all probability, such strivings relate back both to the quality of the first relationships around which the core social self formed in the first place (Bretherton, forthcoming) and to the stage of peer relatedness achieved in each individual's peer development (Mueller and Silverman, forthcoming).

In summary, while the hypothesis of a linear relation between friendship and shared meaning may well prove correct for explaining the relatively superficial and activity-centered friendships of early childhood, it will never be adequate for understanding life's primary socioemotional bonds—specifically the primary bond that develops so early between caregivers and baby and the later intimate ties that develop among individuals and cross-sexed peers (Mueller and Silverman, forthcoming). For this purpose, we must look beyond the mere sharing of interests or knowledge to the recognition that deep within us there are goals for joining others in ways that somehow reflect the core of who we are as individual personalities, and that in their expression place our interpersonal meanings in the order of their true value to us. Such is the complexity, but also the promise, of the study of peer relations from the approach of meaning and shared meaning. I recommend it to you.

Conclusion

In this chapter, I have developed the view that the study of peer relations will progress most quickly if we emphasize the content or meaning of peer relations in place of their formal cognitive properties, such as action coordination and decentration. I went so far as to suggest that structural features of peer interaction, such as coaction versus turn taking and imitation versus complementarity, ultimately will be shown to follow from constraints imposed by the specific meanings of the interactions. Rather than disputing Piaget, such a view seems consonant with his belief in the role of function relative to structure (see Piaget, 1971).

Consider first what work of the past decade may endure in the future. The solid contributions of the past decade might be called cognitive-structural. I think we have done a good job of describing the structure of early peer interaction and its component socially directed behaviors. We know now that the construction of social messages is indeed a process of coordination of actions quite closely akin to that which Piaget described for the child's mastery of physical objects. In this case, the child must coordinate his or her display of content with the communicative signals (such as attention to the face of the partner) that make the content socially communicative.

The past decade has also shown us much about the context of

early peer interaction (Hartup, 1983). For example, we have repeatedly shown that physical objects play some sort of special role in the evolution of peer relations that is unlike their influence on parent-child relations. I believe that this role of objects is related to the differing function of peer relations around exploration and mastery of the world with an "equal," a special feature of the peer world.

Tomorrow

Regarding tomorrow, the most important things we still need to learn concern the relation of the peer world to the parent-child world and to play itself. We need to know whether peer relations can be emotionally compensatory for inadequate parenting (I think not) and whether the abundant time peers spend in play matters at all for their emotional or mastery development (I think so). Play itself has been shown to be important in mental health, yet the processes by which it works are poorly understood. Advances in our knowledge about play process are sure to translate into better understanding of peer process.

A more refined knowledge of the nature of peer relations can only generate better-informed intervention and social policy. The last ten years of work, demonstrating the existence of early peer interaction, are sometimes seen as supportive of day-care centers with small ratios of adults to children. Yet I have never seen convincing work showing that children under about the age of two can relate to two other children at a time, much less to twenty! The material presented in this chapter suggests a very different conclusion: that shared meaning forms first between parent and baby and only later extends to the peer world. Perhaps this is as it should be. Parents should take seriously their role in offering their babies that cradle of meaning on which later peer relations may depend.

References

Bowlby, J. *Attachment.* (2nd ed.) New York: Basic Books, 1982.

Bragg, C. "Before Shared Meaning: The Elicitation and Maintenance of Social Themes Among Toddlers." Paper presented at a meeting of the Society for Research and Child Development, Detroit, April 1983.

Brenner, J., and Mueller, E. "Shared Meaning in Boy Toddlers' Peer Relations." *Child Development,* 1982, *53,* 380–391.

Bretherton, I. "New Perspectives on Attachment Relations in Infancy: Security, Communication and Internal Working Models." In J. Osofsky (ed.), *Handbook of Infant Development.* (2nd ed.) New York: Wiley-Interscience, forthcoming.

Brownell, C. A. "Convergent Developments: Cognitive-Developmental Correlates of Growth in Infant/Toddler Peer Skills." *Child Development,* 1986, *57,* 275–286.

Camaioni, L. "From Early Interaction Patterns to Language Acquisition: Which Continuity?" In J. Cook-Gumperz, W. A. Corsaro, and J. Streeck (eds.), *Children's Worlds and Children's Language.* The Hague, The Netherlands: Mouton de Gruyter, 1986.

Camaioni, L., Baumgartner, E., and Pascucci, M. "Interazioni imitative e complementari tra bambini nel secondo anno di vita" [Complementary and imitative interactions between children aged two]. *Età evolutiva [The evolutionary years],* forthcoming.

Camaioni, L., and Laicardi, C. "Early Social Games and the Acquisition of Language." *British Journal of Developmental Psychology,* 1985, *3,* 31–39.

Duck, S., Miell, D. K., and Gaebler, H. C. "Attraction and Communication in Children's Interactions." In H. C. Foot, A. J. Chapman, and J. R. Smith (eds.), *Friendship and Social Relations in Children.* New York: Wiley, 1980.

Epstein, J. L. "Friendship Selection: Development and Environmental Influences." In E. C. Mueller and C. R. Cooper (eds.), *Process and Outcome in Peer Relationships.* Orlando, Fla.: Academic Press, 1986.

Fenson, L., and Ramsay, D. "Effects of Modeling Action Sequences on the Play of Twelve-, Fifteen-, and Nineteen-Month-Old Children." *Child Development,* 1981, *52,* 1028–1036.

Hartup, W. W. "Peer Relations." In P. Mussen (ed.), *Handbook of Child Psychology.* (4th ed.) Vol. 4. New York: Wiley, 1983.

Hay, D. F. "Learning to Form Relationships in Infancy: Parallel

Attainments with Parents and Peers." *Developmental Review,* 1985, *5,* 122–161.

Howes, C. "Social Competence in Young Children: Developmental Sequences." *Developmental Review,* forthcoming.

Ladd, G. W., and Emerson, E. S. "Shared Knowledge in Children's Friendships." *Developmental Psychology,* 1984, *20,* 932–940.

Lederberg, A. M., Rosenblatt, V., and Vandell, D. L. "Temporary and Longterm Friendships in Hearing and Deaf Preschoolers." *Merrill-Palmer Quarterly,* forthcoming.

Lewis, M. L., and Schaeffer, S. "Peer Behavior and Mother-Infant Interaction." In M. L. Lewis and S. Schaeffer (eds.), *The Uncommon Child.* New York: Plenum, 1981.

Miller, G. A., Galanter, E., and Pribram, K. H. *Plans and the Structure of Behavior.* New York: Holt, Rinehart & Winston, 1960.

Mueller, E. "Shared Meaning in Prelinguistic Communication." In I. Kurcz, G. W. Shugar, and J. H. Danks (eds.), *Knowledge and Language.* North Holland, The Netherlands: Elsevier, 1986.

Mueller, E., and Brenner, J. "The Origins of Social Skills and Interactions Among Playgroup Toddlers." *Child Development,* 1977, *48,* 854–861.

Mueller, E., and Silverman, N. "Maltreatment and Peer Relations." In D. Cicchetti and V. Carlson (eds.), *Handbook of Child Maltreatment.* New York: Cambridge University Press, forthcoming.

Musatti, T., and Mueller, E. "Expressions of Representational Growth in Toddlers' Peer Communication." *Social Cognition,* 1985, *3,* 383–399.

Piaget, J. *Biology and Knowledge.* Chicago: University of Chicago Press, 1971.

Shapiro, D. *Neurotic Styles.* New York: Basic Books, 1965.

Shatz, M., and Gelman, R. "Beyond Syntax: The Influence of Conversational Constraints on Speech Modifications." In C. E. Snow and C. A. Ferguson (eds.), *Talking to Children: Language Input and Acquisition.* Cambridge, England: Cambridge University Press, 1977.

Shugar, G. W., and Bokus, B. "Children's Discourse and Children's Activity in the Peer Situation." In E. C. Mueller and C. R.

Cooper (eds.), *Process and Outcome in Peer Relationships.* Orlando, Fla.: Academic Press, 1986.

Snow, C. E. "Mother's Speech Research: From Input to Interaction." In C. E. Snow and C. A. Ferguson (eds.), *Talking to Children: Language Input and Acquisition.* Cambridge, England: Cambridge University Press, 1977.

Sroufe, L. A. "Infant-Caregiver Attachment and Patterns of Adaptation in Preschool: The Roots of Maladaptation and Competence." In M. Gunnar and W. A. Collins (eds.), *Minnesota Symposia on Child Psychology.* Vol. 16. Hillsdale, N.J.: Erlbaum, 1983.

van der Geest, T. "Some Interactional Aspects of Language Acquisition." In C. E. Snow and C. A. Ferguson (eds.), *Talking to Children: Language Input and Acquisition.* Cambridge, England: Cambridge University Press, 1977.

Chapter 16

Friendships in
Childhood and Adolescence

Thomas J. Berndt

To many adults, the friendships of children and adolescents are endlessly fascinating. At these ages, friendships appear to exist in a kind of never-never-land, a world of fun and adventure that adults rarely if ever enter and cannot fully understand. In this case, appearances mirror reality to a fair degree. Adolescents say that they enjoy the time they spend with friends more than any other part of their days, and when they are with friends, their parents and other adults are usually absent (Csikszentmihalyi and Larson, 1984). Moreover, when children are asked whether adults have any right to control children's friendships—for example, by deciding whether any two children may be friends with each other—the children answer that friendship choice is a private or personal matter that adults should not try to regulate (Tisak, 1986).

The separation between the world of friendships and the world of adult-child relationships has had an impact on psychological research as well. Although research on children's development has a long history, friendships did not become a focus of researchers' attention until the last half of the 1970s (see Hartup, 1978). Since that time, a great deal of evidence about the development of friendships has been gathered. Indeed, a chapter of this size is far too

Note: Preparation of this chapter was supported in part by a grant from the Spencer Foundation. The foundation's support is gratefully acknowledged.

short for a complete review of current knowledge about friendships in childhood and adolescence (but see Berndt, 1988, forthcoming [a], forthcoming [b]; Hartup, 1983). Consequently, I will focus the chapter on two themes that both motivated previous research and pose questions for future research.

The first theme concerns the place of friendship in the child's social world. Friendships can be treated as basic elements in the elaborate social structure that constitutes the social world of peers. How friendships are linked to this larger social structure and how they relate to other facets of the social structure are questions pertinent to this theme. I propose that one question requiring more careful investigation is the relation between friendships and another critical facet of the peer social structure, social status or popularity.

The second theme concerns the influence of particular friends on children's and adolescents' attitudes and behavior. Most of the previous research on friends' influence has been linked to a debate over whether peers have a negative influence on adolescents—for example, by pressuring them to join in delinquent or antisocial behavior (see Berndt, forthcoming [b]; Hartup, 1983). I argue that some influence of friends is inevitable, because human beings are influenced by all other people with whom they form close relationships. I suggest, however, that friends' influence may lead to socially desirable as well as socially undesirable behavior, that the notion of peer pressure oversimplifies the variety of ways in which friends influence each other, and that certain features of friendship actually limit susceptibility to friends' influence. To test these ideas further, more systematic and programmatic research is needed on the processes of social influence among friends.

Friendships in the Social World of Peers

Occasionally, theoretical writings and research reports give the impression that friendships are divorced from the larger social world of peer relationships. Sullivan (1953), for example, emphasized the significance of the close friendships that are formed between pairs of children during the years just prior to puberty. He contrasted these close friendships with the competitive or, less often, cooperative relationships that exist among large groups of peers at earlier ages. Following Sullivan's lead, a number of researchers have attempted to identify preadolescents who have a best friendship of the type described by Sullivan and compare them with those who do not (see McGuire and Weisz, 1982). Moreover, these researchers have established a distinction between best friendships and the wider circle of peer relationships by showing that having or not having an intimate and mutually supportive friendship with another child is not strongly related to a child's popularity in the peer group as a whole. Thus the quality of the friendship between any pair of children seems to have little connection with the children's position in the larger social world of peers (see also Masters and Furman, 1981).

A closer look at both the theoretical and the empirical work on friendship indicates that this view of friendships is misleading at best. Although Sullivan (1953) began his account of preadolescent friendships by talking about the special relationships that develop between pairs of children, he continued by describing the interlocking of these friendship pairs into groups. If Mary has formed close friendships with Marsha and with Molly, for example, then Marsha and Molly are likely to also become friends with each other.

When children are asked to name their best friends, they usually name more than one other person. If they are asked explicitly whether they have one best friend or more than one, they usually say that they have more than one (Berndt and Hawkins, 1987). Children are aware of differences in degrees of friendship— for example, between their very closest friends and their other friends (Berndt and Hawkins, 1987); yet they normally think of friendships not just as relationships between pairs of children but as sets of relationships among small groups of children who frequently interact with one another.

Having more than one best friend is advantageous for children for several reasons. As Davies (1982) noted, a child with a single best friend may be left "friendless" if he or she has a quarrel with this friend and breaks off their relationship for a time. In contrast, children with several friends have someone to turn to when they are in the midst of a conflict with one friend. Similarly, children with a single friend may be left without a playmate if their friend is busy with chores or other activities. Children with more than one friend are assured of more dependable companionship.

Cohen and Wills (1985) summarized a large body of research with adults that illustrates other benefits of having several close relationships. In general, people with more relationships have greater access to valuable information. Adults who need a job, for example, are likely to hear about different job opportunities from different friends. Therefore, the more friends they have, the more opportunities they will hear about. Children do not apply for jobs, of course, but they still value information about enjoyable things to do and places to go. This information is more readily available to children with several friends.

Even friendship groups do not represent the highest level of organization of the peer social world. These groups usually are linked into larger collections or crowds (Brown and Lohr, 1987). Crowds include individuals with similar activities and interests. All of the boys in one grade who share an avid interest in sports might constitute one crowd, for example. Crowds tend to be most visible in the adolescent years, when the social organization of the peer group becomes especially complex. In American high schools, there is often one crowd that is heavily involved in athletics, another crowd known for its largely academic pursuits, a third one whose interests are primarily in social success, and a fourth that is focused on drug use or delinquent activities (Brown and Lohr, 1987).

Crowds do not exist or function in isolation from each other, because some individuals affiliate with more than one crowd. For example, a cheerleader may also be a member of the debate team at his or her school. In addition, some friendships may cross crowd boundaries. A girl who is firmly attached to the socialites in her school may still be friends with another, less popular girl, perhaps because the other girl lives in her neighborhood or because she provides her with answers on her homework assignments. The links between different groups have been charted most carefully in recent years for preschool children. After extensive observations in preschool classrooms, Strayer (1980) outlined the affiliative networks that linked children in each classroom to each other. Some children were part of groups characterized by frequent, mutually initiated interactions. The strong ties between these children seemed to reflect the existence of a close friendship group. Other children had weaker ties with the members of a friendship group, either because they were marginal members of the group or because they fell midway between two groups. In other cases, children had few positive interactions with any of their classmates. These children seemed to be social isolates.

For older children, and for adolescents as well, the organization of the peer social world can be described in terms of affiliative networks. Friendships are important elements in these networks because they represent the strongest mutual links between peers. Nevertheless, the peer social world is still more highly organized than is an affiliative network. Strayer (1980) documented the existence of a second dimension for peer relationships: namely, the dimension of dominance or status. Some children are more often chosen as leaders, more often imitated, more admired, and better liked than are other children. Leadership, imitation, admiration, and liking are not identical (Hartup, 1983), but they overlap with each other. Their overlap defines the dimension of social status. In recent research, social status has been assessed most often in terms of children's popularity.

Although several researchers have emphasized the distinction between friendships and popularity (see McGuire and Weisz, 1982), this distinction cannot be absolute. Popularity is often judged on the basis of the number of peers who name a child as someone with whom they like to play or work. A child who is not named by any other classmate, and thus is socially isolated, both lacks friends and is low in popularity. Conversely, a child who is named by many other classmates not only is popular but is also likely to have many close and mutual friendships (Cauce, 1987).

Nonetheless, there need not be a close connection between how popular children are, or the number of close friendships they have, and the quality of their best or closest friendships. McGuire and Weisz (1982) reported only a weak relation between children's popularity and a measure of the quality of their closest friendship that was derived from Sullivan's (1953) theory. The relation between the measures of popularity and friendship quality was statistically significant, however. In a short-term longitudinal study of adolescents making the transition from elementary school to junior high school, Berndt and Hawkins (1987) found that adolescents' popularity and their perceptions of the supportive features of their closest friendships were not significantly correlated at any single point in time, but adolescents with more supportive friendships at the beginning of their first year in the new junior high school increased in their popularity between the beginning and the end of that first year.

More research on the relations between popularity and the features of close friendships is greatly needed. On the most general level, this research would clarify the connections between the two major dimensions of peer relationships: affiliation and status. Moreover, this research would help integrate the large and growing literature on friendship with the long-standing and increasingly vigorous tradition of research on social status and popularity (see Hartup, 1983; Parker and Asher, 1987).

Two issues regarding the relations between popularity and friendship merit special comment. First, researchers recently have devoted considerable attention to one group of unpopular children: those who are strongly rejected or disliked by many of their peers. This group of children has been studied extensively because there is a large amount of evidence that peer rejection in childhood is predictive of psychological and behavioral problems in adulthood (Parker and Asher, 1987). Yet little is known about the quality of the friendships that rejected children have. For example, do rejected children not only have fewer friendships but also have less satisfying or more conflicted friendships? Most writers who assume that unpopular children are deficient in social skills or prone to maladaptive patterns of social behavior (see Rubin, 1983) would be expected to give an affirmative answer to this question. Therefore, if the correct answer is "no," common assumptions about the causes of unpopularity will need to be abandoned or modified. In addition, assumptions about the most effective interventions for rejected children may need revision.

Second, a few scattered reports imply that popularity influences friendship formation. In particular, some adolescents report that they have attempted to form friendships with more popular peers so that they could gain access to the popular crowd in their school (Hirsch and Renders, 1986). How common this strategic use of friendship is, and how successfully the strategy can be applied, is unknown. Yet the very existence of the strategy calls into question a widely accepted proposition about children's friendships. Following Piaget ([1932] 1965), many theorists and researchers have argued that equality is a guiding principle for friendships in childhood and adolescence (see Berndt, 1982; Youniss, 1980). Friends' interactions are often inconsistent with the principle of equality, however. Children compete with their friends (Berndt, 1982) and complain about their friends' attempts to "boss them around" or assert their superiority over them (for example, "he thinks he's hot stuff"). Faced with these violations of equality, some writers have responded, in effect, that "nobody's perfect" and that young children are less perfect than adolescents or adults (Berndt, 1982), or they have claimed that competition and the quest for superiority are exaggerated in the achievement-oriented society of the United States (as Sullivan, 1953, and many other writers have implied).

A more plausible and better-supported position is that the quest for status and the competition or rivalry it provokes are common in all human groups, even at the preschool age (Strayer, 1980). We can only attain a full understanding of children's friendships if we admit this fact and examine its implications for friendship formation and maintenance. Only in this way will we be able to draw a fully accurate picture of the place of friendships in the social world of children and adolescents.

The Impact of Friends' Influence

Sullivan (1953) and many other theorists have assumed that children's friendships have beneficial effects on their development. In contrast, a number of researchers have raised questions about the influence of friends on children's attitudes and behavior. For example, in the 1960s, Coleman (1961) argued that the norms of the adolescent peer group typically favor athletic or social success in high school at the expense of academic accomplishment. Shortly afterward, Bronfenbrenner (1970) began an extensive program of research that seemed to demonstrate a negative effect of peer pressure on the social behavior of American adolescents. Bronfenbrenner concluded that "where the peer group is to a large extent autonomous—as it often is in the United States—it can exert influence in opposition to values held by the adult society" (1970, p. 189).

The apparent contradiction between hypotheses about the positive effects of friendship and hypotheses about the negative effects of peer influence might be resolved by assuming that close friendships have effects that are different in nature and direction from those of interactions with a larger group of peers. For example, adolescents might receive different messages about the importance of academic achievement from their close friends and from the rest of their classmates. Close friends might encourage adolescents to work hard at school even when their classmates generally place a higher value on popularity or on winning in sports. If so, the two sets of hypotheses would not be contradictory; they would simply refer to distinct and opposing sources of influence. This resolution of the apparent contradiction rests on the assumption that children and adolescents are faced with competing pressures from close friends and from the rest of their peers.

If taken as a general rule, however, this assumption is dubious. On the basis of a review of the research on peer influence, Cohen (1983) concluded that adolescents are most influenced by their close friends and little influenced by the peer group as a whole. Moreover, in my own research (Berndt, 1979), I found little difference in children's and adolescents' responses to items such as those in Bronfenbrenner's research on peer influence when the items referred to "a couple of your best friends" versus "a few of the kids from your school." Finally, other researchers typically have drawn conclusions about peer influence from studies in which children or adolescents were asked specifically about their friends' attitudes and behavior (see Berndt, forthcoming [b]). Taken together, this evidence suggests that the distinction between friends' influence and other peers' influence cannot be used to reconcile the opposing hypotheses about the consequences of friends' or peers' influence. Indeed, the evidence indicates that most peer influence is friends' influence.

Other reviewers have attempted to resolve the opposing hypotheses by questioning the proposition that friends generally have values contrary to those of most adults. For instance, Hartup

(1983) has argued that the values of parents, adolescents, and their friends are more often concordant than discordant. Still more recently, however, Steinberg and Silverberg (1986) revived Bronfenbrenner's (1970) original hypothesis that susceptibility to the antisocial pressure of peers is an important contributor to adolescents' antisocial behavior.

The continuing controversy over the question of friends' influence, coupled with the lack of substantial progress in understanding this phenomenon, suggests that a new approach is needed. In my view, this new approach must treat friends' influence not as a social problem but as a special case of the more general process of interpersonal influence. More than two decades ago, Sherif and Sherif (1964) stated that questions about friends' influence are essentially questions about attitude formation and change. In other words, friends should be seen simply as one source of influence on the formation and modification of children's and adolescents' attitudes and behavior. Viewing friends' influence in the context of more general theories of social influence and attitude change has important implications for the formulation of theories and the planning of research (see Berndt, forthcoming [b]). Three implications are especially significant.

First, whether friends have positive or negative effects on children's attitudes and behavior is not predictable in general because friends' influence can and does have both types of effects. Thus researchers cannot assume that friends' influence leads invariably either to undesirable behavior or to desirable behavior. Rather, they must specify the conditions under which each of these outcomes might be expected.

This perspective on friends' influence is not novel, although it has often been overlooked in the heat of debate. Bronfenbrenner (1970) himself assumed that peer influence can lead to behaviors approved by adult society. In discussing the role of peers in Soviet schools, Bronfenbrenner emphasized the power of peer groups to reinforce the values and behaviors endorsed by school officials and other adults. Moreover, interactions with friends may influence the formation of behavior patterns that are viewed positively by some adults and negatively by other adults. Hartup (1983) summarized evidence indicating that friends and other peers encourage children and adolescents to behave in ways consistent with traditional sex stereotypes. Some adults would regard this outcome as desirable; other adults would seek ways to alter friends' interactions so that friends' influence promoted less traditional and more egalitarian roles for the two sexes.

The conditions that determine whether friends' influence will lead to desirable or undesirable behaviors are not well understood. The direction of influence must certainly depend on the attitudes and behavior of the friends who are the source of influence. Bronfenbrenner's research indicates that the direction of friends' influence also depends on the social context for their interactions (for example, American high schools versus Soviet residential schools). Researchers should attempt in the future to identify the characteristics of friends and of social contexts that are associated with specific effects of friends' influence on specific attitudes and behaviors.

Second, the net effect of friends' influence is the resultant of multiple influence processes. In previous research, processes of influence were rarely described with any precision. Many authors referred to a single process of influence—social pressure—which they neither defined precisely nor analyzed carefully (see, for example, Berndt, 1979). Yet more complex and more accurate descriptions of the processes of influence in children's and adolescents' friendship groups have been available for some time. Sherif and Sherif (1964), for example, suggested that pressure based on overt sanctions or threats of sanctions is but one means used to control the behavior of group members. More frequently, adolescents' behavior is controlled by the friends' positive reinforcement in the form of praise or approval. Furthermore, friends often influence adolescents' behavior without actively attempting to exert influence at all. Adolescents may simply become aware of the norms for behavior within a particular group and comply with those norms because they value membership in the group. Finally, the conversations that are such a large part of friends' interactions (Csikszentmihalyi and Larson, 1984) may also influence adolescents' attitudes and behavior. Piaget ([1932] 1965) suggested long ago that the information exchange in these conversations can encourage children or adolescents to reexamine their own views of social norms or moral issues (see also Berkowitz, 1985).

In short, the processes by which friends influence each other are more varied and complex than is implied by notions of peer pressure. Friends may exert influence on an individual child by explicitly reinforcing or punishing certain behaviors, by making the child aware of the behaviors that lead to acceptance and status, or by discussing issues with the child in a mutual search for the best possible conclusion. Although previous research has demonstrated that these influence processes operate during friends' interactions (Sherif and Sherif, 1964), additional research is needed on their relative importance in friendship groups that differ in age, sex, or other characteristics.

Third, most theorists and researchers have assumed that friends' influence declines only in late adolescence, when individuals develop true autonomy (see Berndt, 1979). Yet scattered evidence suggests that, even earlier, certain features of the relationship between friends may limit their influence on each other. Recent research indicates that even seventh graders are tolerant of individuals whose beliefs are different from their own (Enright, Lapsley, Franklin, and Steuck, 1984): That is, seventh graders grant other people the right to their own opinions and do not consider them bad or wrong simply because the others' opinions differ from their own.

This tolerance of differing views may be especially great among friends. When one sample of seventh graders were asked directly about their friends' influence on their attitudes toward school and their behavior in school, they often said that their friends had not changed their attitudes and behavior or vice versa (Berndt, Miller, and Park, 1988). One reason they gave for this lack of influence was that "we don't try to change each other's feelings," or "I have my own ideas, and they do, too." These responses seem to represent one facet of the mutual respect that Piaget ([1932] 1965) described as prototypical of close peer relationships in later childhood and adolescence. The existence of a belief that children must respect their friends' opinions, even when they conflict with their own, may act as a constraint on some forms of friends' influence.

The degree to which this belief reflects reality has yet to be determined, however.

Conclusion

The two themes discussed in this chapter illustrate the range of issues relevant to research on friendships in childhood and adolescence. In the discussion of the first theme—the place of friendships in the social world of peers—friendship was seen as the basic element or building block of a large and complex social structure. Children and adolescents typically see themselves as having a few best friends, not just one. These friends often know each other and form a small friendship group. These groups, in turn, are linked to other groups by children who are members of or on the fringes of multiple groups. These interconnections define an affiliative network.

Researchers have also looked at the peer social world from a different perspective that emphasizes differences in social status or popularity within a peer group. Occasionally, researchers have claimed that children's popularity and the quality of their friendships bear little relation to each other. Although some evidence supports this contention, there are important questions to be investigated about the interplay between the affiliative and the status dimensions of peer relationships. For example, the features of the friendships among children who are rejected by many of their peers have not been examined systematically. In addition, the degree to which children's overall popularity influences their selection of friends is largely unknown. Research on these questions would help bridge the gap between studies of friendship and studies of popularity. More generally, this research could lead beyond the investigation of friendships per se or popularity per se to the analysis of the overall structure of peer relationships in particular groups of children and adolescents. These analyses ultimately could lead to the development of techniques for assessing not just children's popularity or the quality of their friendships but their exact position in each peer group that they have at school, in their neighborhoods, or in other settings. These assessments would clarify both the consistency and the variability in children's relationships and, indirectly, address questions about consistency in personality and behavior as well.

In the discussion of the second theme, the focus was placed not on friendship as a relationship but on friends as sources of influence on children's and adolescents' attitudes and behavior. The controversy over the putative effects of peer pressure on adolescents' behavior was the starting point for a new approach to the understanding of friends' influence. In this new approach, the influence of close friends is seen as a particular instance of the general phenomenon of social influence. Children are influenced by friends because they are influenced by all individuals with whom they have formed close relationships. The direction of this influence—toward socially desirable or undesirable attitudes and behavior—cannot be defined without further knowledge of the friends' own characteristics and the social context for their influence on each other. The processes of influence that operate among friends are more diverse and complex than the notion of peer pressure suggests. Moreover, friends' influence on each other may be restrained by one feature of their relationship: their belief that friends must respect each other's rights to make their own decisions and to hold to their own opinions.

This new approach to the understanding of friends' influence raises many questions for future research. The conditions under which friends' influence contributes to undesirable behaviors or, conversely, to desirable behavior need to be identified, both for theoretical and for practical reasons. The processes of influence that might account for the effects of friends on one another's behavior can be defined in the abstract, but their relative importance for an understanding of friends' influence remains to be determined. Previous research suggests that overt pressure based on threats or ridicule is not the primary means by which friends control each other's behavior, but the influence processes that are most powerful in general or at particular ages have not been investigated. Children's own impressions of friendship as a relationship that demands tolerance of differences in perspectives is intriguing but difficult to interpret. It would be valuable, for example, to know whether tolerance of differences or respect of opposing views is discussed explicitly in friends' conversations.

Tomorrow

As already noted, many questions relevant to the themes discussed in this chapter will only be answered in the future. Predicting which of these questions will ultimately have the most significant answers is difficult. Even so, two possibilities are worth mentioning.

First, the recent evidence that children's popularity is not strongly related to the closeness and harmony of their friendships not only illustrates an important feature of the peer social world but also raises questions about the personal consequences of social status in the peer group. Are those popular children who lack close friendships exemplars of the adage "it's lonely at the top"? Are those unpopular children who have close friendships—perhaps with other unpopular children—drawn together by a feeling that "it's us against the world"? Exploring the attitudes, social perceptions, and self-concepts of children who differ in their peer status and the qualities of their friendships would provide a fuller profile of children's social adjustment than do measures of status or friendship alone. This fuller profile, in turn, could be useful in identifying children with severe problems in social adjustment and designing interventions for those specific problems.

Second, the proposal that friends' influence is best viewed as one instance of the general phenomenon of social influence seems to resolve several old issues in the literature. Yet some important questions are not adequately addressed by the new approach. Probably the most salient of these questions concerns the developmental course of friends' influence. Although many reviewers have concluded that friends' influence peaks in early or middle adolescence (see Hartup, 1983), the data base for this conclusion is fairly weak. One general hypothesis that seems undoubtedly true is that the developmental changes in friends' influence are partly determined by developmental changes in friendships themselves. But what changes in friendships are most significant? Does the increase in the intimacy of friendships between childhood and adolescence (Berndt, 1982) lead to an increase in friends' power to influence one another? Alternatively, does the increase in tolerance and mutual respect during the same age range (Enright, Lapsley, Franklin, and

Steuck, 1984; Piaget, [1932] 1965) lead to a decrease in actual influence? Determining the answers to these questions will require a substantial effort in theoretical analysis and empirical research. Nevertheless, the effort seems justified, for the eventual payoff will be an increase in understanding of the contributions of peer relationships to children's development.

References

Berkowitz, M. W. (ed.). *Peer Conflict and Psychological Growth.* New Directions for Child Development, no. 29. San Francisco: Jossey-Bass, 1985.

Berndt, T. J. "Developmental Changes in Conformity to Peers and Parents." *Developmental Psychology,* 1979, *15,* 608–616.

Berndt, T. J. "The Features and Effects of Friendship in Early Adolescence." *Child Development,* 1982, *53,* 1447–1460.

Berndt, T. J. "The Nature and Significance of Children's Friendships." In R. Vasta (ed.), *Annals of Child Development.* Vol. 5. Greenwich, Conn.: JAI Press, 1988.

Berndt, T. J. "Obtaining Support from Friends in Childhood and Adolescence." In D. Belle (ed.), *The Social Support Needs of School-Age Children.* New York: Wiley, forthcoming (a).

Berndt, T. J. "Peer Influence in Middle Adolescence." In A. L. Greene and A. Boxer (eds.), *Transitions Through Adolescence: Research and Theory in Life-Span Perspective.* Hillsdale, N.J.: Erlbaum, forthcoming (b).

Berndt, T. J., and Hawkins, J. A. "The Contribution of Supportive Friendships to Adjustment After the Transition to Junior High School." Unpublished manuscript, Department of Psychological Sciences, Purdue University, 1987.

Berndt, T. J., Miller, K. E., and Park, K. "Adolescents' Perceptions of Friends' and Parents' Influence on Their School Orientation." Unpublished manuscript, Department of Psychological Sciences, Purdue University, 1988.

Bronfenbrenner, U. "Reaction to Social Pressure from Adults Versus Peers Among Soviet Day School and Boarding School

Pupils in the Perspective of an American Sample." *Journal of Personality and Social Psychology,* 1970, *15,* 179-189.

Brown, B. B., and Lohr, M. J. "Peer Group Affiliation and Adolescent Self-Esteem: An Integration of Ego Identity and Symbolic Interaction Theories." *Journal of Personality and Social Psychology,* 1987, *52,* 47-55.

Cauce, A. M. "School and Peer Competence in Early Adolescence: A Test of Domain-Specific Self-Perceived Competence." *Developmental Psychology,* 1987, *23,* 287-291.

Cohen, J. "Commentary: The Relationships Between Friendship Selection and Peer Influence." In J. L. Epstein and N. Karweit (eds.), *Friends in School.* Orlando, Fla.: Academic Press, 1983.

Cohen, S., and Wills, T. A. "Stress, Social Support, and the Buffering Hypothesis." *Psychological Bulletin,* 1985, *98,* 310-357.

Coleman, J. S. *The Adolescent Society.* New York: Free Press, 1961.

Csikszentmihalyi, M., and Larson, R. *Being Adolescent.* New York: Basic Books, 1984.

Davies, B. *Life in the Classroom and Playground.* Boston: Routledge & Kegan Paul, 1982.

Enright, R. D., Lapsley, D. K., Franklin, C. C., and Steuck, K. "Longitudinal and Cross-Cultural Validation of the Belief-Discrepancy Reasoning Construct." *Developmental Psychology,* 1984, *20,* 143-149.

Hartup, W. W. "Children and Their Friends." In H. McGurk (ed.), *Issues in Childhood Social Development.* London: Methuen, 1978.

Hartup, W. W. "Peer Relations." In P. Mussen (ed.), *Handbook of Child Psychology.* (4th ed.) Vol. 4. New York: Wiley, 1983.

Hirsch, B. J., and Renders, R. J. "The Challenge of Adolescent Friendships: A Study of Lisa and Her Friends." In S. E. Hobfoll (ed.), *Stress, Social Support, and Women.* Washington, D.C.: Hemisphere, 1986.

McGuire, K. D., and Weisz, J. R. "Social Cognition and Behavior Correlates of Preadolescent Chumships." *Child Development,* 1982, *53,* 1478-1484.

Masters, J. C., and Furman, W. "Popularity, Individual Friendship Selection, and Specific Peer Interaction Among Children." *Developmental Psychology,* 1981, *17,* 344-350.

Parker, J. G., and Asher, S. R. "Peer Relations and Later Personal

Adjustment: Are Low-Accepted Children 'At Risk'?" *Psychological Bulletin,* 1987, *102* (3), 357–389.

Piaget, J. *The Moral Judgment of the Child.* New York: Free Press, 1965. (Originally published 1932.)

Rubin, K. H. "Recent Perspectives on Social Competence and Peer Status: Some Introductory Remarks." *Child Development,* 1983, *54,* 1383–1385.

Sherif, M., and Sherif, C. *Reference Groups: Exploration into Conformity and Deviance of Adolescents.* New York: Harper & Row, 1964.

Steinberg, L., and Silverberg, S. B. "The Vicissitudes of Autonomy in Early Adolescence." *Child Development,* 1986, *57,* 841–851.

Strayer, F. F. "Social Ecology of the Preschool Peer Group." In W. A. Collins (ed.), *Minnesota Symposium on Child Psychology.* Vol. 13. Hillsdale, N.J.: Erlbaum, 1980.

Sullivan, H. S. *The Interpersonal Theory of Psychiatry.* New York: Norton, 1953.

Tisak, M. S. "Children's Conceptions of Parental Authority." *Child Development,* 1986, *57,* 166–176.

Youniss, J. *Parents and Peers in Social Development.* Chicago: University of Chicago Press, 1980.

Chapter 17

Rearing
Competent Children

Diana Baumrind

In this chapter I will discuss the effects on children of parental *demandingness* and parental *responsiveness* and of patterns of parental behavior representing the intersection of the two dimensions. My emphasis will be on middle childhood (Time 2, or age nine). However, I will also provide a context by summarizing findings from my longitudinal program of research when the children were of preschool age (Time 1, or T1), as well as when they were nine years of age (Time 2, or T2).

I began my ongoing work on child rearing in 1959 with the first of three studies, using as participants middle-class Caucasian parents and their preschool children enrolled in one of thirteen nursery schools in Berkeley and Oakland, California. My long-range objective was to identify the familial antecedents of optimal competence in children and adolescents. At each of three developmental periods—preschool (T1), middle school (T2), and early

Note: During the preparation of this chapter, the author was supported by a Research Scientist Award (1-K05-MH00485-01) and a research grant (1-R01-MH38343-01) from the National Institute of Mental Health. During the adolescent phase of the research, the project was supported by a research grant from the National Institute on Drug Abuse (1-R01-DA-1919) and by one from the John D. and Catherine T. MacArthur Foundation. The William T. Grant Foundation has provided consistent and generous support of this longitudinal program of research, including the present phase of analysis of the early adolescent data (Grant 84044973).

adolescence (T3)—my colleagues and I collected comprehensive data from ecologically valid sources. These sources consisted of direct observation in naturalistic and laboratory settings, intensive structured interviews, and standardized and project-designed psychological tests. With each successive developmental stage, additional measures were included in the battery to match the increasingly differentiated status of the maturing child. At all three time periods, the subsequent observations and ratings of parents and children were collected by separate teams of observers. The Q-sorts and Likert-type rating scales based on the observations and interviews for children were reduced via cluster and factor analyses to two primary interpersonal modalities assessing *agency* and *communion*. For parents, these two underlying modalities are called *demandingness* and *responsiveness*.

In the psychological literature (for example, Bakan, 1966), agency refers to the drive for independence, individuality, and self-aggrandizement, and in the sex-role literature (for example, Spence and Helmreich, 1978) it is identified as the masculine principle; communion refers to the need to be of service and to be engaged with others and is identified as the feminine principle. The social dimensions of status (dominance, power) and love (solidarity, affiliation), which emerge as the two orthogonal axes from almost all factor analyses of human behavior (see, for example, Baumrind and Black, 1967; Lonner, 1980; Leary, 1957; Schaefer, 1959; Wiggins, 1979), are manifestations of agency and communion. In practical endeavors, the integration of the two modalities is represented by actions that resolve social conflicts in a manner that is both just and compassionate. In the sex-role literature, such integration is regarded as androgynous. Optimal competence is defined in this study as high levels of both agency and communion and incompetence as low levels of both agency and communion, whereas either unmitigated agency *or* communion is considered to be partially competent behavior.

My early work (Baumrind and Black, 1967; Baumrind, 1967, 1971a, 1971b, 1972) was designed to overcome the shortcomings of previous research on socialization effects, which had relied on retrospective reports and an inadequate data base and which had confounded observations of parent and child behavior. The

vigorous introduction into educational philosophy of permissive
and child-centered attitudes began about sixty years ago (Coriat,
1926; Naumberg, 1928) as a partial outgrowth of the psychoanalytic
theory of psychosexual development. Following Lewin's work with
authoritarian, democratic, and laissez-faire social climates (Lewin,
Lippitt, and White, 1939) and the publication of *The Authoritarian
Personality* (Adorno, Frenkel-Brunswik, Levinson, and Sanford,
1950), the neutral definition of an authority as an expert qualified to
designate a behavioral alternative for another where the alternatives
are perceived by both became infused with the prejudicial connota-
tions appropriate to the authoritarian personality syndrome. The
introduction of the "authoritarian personality syndrome" into the
lexicon of the psychologist, probably by Fromm (1941), provided a
convenient label to apply to the controlling parent. Fromm,
however, had distinguished between rational and inhibiting
authority, reserving the term *authoritarian personality* for the
syndrome in which enactment of the role of inhibiting authority,
not rational authority, characterizes the individual's interpersonal
relations.

The Preschool Years

Three separate samples of preschool children and their
families were studied. The first small sample of thirty-two families
was selected from a larger sample after prolonged observations in
the nursery school setting of the children's patterns of behavior.
Three prototypic patterns of parental authority—authoritative,
authoritarian, and permissive—associated with each of three child
types emerged from this study (Baumrind, 1967). Parents of the
children who were the most self-reliant, self-controlled, explorative,
and content were themselves controlling and demanding; but they
were also warm, rational, and receptive to the child's communication. This unique combination of high control and positive
encouragement of the child's autonomous and independent striving
associated with optimal competence was called *authoritative*
parental behavior. Parents of children who, relative to the others,
were discontented, withdrawn, and distrustful were themselves
detached and controlling and somewhat less warm than the other

parents. These parents of dysphoric and disaffiliative children were called *authoritarian*. Parents of the least self-reliant, explorative, and self-controlled children were themselves noncontrolling, nondemanding, and relatively warm. These parents of immature children were called *permissive*.

Dimensional analyses were conducted on a second sample of ninety-five families (Baumrind and Black, 1967). Data were analyzed separately for boys and for girls. From this study, we learned that parental practices that were stimulating and even tension producing (for example, maternal maturity demands for boys; paternal confrontation and maternal socialization demands for girls) were associated in the young child with self-assertiveness and adaptability. Firm, consistent paternal discipline was associated with self-confident, exploratory behavior for boys and with friendly, cooperative behavior for girls. Overprotective and intrusive control, in contrast to the effects of firm, consistent control, was associated with dependent and stereotyped behavior for boys. Parents' psychological differentiation—that is, their use of reason to obtain compliance and their encouragement of exploratory behavior and verbal assertiveness—was associated with stable, adaptive behavior for girls and with independent and nonconforming behavior for boys. Coercive use of power—that is, superfluous demands and use of power to enforce them—had a negative effect on girls' emotional stability in contrast with direct confrontation around disciplinary issues, which was associated with socially assertive behavior. Affective warmth was virtually uncorrelated with preschool behavior in this study.

Typological analyses were used to analyze the data from the third study. This, the most comprehensive of my studies of preschool children, also constitutes the first wave of the ongoing longitudinal study, which we refer to as the Family Socialization and Developmental Competence Project (FSP). The 134 middle-class Caucasian children in this longitudinal sample were born in 1964 and were first studied in 1968–69, when they were four to five years of age. The complex results from this study, described in detail in a monograph (Baumrind, 1971a), are summarized here.

Whereas in the pilot study families were selected on the basis of their children's patterns of behavior and their parents were then compared, in this study the families were classified on the basis of the parents' patterns of behavior and the characteristics of their children were then compared. The theory-derived parent classification was based on the profiles that had previously emerged from the pilot study: Families were classified into (variations of) the authoritarian, authoritative, and permissive prototypes. Both parents' patterns of scores on item clusters that had emerged after factor analyzing each parent's scores on seventy-five parent behavior rating scales were used to classify each family. After first describing each prototype, I will then summarize the results for that prototype.

Authoritarian parents attempt to shape, control, and evaluate the behavior and attitudes of the child in accordance with a set standard of conduct—usually an absolute standard that is theologically based or formulated by a higher secular authority. Authoritarian couples value obedience as a virtue and favor punitive, forceful measures to curb self-will at points at which their children's actions or beliefs conflict with their standards of acceptable conduct. These parents attempt to inculcate such conventional values as work, respect for authority, and preservation of order and traditional structure. They do not encourage verbal give and take, believing that children should accept parents' word for what is right. Couples were assigned to the authoritarian pattern if they had high scores on the clusters measuring firm enforcement and maturity demands and low scores on the clusters measuring responsiveness and psychological differentiation.

Children of authoritarian couples did not have a distinctive profile when compared to all other children. However, when children from authoritarian homes were compared specifically with their same-sex peers from authoritative homes, boys from the authoritarian households were found to be relatively hostile and resistive and girls were found to be relatively lacking in independence and dominance.

Authoritative parents, in contrast with authoritarian parents, attempt to direct their children's activities in a rational, issue-oriented manner. They encourage verbal give and take and share with their children the reasoning behind their policies. They value both expressive and instrumental attributes, both autonomous self-will and disciplined conformity. Therefore, they exert firm control at points of parent-child divergence but do not hem their children in with restrictions. Authoritative parents are demanding in that they guide their children's activities firmly and consistently and require them to contribute to family functioning by helping with household tasks. They willingly confront their children in order to obtain conformity, state their values clearly, and expect their children to respect their norms. Authoritative parents are affectively responsive in the sense of being loving, supportive, and committed and cognitively responsive in the sense of providing a stimulating and challenging environment. They recognize their own special rights as adults, but they also respect their children's individual interests and special ways. These parents affirm their children's present qualities but also set standards for future conduct. They do not base their decisions on group consensus or on the individual child's desires, but they also do not regard themselves as infallible or divinely inspired. Couples assigned to the authoritative pattern, like authoritarian parents, scored high on firm enforcement and maturity demands. But by contrast with authoritarian parents, authoritative parents were responsive and psychologically differentiated.

Preschool children from authoritative homes were consistently and significantly more competent than other children. For girls, authoritative parental behavior was associated with purposive, dominant, and achievement-oriented behavior; and for boys it was associated with friendly, cooperative behavior.

Permissive parents are less controlling than they are warm and autonomy granting. Permissive parents attempt to behave in a nonpunitive, accepting, and affirmative manner toward their children's impulses, desires, and actions. They make few maturity demands. They present themselves as resources to be used as their children wish, not as active agents responsible for shaping or altering their children's ongoing or future behavior. They allow their children to regulate their own activities as much as possible, avoid the exercise of control, and do not insist that their children obey externally defined standards. Permissive parents avoid the use of overt power to accomplish their ends.

Preschool children of permissive couples did not differ significantly from children of authoritarian couples. However, compared with children from authoritative homes, girls were markedly less socially assertive, and both sexes were less achievement oriented.

Middle Childhood

At T2, when the children were nine years of age, we collected a second wave of data. At T2, the sample consisted of 164 children and their parents, 104 of whom had been studied at T1 and 60 of whom had been added in order to provide an enhanced sample for future waves. Based on their scores on the child and parent clusters, child and parent types were identified.

Children were classified into five types, based on the balance between "social assertiveness" (socially confident, peer ascendant clusters) and "social responsibility" (friendly, cooperative clusters): (1) *competent* children were high on both dimensions, (2) *incompetent* children were low on both dimensions, (3) *oversocialized* children were high on social responsibility and low on social assertiveness, (4) *undersocialized* children were low on social responsibility and high on social assertiveness, and (5) *average* were the remaining children.

Each family was assigned to a pattern on the basis of both mother's and father's profiles on specific parent behavior rating composites measuring "demandingness" and "responsiveness." To be included in a pattern, both parents in a family had to fit the definition (except that one parent could depart by two points, provided that the other parent's scores compensated). For purposes of classification, demandingness was defined as the average of the scales called "firm" and "requires household help," and responsiveness was defined as the average of the scales called "responsive" and a separate scale called "loving-supportive." Nine T2 parent types were identified on the basis of parents' scores (high, medium, or low) on the demandingness and responsiveness indexes. Scores were considered high or low if they were one-half standard deviation or more above or below the mean. These parent types were called (1) authoritative, (2) demanding, (3) traditional, (4) authoritarian, (5) undifferentiated, (6) democratic, (7) permissive, (8) nondirective, and (9) rejecting-neglecting. Five of the nine parent types—

authoritative, traditional, authoritarian, permissive, and rejecting-neglecting—were hypothesized to have the clearest and most distinctive impact on children's development and were therefore considered prototypes. Of these, all but one—traditional—had already been identified at T1 (Baumrind, 1971a). The nine parent types were further grouped into four higher-order patterns (engaged, restrictive, lenient, and unengaged). In operationally defining the patterns, I will describe only the prototypes in detail.

By definition, parents in the *engaged* pattern, consisting of *authoritative, traditional,* and *demanding* parents and exemplified by the *authoritative* prototype, were high demanding and high or medium responsive. Empirically, authoritative parents were also noncoercive, nonrestrictive, and psychologically differentiated (that is, intellectually stimulating, individuated, and self-confident). They were also confronting (expresses anger) and somewhat conventional. Thus the types designated as authoritative at T1 and T2 are conceptionally and empirically very similar. The traditional prototype was discovered while classifying families into the other categories and exhibited a structural role differentiation between mothers and fathers. Mothers were highly responsive but relatively undemanding, whereas fathers were highly demanding but quite coercive and nonresponsive. Demanding parents were medium responsive and high demanding.

Parents in the *restrictive* pattern, exemplified by the *authoritarian* prototype, were by definition high demanding and low responsive. Empirically, authoritarian parents were also highly confronting, monitoring, and conventional and somewhat coercive and lacking in psychological differentiation. As with the authoritative prototype, the types designated as authoritarian at T1 and T2 are conceptually and empirically very similar.

Parents in the *lenient* pattern, consisting of *democratic* and *permissive* parents and exemplified by the *permissive* prototype, were by definition low or medium demanding and high responsive. Empirically, permissive mothers avoided disciplinary confrontations, and both parents were noncoercive, unconventional, and moderately individuated and self-confident. At T2, the parents classified as permissive fit the prototype rather well, except that mothers were somewhat directive and some fathers were easily angered. Democratic families were high responsive and medium demanding. Individual undifferentiated families did not meet the criteria for any classification. However, their *mean* scores on the definers did not differ significantly from the mean scores of families in the lenient pattern, and they were therefore included in that pattern.

Parents in the *unengaged* pattern, consisting of *nondirective* and *rejecting-neglecting* parents and exemplified by the *rejecting-neglecting* prototype, were, by definition, low demanding and low or medium responsive. Empirically, they were highly coercive, nonindividuated and lacking in intellectual stimulation, and rather conventional, and they did not monitor their children's activities. The types designated as rejecting-neglecting were quite similar at T1 and T2. Rejecting-neglecting parents were low demanding and low responsive, whereas nondirective parents were low demanding and medium responsive.

The T2 data were analyzed using both the dimensions and the types. The results are very detailed and complex, but I will summarize both kinds of analyses briefly.

Dimensional Analyses. The impact on children's competence of two manifestations of parental *demandingness*—firm control and restrictiveness—and of two manifestations of parental *responsiveness*—warmth and noncoerciveness—were examined.

In general, firm control was associated with high levels of competence and restrictiveness with average or low levels of competence.

1. Firm control predicted social assertiveness in girls but not in boys and, conversely, social responsibility in boys but not in girls. Thus at T2, firm control facilitated those aspects of competence that are not sex typed.

2. Restrictive parenting had its primary impact on social assertiveness. Two kinds of restrictive practices were identified: "monitors" and "intrusive-directiveness." Monitors refers to the provision by parents of an orderly, supervised environment, whereas intrusive-directiveness refers to imposition by parents on the child of stage-inappropriate restrictions. With the impact of monitoring controlled, intrusive-directiveness had a negative effect on boys' social assertiveness and general competence. With the

impact of intrusive-directiveness controlled, monitoring, as was the case with firm control, had a positive impact on girls' social assertiveness.

In general, for both sexes, warmth and noncoerciveness were related negatively to emotional disability, and positively or nonlinearly to competence; and the relations were stronger for boys than for girls.

1. For both sexes, warmth and noncoerciveness were related linearly and positively to social responsibility.

2. For girls, no linear relations were found between warmth or noncoerciveness and social assertiveness. For boys, a nonlinear relation was found for warmth, such that sons of parents who were moderately warm were more assertive than sons of parents who were very warm or very cold; and a *negative* linear relation was found between fathers' noncoerciveness and sons' social assertiveness.

3. For boys but not for girls, warmth and noncoerciveness were positively related to cognitive competence.

4. For boys but not for girls, warmth was related linearly to general competence. For boys, the nonlinear relation reported under point 2 above between warmth and social assertiveness was also present for general competence. However, noncoerciveness was linearly and positively related to general competence, especially for girls, a finding that the reader will recall emerged with a different sample at a younger age.

Typological Analyses. The results of the typological analyses help clarify the results of the dimensional analyses. The effects of the parent types on both the child types and child dimensions were examined—the former with prediction analyses and the latter with nonparametric a priori contrasts:

1. Parents who were both demanding and responsive (the engaged pattern and the authoritative prototype) produced children who were socially responsible and socially agentic.

2. Parents who were low on both dimensions (the unengaged pattern and the rejecting-neglecting prototype) produced children who were either (a) low on *both* social responsibility and social assertiveness or (b) low on non-sex-normed competence (that is, social responsibility for boys and social assertiveness for girls).

3. Parents who were highly demanding but not responsive

(the restrictive pattern and the authoritarian prototype) produced daughters who were socially assertive and not highly socially responsible but sons who did not differ from other boys.

4. Parents who were highly responsive but not demanding (the lenient pattern and the permissive prototype) produced daughters who were not socially assertive but who were moderately socially responsible but sons who were similar to sons from authoritarian families and who did not differ significantly from other boys.

Table 17.1 provides a convenient summary of comparisons across the five prototypic parent types for three groups of girls and boys distinguished by their level of competence.

In Table 17.1, the optimally competent children are those who are highly agentic *and* communal (that is, "socially assertive" and "socially responsible"); the incompetent children are those who are neither agentic nor communal; and the partially competent children are those who obtained either average scores on both dimensions or high scores on one dimension and low scores on the other dimension.

Comparisons of the children's competence levels across the five parent prototypes using the Kruskal-Wallis test were highly significant for girls (chi square 17.43; $p < .002$) and for boys (chi square 19.31; $p < .001$). No child raised by an authoritative couple, no girl raised by an authoritarian couple, and no boy raised by a traditional couple was incompetent. No child raised by a rejecting-neglecting couple and no girl raised by a permissive couple was optimally competent. In contrast, 67 percent of boys raised by a rejecting-neglecting couple were incompetent and over 85 percent of children raised by authoritative couples were optimally competent. In addition, compared with each other, more children from nondemanding families (permissive and rejecting-neglecting) were incompetent and more children from demanding families (authoritative; traditional and authoritarian) were optimally competent (Fisher Exact test [Bradley, 1968] for girls, $p < .001$, and for boys, $p < .008$).

At this developmental stage, demanding parenting is highly related to general competence for both sexes, and it is a sufficient condition for the acquisition of a high level of agency for girls.

Table 17.1. Parent Prototype by Child Competence Levels.

Parent Prototype	n Girls	Boys	Optimal Girls %	n	Boys %	n	Partially Competent[1] Girls %	n	Boys %	n	Incompetent Girls %	n	Boys %	n
Authoritative	7	6	86	6	83	5	14	1	17	1	00	0	00	0
Traditional	6	14	50	3	43	6	33	2	57	8	17	1	00	0
Authoritarian	12	11	42	5	18	2	58	7	55	6	00	0	27	3
Permissive	7	5	00	0	20	1	71	5	60	3	29	2	20	1
Rejecting-Neglecting	8	9	00	0	00	0	63	5	33	3	27	3	67	6

Note: Based upon Table VI-10, from "Familial Antecedents of Social Competence in Middle Childhood" (Baumrind, under review).

[1]Three child types—oversocialized, undersocialized, and average—have been combined into "partially competent" here in order to convert the types into competence levels.

However, in order for boys to be socially responsible or optimally competent, it is necessary for parents to be responsive as well as demanding. High responsiveness paired with high demandingness appears to facilitate, perhaps by reinforcing, the effect of demandingness on girls; but even when demanding parents were not responsive, girls were more socially assertive than were other girls. High responsiveness and low demandingness accentuated sex-normed competence (that is, social responsibility) in girls. When parents were neither responsive nor demanding, both girls and boys tended to be either incompetent or sex normed.

In the following sections, I will discuss the important differentiations that have been made over the past decade in the realms of *demandingness* and *responsiveness*. Although parental control and parental love generally emerge as uncorrelated factors from two-dimensional factor analyses, investigators differ in how they define the component constructs, with the consequence that it is not always clear within which realm a construct such as "coerces" or "confronts" that probes the limits of the demanding or responsive realms belongs.

Demandingness

In this section, I will discuss the impacts on children and the meanings of the following constructs in the demandingness realm: direct confrontation, monitors, intrusive-directiveness, and a pattern of firm, consistent discipline with high maturity demands.

Parents are *confronting* when they openly oppose a child's wishes or persist in a demand even if this results in open conflict with the child. Parents who are confronting are not necessarily coercive: Parents are coercive when they issue a stream of superfluous commands accompanied by threats and promises—that is, when they use power without reason. The data already presented suggest that parents are well advised to minimize coercive use of power but to not avoid direct confrontation: Coerciveness undermines internalization by focusing the child's attention on the powerful status of the parent rather than on the harmful consequences of the act that the parent opposes, thus irking the child and provoking opposition; direct but rational confrontation encourages rational give and take. Confrontation that results in resolution or negotiation of the conflict appears to enhance a healthy child's self-assertiveness and expand the child's repertoire of communication skills. In the general population, playful confrontational engagement occurs more commonly between fathers and sons engaged in rough-and-tumble play or competitive sport than between parents and daughters. Reciprocal playful interaction in which emotional arousal is moderately high, although normative for boys, also appears to benefit many girls when it does occur. However, not all parents or all children are temperamentally suited to enjoy or benefit from intense expressivity or abrasive confrontation, even in play: A normally resilient, hardy child will be stimulated, whereas an introverted, vulnerable child may be disrupted, by the high emotional expressivity (Goldstein and Rodnick, 1975) that accompanies spirited confrontation. Parents' responsiveness may be evaluated by the extent to which their emotional expressivity matches the temperament and state of the child.

According to Lepper (1981, 1983), covert techniques of parental control that are minimally sufficient to produce behavioral compliance will deter the child from attributing compliance to an extrinsic source and thereby induce the child to become intrinsically interested in the desired behavior. Both Lepper and Grusec (1983) assert that confrontational social control techniques deter internalization of prosocial attitudes, whereas covert influence techniques do not. The data presented here suggest that confrontational techniques deter dispositional compliance but not prosocial proclivities. We have found no evidence indicating that parents discourage empathy and friendliness by encouraging assertive verbal give and take. Although a confrontational atmosphere does not seem to attenuate prosocial tendencies, it is likely to deter dispositional compliance by discouraging what Ausubel (1957) calls "satellization." Satellization is a noncognitive process in which emotionally dependent attachments to authorities result in compliance to avoid the caregiver's displeasure and in willingness to forgo the acquisition of status or development of abilities that might threaten the relationship with the primary caregiver. Diversion or redirection, in contrast, permits satellization to occur, encouraging dispositional compliance.

However, dispositional compliance is not consistent with optimal competence in the educated middle-class children we sampled, and it therefore is not the primary socialization objective of such parents. The ultimate objective of most such parents is to develop in their children enduring dispositional tendencies that ensure optimal competence—including a history of successful accomplishments, positive self-attributions, and socially responsible coping strategies.

With this in mind, I conclude, in contrast to the advice proffered by Lepper and Grusec, that there are at least five moral and practical reasons to confront children directly about their misdeeds, using both reason and power to persuade:

1. It is known from the work of Krebs (1975) and Maccoby (1983), for example, that children suffer natural empathic responses to another's distress. Parents' failure to confront the child about actions that harm others may extinguish such concern.

2. An explicit, forceful directive to share has been shown to increase rather than decrease the likelihood that young children will continue to share after instructions and surveillance are discontinued (Israel and Brown, 1979), which suggests that confrontation

does not necessarily interfere with internalization. Further, as Staub has shown in a series of studies (1971a, 1971b, 1975a, 1975b), parents' insistence that children take on responsibilities raises rather than lowers the level of their prosocial proclivities. As Hoffman (1970, 1983) suggests, some show of force is often necessary for the voice of reason to be noticed. Parents who habitually use reason without power signal to the child that they are indecisive about requiring compliance.

3. Manipulative parents are likely to produce manipulative children. Parents' subtle manipulation of children's motivation models dishonest behavior, which is likely to be detected by children in the home setting.

4. Children who are not made clearly aware that behavioral compliance is expected do not learn that there is a norm that they are expected to internalize requiring obedience to legitimate authority. Middle school-aged children seek information to discern whether they are being "good" or "bad." When parents articulate explicit norms and then reinforce an act the child is already performing, the child's identity as a "good" child is confirmed.

5. If a child clearly recognizes that the parent has the ability to mediate rewards and punishments, the value to the child of receiving nurturance from that parent is increased (Homans, 1967; Rollin and Thomas, 1975). Power to reinforce not only legitimizes parental authority in a young child's mind but also makes the parent an attractive model (see Burton and Whiting's [1961] elaboration of the status-envy hypothesis). Also, if the powerful parent both models and rewards prosocial behaviors, his or her ability to generate prosocial behavior is likely to be amplified.

Monitoring the child's activities and intrusively directing them, although highly correlated parental variables (.60 for girls and .47 for boys), have different correlates when mutually controlled. *Monitoring* measures the extent to which parents provide an orderly, safe environment for the child, whereas *intrusive-directiveness* measures the extent to which parents constrain and constrict the child's activities, preventing stage-appropriate exploration. When mutually controlled, the effect of monitoring, particularly on girls, was clearly positive (.32 with social assertiveness and .32 with cognitive competence), whereas the effect of intrusive-directiveness, particularly on boys, was negative (-.28 with social assertiveness and -.34 with optimal competence).

Lewis (1981) has challenged the importance I attach to the *pattern of firm control and high maturity demands.* In her thoughtful critique of my interpretation of the effects of firm control, she suggested that neither demanding practices nor authoritative child rearing is necessary to the development of optimal competence. She is correct. As we have seen, authoritative child rearing was sufficient but not necessary to produce competence and to prevent incompetence, as these terms are defined in this study; and demanding practices were sufficient but not necessary to produce social assertiveness in girls. Authoritative child rearing was the only pattern that consistently produced optimally competent children and failed to produce incompetent children in the preschool years and in middle childhood, and this was true for both girls and boys. However, most of the optimally competent children did not come from authoritative homes. Some came from *harmonious* homes (Baumrind, 1971b). Harmonious parents are highly responsive and moderately firm but attach little importance to obtaining obedience.

Lewis and other investigators are particularly interested in the offspring of harmonious parents in this culture. Lewis noted correctly that at T1 the daughters of harmonious parents were as competent as were those with authoritative parents. All six children (four girls and two boys) whose parents were classified as harmonious at T1 remained exceptionally socially responsible at T2. One boy, however, was very unassertive, and all four of the girls were only moderately assertive. Thus the children from harmonious families, in comparison with those from authoritative families, were somewhat less assertive than they were socially responsible.

Despite the importance of firm control and high maturity demands in generating competence, especially in promoting social assertiveness in girls, I do not believe that *any* single variable taken out of context can be considered a necessary cause of children's competence. Parents may accomplish a similar child rearing objective by more than one means. Further, optimal competence varies in its definition within the culture. Thus Japanese mothers, by means of an indulgent, harmonious mother-child relationship that by Western standards is imbalanced in the direction of responsiveness, intentionally encourage a strong sense of dependence and an imbalance in the direction of communion—an outcome valued more in Japanese than in American culture (Azuma, 1986).

Just as the definition of optimal competence varies with the culture, so, as Bronfenbrenner (1985) has shown, does the optimal balance of freedom and control vary with the modal level of stability of the larger society within which the family is embedded. Because the social structure in which families are embedded has become increasingly unstable over the last forty years, there has been a correspondingly increased need for family structure, engagement, and discipline.

In sum, certain demanding disciplinary practices are beneficial to children, whereas others are not. Those that are beneficial include firm control, high maturity demands, direct confrontation, and monitoring. Those that are not beneficial include coercive control and intrusively directive demands that interrupt the child's ongoing activities.

Responsiveness

In this section, I will differentiate among the meanings and the impacts on children of the following constructs in the responsiveness realm: affective warmth, cognitive responsiveness, attachment and bonding, unconditional acceptance or noncontingent positive reinforcement, sensitive attunement, involvement, and reciprocity. The process of making differentiations within the responsiveness realm began in earnest about five years ago with the Maccoby and Martin (1983) chapter in the Mussen handbook. Meanings of terms in the responsiveness realm are still quite diffuse and overlapping, and different investigators use the same term to refer to different processes. It is to be hoped that as the empirical work that examines these processes proceeds, the terms will come to have more univocal meaning.

The seminal meaning of "responsiveness" comes from ethological theory and pertains to the meshing or mutual shaping of infant and caretaker behavior to achieve synchrony (Bowlby,

1969; Hinde, 1974). Prior proclivities of the caretaker are crucial determinants of the quality of attachment. These prior proclivities include warmth, sensitivity, and willingness to become involved in caregiving activities—all of which are aspects of what we now include in the meaning of parental responsiveness. After achieving object permanence, the infant can anticipate how its caretaker is likely to act in certain situations; thus not only can it adjust its behavior accordingly but it also can use its repertoire of responses to induce its caretaker to adjust his or her plans to take its needs into account. However, the infant can have only as much influence as the caretaker permits.

      Until recently, the responsiveness realm was operationally defined by the warmth/hostility factor that emerged from the analyses of Schaefer (1959) and Becker (1964). In our own work, my colleagues and I were able to distinguish empirically between affective warmth and cognitive responsiveness. By *affective warmth* I refer to a parent's emotional expressiveness, usually of love. Affective warmth does not imply unconditional acceptance or passivity, but it may be accompanied by both. However, ready expressions of affection may coexist instead with ready expression of anger and with willingness to confront the child over disciplinary matters. *Cognitive responsiveness* refers to intellectual stimulation and to encouragement of the child to express his or her point of view, often in the context of a disciplinary encounter. It implies verbal reciprocity (that is, give and take) and negotiation of differences but does not imply that the parent relinquishes control in disciplinary encounters. As data presented earlier documented, affective warmth was linearly related to social responsibility for both sexes, but to social assertiveness for neither (for boys a quadratic relation is present), and to cognitive competence and general competence only for boys. Cognitive responsiveness was correlated for both sexes with cognitive competence, social assertiveness, and general competence; and for boys only with social responsibility. However, the large impact of cognitive responsiveness was mediated by affective warmth and firm control: When these two variables were jointly controlled by including them in a multiple regression equation, the independent contribution of cognitive responsiveness to children's competencies was no longer significant.

For ethologists such as Ainsworth (1973) and Hinde (1974), attachment figures provide a secure base from which children can explore their world; *attachment* implies "letting go" for both participants. But attachment is based on strong caretaker bonding to the infant, and such *bonding* implies adhering to, not letting go. In their analysis of the Parental Bonding Instrument, Parker, Tupling, and Brown (1979) identified two component dimensions: (1) care and empathy (corresponding to affective warmth) and (2) overprotection and intrusiveness (its negative pole corresponding to cognitive responsiveness). Affective warmth and firm bonding are necessary to the well-being of the infant. But overprotectiveness and intrusiveness encourage dependency and separation problems in the toddler (Eisenberg, 1958). It is a wise and altruistic mother indeed who can be maximally warm but minimally overprotective and intrusive. Thus it may be beneficial for primary caretakers to have important attachments to others besides infants so that they may be motivated to "let go" in appropriate ways after forming a strong bond of attachment to the infant. Neither attachment nor responsiveness implies unconditional acceptance.

The concept of *unconditional acceptance* or *noncontingent positive reinforcement* is akin in its expression and effects to oversolicitous protection and excessive involvement. The view that the effects of contingent approval (by contrast with unconditional approval) on the child are inhibiting and neurotogenic, as well as indefensible ethically, was promoted in the 1960s by articulate spokespersons in the fields of education and child rearing, such as Goodman (1964), Neill (1964), and Rogers (1960). However, a number of studies that analyzed the effects of noncontingent positive stimulation on young children (see, for example, Millar, 1972; O'Brien, 1969; and Watson, 1971) found that children's responses were highly consistent with those obtained using noncontingent aversive stimulation. Commenting on the deleterious effects of noncontingent positive stimulation on the future learning of young infants, Watson (1977, p. 128) suggested that the "eventual failure to initiate instrumental activity appears to be a consequence of experiencing an event that is not dependent on behavior as opposed to being a consequence of a lack of experience with an event dependent on behavior." Similarly, I have found that unconditional approval is not associated with competence in preschool children (Baumrind, 1967, 1971a; Baumrind and Black, 1967). In these and other studies—including those of Hoffman, Rosen, and Lippitt (1960), Kagan and Moss (1962), and Rosen and D'Andrade (1959)—among children of various ages, passive acceptance and overprotective parental practices were associated with dependence, especially in girls, and with other indexes of low competence. The impact on children's social development of noncontingent reinforcement appears to be negative whether the noncontingent reinforcement is positive, in the form of approval, or negative, in the form of disapproval. An environment of noncontingent approval may function as noncontingent positive stimulation did in Watson's experiments. Unconditional approval, like noncontingent rejection, leads children to conclude that the environment is not responsive to their behavior and that social causes and effects are not reliably related. Such beliefs about causality appear to deter children from trying harder when confronted with an obstacle to goal achievement. Contingency in parent-child relations, in both nondisciplinary and disciplinary encounters, provides children with opportunities to engage in coping behaviors to repair a mismatch or to be instrumental in engaging the caretaker's attention.

A response is contingent when it is timely, consistent, and carefully targeted. In order for a caregiver to use contingent reinforcement effectively in a disciplinary context, she or he must be *sensitively attuned* to the child's motivational system. But not all caregivers who use contingent reinforcement effectively in a disciplinary context are warm or sensitively attuned to the child's moods, needs, and signals in nondisciplinary situations. Affective warmth implies noncontingent as well as contingent expressions of affection. If parental involvement and commitment are manifested only by demands and attempts to shape the child's behavior, the interactions will be experienced as arid and punitive, and the child will seek to escape rather than to engage the caretaker. Contingent disapproval, unless balanced by contingent approval and noncontingent expressions of love and commitment, will demoralize a child. Furthermore, persistent child misbehavior eliciting persistent parental disapproval is likely to reflect a past history of parental mismatch and lack of attentiveness.

Low parental *involvement*—that is, emotional detachment, withdrawal, or indifference—has more deleterious effects even than an imbalance in favor of contingent disapproval over contingent approval. The negative effects of lack of involvement have been documented at all ages, with cognitive and personality deficits evident in infancy (see Egeland and Sroufe, 1981a, 1981b) and throughout childhood and adolescence (see Baumrind, 1971a; Block, 1971; and Pulkkinen, 1982).

Maccoby and Martin (1983) and Parpal and Maccoby (1985) used the term *reciprocity* to refer to the extent to which caretakers take into account the wishes and feelings of the child. Maccoby and Martin (1983) distinguished conceptually between reciprocity based on willing compliance, which they saw as characteristic of harmonious (Baumrind, 1971b) as well as of authoritative families, and reciprocity based on expectations of contingent reinforcement or exchange, which they saw as occurring both in noncommunal and in communal relationships. When what is exchanged is the relationship itself, as is the case in the family, the distinction between simple exchange and cooperation to attain a mutual goal is less important. Therefore, after making the distinction, Parpal and Maccoby considered the two kinds of reciprocity jointly in a study designed to test the hypothesis that "a child's willing cooperation with a parent will be enhanced by the parent's having previously demonstrated a willingness to cooperate with the child" (1985, p. 1327). Bugenthal and Shennum (1984) invoked a similar construct of reciprocal responsiveness to contrast transactions (with "difficult" and "easy" children) in which parents attributed more power to *either* the parent or the child with transactions in which parents attributed power to *both* the parent and the child. The notion of caregiver-child reciprocity also encompasses those of synchrony or attunement in parent-infant interactions (see Martin, 1981; Tronick, Ricks, and Cohn, 1982).

Parpal and Maccoby made two observations that support serendipitous findings of our own, although the observational conditions were quite different. First, in a condition referred to as "free play," children reacted to positive reinforcement as if it were coercive: They cooperated less with adults under the condition of free play, in which mothers dispensed more reinforcement than in the other two conditions, even though the reinforcement was generally positive. Similarly, in our study, daughters whose mothers used a great deal of positive (or negative) reinforcement were less cooperative. Second, in the Parpal and Maccoby experiment, a multiple regression entering both kinds of variables ruled out affective warmth rather than behavioral responsiveness as the causative factor in obtaining compliance. Other studies (for example, Lytton, 1977) confirm their finding (and ours) that parental responsiveness to the young child's wishes rather than affective warmth generates prosocial behavior. Reciprocity and responsiveness in the parent-child relationship may coexist in an affective atmosphere of mild-mannered warmth or one of abrasive confrontation or a mixture of both.

Authoritative Caregiving

Maccoby and Martin (1983) emphasize the importance of reciprocity in their description of what they call the "authoritative-reciprocal" pattern, describing it as "a pattern of family functioning in which children are required to be responsive to parental demands and parents accept a reciprocal responsibility to be as responsive as possible to their children's reasonable demands and points of view" (p. 46).

Reciprocity in a family requires that parents maintain the balance between agency and communion and encourage the same in their children: An imbalance favoring agency in either parent or child (that is, demanding more than one is willing to give) results in a focus on rights rather than on obligations, whereas an imbalance favoring communion (that is, giving more than one expects to receive) results in a focus on one's obligations to the neglect of one's rights. Authoritative parents represent a balance between agency and communion, as does the competent child type. Accordingly, families high in reciprocity among family members are those with authoritative parents and competent children.

The optimal parent-child relationship at any stage of

development can be recognized by its balance between parents' acknowledgment of the child's immaturity—shown by providing structure, control, and regimen (demandingness)—and the parents' acknowledgment of the child's emergence as a confident, competent person—shown by providing stimulation, warmth, and respect for individuality (responsiveness). Authoritative parents take a functional-rational approach to discipline, in which their exercise of control is grounded in intimate knowledge of their child and his or her circumstances rather than in arbitrary rules. In the various observable areas of the child's life—education, personal and health care, cooperating with other family members, handling resources, and social life—the success of the parent-child interaction can be assessed by how well the parent balances disciplinary demands with respect for the child and by how well the child balances reliance on parental care with willing progress toward emancipation.

Tomorrow

Although the population from which my sample was drawn is more educationally and socially advantaged than is the general population, investigators such as Reginald Clark (1983) and Sanford Dornbusch and his colleagues (Dornbusch and others, 1987) have found that our basic findings contrasting the impact on young children of authoritative, authoritarian, permissive, and rejecting-neglecting families have wide applicability to a heterogeneous population. In looking ahead, however, we will want to specify more precisely how the authoritative balance is achieved at various stages of the child's development in various subcultures. Our sample of predominantly Berkeley families were harbingers of secular changes. These secular changes—in particular those associated with the women's movement, which left many children undersupervised—may help explain why the optimal level of control in our sample was even higher than expected at T2, when the children were age nine. At that developmental stage, even rather strict authority was not associated with ill effects. During adolescence, the appropriate balance is likely to shift so as to favor responsiveness over demandingness as the child's need for parental guidance decreases and his or her need for autonomy increases.

However, during periods of social instability or in subcultures that pose special risks, the appropriate balance at all stages of development may require greater parental monitoring than during periods of social stability or than in subcultures that provide a protective environment.

Rapidly accelerating demographic and socioeconomic changes have resulted, according to Bronfenbrenner (1985, p. 337), in an "unravelling of the social fabric in which families, schools, and other immediate contexts of development are embedded." Bronfenbrenner posited that the optimal ratio of control relative to freedom within the family increases as the modal level of stability and structure in the larger society decreases. It follows from his analysis that in a context of social instability there is increased need for parental supervision. In view of this increased need, the changes brought about by the women's movement—as liberating as they have been for adults—do have possible negative consequences for children. Commitment to vocation may be accompanied by lessened commitment to parenting for many mothers. This lessened commitment can enable mothers to "let go" in appropriate ways. But it may also result in neglect unless there is commensurate commitment to parenting by fathers or other primary caretakers.

The importance of secure attachment to trustworthy adults has been documented in adolescence, as well as in early childhood. A secure attachment may be difficult to achieve with multiple caretakers, unless one parent assumes responsibility for carefully coordinating and supervising the multiple caretakers and the child feels truly special to at least one of them. Class distinctions, to the extent that they are based on different patterns of cognitive and interpersonal competence, can be expected to diminish as the home environment of middle-class children comes to resemble more closely the home environment of working-class children, who have always had to be self-sufficient because their mothers worked by necessity, if not by choice. Prospective parents and child advocates need information about what constitutes "good enough" parenting in our changing society.

In light of the secular changes already mentioned, I would like to see research on early and middle childhood focus on the following four issues:

1. Careful specification of the conditions that generate competence and deter pathology in children of various ages who are receiving primary care from caretakers other than their mothers, and in settings other than their home.
2. Identification of the parenting processes and patterns in ethnic families of color and of how these facilitate successful survival strategies in children. Such identification should take into account the factor of bicultural identity, which is not present in the majority culture.
3. Specification of the optimal ratio of freedom to control or of responsiveness to demandingness at successive developmental states, in changing secular conditions, and in diverse subcultures.
4. Examination of sex-differentiated socialization effects as gender roles are redefined.

References

Adorno, T. W., Frenkel-Brunswik, E., Levinson, D. J., and Sanford, R. N. *The Authoritarian Personality.* New York: Harper & Row, 1950.

Ainsworth, M. D. "The Development of Infant-Mother Attachment." In B. M. Caldwell and H. N. Ricciuti (eds.), *Review of Child Development Research.* Vol. 3. Chicago: University of Chicago Press, 1973.

Ausubel, D. P. *Theory and Problems of Child Development.* Orlando, Fla.: Grune & Stratton, 1957.

Azuma, H. "Why Study Child Development in Japan?" In H. Sherman, H. Azuma, and K. Hakuta (eds.), *Child Development and Education in Japan.* New York: W. H. Freeman, 1986.

Bakan, D. *The Duality of Existence: Isolation and Communion in Western Man.* Boston: Beacon Press, 1966.

Baumrind, D. "Child Care Practices Anteceding Three Patterns of Preschool Behavior." *Genetic Psychology Monographs,* 1967, *75,* 43–88.

Baumrind, D. "Current Patterns of Parental Authority." *Developmental Psychology Monographs,* 1971a, *4* (no. 1, part 2).

Baumrind, D. "Harmonious Parents and Their Preschool Children." *Developmental Psychology*, 1971b, *4* (1), 99–102.

Baumrind, D. "Some Thoughts About Childrearing." In U. Bronfenbrenner (ed.), *Readings in the Development of Human Behavior*. New York: Dryden Press, 1972.

Baumrind, D., and Black, A. E. "Socialization Practices Associated with Dimensions of Competence in Preschool Boys and Girls." *Child Development*, 1967, *38*, 291–327.

Becker, W. C. "Consequences of Different Kinds of Parental Discipline." In M. L. Hoffman and L. W. Hoffman (eds.), *Review of Child Development Research*. Vol. 1. New York: Russell Sage Foundation, 1964.

Block, J. *Lives Through Time*. Berkeley, Calif.: Bancroft Books, 1971.

Bowlby, J. *Attachment and Loss*. Vol. 1: *Attachment*. New York: Basic Books, 1969.

Bradley, J. V. *Distribution-Free Statistical Tests*. Englewood Cliffs, N.J.: Prentice-Hall, 1968.

Bronfenbrenner, U. "Freedom and Discipline Across the Decades." G. Becker, H. Becker, and L. Huber (eds.), *Ordnung und Unordnung* [Order and disorder]. Weinheim, West Germany: Beltz Verlag, 1985.

Bugenthal, D. B., and Shennum, W. A. " 'Difficult' Children as Elicitors and Targets of Adult Communication Patterns: An Attributional-Behavioral Transactional Analysis." *Monographs of the Society for Research in Child Development*, no. 205, 1984, *49* (1).

Burton, R. V., and Whiting, J.W.M. "The Absent Father and Cross-Sex Identity." *Merrill-Palmer Quarterly*, 1961, *7*, 85–95.

Clark, R. *Family Life and School Achievement: Why Poor Black Children Succeed or Fail*. Chicago: University of Chicago Press, 1983.

Coriat, I. H. "The Psychoanalytic Approach to Education." *Progressive Educator*, 1926, *3*, 19–25.

Dornbusch, S. M., and others. "The Relation of Parenting Style to Adolescent Performance." *Child Development*, 1987, *58*, 1244–1257.

Egeland, B., and Sroufe, L. A. "Attachment and Early Maltreatment." *Child Development,* 1981a, *52,* 44–52.

Egeland, B., and Sroufe, L. A. "Developmental Sequelae of Maltreatment in Infancy." In R. Rizley and D. Cicchetti (eds.), *Developmental Perspectives on Child Maltreatment.* New Directions for Child Development, no. 11. San Francisco: Jossey-Bass, 1981b.

Eisenberg, L. "Social Phobia: A Study in the Communication of Anxiety." *American Journal of Psychiatry,* 1958, *114,* 712–718.

Fromm, E. *Escape from Freedom.* New York: Holt, Rinehart & Winston, 1941.

Goldstein, M. J., and Rodnick, E. H. "The Family's Contribution to Schizophrenia: Current Status." *Schizophrenia Bulletin,* 1975, *1,* 48–63.

Goodman, P. *Compulsory Mis-Education.* New York: Horizon, 1964.

Grusec, J. E. "The Internalization of Altruistic Dispositions: A Cognitive Analysis." In E. T. Higgins, D. N. Ruble, and W. W. Hartup (eds.), *Social Cognition and Social Development.* New York: Cambridge University Press, 1983.

Hinde, R. A. *Biological Bases of Social Behavior.* New York: McGraw-Hill, 1974.

Hoffman, M. L. "Conscience, Personality and Socialization Techniques." *Human Development,* 1970, *13,* 90–126.

Hoffman, M. L. "Affective and Cognitive Processes in Moral Internalization." In E. T. Higgins, D. N. Ruble, and W. W. Hartup (eds.), *Social Cognition and Social Development.* New York: Cambridge University Press, 1983.

Hoffman, M. L., Rosen, S., and Lippitt, R. "Parental Coerciveness, Child Autonomy, and Child's Role at School." *Sociometry,* 1960, *23,* 15–22.

Homans, G. C. "Fundamental Social Processes." In N. J. Smelser (ed.), *Sociology: An Introduction.* New York: Wiley, 1967.

Israel, A. C., and Brown, M. S. "Effects of Directiveness of Instructions and Surveillance on the Production and Persistence of Children's Donations." *Journal of Experimental Child Psychology,* 1979, *27,* 250–261.

Kagan, J., and Moss, H. A. *Birth to Maturity: A Study in Psychological Development.* New York: Wiley, 1962.

Krebs, D. "Empathy and Altruism." *Journal of Personality and Social Psychology,* 1975, *32,* 1134–1146.

Leary, T. *Interpersonal Diagnosis of Personality: A Functional Theory and Methodology for Personality Evaluation.* New York: Ronald Press, 1957.

Lepper, M. "Intrinsic and Extrinsic Motivation in Children: Detrimental Effects of Superfluous Social Controls." In W. A. Collins (ed.), *Aspects of the Development of Competence: The Minnesota Symposium on Child Psychology.* Vol. 14. Hillsdale, N.J.: Erlbaum, 1981.

Lepper, M. "Social Control Processes and the Internalization of Social Values: An Attributional Perspective." In E. T. Higgins, D. N. Ruble, and W. W. Hartup (eds.), *Social Cognition and Social Development.* New York: Cambridge University Press, 1983.

Lewin, K., Lippitt, R., and White, R. K. "Patterns of Aggressive Behavior in Experimentally Created 'Social Climates.' " *Journal of Social Psychology,* 1939, *10,* 271–299.

Lewis, C. C. "The Effects of Parental Firm Control: A Reinterpretation of Findings." *Psychological Bulletin,* 1981, *90* (3), 547–563.

Lonner, W. J. "The Search for Psychological Universals." In H. C. Triandis and W. W. Lambert (eds.), *Handbook of Cross-Cultural Psychology.* Vol. 1. Newton, Mass.: Allyn & Bacon, 1980.

Lytton, H. "Correlates of Compliance and the Rudiments of Conscience in Two-Year-Old Boys." *Canadian Journal of Behavioral Science,* 1977, *9,* 243–251.

Maccoby, E. E. "Let's Not Overattribute to the Attribution Process: Comments on Social Cognition and Behavior." In E. T. Higgins, D. N. Ruble, and W. W. Hartup (eds.), *Social Cognition and Social Development.* New York: Cambridge University Press, 1983.

Maccoby, E. E., and Martin, J. A. "Socialization in the Context of the Family: Parent-Child Interaction." In P. Mussen (ed.), *Handbook of Child Psychology.* (4th ed.) Vol. 4. New York: Wiley, 1983.

Martin, J. A. "A Longitudinal Study of the Consequences of Early

Mother-Infant Interaction: A Microanalytic Approach." *Monographs of the Society for Research in Child Development*, no. 190, 1981, *46* (3).

Millar, W. S. "A Study of Operant Conditioning Under Delayed Reinforcement in Early Infancy." *Monographs of the Society for Research in Child Development*, 1972, *37* (2).

Naumberg, M. *The Child and the World*. San Diego, Calif.: Harcourt Brace Jovanovich, 1928.

Neill, A. S. *Summerhill*. New York: Hart, 1964.

O'Brien, R. A. "Positive and Negative Sets in Two-Choice Discrimination Learning by Children." Unpublished master's thesis, University of Illinois, Urbana, 1969.

Parker, G., Tupling, H., and Brown, L. B. "A Parental Bonding Instrument." *British Journal of Medical Psychology*, 1979, *52*, 1-10.

Parpal, M., and Maccoby, E. E. "Maternal Responsiveness and Subsequent Child Compliance." *Child Development*, 1985, *56*, 1326-1334.

Pulkkinen, L. "Self-Control and Continuity from Childhood to Adolescence." In P. B. Baltes and O. G. Brim (eds.), *Life-Span Development and Behavior*. Vol. 4. Orlando, Fla.: Academic Press, 1982.

Rogers, C. R. "A Therapist's View of Personal Goals." In *Pendle Hill Pamphlet 108*. Wallingford, Pa.: Pendle Hill, 1960.

Rollin, B. C., and Thomas, D. L. "A Theory of Parental Power and Child Compliance." In R. E. Cromwell and D. H. Oldson (eds.), *Power in Families*. Beverly Hills, Calif.: Sage, 1975.

Rosen, B. C., and D'Andrade, R. "The Psychological Origins of Achievement Motivation." *Sociometry*, 1959, *22*, 185-218.

Schaefer, E. S. "A Circumplex Model for Maternal Behavior." *Journal of Abnormal and Social Psychology*, 1959, *59*, 226-235.

Spence, J. T., and Helmreich, R. L. *Masculinity and Femininity: Their Psychological Dimensions, Correlates, and Antecedents*. Austin: University of Texas Press, 1978.

Staub, E. "A Child in Distress: The Influence of Nurturance and Modelling on Children's Attempts to Help." *Developmental Psychology*, 1971a, *5*, 124-132.

Staub, E. "Use of Role Playing and Induction in Training for Prosocial Behavior." *Child Development,* 1971b, *42,* 805–816.

Staub, E. *The Development of Prosocial Behavior in Children.* Morristown, N.J.: General Learning Press, 1975a.

Staub, E. "To Rear a Prosocial Child: Reasoning, Learning by Doing, and Learning by Teaching Others." In D. DePalma and J. Foley (eds.), *Moral Development: Current Theory and Research.* Hillsdale, N.J.: Erlbaum, 1975b.

Tronick, E., Ricks, M., and Cohn, J. "Maternal and Infant Affective Exchange: Patterns of Adaptation." In T. Field and A. Fogel (eds.), *Emotion and Interaction: Normal and High-Risk Infants.* Orlando, Fla.: Academic Press, 1982.

Watson, J. S. "Cognitive-Perceptual Development in Infancy: Setting for the Seventies." *Merill-Palmer Quarterly,* 1971, *17,* 139–152.

Watson, J. S. "Depression and the Perception of Control in Early Childhood." In J. G. Schulterbrandt and A. Raskin (eds.), *Depression in Childhood: Diagnosis, Treatment, and Conceptual Models.* New York: Raven Press, 1977.

Wiggins, J. S. "A Psychological Taxonomy of Trait-Descriptive Terms: The Interpersonal Domain." *Journal of Personality and Social Psychology,* 1979, *37,* 395–412.

Chapter 18

Parent-Adolescent Relationships

James Youniss

This chapter focuses on parent-adolescent relationship and the concept of *social capital*. The aims of this chapter are, first, to show how this concept helps ground findings on relationship in social context and, second, to show how findings on relationship help explicate the concept. James Coleman (1987, p. 36) has defined social capital, in terms of child rearing, as: "the norms, the social networks, and the relationships between adults and children that are of value for the child's growing up." Sociological theorists usually have either emphasized socialization techniques to the minimization of relationship or subordinated parent-adolescent relationship to social-structural determinants. Coleman, in contrast, makes the relationship a key mediator between adolescents, who are trying to enter society, and society, which consists of structures to which young adults must accommodate. In Coleman's view, the relationship functions to connect the generations as parents, who are members of society, share their knowledge and values with youths who seek adult status.

Coleman has introduced the concept of social capital, in part, to address a problem in our culture: Children need capital if they are to enter society with the shared viewpoint most adults hold. To acquire it, they need to have meaningful contact with adults who have capital and who consciously transmit it to children. Coleman notes, however, that many children either lack contact with adults or experience only narrow exchanges with them regarding important matters of religion, economics, schooling, politics, and cultural values. Capital can also come from sources other than the family. Schools and churches are capital-promoting institutions. However, such institutions often are not coordinated with one another or with the family, and, as a consequence, their potential advantages are diminished. Coleman cites the case of disadvantaged black youths, who frequently come from single-parent homes. In some communities, the most powerful institution is the church. However, by law, the church is prohibited from helping the school help children, "through, for example, after-school programs and youth organizations. Thus, the disadvantaged are harmed, and the black disadvantaged are especially harmed by making impossible the use of social capital that does exist in a setting where this capital is not abundant" (Coleman, 1987, p. 37).

As will be shown in this chapter, there seems to be a division of specializations such that contemporary households that produce income are separated from households that rear children. Moreover, some households provide abundant social capital through a two-parent effort that is integrated with private schooling and peer organizations, while other households provide little capital through one parent, schooling that is not accountable, and a community that does not uphold standards for conduct. The concept, then, offers psychologists a way to view parent-adolescent relationships within a social framework and, at the same time, to explore the variations in relationship that differentiate adolescents' experience of contemporary society. If one is to take seriously the proposition that development is socially mediated (see Wertsch, 1985), it is necessary to study variations among adolescents and to trace them back to social origins. The concept of social capital seems appropriate for this task.

This chapter begins with a description of social capital and its place in Coleman's broader perspective on contemporary society. Next, empirical findings on parent-adolescent relationship are reviewed so that key aspects of the transfer of social capital between generations can be assessed. Coleman suggests how the process might work but also raises the question of whether the process is functioning in families today. Findings are summarized, therefore, in terms of parent-adolescent communication, parental authority, and mutual respect. Lastly, an attempt is made to project implications of the concept to the short-term future of the next twenty years.

Coleman's View

One of Coleman's abiding interests as a researcher has been American education—especially the education of minorities. Of present concern are variations in family structure in minority populations, public and private schooling, and the demographic makeup of school students. For example, only 20 percent of the current United States population under nineteen years of age is composed of white males. This entails a challenge for schools, which must learn to deal with students who, unlike those in the past, have not come to them from advantaged positions or with strong academic motivation. This issue may be conjoined with another concern regarding family support for these populations: In some areas of the nation, minority students frequently come from single-parent households and communities that do not provide strong supporting structures for achievement. Coleman realizes that there are variations in this pattern such that some groups of students succeed academically despite these circumstances. One example is of low-income students whose parents have sent them to private parochial schools, and another is of Asian students whose parents have co-taught themselves as their children have learned. It has not escaped Coleman's attention that these successes share the feature of parental involvement in learning and parental support of the schools their children attend.

Coleman proposes that capital comes from within the family, from outside institutions, and through their conjunction. Inputs that come from family relations include "attitudes, effort, and conception of self"; inputs from institutions, such as schools, include "opportunities, demands, and rewards" (Coleman, 1987, p. 35). Their conjunction, such as with the family-school relation, provides still other inputs that may form a community structure that would value, for example, academic achievement or adherence to communal standards for behavior, as is true for some Asian immigrant groups. Viewing society in a macro sense, Coleman sees a depletion of social capital insofar as American families are giving up one of their historic functions—providing for the welfare of its members. This is due in part to an income redistribution away from families with children. Given that an estimated 50 percent of dependent children are not living with both biological parents (Glick, 1980), the issue of depletion becomes real for a large segment of the population. Weiss (1982) and Weitzman (1985) have documented the immediate and long-term income differential between divorced mothers who have custody of their children and their former husbands who live apart from them. Coleman puts these findings into a broader perspective by proposing that an unusual division of labor has evolved such that "adults in a portion of the nation's households are occupied in having children, and adults in another portion are occupied with making money; . . . increasingly, households are specializing in one of these two activities" (1987, p. 33). A sign of this division is found in the call for government assistance in the task of rearing children via day care, school lunches, compensatory education, job training, and health insurance.

In describing the erosion of social capital within the household, Coleman notes the importance of relations with adults that can provide youths with a set of experiences and associated views that facilitate their entrance and incorporation into adult society. He highlights elemental processes, such as family recreation, which mixes persons of diverse ages in common enjoyment, or discussion, during which ideas are exchanged about important social and political topics. For Coleman, an advantage is implied for youths whose participation includes exposure to adults' norms as criteria of worth. While at one time this accrued naturally, as adults and children worked side by side, now the process has to be mediated through other means. In completing this idea, Coleman returns to a position he took some years ago in his well-known statement on the segregation of youths from adults and adult society (Coleman, 1961). The argument remains essentially intact that when youths are focused on their own subculture, they forfeit opportunities for gaining capital that adults could share with them. That argument can now be expanded because of the increased segregation that comes from the identification of youth as a consumer group for music, clothes, food, and recreation (see Gilbert, 1986). Insofar as shopping malls have replaced neighborhood shops and commercialized recreational events have replaced family social gatherings, the environment overall has become increasingly "inhospitable to the relations between adults and children that constitute social capital for children's growth" (Coleman, 1987, p. 37).

General Characteristics of Parent-Adolescent Relationship

The review that follows will present findings that illustrate general characteristics of the relationship insofar as they inform the concept of social capital.

Closeness. Ketterlinus (1987) reported on a sample of about six hundred high school students from Baltimore, Maryland, who were asked to say how "close" they felt to their mothers and fathers. Scores were near to ceiling for both parents. Youniss and Ketterlinus (1987) and Smollar and Youniss (1985) found that, after divorce, closeness to custodial mothers remained at ceiling while closeness to fathers dropped precipitously, especially for female adolescents. Closeness has been measured through other means and found to be rather strong throughout the adolescent period. Youniss and Smollar (1985) found that "just talking" with parents was a favorite activity for adolescents. Closeness has a counterpart in what Grotevant and Cooper (1986) have termed "connectedness." They propose that adolescents remain connected to their parents during the extended process of transforming their relationship from a state of dependence to one of mutual interdependence, which will be developed further in adulthood (White, Speisman, and Costos, 1983). The concept of connectedness may have an equivalent in Greenberg, Siegel, and Leitch's (1983) concept of adolescents' "attachment" to parents.

Topics of Discussion. Part of Coleman's concern devolves on the question of whether, in a time of increasing age segregation, adolescents talk to adults and learn what adults are thinking. Relevant empirical findings are clear and consistent. First, adolescents spontaneously say that they have conversations about their lives with their parents, and in particular with their mothers (Youniss and Smollar, 1985). Second, when adolescents have been asked whom they seek out for advice about various areas of their lives, they have regularly nominated parents as advisers regarding career options, schooling, financial matters, and personal problems (see Kandel and Lesser, 1972; Wintre, Hicks, McVey, and Fox, 1988). Sebald (1986) has added to this finding with data on advice seeking from three adolescent cohorts, which were seen in 1963, 1976, and 1982, respectively. Parents were advisers of choice on the above matters for all three cohorts, although there was a drop-off in the 1976 sample. However, the 1983 sample showed recovered levels of parental advice seeking that matched 1963 levels. Hunter (1985) reported that most of the 180 adolescents in her sample said that they had discussed school, career, family problems, and friendship with their parents as well as with their friends. About one-half of these adolescents had discussed social-political issues and religion with their parents.

Forms of Communication. Coleman has questioned whether parents discuss their views with adolescents so as to communicate that there are distinctions among better and worse views toward society. The question is whether, in becoming "friends" with their sons and daughters, parents might neglect to express preferences or articulate standards. There are several kinds of data that bear on this issue. First, a number of researchers have directly observed on-line interactive discussions between adolescents and parents. Although diverse tasks and coding schemes have been employed, it has been generally found that parents assert their viewpoints and point out why they disagree with the views that adolescents express (see Bell and Bell, 1983). Cooper, Grotevant, and Condon (1983) reported also that parents ordinarily solicited further discussion of differences, implying a desire for engagement rather than disinterest (see Zahaykevich, 1987). Second, several investigators have reported family members' descriptions of the forms of interactions that occur in discussion. Chaffe, McLeod, and Wackman (1973) reported four types of family discussion of political-social issues, two of which, "pluralistic" and "consensual," entailed serious exchanges of views. Third, Youniss and Smollar (1985) asked adolescents to describe disputes with parents and then to say how these disputes were resolved. In the main, resolution involved complying with parents' wishes; however, compliance was often preceded by give and take during which rationales for the conflicting views were discussed.

Authority. Damon (1977) found that young children perceived their parents as naturally having all-encompassing authority, while preadolescents qualified parental authority so that it was dependent on expertise. Huard (1980) extended Damon's interview to adolescent subjects and found that they recognized parents' authority and also identified it with expertise. Hunter (1984) approached authority another way by asking adolescents to describe the ways in which their parents dealt with differences in opinions when they wanted adolescents to comply with their positions. The typical response was that parents took the role of unilateral authorities by demanding compliance. Parents were identified with the statements: "my father says I'm supposed to do what he tells me to do," and "my mother tells me she points out where I'm wrong for my own good." The fact that parents set themselves up as authorities was attested to in still another way by adolescents who called parents "judgmental," on the one hand, and said that parents insisted on compliance because "they know better than I do," on the other (Smollar and Youniss, 1985). Smith (1983) reported data from parents who were asked to describe the complementary side of Hunter's situation of parent-adolescent differences of opinion. Parents said that the procedure they used most frequently was to demand compliance but to cushion it with statements that gave assurances that the adolescent's welfare was at stake. The second most used procedure was sheer demand for compliance without a cushion. Lastly, Harris and Howard (1981) reported responses from 844 teenagers who were asked whether there was a boss in their families and whether the boss exercised authority with or without reasonableness. Forty percent of the students nominated the father as the boss, while 34 percent nominated both parents. Forty percent of the students said that the boss exercised authority in a very reasonable manner, while 25 percent believed that the family boss was not so reasonable.

Discipline. There is a small supplemental literature that is based on parents' own descriptions of how they go about disciplining their adolescent children. McHenry, Price-Bonham, and O'Bryant (1981) reported data from 106 mother-father pairs.

Mothers and fathers agreed on the rank order of the most commonly used disciplinary techniques: talk out problems, withdraw privileges, use physical punishment, and isolate children. DeSantis (1986) found that parents stated that they used direct or indirect techniques depending on the direness of the situation they were confronting. Direct intervention was used with alcohol problems and failing school performance. These data are congruent with adolescents' perceptions (DeTurk and Miller, 1983) that parents use a variety of procedures in trying to persuade their adolescent sons and daughters to act as they desire. Techniques range from threats to promises of rewards and are sometimes expressed with raw power, while at other times they are couched in persuasive rationales (see Hunter, 1984). Supporting data are available from adolescents who judged a list of potential misbehaviors and said which would evoke parental intervention (Youniss and Smollar, 1985). About half of the items, which included coming home late or not doing house chores, were judged as likely to incur parents' disciplinary actions.

Respect and Mutual Understanding. Youniss and Smollar (1985) found that adolescents felt respect for their parents, whom they described as working and sacrificing for the family's welfare. This result was accompanied by appreciation of parents as individuals and by a sense of obligation toward parents. White, Speisman, and Costos (1983) reported similar data from young adults who showed an advanced appreciation of their parents' individuality. Other investigators have reported supporting findings that youths believe that their parents understand them (Hunter, 1985; Ketterlinus, 1987; Mortimer, Lorence, and Kumka, 1986). The last result is interesting in that college-aged males who said they felt that their fathers understood them showed successful career patterns over the ensuing decade. Lastly, there is a literature on parent-youth agreement that is exemplified by Acock and Bengtson's (1978) finding of high agreement among 653 mother-father-youth triads on religiosity, political conservatism, the work ethic, and norms for sexual behavior.

Parents and Peers. There is an extensive literature that was previously framed by the question of whether adolescents are influenced more by parents or by peers. Recent studies are cited to show that this may be an inappropriate question because, among other things, adolescents tend to choose peers who are similar to themselves and who share values that their parents endorse (Fasick, 1984). Berndt (1979) found that older adolescents believe that their parents and the adolescents' friends share common values. Hunter and Youniss (1982) found that adolescents judged their parents to be similar to peers on major dimensions of relationship. Finally, Brown, Clasen, and Eicher (1985) reported that adolescents differentiated peer groups according to types that implied varying degrees of compatibility with dominant societal values. In sum, these findings illustrate that peer associations may be seen as extensions of parental relationships rather than as counterforces that introduce youths to anticultural values.

Conclusion

The foregoing review has helped explicate the concept of social capital as it applies to parent-adolescent relationship. An impressive array of results illustrates that the relationship still provides a bridge for knowledge and values across the generations. The data also show that parents take authority and their generational responsibility seriously and that adolescents respect parents enough to take seriously the values that parents espouse. Parents communicate beliefs that are substantive. These beliefs are explained, argued over, and held up as standards against which adolescents' views are judged. Parents have not given up their roles as authorities, but they assert their knowledge as being grounded in societal experience. In turn, adolescents respect their parents and feel close to them. Further, they are secure in the belief that parents typically work for their best interests. Parents are advisers and confidants, but not for all matters. There is overlap between the issues that adolescents take up with parents and with friends. Moreover, adolescents say that their parents and friends hold similar values; in this regard, peers seem to extend rather than contradict parental relations.

Coleman's concept may help broaden psychologists' understanding of the parent-adolescent relationship so that it is seen as leading the younger generation toward a commitment to carry on what the older generation has preserved. While the relationship can be studied for the intrasubject skills it might engender, or for the specific knowledge that is transmitted through it, social capital adds a further dimension. In the sense viewed here, the relationship provides adolescents with a commitment to social standards and values, as well as interest in wanting to explore the society their parents value. As David Riesman (1953) noted some time ago, modern parents realize that their offspring are likely to live in a society that is different from theirs, has new problems, and is open to changing standards. They do not, therefore, seek to duplicate themselves through their offspring by transmitting specific knowledge; that would be dysfunctional. The concept of social capital puts the focus on parents' helping their sons and daughters gain entrance to society and achieve advantageous positions in it. Once in society, this new generation, knowing whence it came, can help redirect it where it sees best.

Tomorrow

From the point of view of parent-adolescent relationship, two areas of concern are evident. One is divorce, insofar as father-adolescent relations often deteriorate to such an extent that little if any capital may be conveyed through them. Adolescents often feel distant from and hostile toward their fathers following their parents' divorce. This is understandable given that, after divorce, fathers typically experience income gains while custodial mothers and the children suffer income reduction. Further, communication between these fathers and their teenagers is often constricted. Youths whose family situations follow the above pattern are likely to suffer an obvious loss of social capital relative to youths who maintain close, positive relations with fathers. This source of loss may be exacerbated when youths are situated in a community that lacks the presence of norm-bearing adults and supporting institutions. For many middle-class youths, mother's remarriage or geographic relocation near to extended family members can provide compensatory social capital. For many other youths, however, loss of paternal relationship entails a larger cutoff from capital sources that our society has yet to remedy.

A second potential problem is seen in the area of work, which is undergoing structural transformation in the United States. Families historically have served as means for gaining jobs. Economists estimate that jobs as we presently know them may be shifting such that, for example, the twenty-five million positions in manufacturing today will become three million by 2010. Replacement positions are most likely to come from the growing service sector as demands for janitors, fast food workers, and the like increase. Technology is largely responsible for the changing structure, and technically sophisticated personnel will be needed. In fact, demand will be high for two reasons. First, the post-*Sputnik* cohort of scientists and engineers will reach retirement age in the mid 1990s. Second, their replacements will have to come from the current population of children and the unknown factor of future immigrants. In the current population of children under nineteen years of age, white males, the group that historically has provided technical personnel, are a minority. The remainder is constituted mainly of females, blacks, and Hispanics, who traditionally have not entered these fields. In the future, new opportunity will exist for these groups. The question is whether sufficient social capital will be available to encourage these youths to take up the educational challenge that is prerequisite to their taking advantage of the opportunity.

References

Acock, A. C., and Bengtson, V. L. "On the Relative Influence of Mothers and Fathers: A Covariance Analysis of Political and Religious Socialization." *Journal of Marriage and the Family,* 1978, *40,* 519–530.

Bell, D. C., and Bell, L. G. "Parental Validation and Support in the Development of Adolescent Daughters." In H. D. Grotevant and C. R. Cooper (eds.), *Adolescent Development in the Family.* New Directions for Child Development, no. 22. San Francisco: Jossey-Bass, 1983.

Berndt, T. J. "Developmental Changes in Conformity to Peers and Parents." *Developmental Psychology,* 1979, *15,* 608–616.

Brown, B. B., Clasen, D. R., and Eicher, S. A. "Perceptions of Peer

Pressure, Peer Conformity Dispositions, and Self-Reported Behavior Among Adolescents." Paper presented at the biennial meeting of the Society for Research in Child Development, Toronto, Canada, April 1985.

Chaffe, S. H., McLeod, J. M., and Wackman, D. B. "Family Communication Patterns and Adolescent Political Participation." In J. Dennis (ed.), *Socialization to Politics*. New York: Wiley, 1973.

Coleman, J. *The Adolescent Society*. New York: Free Press, 1961.

Coleman, J. S. "Families and Schools." *Educational Researcher*, 1987, *16*, 32–38.

Cooper, C. R., Grotevant, H. D., and Condon, S. M. "Individuation and Connectedness in the Family as a Context for Adolescent Identity Formation and Role-Taking Skill." In H. D. Grotevant and C. R. Cooper (eds.), *Adolescent Development in the Family*. New Directions for Child Development, no. 22. San Francisco: Jossey-Bass, 1983.

Damon, W. *The Social World of the Child*. San Francisco: Jossey-Bass, 1977.

DeSantis, J. P. "Parents' Socialization Procedures for Adolescent Friend Associations and Alcohol Use." Unpublished master's thesis, Department of Psychology, Catholic University of America, 1986.

DeTurk, M., and Miller, G. R. "Adolescent Perceptions of Parental Persuasive Message Strategies." *Journal of Marriage and the Family*, 1983, *45*, 543–552.

Fasick, F. A. "Parents, Peers, Youth Culture and Autonomy in Adolescence." *Adolescence*, 1984, *19*, 143–157.

Gilbert, J. *A Cycle of Outrage: America's Reaction to Juvenile Delinquency in the 1950s*. New York: Oxford University Press, 1986.

Glick, P. C. "Remarriage: Some Recent Changes and Variations." *Journal of Family Issues*, 1980, *1*, 455–478.

Greenberg, M. T., Siegel, J. M., and Leitch, C. J. "The Nature and Importance of Attachment Relationships to Parents and Peers During Adolescence." *Journal of Youth and Adolescence*, 1983, *12*, 373–386.

Grotevant, H. D., and Cooper, C. R. "Individuation in Family

Relationships: A Perspective on Individual Differences in the Development of Identity and Role-Taking Skill in Adolescence." *Human Development,* 1986, *29,* 82–100.

Harris, I. D., and Howard, K. I. "Perceived Parental Authority: Reasonable and Unreasonable." *Journal of Youth and Adolescence,* 1981, *10,* 273–286.

Huard, C. A. "A Cognitive-Developmental Analysis of Children's Conceptions of Interpersonal Authority." Unpublished doctoral dissertation, Department of Psychology, Catholic University of America, 1980.

Hunter, F. T. "Socializing Procedures in Parent-Child and Friendship Relations During Adolescence." *Developmental Psychology,* 1984, *20,* 1092–1099.

Hunter, F. T. "Adolescents' Perceptions of Discussions with Parents and Friends." *Developmental Psychology,* 1985, *21,* 433–440.

Hunter, F. T., and Youniss, J. "Changes in Functions in Three Relations During Adolescence." *Developmental Psychology,* 1982, *18,* 806–811.

Kandel, D. B., and Lesser, G. S. *Youth in Two Worlds: U.S. and Denmark.* San Francisco: Jossey-Bass, 1972.

Ketterlinus, R. D. "Transformations in Adolescents' Relationships with Parents, Friends, and Peers and Their Behavioral Correlates." Unpublished doctoral dissertation, Department of Psychology, Catholic University of America, 1987.

McHenry, P. C., Price-Bonham, S., and O'Bryant, S. L. "Adolescent Discipline: Different Family Members' Perceptions." *Journal of Youth and Adolescence,* 1981, *10,* 327–337.

Mortimer, J. T., Lorence, J., and Kumka, D. S. *Work, Family, and Personality: Transition to Adulthood.* Norwood, N.J.: Ablex, 1986.

Riesman, D. *The Lonely Crowd.* Garden City, N.Y.: Doubleday, 1953.

Sebald, H. "Adolescents Shifting Orientation Toward Parents and Peers: A Curvilinear Trend over Recent Decades." *Journal of Marriage and the Family,* 1986, *48,* 5–13.

Smith, T. E. "Adolescents' Reactions to Attempted Parental

Control and Influence Techniques." *Journal of Marriage and the Family,* 1983, *45,* 533–542.

Smollar, J., and Youniss, J. "Parent-Adolescent Relations in Adolescents Whose Parents Are Divorced." *Journal of Early Adolescence,* 1985, *5,* 129–144.

Weiss, R. S. "The Impact of Marital Dissolution on Income and Consumption in Single-Parent Households." *Journal of Marriage and the Family,* 1982, *46,* 115–127.

Weitzman, L. J. *The Divorce Revolution: The Unexpected Social and Economic Consequences for Women and Children in America.* New York: Free Press, 1985.

Wertsch, J. V. *Vygotsky and the Social Formation of Mind.* Cambridge, Mass.: Harvard University Press, 1985.

White, K. M., Speisman, J. C., and Costos, D. "Young Adults and Their Parents: From Individuation to Mutuality." In H. D. Grotevant and C. R. Cooper (eds.), *Adolescent Development in the Family.* New Directions for Child Development, no. 22. San Francisco: Jossey-Bass, 1983.

Wintre, M. G., Hicks, R., McVey, G., and Fox, J. "Age and Sex Differences in Choice of Consultant for Various Types of Problems." *Child Development,* 1988, *59,* 1211–1231.

Youniss, J., and Ketterlinus, R. D. "Communication and Connectedness in Mother- and Father-Adolescent Relationships." *Journal of Youth and Adolescence,* 1987, *16,* 265–280.

Youniss, J., and Smollar, J. *Adolescent Relations with Mothers, Fathers, and Friends.* Chicago: University of Chicago Press, 1985.

Zahaykevich, M. "An Object Relations View of Adolescent Gender Formation in Maternal Discourse." Paper presented at the biennial meeting of the Society for Research in Child Development, Baltimore, Md., April 1987.

Chapter 19

Interpersonal Competence Training

Myrna B. Shure

Interpersonal, or social, competence can mean different things to different people, including specific behaviors, rates of interaction, self-concept, and so forth (Dodge, 1985). Regarding definition, Dodge also comments that "one reasonable research path is to study the correlates and outcomes of specific behaviors, and to declare as incompetent those behaviors that indicate a degree of risk for later maladaptation" (1985, p. 9). Clearly, some children display behaviors that make them appear to be at greater risk than others for later, more serious problems.

The eloquent and sensitive review by Parker and Asher (1987) and research by Smith and Fogg (1979) suggest that while much more needs to be learned, the most clearly identified risk factors for psychopathology, delinquency, substance abuse, or all three appear to be: (1) antisocial, rebellious, and defiant behaviors, (2) poor peer relations, (3) poor academic skills, and (4) low self-esteem. The risk status of shy, withdrawn behavior is, at present, still unclear; but shy, withdrawn second to fifth graders report significantly more depressive symptoms and higher rates of anxiety than do sociable children (Straus, Forehand, Smith, and Frame, 1986), and extreme withdrawal that persists over several years might well represent a population at risk for internalizing problems (Rubin, 1985).

In addition to behaviors, or what people *do*, my view of interpersonal competence gives equal weight to how people think,

393

because I believe that how people think affects what they do—not just in adults but, as far as we can measure it, in children as young as four years of age.

Using my own and others' research in interpersonal cognitive problem solving (ICPS) as one example, this chapter will address (overlapping) issues about how intervention to enhance interpersonal *cognitive* competence may improve interpersonal *behavioral* competence and ultimately, perhaps, promote positive mental health and prevent later psychopathology, delinquency, substance abuse, or all three.

Regarding intervention, issues that developmental, community, and clinical psychologists, as well as educators and members of related disciplines, have been grappling with over the past decade include: (1) who should be trained, (2) how to intervene, (3) when to intervene, and (4) how long an intervention should be. While strategies regarding these are guided by one's theoretical orientation and research priorities, some choices may contribute to why some interventions may show greater impact than others.

Who Should Be Trained?

In normal populations, the question is whether only those who already show particular developmental deficits identified as predictors of later dysfunction should receive individualized or small-group intervention or whether mass targeting (training, for example, an entire classroom) might be more effective in the long run.

Advocating the individualized, or specifically targeted, approach, Dodge (1985), Coie (1985), and Asher (1985) believe that interventions should be tailored to the specific cognitive or behavioral deficits displayed by the individual child or subgroup. At the cognitive level, Dodge believes that a child who, for example, inaccurately perceives another's intention as hostile (Dodge and Frame, 1982) should not receive the same intervention as one who correctly encodes such social cues but is unable to generate more than one effective behavioral response to those interpreted cues. At the behavioral level, for example, actively rejected children display different behaviors than do neglected ones, behaviors such as increased aggression, disruptiveness, and sometimes poorer academic skills. Because these behaviors place rejected children at greater risk than youngsters who are neglected—primarily ignored—they are not only in greater need of intervention but clearly in need of different ones.

The other option, to mass target, may provide advantages that individualized or subgroup (that is, tailored) interventions may not. Assessing each child's cognitive and behavioral deficiencies would produce the need for many different interventions; mass targeting would reach more youngsters in a shorter period. Tailored interventions are designed to treat only those already showing high-risk behaviors; mass-targeted interventions may *prevent* such behaviors from occurring at all. Tailored interventions often require removing children from the classroom, possibly making them feel picked on or special or leaving those not "chosen" to feel that they are missing something or to feel left out.

Regarding group versus individualized interventions, Rose (1982) adds that a group setting is generally more attractive to children than is one-on-one interaction with an adult. Also, a group setting affords multiple opportunities to learn from other, more competent classmates. Importantly for those more competent classmates, helping others can further strengthen their own self-esteem and social competence. Of course, there is the question of whether an intervention given to someone who does not need it can actually do that person harm—and whether all recipients, say in a classroom, can have equal opportunity to respond and therefore to benefit. Can quality control be adequately maintained? That is, are the training agents doing a good job?

In our ICPS interventions, we designed programs that could be conducted in small groups within the classroom (Shure and Spivack, 1971, 1974). In preschool classes, teachers were able to conduct each lesson twice daily, once in the morning and once in the afternoon, with groups of six to eight youngsters each (only twelve to eighteen youngsters were in any given classroom). Demonstrations and observations in each classroom were made on a regular basis, at least once a week. This procedure not only monitored quality control but created improvements in the intervention by enabling us to watch the teachers implement the techniques and observe how the children responded (or did not respond) to those techniques. What we did to teach how to think through and solve real-life problems would probably not really hurt anyone, or it would, as Bell has expressed, "at worst be ineffective for those not at risk and, hopefully, benefit those who are" (Richard Bell, personal communication, 1984).

Based on the theoretical position that ICPS skills—namely, alternative problem solving and consequential thinking—could be taught and that behavior could be guided by cognitive mediators rather than the other way around, we found evaluation, at least in very young children, to be more meaningful with the mass-targeted approach. Here is what we found. For those who started out *not* at risk (not behaviorally impulsive or inhibited) at the beginning of preschool, there was no difference between trained and nontrained control youngsters in terms of the percentage of those still not at risk at the end of the preschool year—thirty-seven of forty-one trained, forty-three of fifty controls. But in kindergarten, only eighteen, or 58 percent of the thirty-one remaining controls, were still not at risk. So thirteen children got worse (about 42 percent). But for those who were trained, the picture was different. Of twenty-nine who began not at risk, twenty-five were still not at risk (86 percent) at the end of the preschool year—significantly more than the nontrained controls—and only four (14 percent) got worse—significantly fewer than the nontrained controls (Shure and Spivack, 1982).

For us, mass targeting had a major advantage in that it may have prevented withholding of help from unidentified false negatives in the preschool year (that is, those incorrectly identified to be not at risk). Further, the intervention may have prevented inhibited youngsters from developing extreme withdrawal, which might have endured over several years and which, as noted earlier, might have put these children at risk for internalizing problems.

Because our intervention strategies guided the children to respond (and not be given ideas or suggestions by the teacher), it was important to have ICPS-competent as well as ICPS-deficient youngsters in a group—to help avoid group silence. So it was both research and intervention strategies that guided us toward mass targeting. Then, once we identified the teacher as training agent, we found it much more feasible to train all of his or her students and not select just some of them. No one felt special, picked on, or left out.

Could Dodge, whose social cue encoding and generating of solutions (called response search) are part of a progressive five-step model of social competence, apply that model to all youngsters in a classroom? It would be important to test the preventive impact of that model (which includes evaluating options [consequences], choosing among those options, and finally carrying out the "best" solutions), an impact that could help unidentified false positives benefit over time. It is possible that adding attributional training (Dodge steps 1 and 2) to generating, evaluating, and carrying out solutions (steps 3 through 5)—steps similar to those of ICPS intervention—could reduce or prevent aggression more than could steps 3 through 5 alone. It seems reasonable to assume that such an addition could benefit aggressive children whether the aggression is based on inaccurately perceived hostile intentions of another (see Dodge, 1986) or whether aggression, reduced or prevented via increased solution and consequence competencies, could, in turn, modify the accuracy of the attributions. It is possible that other, as yet unidentified, high-risk behaviors could be reduced or prevented by inclusion of the entire model in an entire classroom.

How to Intervene

The issue of how to intervene cuts across the issue of whom to train. Specifically tailored interventions are generally conducted outside the classroom. We believe that one way to capitalize on the above-mentioned consistent-reinforcement advantage brought out by Hawkins and Weis (1985) is to have the teacher who is with the youngsters all day supplement the formal lessons with informal use of the approach when real problems come up during the day. We have done that with a technique we call problem-solving communication, or dialoguing.

While dialoguing follows no prescribed recipe and the content varies with the particular problem at hand, the underlying process generally includes guiding the person to: (1) identify the problem, (2) consider how she or he, and others involved, might feel, (3) anticipate what might happen next, and (4) recognize that there is more than one way to solve a problem. Focusing on a process rather than on a content of thought, the goal is to help a person learn to apply ICPS skills to new problems, with different people, in different places.

Here is how an ICPS-trained teacher talked with four-year-old Robert, who had snatched some magnets from Erik:

Teacher: Robert, what happened when you snatched those magnets from Erik?

Robert: He hit me.

Teacher: How did that make you feel?

Robert: Sad.

Teacher: You wanted to play with magnets, right?

Robert: Right.

Teacher: Snatching it is one way to get him to give them to you. Can you think of a different idea?

Robert: Ask him.

Teacher: (*Calls Erik over.*) Robert, you thought of asking him for the magnets. Go ahead and ask him.

Robert: (*to Erik*) Can I hold the magnets?

Erik: No!

Teacher: Oh, Robert, he said no. Can you think of a *different* way?

Robert: (*Starts to cry.*)

Teacher: I know you're feeling sad now, but I bet if you think real hard, you'll find a different idea. You could ask or . . . ?

Robert: (*after several seconds*) I'll give 'em back when I'm finished.

Erik: (*reluctantly*) Okay.

Teacher: Very good, Robert. You thought of another way to get Erik to let you play with those magnets. How do you feel now?

Robert: (Smiles.) Happy.

Teacher: I'm glad, and you thought of that all by yourself.

Source: Spivack and Shure, 1974, p. 62.

Robert was encouraged to think of other solutions to his problem. With a little guidance and encouragement, Robert was able to carry his thought process to completion.

While it is possible that dialoguing in the absence of formal structured lessons may enhance behavioral adjustment (a speculation that has not yet been researched), there are studies that did not show behavior change with structured lessons in the absence of dialoguing (see Durlak and Sherman, 1979; Sharp, 1981). With dialoguing combined with the ICPS structured program script showing behavior gains in preschool children (Allen, 1978; Feis and Simons, 1985; Spivack and Shure, 1974; Nancy Wowkanech, personal communication, 1978) and in school-aged youngsters (Weissberg and others, 1981), it appears thus far that dialoguing really is an essential ingredient. While other factors may account for behavior change or lack of it in these investigations, dialoguing introduces an in vivo quality by encouraging children to exercise their ICPS skills so as to bring about more effective use of ICPS thought when faced with real problems of their own. Regarding this, Weissberg and Gesten (1982) note that teachers of school-aged children report that dialoguing may be the key to independent problem-solving thought, and Weissberg and others (1981) attribute behavior change in their latter studies, at least in part, to more systematic incorporation of dialoguing into their overall training format. Perhaps the real issue for any intervention is whether use of the concepts taught or coached during the day when the situation is relevant will help children incorporate what they are learning (in our case, how they think) into what they do and how they behave.

When to Intervene

Unquestionably, basic research must seek to identify who is at risk for particular dysfunctions, identify transition points at which that risk may be heightened, and address the issue of how to improve prediction in order to permit intervening at optimal developmental stages. A study by Smith and Fogg (1979) can illustrate for us how identification and prediction research can guide developmentally and conceptually appropriate interventions at appropriate sensitive periods. Smith and Fogg found that the combination of low grades, extreme rebelliousness, and attitudes about and incidence of cigarette smoking in seventh grade can predict substance abuse of several classifications of drugs in ninth grade. The question now becomes whether intervention should be given only to those who show those predictor deficits in seventh grade or whether appropriate competency intervention should be implemented even earlier to prevent those predictor deficits from first occurring. Thus, in addition to the question of who the recipients should be (another argument for mass targeting), the issue of timing becomes crucial as well. For ICPS research, it appears clear that very early intervention has preventive impact. Because behavior patterns that can predict later problems show up as early as kindergarten (Spivack, Marcus, and Swift, 1986), it seems reasonable and logical to begin intervention, as my colleagues and I did, even before that.

How Long Should an Intervention Be?

Overlapping with the issue of when to intervene in a child's life, the length of an intervention will depend on how long it takes to reach its goals, which may itself depend on the age group being trained. In our ICPS research, preschool and kindergarten youngsters decreased in both impulsive and inhibited behaviors and increased in positive, prosocial behaviors after one four-month exposure. In older children, we found in two separate studies (Shure, 1984, 1986) that fifth graders improved in positive behaviors after one four-month exposure but decreased in negative ones, especially impulsive behaviors, only after another four-month exposure in sixth grade.

It is possible that negative behaviors *are* more difficult to change in older than in younger children because more habitual patterns of behavior might be more resistant to change. Or it is possible that the logistics of incorporation in the grades is more difficult due to curriculum and other demands being greater than in preschool or in kindergarten. While teachers could implement ICPS every day with the younger children, three times a week was the maximum the fifth and sixth grade teachers could muster. And dialoguing, so important to ICPS intervention, often could not occur on the spot, when the effects would be most potent.

Gesten and others (1982) found some interesting results with a mass-targeted ICPS program (called social problem solving, or SPS, by this research team) for second and third graders. First, both positive and negative (acting out) behavior gains did not show up in ratings of teachers until one year later. The fact that immediate behavior gains of controls—a group whose ICPS (SPS) skills never improved—returned to baseline at follow-up does support the mediational role that interpersonal cognitive skills play in behavior. But what might have been happening here with the trained groups? It is possible that it really did take another year for behavior gains to emerge. It is also possible that once teachers are pressured to prioritize curriculum demands above all else, they become less sensitive or more resistant to observing behavior change if it does occur (Allen and others, 1976). If this is the case, perhaps real change did occur in the first year of the study by Gesten and others but was observed only by new teachers unaware of (and thus unbiased about) behavior as it existed a year earlier.

If the issue of how long to intervene is tied to *when* the intervention is conducted, perhaps the younger the child, the greater will be the impact in the shortest period. The verdict will not be in, however, until much more longitudinal research is done.

Further Thoughts

The follow-up data presented by Gesten and his colleagues can make a further case for mass-targeted rather than tailored interventions for specifically high-risk individuals. If, for example, we were to learn that particular subgroups benefit the most *immediately* following an intervention, any latent effects on the youngsters that might have followed still later would never be known because those youngsters would never have been trained in the first place.

In a series of anger-coping/ICPS interventions targeted for disruptive, aggressive fourth to sixth grade boys, Lochman and Lampron (1983) found that comparable no-treatment boys who demonstrated the greatest relative improvement were those who were best at generating alternative solutions to begin with and who exhibited a high level of self-esteem at the outset. No-treatment boys low in solution thinking and self-esteem tended to become even more disruptive during the school year. But for trained boys, the reverse was true. Those who initially generated the fewest alternative solutions and who were the most disruptive and aggressive were the ones who most often showed reduced aggression following intervention. Thus, the intervention "had the greatest impact on those who apparently would have demonstrated the greatest increase in disruptive and aggressive behavior if left untreated" (Lochman and Lampron, 1983, p. 8). These findings are very important because they not only support the ICPS/behavioral mediation theory, but they tell us which subgroups are most likely to show *immediate* benefits. However, had Lochman and Lampron trained all youngsters in the classroom, they might have learned more about: (1) latent impact on children displaying high-risk behaviors other than aggression, (2) potential impact a year later on other trained aggressive boys whose behavior did not immediately improve, and, importantly, (3) (as we did) possible unidentified false negatives in what became the unstudied control group.

While we have begun to address some important issues in the arena of interpersonal competence training, there is still more to learn. If, for example, programs are mass targeted, how can they best be implemented to meet both our research demands (for scientific validity) and the needs and values of the recipients (a constituent validity)? While this is grist for another chapter and has been thoughtfully discussed by Weissberg (1985), the issue of whom to train also has relevance for another unanswered question: that of who *else* might benefit—that is, what are the potential spillover effects? For example, early intervention designed in part to improve IQ also improved the IQ of the target children's younger siblings (Klaus and Gray, 1968). Would benefits of any intervention, whether tailored or mass targeted, spill over to younger brothers and sisters, too?

Still other unanswered questions include how long an intervention (however administered) will really last. We need to examine when whatever impact does occur might begin to wear off and, as Wienckowski (1982) has suggested, add intermittent "booster shots" to maximize that impact. It will also take further longitudinal research to determine optimal developmental timing for any interpersonal competence intervention, as well as, in the end, who will really benefit the most and for the longest time.

Tomorrow

In this chapter, I have presented an interpersonal competence approach to children's development, its potential for prevention of psychological dysfunction, and probable advantages of applying it as early in life as possible.

In addition to still-unanswered questions already addressed—such as the optimal timing of an initial intervention, the subsequent introduction of "booster shots," the pros and cons of mass versus individualized targeting, potential side effects (who else might benefit), and how a research intervention can meet the needs and values of both the researcher and the recipients—there are still many, many more issues to be considered.

Regarding the specific ICPS technology I described, we first asked how various processes of ICPS skills relate to maladjustment. Now we're asking, what *is* maladjustment? For example, is being aggressive really high-risk, or is it really aggression *combined* with, say overemotionality and/or impatience? We ask this because we discovered in pilot work that some aggressive youngsters care about their friends, are perceived as good leaders, and are well liked. These aggressive but otherwise prosocial youngsters are often good problem solvers—especially boys. Is it possible that in the inner-city culture of these older children, at least some aggressive behavior may be adaptive? Perhaps we need to look at *patterns* of behaviors before we can know what really can be called maladjustment. But, on the other side of the coin, if ICPS skills predict behaviors, perhaps we should look at patterns of these cognitive skills, not just one at a time. Are youngsters who are competent in more than one

ICPS skill, or in specific combinations, less likely to show behaviors at risk for psychological dysfunction?

As Margaret Ensminger (1987, p. 144) has noted: "Evaluations of prevention strategies that focus on only one narrow outcome may miss important effects of the prevention program. Prevention studies of a broad range of outcomes are likely to be more fruitful in both understanding the developmental course leading to various outcomes as well as determining the effectiveness of the prevention strategy. By focusing on a broad range of outcomes, unanticipated effects become more apparent." In our research with fifth graders (Shure, 1984), my colleagues and I noted that one outcome (positive behavior gains) had an unexpected impact on another (academic gains), accomplished indirectly through ICPS enhancement. With initial IQ controlled, once behaviors mediated through ICPS skills did improve, youngsters could better absorb the task-oriented demands of the classroom and subsequently do better in school. With the literature reviewed by Parker and Asher (1987) suggesting that academic achievement is also a predictor of later outcomes, this serendipitous finding takes on added importance. All of these questions address some issues that can add to our knowledge about the ICPS approach and about whom it can help, how long it might take, and how long the results might last. As we told our colleagues not too long ago (Spivack and Shure, 1985, p. 235): "It is not simple. It is not as simple as we first thought."

Perhaps the ultimate question is what future action may result from all this research. Amidst the relatively austere and conservative climate of the 1980s, priorities of politicians and policymakers are still primarily for treatment. As Albee (1983, p. xi) has noted: "Every assessment of the distribution of disturbance in the society arrives at an estimate of approximately 15 percent of the population." And the number is still growing. As the growth of new diagnosable cases exceeds the capacity of mental health professionals to treat them, the cost to our society will be incalculable, not only in dollars but in personal agony. If the emphasis today is on treatment, perhaps tomorrow the pressing need will shift the emphasis to prevention; because interpersonal problems are among the most common symptoms found across all psychiatric diagnostic groups

(Rutter, Tizard, and Whitmore, 1970), and because low degrees of social competence in children seem to be importantly related to psychopathology (White, 1979), we believe that interpersonal competence training is one very productive way to do just that.

References

Albee, G. W. "Foreword." In R. D. Felner, L. A. Jason, J. N. Moritsugu, and S. S. Farber (eds.), *Preventive Psychology: Theory, Research and Practice.* Elmsford, N.Y.: Pergamon Press, 1983.

Allen, G., and others. *Community Psychology and the Schools: A Behaviorally Oriented Multilevel Preventive Approach.* Hillsdale, N.J.: Erlbaum, 1976.

Allen, R. J. "An Investigatory Study of the Effects of a Cognitive Approach to Interpersonal Problem Solving on the Behavior of Emotionally Upset Psychosocially Deprived Preschool Children." Unpublished doctoral dissertation, Center for Minority Studies, Union Graduate School, Brookings Institution, 1978.

Asher, S. R. "An Evolving Paradigm in Social Skill Training Research with Children." In B. H. Schneider, K. H. Rubin, and J. E. Ledingham (eds.), *Children's Peer Relations: Issues in Assessment and Intervention.* New York: Springer-Verlag, 1985.

Coie, J. D. "Fitting Social Skills Intervention to the Target Group." In B. H. Schneider, K. H. Ruben, and J. E. Ledingham (eds.), *Children's Peer Relations: Issues in Assessment and Intervention.* New York: Springer-Verlag, 1985.

Dodge, K. A. "Facets of Social Interaction and the Assessment of Social Competence in Children." In B. H. Schneider, K. H. Rubin, and J. E. Ledingham (eds.), *Children's Peer Relations: Issues in Assessment and Intervention.* New York: Springer-Verlag, 1985.

Dodge, K. A. "A Social Information Processing Model of Social Competence in Children." In M. Perlmutter (ed.), *Minnesota Symposium on Child Psychology.* Vol. 18. Hillsdale, N.J.: Erlbaum, 1986.

Dodge, K. A., and Frame, C. L. "Social Cognitive Biases and

Deficits in Aggressive Boys." *Child Development*, 1982, *53*, 620–635.

Durlak, J. A., and Sherman, D. "Primary Prevention of School Maladjustment." Paper presented at the meeting of the American Psychological Association, New York, September 1979.

Ensminger, M. E. "Implication of Longitudinal Studies of Delinquency for Prevention Research." In J. A. Steinberg and M. Silverman (eds.), *Preventing Mental Disorders: A Research Perspective* (DHHS Publication No. ADM 87-1492). Rockville, Md.: National Institute of Mental Health, 1987.

Feis, C. L., and Simons, C. "Training Preschool Children in Interpersonal Cognitive Problem-Solving Skills: A Replication." *Prevention in Human Services*, 1985, *4*, 59–70.

Gesten, E. L., and others. "Training Children in Social Problem-Solving Competencies: A First and Second Look." *American Journal of Community Psychology*, 1982, *10*, 95–115.

Hawkins, J. D., and Weis, J. G. "The Social Development Model: An Integrated Approach to Delinquency Prevention." *Journal of Primary Prevention*, 1985, *6*, 73–97.

Klaus, R. A., and Gray, S. W. "The Early Training Project for Disadvantaged Children: A Report After Five Years." *Monographs of the Society for Research in Child Development*, no. 120, 1968, *33* (4).

Lochman, J. E., and Lampron, L. B. "Client Characteristics Associated with Treatment Outcome for Aggressive Boys." Paper presented at meeting of the American Psychological Association, Anaheim, Calif., August 1983.

Parker, J. G., and Asher, S. R. "Peer Relations and Later Personal Adjustment: Are Low-Accepted Children 'At Risk'?" *Psychological Bulletin*, 1987, *102* (3), 357–389.

Rose, S. R. "Promoting Social Competence in Children: A Classroom Approach to Social and Cognitive Skill Training." *Child and Youth Services*, 1982, *5*, 43–59.

Rubin, K. H. "Socially Withdrawn Children: An 'At Risk' Population?" In B. H. Schneider, K. H. Rubin, and J. E. Ledingham (eds.), *Children's Peer Relations: Issues in Assessment and Intervention.* New York: Springer-Verlag, 1985.

Rutter, M., Tizard, J., and Whitmore, K. *Education, Health and Behavior.* London: Longman, 1970.

Sharp, K. C. "Impact of Interpersonal Problem-Solving Training on Preschoolers' Social Competency." *Journal of Applied Developmental Psychology,* 1981, *2,* 129-143.

Shure, M. B. "Social Competence Through Problem Solving in Inner-City Fifth-Graders: Is It Too Late?" Paper presented at the meeting of the American Psychological Association, Toronto, Canada, August 1984.

Shure, M. B. "Problem Solving and Mental Health of Ten- to Twelve-Year-Olds." Final Summary Report, no. MH 35989. Washington, D.C.: National Institute of Mental Health, 1986.

Shure, M. B., and Spivack, G. "Interpersonal Cognitive Problem Solving (ICPS): A Mental Health Program for Four-Year-Old Nursery School Children: Training Script." Philadelphia: Department of Mental Health Sciences, Hahnemann University, 1971.

Shure, M. B., and Spivack, G. "Interpersonal Cognitive Problem Solving (ICPS): A Mental Health Program for Kindergarten and First Grade Children: Training Script." Philadelphia: Hahnemann University, Department of Mental Health Sciences, 1974.

Shure, M. B., and Spivack, G. "Interpersonal Problem Solving in Young Children: A Cognitive Approach to Prevention." *American Journal of Community Psychology,* 1982, *10,* 341-356.

Smith, G. M., and Fogg, C. G. "Psychological Antecedents of Teenage Drug Use." In R. G. Simmons (ed.), *Research in Community and Mental Health.* Vol. 1. Greenwich, Conn.: JAI Press, 1979.

Spivack, G., Marcus, J., and Swift, M. "Early Classroom Behaviors and Later Misconduct." *Developmental Psychology,* 1986, *22,* 124-131.

Spivack, G., and Shure, M. B. *Social Adjustment of Young Children.* San Francisco: Jossey-Bass, 1974.

Spivack, G., and Shure, M. B. "ICPS and Beyond: Centripetal and Centrifugal Forces." *American Journal of Community Psychology,* 1985, *13,* 227-243.

Straus, C. C., Forehand, R., Smith, K., and Frame, C. L. "The Association Between Social Withdrawal and Internalizing

Problems in Children." *Journal of Abnormal Child Psychology,* 1986, *14,* 525–535.

Weissberg, R. P. "Designing Effective Social Problem-Solving Programs for the Classroom." In B. H. Schneider, K. H. Rubin, and J. E. Ledingham (eds.), *Children's Peer Relations: Issues in Assessment and Intervention.* New York: Springer-Verlag, 1985.

Weissberg, R. P., and Gesten, E. L. "Considerations for Developing Effective School-Based Social Problem-Solving (SPS) Training Programs." *School Psychology Review,* 1982, *11,* 56–63.

Weissberg, R. P., and others. "Social Problem-Solving Skills Training: A Competence-Building Intervention with Second- to Fourth-Grade Children." *American Journal of Community Psychology,* 1981, *9,* 411–423.

White, R. W. "Competence as an Aspect of Personal Growth." In M. W. Kent and J. E. Rolf (eds.), *Primary Prevention of Psychopathology.* Vol. 3. Hanover, N.H.: University Press of New England, 1979.

Wienckowski, L. *Research Planning Mini-Conference in Primary Prevention.* Sponsored by the Office of Prevention and the Center for Prevention Research at the National Institute of Mental Health and the Community Psychology Training Program, University of Texas, Austin. February 24–26, 1982.

Chapter 20

Fostering
Intimacy and Autonomy

Robert L. Selman

 Arnie, at age thirteen, claims to need no friends. In class, he sits off in a corner by himself; at lunch, he usually chooses to eat alone; and as he walks down the corridors, his eyes are cast down, his vision turned inward. His "interpersonal life" is filled not with friends but with fictional characters from the science fiction and horror comics and books he carries everywhere. Half kidding and half serious, he is preoccupied with his need to be able to "stand alone," to protect himself from these characters, and he is obsessed with his own extreme form of autonomy ("I don't need to rely on nobody"). But this is often belied by his intense and sudden anger when a counselor he does talk to is a few minutes late for a meeting or when a teacher he depends on does not give him the attention he demands. Often Arnie appears sad and lonely.

Arnie's classmate Mitchell is also thirteen and friendless, but not for lack of effort. Mitchell would desperately like to have a friend, but he does not know now, nor does he ever seem to have

Note: This chapter was written with support from the William T. Grant Foundation and from the Spencer Foundation. I would like to acknowledge the help and support of: the clinical and educational staff of the Manville School; Stanley Walzer, director of the Judge Baker Children's Center; Brina Caplan and Kathy Schantz, who observed and provided feedback on this clinical/research case; Lynn Schultz and Anne Selman, for providing feedback on earlier drafts; and Matthew and Jesse Selman, for first involving me in the game of "Wizardry."

409

learned, how to go about making or keeping one. Mitchell virtually throws himself onto peers, trying to be included in the interactions of his classmates, but he seldom if ever succeeds. Part of the problem is that his style of interacting is more like that of someone half his age. He giggles uncontrollably, does not focus his attention on the social scene, and often misunderstands the social subtleties and nuances of his peers' interactions. He tattles one day and expects his victims to be his friends the next. When even slightly rebuffed, he reacts with epithets and curses, only to expect forgetfulness if not forgiveness. Desperate for early adolescent intimacy, Mitchell is confused and lonely.

The Clinical Context and Its Theoretical Underpinnings

Mitchell and Arnie are in therapy together—pair therapy. Almost ten years ago, we began the Pair Therapy Project, a program of clinical and developmental research at the Manville School, the day treatment school I direct for children with emotional and interpersonal difficulties at the Judge Baker Children's Center in Boston. The aim of pair therapy is to help children with troubled or virtually no peer relationships to be able to both like and be liked by other children, to develop the capacity to establish and maintain close friendships. The term *pair therapy* is somewhat misleading; actually, a triad is involved in this approach to treating psychosocial problems in the young. This treatment requires two pre- or early adolescents to meet regularly (typically once a week for about an hour) with a pair therapist, who plays a crucial role, providing the two with a third-person perspective on and facilitative mediation for the pair's social interaction processes.

The theoretical underpinnings of the therapeutic perspectives and techniques in this form of treatment are essentially developmental in nature. Although the children with whom we work have emotional and interpersonal difficulties severe enough to qualify for a host of psychiatric labels, our orientation does not rely primarily on diagnostic categories or look specifically for syndromes (although the children receive this kind of assessment in the course of other aspects of their program at the school). For the purposes of pair therapy intervention and research, we describe communicative and psychosocial functioning (and malfunctioning) in developmental terms. Accordingly, we do not see pair therapy primarily as curing specific psychiatric disorders but instead as facilitating the general process by which one's potential is achieved in interpersonal development, taking the range of each individual's abilities and disabilities into account. Subtle as the difference may seem, there is an important distinction to be drawn between approaches that intend to correct injury or illness in a previously healthy individual, and those, such as pair therapy, that aim to promote the continued development and maturation of an individual whose psychosocial functioning is regressed to or fixated at a level characteristic of younger children.

Furthermore, pair therapy differs to some degree from more traditional kinds of individual child psychotherapies insofar as it is both social interaction based *and* insight oriented. An important focus of the treatment throughout its course is on fostering psychosocial and personality development through a program that encourages the pair to do things together and then, with the crucial help of the therapist, to reflect on both the degree of success and the level of maturity of "how we did." This aim is to provide what Harry Stack Sullivan (1953) described as a "corrective interpersonal experience" for youngsters who have immature interpersonal functioning.

But, specifically, what kind of development does pair therapy try to foster? It provides a context in which individuals can move along the road toward, if not ultimately achieve, the long-term goal of using mutual and collaborative methods to deal with other individuals in close and ongoing one-to-one relationships. This capacity for mutual collaboration, as it is conceptualized in our developmental model, is based on the developing ability to coordinate perspectives on the social interaction between the self and a significant other, in both a cognitive and an emotional sense. Ordinarily achieved in pre- or early adolescence, essentially it is the capacity to reflectively step outside of the self and fully experience the interaction between self and other from what I have called a "third-person point of view" (Selman, 1980) or what Anna Freud, in *The Ego and the Mechanisms of Defense* (1966), termed (in a somewhat different context) the development of the "observing ego."

Whatever this capacity is called, it requires strength of character to act on the basis of the cognitive and affective understanding it embodies, and it functions best when both parties in a relationship are able to use it. Pair therapy is a context in which socially immature—but cognitively capable—youngsters can take the often shaky first steps in this direction, putting their most competent level of interpersonal understanding into action in an emotionally meaningful context.

Intimacy and Autonomy: Functions and Forms

Although the reflective capacity for mutual collaboration normally develops in early or middle adolescence, its use and refinement thereafter constitute a lifelong process. Mutual collaboration is a reflective method of relating—an approach the self uses to deal with self and other. It can be recognized in the way an individual interacts with another (communicating and resolving differences), demonstrating in both words and deeds, in thoughts and feelings, a respect for self and other in his or her relating. Accordingly, it continues to broaden, deepen, and be transformed as a function of the developmental tasks and contextual challenges of social interactions encountered across one's lifetime. And, from our perspective on the nature of personality development, it is the result of the codevelopment of the capacity for *intimacy*, operationally defined in our work in pair therapy as the ability to share experiences with another person, and the capacity for *autonomy*, defined, perhaps somewhat idiosyncratically, not as a need to establish a separate and distinct identity, as emphasized by Erik Erikson (1968), but as the ability, as one attempts to define the self's interests and achieve one's goals, to understand, coordinate, and negotiate one's own needs with the needs of another person, particularly when they may conflict.

In this view, the terms *intimacy* and *autonomy* do not describe static phenomena, nor are they early, late, or final achievements. Instead, these terms describe psychological processes that function throughout life, from infancy to old age. They are not simply achieved (have/don't have) products or properties within an individual but aspects of the self's actions in ongoing relationships with others. Infants, as well as young adults, achieve a form of intimacy with parents, even if infants do not fully understand the basis of their own feelings or of their parents' feelings toward them (Stern, 1985; White, Speisman, and Costos, 1983); both toddlers and adolescents struggle with parents for a type of autonomy, even if toddlers cannot function in as fully independent a manner as can adolescents (Erikson, 1963); both preschoolers and preadolescents (Brenner and Mueller, 1982; Gottman, 1983) have meaningful and deep attachments with peers, even if younger children define their friendships in superficial or nonpsychological terms. The point is that all intact individuals in social relationships continually seek to establish and maintain both a sense of intimacy and a sense of autonomy with the significant other persons in their lives. But although these two component processes of interpersonal growth and development function from birth onward, the forms they take change and fluctuate with time and experience. Furthermore, these forms can become fixated (as in Mitchell's case) or regressive or unstable (as in Arnie's).

If each component is developing adequately, both separately and together, the child growing into adolescence can begin to move toward utilizing a collaborative attitude, exercising mutually collaborative methods of relating to the significant other people in his or her life. As Blatt and Shichman pointed out in their 1983 theoretical article, "Two Primary Configurations of Psychopathology," the developmental lines toward higher forms of intimacy and autonomy normally develop as a complex dialectical process (see Cooper, Grotevant, and Condon, 1983; Gilligan, 1982). Accordingly, various forms of psychopathology are considered as distortions of both processes but are more blatantly manifest in one or the other of these two fundamental developmental lines. But what does "developing adequately" mean in concrete and observable terms, and what do distortions actually look like? It is at this level of specificity that theory usually gives way. In a modest way, we have attempted to use the context of pair therapy to pick up some of the slack.

In previous work (for example, Selman and Schultz, forthcoming), my colleagues and I examined extensively one critical manifestation of the capacity for autonomy: the strategies children use for interpersonal negotiation. Our work construes normal children growing up as developing an expanding repertoire of *interpersonal negotiation strategies,* the forms of which can be characterized as evolving through a sequence of levels and the foundations of which rest upon levels in the child's developing capacity to coordinate psychosocial perspectives (Selman, 1980). Interpersonal negotiation strategies classified as level 0 are primarily impulsive, physicalistic strategies (for instance, impulsive fight or flight). They connote a lack of clear distinction and acknowledgment of the perspectives of the self and the significant other in the consideration of a particular problem.

Level 1 strategies indicate recognition that the significant other's perspective may differ from the self's in the particular context. However, these strategies do not coordinate—that is, simultaneously consider—the perspectives of the self and the significant other. Thus, strategies classified as level 1 include one-way commands and assertions and, conversely, simple and unchallenging accommodation (or giving in) to the perceived needs and requests of the significant other.

Strategies classified as level 2 (psychologically based reciprocal exchanges) are based on an understanding of both the self and the significant other as planful, capable of reflection, and having opinions, feelings, and behaviors that influence the other person. These strategies indicate an ability to reflect upon the self's needs from a second-person perspective. They focus primarily on trades, exchanges, verbal persuasion, convincing others, making deals, or suggesting other behaviors designed to protect the subjective interests of the self in negotiation. The self may go second, but he or she will not yield completely; or go first, but not dominate totally.

Level 3 strategies, akin to Sullivan's notion of collaboration, indicate consideration of a need for integration of the interests of the self and the significant other as viewed from a third-person perspective. These strategies involve compromise, dialogue, process analysis, and the development of shared goals. They indicate an understanding that concern for the relationship's continuity over time relates to the solution of any immediate problem.

Specific strategies falling into each of these four levels (0 to 3) can be further classified according to which predominant interpersonal style or orientation the child adopts. In strategies in the *self-transforming orientation,* the self acts predominantly on the self to accommodate to the other; in strategies in the *other-transforming orientation,* the self acts to change the other to accommodate to the self. At advanced developmental levels, the interpersonal orientations become less polarized, culminating in a collaborative orientation whereby strategies are neither self- nor other-transforming but balanced and integrated. Table 20.1 summarizes this developmental classification system.

More recently, we have utilized pair therapy to explore an important manifestation of intimacy; here our interest has been in delineating evolving forms or levels of *shared experience* (see Selman and Yeates, 1987). Within the history of the Pair Therapy Project, our interest in shared experience developed relatively late. The project began, as I noted earlier, with a focus on helping children with poor peer relationships become more adept at getting along; thus it was the fights and disagreements, the conflicts these children were getting into, that caught our eye and called for our attention. The intensive focus of our initial years of theoretical, empirical, and clinical work on the autonomy-related processes of interpersonal negotiation obscured somewhat the complementary difficulties these children were having establishing and maintaining a sense of closeness with peers. Once our attention was refocused in this direction, the possibility—indeed the likelihood—occurred to us that the difficulty or discomfort these youngsters had in achieving a sense of closeness or intimacy actually may have played a role in generating many of the conflicts (contexts for negotiation) they resolved so inadequately with their truncated and immature range and repertoire of interpersonal strategies.

In addition, even as we were refining our techniques for helping children improve their negotiation and conflict resolution skills, we could not help but speculate that the closeness and intimacy the children were beginning to demonstrate with one another in this therapeutic context—one made safe, sound, dependable, and continuous by the pair therapist—was a major factor in encouraging the children to venture to try new and unfamiliar (or at least more reciprocal, if not collaborative) negotiation strategies.

Table 20.1. Levels of Intimacy (Shared Experience) and
Autonomy (Interpersonal Negotiation) Processes.

Intimacy function (sharing experience)	Core developmental levels in the capacity to coordinate social perspectives	Autonomy function (negotiating interpersonal conflict)
Shared experience through collaborative empathic reflective processes	Mutual/ Third-Person level (3)	Negotiation through collaborative strategies oriented toward integrating needs of self and other
Shared experience through joint reflection on similar perceptions or experiences	Reciprocal/ Reflective level (2)	Negotiation through cooperative strategies in a persuasive or deferential orientation
Shared experience through expressive enthusiasm without concern for reciprocity	Unilateral/ One-Way level (1)	Negotiation through one-way commands/ orders or through automatic obedience strategies
Shared experience through unreflective (contagious) imitation	Egocentric/ Impulsive level (0)	Negotiation through unreflective physical strategies (impulsive fight or flight)

Development

We therefore returned to our corpus of data, the videotapes and narratives in our library of past pair therapy sessions, to seek instances of social interactions that might be considered exemplars of different forms of shared experience.

To our surprise, in addition to instances that one might commonly expect, such as two boys giving each other "high signs" after working cooperatively to defeat the pair therapist at a game of tag, we found some experiences that were clearly intensely shared, even though they seemed to us somewhat primitive and even unbalanced. For example, in many of our pairs, much glee was generated by some pairs as they simultaneously produced bodily function sounds (for example, fake burps) in close harmony with one another. And in some of our youngest and/or most immature pairs, we observed a kind of unreflective mutual mimicry or imitation, more like follow-the-leader than anything truly mutual. Nevertheless, the members of the pair seemed to experience a soothing effect through sharing even this motoric and repetitive activity.

Our next task, following guidelines first laid down by Heinz Werner in his classic, *The Comparative Psychology of Mental Development* (1948), was to attempt to group instances of shared experience into classes or categories that could be ordered along developmental lines, from the primitive, global, and undifferentiated to the psychologically complex, hierarchically integrated, and differentiated. Once again, as when developing the levels of interpersonal negotiation strategies, we relied on our earlier work on levels in the coordination of social perspectives as an analytic tool to generate the following four tentative forms (or levels) of shared experience.

At the most primitive level (level 0), what seems to be shared (more literally "spread" in an unreflective way) is one child's impulsive and motoric activity. The experience often starts with one actor's expressiveness and appears to be transmitted to the other through a *process of contagion*. For example, Korey and David, both age nine, have developed a form of sensorimotor imitation. If Korey reaches for a drink, David does the same; if David bounces a ball or crosses his legs, Korey automatically does so too. Neither seems to be aware of the imitation, but each appears to be soothed by it. This kind of activity is often poorly regulated, such that often an outside agent is needed to control the expression of the common action should it become overstimulating.

At a higher level (level 1), children appear to "share" actions more consciously, but in a somewhat paradoxical way: one actor "commands" the other to participate, not necessarily or only through orders or dictates but rather through a kind of expressive enthusiasm. And the other takes pleasure in following. Often this *unilateral* form of shared experience—a term meant to capture its paradoxical nature—was seen in fantasy or role-play situations in which turns were taken at being in control (although one partner usually determined the switching of roles). For example, Kenny (age nine) and Peter (age eight) play a fantasy game (of Kenny's design) in which each has a chance to exert "laser power" over the will and behavior of the other. They alternate as controller and controllee, although Kenny always determines when the switch occurs.

In contrast, shared experiences at the next level (level 2) involve *reciprocal reflection* on the experience of actions. In other words, the accent falls on reflecting with another who has had the same or a similar experience. Both children participate equally; however, the experience still is shared primarily for the sake of each self's own satisfaction, without a strong or clear sense of interconnecting. A common kind of shared experience at this level is one in which each member of the pair is intent on gaining consensual validation on the meaning of the actions of a third party (such as a teacher both participants share or a peer with whom each interacts). For example, Brenda (age twelve) asks Karen (also twelve), "Do you like Harriet?" in a tone that conveys that Brenda clearly does not. Karen reads the meaning correctly, and the two go on to gossip merrily about Harriet's weaker features.

A more *mutually collaborative* form of reflective shared experience consists of communications in which the other person's concerns are felt to be as significant as one's own. At this level (level 3), each participant clearly regards the other as part of a mutually experienced "we." For example, Jessica (age fourteen) and Heather (age thirteen) share their anxiety about moving from junior high school to high school next year. They discuss why each of them will miss their favorite teacher, experiencing each other's feelings and listening to each other empathically. Finally, each adds that she is glad she will have the other as company in this transition.

Distinguishing, or diagnosing, the subtle but crucial difference between cooperation for self-interest (level 2, reciprocal reflective) and collaboration for mutual interest (level 3) is a challenge—theoretically, empirically, and clinically. The difference is not just in the words that are used but in the meanings these words express and in the interpersonal feelings that underlie them. A collaborative attitude in the context of the intimacy of shared experience, no less than in the autonomy of interpersonal negotiation, can be best observed in social interactions over time, in the cues and clues that are observed in the course and context of the ongoing relationship (see Hinde, 1979; Sroufe and Fleeson, 1986).

The levels we have tentatively identified are from admittedly limited resources. Undoubtedly, much developmental research needs to be done to better understand the various forms, functions, and fluctuations of these phenomena. And most likely, forms of shared experience more advanced than these can be articulated. Clinically, however, our interest is in using what we have come to understand of forms of shared experience *and* levels of interpersonal negotiation as guides to the broad and long-range goals of pair therapy. On the one hand, we ask, what can the therapist do to facilitate the "glue" of pair therapy, the fostering of higher-level forms of shared experience? On the other hand, our question is how can the therapist help both members of the pair to "structure" their own autonomy, to act with a greater sense of collaboration in sorting out their own needs and the needs of their pair partner in interpersonal negotiation?

These opportunities for shared experience and contexts for interpersonal negotiation do not occur haphazardly or appear out of thin air. Therapeutic environments for the development of advanced forms of intimacy and autonomy must be created. In this treatment, as in most, the therapist must create an atmosphere of safety, consistency, clear limits, warmth, and possibilities. He or she must also be prepared to serve as a "communications mediator" for the pair, in addition to a number of other functions. However, what I wish to emphasize here is that the likelihood of the pair progressing along both these developmental lines (intimacy and autonomy) is greatly enhanced if the pair, with the therapist's help, develops what we call a *home base activity*.

The home base activity comprises several key properties. First, and simplest, the pair "is engaged in it" much or most of the time over a period of months or longer. Second, at minimum, through constant play or rehearsal, both members come to feel a high degree of comfort with and competence in the activity. A typical example is two preadolescent children who repeatedly play a board game, such as Sorry, until each knows all the strategies involved. In this sense, it has a home base or security-oriented function. It provides a safe and familiar ground against which the "real" interpersonal content of therapy is played out. And the pair can always refocus its attention on the game when the interpersonal situation, the reflection or conversation, becomes too stressful. Third, ideally a home base activity repeatedly provides for the pair both contexts for serious negotiations and opportunities for meaningful shared experiences. Fourth, it is an activity through which the adult therapist can provide the pair with challenges, examples, mediation, or other facilitating stimulation that is above the pair's current functioning. That is, the activity needs to be complex enough that it can be "played" or approached at a number of levels. As a result, in a way that is similar to the way Griffin and Cole (1984) describe what Vygotsky (1978) called "the zone of proximal development," there is always an area available to the therapist to target his or her efforts.

In some cases, a home base activity can be established that enables the pair to take crucial steps on behalf of its own development. It then becomes a truly developmental activity, what we call a "developmental project," in several senses. First, it becomes compelling enough for both partners over a significant period of time that it assumes properties of a "quest." Second, this level of involvement creates a zone of proximal development between, by, and for the partners themselves. And third, and perhaps most significantly, the activity itself provides a series of developmental challenges of increasing complexity, both socioemotional and intellectual, both to the pair and to each partner. The activity has a developmental inner structure that can unfold over time. And it challenges the participants increasingly as they become increasingly involved. Such an activity, when the therapist can keep it safe and the partners are deeply drawn in, is an optimal context for fostering the integration and development of intimacy and autonomy processes and movement toward a collaborative attitude. Toward the end of their first year in pair therapy together, Arnie and Mitchell, the two early adolescent boys introduced earlier, became engaged in such an activity.

The Quest for the Amulet: A Case Study
of a Developmental Project

The remainder of this chapter will provide the reader with a sense of how the principles of this developmental approach actually and actively guide treatment. Described in some detail are the properties of a particular developmental project that was used to foster more mature levels of intimacy and autonomy in Arnie and Mitchell.

In our data collection on the social interaction and individual development of these boys, two observers together watched each session from an adjacent room through a one-way mirror. Each had a primary focus on one of the pair partners, in interaction with the other and with the therapist. Each session was also recorded on videotape. After every session, the pair therapist met with the two observers to review the tape and discuss whether perspectives from inside and beyond the pair therapy room revealed the same interpretation of events. At times it was necessary to discuss at some length what had been seen in order to arrive at a consensus about how best to describe and interpret what the observers and the therapist might have seen differently. Our analysis of the first period of treatment for Arnie and Mitchell can be synopsized as follows:

The initial two-thirds of the first year of treatment was essentially a period of challenges, in which the two boys slowly began to feel comfortable with each other. At each session, Arnie would arrive with his tote bag full of comics and books that interested him but that did not necessarily interest Mitchell. The first session was typical of many that followed. The therapist asked Arnie what was in the bag, and Arnie revealed some fantasy role-play games. When asked by the therapist whether he would like to learn them, Mitchell responded somewhat passively, "I don't care." Arnie then proceeded to dictate how to play, without any apparent consideration of whether Mitchell was comprehending the instructions. But Mitchell did not venture to communicate the degree of either his understanding of or his interest in the game; he simply went along.

At this point, negotiation was at a relatively low (unilateral) level and in rigid, polarized orientations. Initially, Arnie took control (in our terms, was other-transforming) and Mitchell stepped into the passive, subordinate (self-transforming) role. During this initial six-month period, Arnie slowly yielded some control. For instance, early on he would sit off to one side of the room and refuse to directly compete in "Trivial Pursuit," a game Mitchell enjoyed playing. However, as Arnie began to see that he could do well in the game, he moved closer, both physically and psychologically, even "allowing" Mitchell to set some of the pace. In fact, within three months, Arnie and Mitchell were cracking jokes together—a significant and new shared experience for each of them. As with many of the pairs we have worked with, it seemed that once an initial dominance pattern was set (here, Arnie in the ascendant position) and a negotiation style established (mostly "level 1" orders and commands), the partners could begin to feel safe enough to explore the less familiar and hence more frightening waters of closeness and intimacy.

While the setting of a dominance pattern is fairly common in pair therapy, particularly in the early phases of treatment, eventually the therapist will look to break (and restructure) this pattern. He or she will try to help each member of the pair utilize a higher level of functioning and in so doing become more integrative in interpersonal orientation. But for many months this pair seemed to meander in the waters of this initial phase. No one activity seemed to be truly compelling enough to "grab" both of them, none engaging enough for them to catch the wind and move decisively in a "developmental direction." It was not until the late spring of the first year that a true home base activity was found. At that time, the therapist introduced the pair to a computer software fantasy adventure game that not only appealed to each boy's particular preoccupations but also met the requirements of a "developmental project."

When the boys arrived at the pair therapy room, they found a Macintosh Plus computer and a game called "Wizardry" awaiting them. The boys were familiar with the computer from their classwork, but the software package was new to them. For the next several sessions, the therapist functioned primarily as an instructor, acknowledging the necessity to teach the boys to interact with the computer and learn the rules of the game. At the same time, he continued to facilitate their interactions with one another. And in "Wizardry," interactions become intense. The game, the seating arrangement of which is schematized in Figure 20.1, became a developmental project not only for the waning sessions of this first year of pair therapy but consistently (although not during every session) throughout the second year.

To describe how this activity provides a context in which the development of both intimacy and autonomy processes can be facilitated for the pair and for each of the boys, it is necessary to

Figure 20.1. Seating Arrangement for "Wizardry."

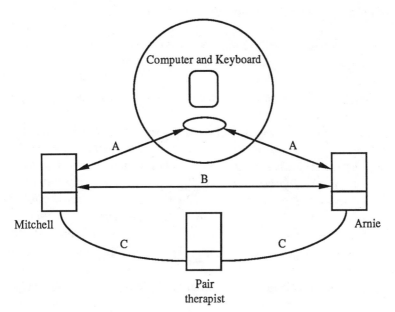

describe the actual game procedure in some detail. The first step in the game is for the boys to create or develop between them six characters, whose function, as a party, is to master a series of ten increasingly complex levels of a maze below their castle, going down deeper and deeper into a dungeon. The goal is for the party to capture a magic amulet hidden somewhere in the maze at the tenth level. The forms of the maze levels are unknown and invisible; the only part that can be seen on-screen at a given time is the area of several steps around the party's current location.

The various members of the search party have different "innate" characteristics and functions. Some are Fighters, with greater "degrees" of strength and endurance and concomitantly lower "degrees" of luck and agility. Others are Mages, with more wisdom but less strength; or Priests, with greater piety; or Thieves, with more luck and agility (the better to open gold-filled but booby-trapped treasure chests found in the maze) but with little strength or piety. Each of these character traits can be put to good use, cooperatively, in the party's quest for the amulet. The longer the team stays together and does not get lost in the mazes or defeated in battle with the antagonists they meet there, the more strength, endurance, piety, wisdom, and so on their characters develop or acquire. Through successful encounters (battles) with the denizens of the mazes, for example, Priests may progress to the status of Bishops, with qualitatively greater healing powers (for example, the power to restore life rather than merely to heal a member of the party injured during a battle). Each member of the team develops through experience.

From a developmental perspective, successfully reaching the deepest level of the maze requires a match between the level of character development of the members of the party (in terms of their developing levels of strength, intelligence, agility, and so forth) and the level of complexity of the tasks they must accomplish at each subsequent level of the maze. Only when the players have experientially acquired wisdom, weapons, wealth, and strength for their party by winning many battles and mapping the maze at one level are they in a position to take the party to the next level. And since each maze level is not simply quantitatively more difficult than the previous one but also qualitatively more complex, the player(s) of the game must master each maze level completely—and in a consolidated manner—before members of the party are "developmentally" ready to go to the next maze level. Impulsive and premature attempts to master deeper levels of the maze, when the search party is not "developmentally ready" or the current maze level has not been fully explored and mapped, almost surely will lead to disaster in the form of battles with opponents with strengths and skills beyond the abilities of the party or the specter of becoming hopelessly lost in the maze.

Exploring all aspects of a given level of the maze, systematically mapping each level as the party walks through it, is important to avoid becoming lost, but it also is crucial because there are certain "keys" to success at later levels that must be found at the earlier ones. For example, without the key to the elevator found at level 4, the party will not easily reach level 5, whereas at the previous levels all that was needed was to find the stairs going down to go from level 1 to level 2, level 2 to level 3, and so on.

One final bit of information is worth noting. Although the quest for the amulet itself lasts many hours (a conservative estimate would be at least fifty hours), it is not one continuous journey. Multiple trips into and out of the different maze levels are made, and each trip takes its inevitable toll on the members of the party: in injuries, poisonings, and even death. The party must return regularly to the starting point—the castle above the ten levels of the maze—in order to perform certain restorative and character-developing functions. Essentially, the castle above the maze becomes the home base for the party and hence, symbolically, for the two players. For instance, the team members need to return, on occasion, to the castle hotel to receive the proper credits for the battles and other experiences they have had and hence to develop further their party members. (Indeed, development for each character on the team occurs only at these periods of rest and consolidation in this game—as it well may in the real game of life.) And each time the party "comes up for air" to receive the new spells or to move to the higher levels of functioning it has earned in a successful expedition, the previously assimilated levels of the maze, initially experienced by the players as perilous or challenging, become more mundane and routine. But if the new level proves too much of a challenge, the previous level can take on the quality of a home base.

The game has certain developmental features that parallel, if not symbolize, processes of socialization and maturation. First, there are hierarchically ordered and qualitatively distinct levels of complexity, both for the characters and for the maze environment. Second, there is a need for characters to consolidate skills and achievements at one level before developing competence at the next. Third, in the course of the game, there naturally emerge periods that call for consolidation of the "cutting-edge" level or even regression to a lower level of game play. These are features that are built into the game's internal "structure," whether it is played together by two or more players or alone. Thus in a less conscious— but no less meaningful—way, the two boys sought character development of the members of their party (interactions A in Figure 20.1) just as the therapist sought character development of the members of the pair (interaction C). In both instances, the name of the game is the acquisition of newer "inner" capabilities through the adaptive processing of "social" experiences. The function of these capabilities is to help the characters (the live ones as well as the electronic ones) master life's developmental tasks.

Although the game has a great deal more complexity than just described, one can begin to understand how well it fit with the dynamics of Mitchell and Arnie, both as individuals and as a pair. The rich detail of the fantasy world of the game, the inherent complexities of the techniques, and the excitement of the quest attracted and motivated them very powerfully. And as a "therapeutic task," at the very least, it challenged them to cooperate and to persist. In addition, now instead of a triadic system, with a pair and a therapist, it became a quartet, with two "game players," a therapist, and a computer with its own strict parameters and a great deal of patience. The therapist functioned for the two boys both as a guide (who had played the game to its completion before) and as a facilitator (who encouraged functioning in a "zone of proximal development"), but he did not lead them directly in their quest for the amulet.

For example, although he knew that carefully mapping each level of the maze was crucial, rather than directing the boys to do so, the therapist briefly modeled this activity and merely suggested that it would be helpful. However, initially neither boy wanted to map, both because it took away from the impulsive excitement of the game and because it generated anxiety by causing them to acknowledge taking the game seriously. But when Arnie and Mitchell were allowed to codiscover, through sometimes bitter experience, the value of carefully mapping, of alternating between mapping and exploring, and of doing both tasks together rather than alone, they in effect took advantage of a zone of proximal development for persistence and self-control, and they experienced an enormous sense of mutual achievement.

From a therapeutic perspective, the ways in which the game fostered interaction between the pair members (interaction B in Figure 20.1) stimulated and motivated interpersonal development in each. Because the likelihood of success at this game is greatly enhanced if it is played by two people (as it is difficult to simultaneously explore and map the maze by oneself), the motivation for Arnie and Mitchell to discover cooperative techniques was very high. Among the many contexts for negotiating their autonomy were conflicts over: which player could use the computer's "mouse" to "walk" the party through the maze, how the gold acquired during a successful expedition would be spent, whether to fight or flee a battle with unfamiliar foes, which spells to cast, when was the best time to return from the maze to the castle for rest, recuperation, and character development. Again and again, the characteristics of the developmental project and the therapist's support were such that Arnie and Mitchell persisted in reaching solutions.

Beyond cooperation and higher-level negotiation, Mitchell and Arnie began to develop something emotionally deep as well: a sense of mutuality with a peer, fostered by the many hours facing danger, disappointments, decisions, and victories together. Although this game could have been played alone and would still have provided many of the same "individual" developmental challenges, the sense of shared experience, consensual validation, and collaboration that was achieved by engaging in the quest as a pair—which would be valuable for most early adolescents—was critical for Arnie and Mitchell.

As further examples, during the game the pair often found

itself in a situation in which a tough decision needed to be made. When the stairway to the next level of the maze was found, was the party ready to take the risk and explore the new territory? Or serious anxiety and panic could be generated by the realization that the party was in a battle that was over its collective head or lost somewhere in the maze. At best, these tense decisions or moments of potential panic were situations in which the pair, with some assistance from the therapist, worked out the problem together while at the same time learning to deal with their own very real feelings. Although panic can lead to the loss of the party and all that it has come to mean to the players, there are often subtle ways out of tough situations that can be perceived if one's mind is not clouded by fear. Over time, Mitchell and Arnie found that two heads really were better than one in slowing things down and not acting out of impulse or panic. Thus, on the "good days," an affective "zone of proximal development," as well as an intellectual one, was created.

However, boys like Arnie and Mitchell, who have not had much experience with cooperation, let alone collaboration, particularly in situations in which affect is heightened, might not, if left to their own devices, have made the best use of the opportunity to support each other in a positive spirit. This is where the therapist played an important linking role, helping the two boys see how a friend can help one out in a tough situation and providing a context for their having the experience of a successful two-person endeavor, whether it was a single battle or an extended expedition into the maze.

There are many more general inherent opportunities for shared experience in this developmental project. On the one hand, any successful expedition into the maze was successful not for just one but for both players. Feelings of excitement occurred not alone but together, and they often were shared. On the other hand, there is also always the possibility—indeed, for the boys as novices, the probability—that a party will become hopelessly lost in the maze or be completely defeated in battle. Thus they had many occasions of the shared bitterness of defeat (and the subsequent possibility of guilt or blame). The therapist endeavored to help each boy work through these real-life feelings in the interaction, feelings that they needed to learn to deal with if they were to achieve a more mature level of intimacy and closeness.

The therapist's goal was to work to help the pair become a partnership, to foster a tempo of mutual social regulation. The therapist was there to facilitate and mediate, both emotionally and intellectually, not to tell them how to win the game. By the same token, he was there to support, provide boundaries for, and ease their interactions, not to solve their conflicts and upsets for them. Following is a summary of the year and a half of Arnie and Michell's pair therapy after "Wizardry" was introduced.

Initially, Arnie was more proficient at the game than Mitchell; this was clearly evident when the activity was first being introduced. Mitchell was intimidated not only by the game's inherent complexity but also by the demands of the computer's exactitude. He had difficulty with the keyboard, with the mouse, and with the general level of precision necessary for computer activities. Often he would allow his frustration to express itself as a rageful disparagement of the "stupid computer," and he would pound the keyboard in frustration or flee in dismay. On occasion, he would blame himself for being unable to master some of the basics immediately; he desired instant proficiency but was not willing to expend the personal effort or tolerate the anxiety necessary to obtain it. Arnie, on the other hand, was more confident as well as more computer literate, so he often took the lead. And with some wisdom, Mitchell chose to step back on occasion and let Arnie run the game.

Mitchell gained a great deal through observation. At first, he would utilize old interpersonal patterns, barking intrusive orders to Arnie and then, when he was not listened to immediately, withdrawing, pouting, and whining. But by the halfway point of the second year, he was feeling comfortable enough with the dynamics of the trio, as well as with the technical aspects of the activity, to use higher-level autonomy skills in his social interactions: to speak up for his fair share of computer time and to be constructively involved in decisions and choices. Rather than yelling or screaming or, conversely, not expressing his interests at all, he would more persistently and steadily make his interests known, patiently but insistently repeating his desire to get "on-line."

At first, Arnie also utilized his old interpersonal patterns, insisting that he play the game all alone, that he did not need any help from "a nerd like Mitchell." However, with time, he seemed to learn to feel comfortable working with Mitchell, and he could even acknowledge the value of depending on his help. Occasionally, both boys resorted to lower-level forms of negotiation, grabbing or demanding, but most of the time the therapist was able to encourage due process and reciprocity as the medium of negotiation for computer time. This provided a powerful exercise in self-control as well as in self-assertion that by the end of the second year showed signs of being internalized by both boys.

There were, as noted before, setbacks and defeats. The pain and despair each boy suffered early in the beginning of the second year of pair therapy when a party, whose quest for the amulet had begun four weeks earlier, was lost in the maze was so tangible that neither boy could return to the game for almost a month, and then only with the therapist's gentle prodding. But the inherent excitement and powerful developmental lure of this activity won out, and throughout the rest of the year, the boys, with greater patience and wisdom, increased the strength of their characters and made progress in the game—and in the way each dealt with the other. At times, the boys temporarily lost interest in the activity or became frustrated by setbacks or lack of obvious progress. At times, they simply wanted some variety—to take a walk, to visit a store, to celebrate a birthday with a trip to the local fast-food emporium. But in true home base fashion, the quest was always there to fall back on, and it waited patiently in its floppy disk for them to call it out at the point at which they had left it.

Conclusion

This chapter has told a story of how an emphasis on the dual processes of personality development has helped expand the vision of our program of relationship therapy for pairs of children and early adolescents—a program in which we have been engaged for almost a decade. The case just recounted amplifies a thesis: that movement toward attaining methods of relating to others that are based on the capacity for mutual collaboration requires the development of both autonomy and intimacy processes. Mitchell cannot share experiences with Arnie at a higher level unless he feels empowered to negotiate his participation in the developmental project with some sense of equality. He must feel a strong enough sense of autonomy to be able to express and defend his own needs and interests if he is to feel safe enough to allow himself to get close to Arnie and to share the tragedies and triumphs of the activity. Arnie will not be motivated to negotiate conflict at a higher level with Mitchell ("you go first this time, Mitchell; I did the last time" rather than, "out of my way, nerd") unless he can begin to feel some familiarity with Mitchell's perspective—to see Mitchell more fully and completely. To strive for this, he needs to be convinced of the positive effects of social interaction. At first, this may simply be filtered through a defensive structure that can only acknowledge the need for a partner in a unilateral way: someone to assist in playing the game more successfully. But it is to be hoped that the positive affect associated with this kind of peer interaction will stimulate the desire to share experience at a more collaborative level.

The story of Mitchell and Arnie suggests that the establishment of autonomy through negotiation on the one hand and intimacy through sharing on the other were the significant themes in the development of their relationship. We can speculate that these two themes may attain ascendancy in a specific order, with concerns around autonomy preceding intimacy and intimacy gaining a clearer ascendancy after the establishment of a home base—that is, a shared activity in which both participants clearly understand the guidelines and explicit rules and in which each feels very comfortable and at least minimally competent. This suggests that perhaps in the therapeutic process of relationship building, when autonomy structures and boundaries at a given level are established, the mechanisms for the development of new structures at a higher level may involve the "interpenetrating" of these boundaries and the commingling of affect, which can best be brought about through processes of intimacy and sharing. However, not all close relationships develop in this way, with autonomy processes initially predominating. Although defining boundaries may be the dominant first function in many kinds of developing relationships, in others (for example, boy meets girl) intimacy functions seem to be ascendant at first, followed only later by boundary-oriented processes.

At the beginning of their journey together in pair therapy, the vague shape and form of a sense of mutuality and a collaborative method of relating was a star too many light-years away for these two youngsters even to see, let alone grasp. But as they strove for the amulet, a closer, more attainable body of light, they also came to strive for cooperation and reciprocity. And we could see in their interaction the interplay between the autonomy function (the negotiation of the needs of self and other) and the intimacy function (the sharing of experience).

Equally striking, perhaps, are the many functions the pair therapist performed in his role as a connecting link between the two boys. But ultimately his function is analogous to the natural but less structured function of adults in our society, where elders tutor and mediate interactions among the young, even as they are the foil for the young's discomforts. The therapist's job is to help each boy experience a new level of success in those social functions that are basic to the tasks of later adolescence and adulthood: the capacity to develop and maintain collaborative forms of both autonomy and intimacy in close, ongoing personal relationships.

For Arnie and Mitchell, from our clinical perspective, things have changed. Arnie has long since abandoned his cache of fantasy comics, and Mitchell usually makes it through lunch without antagonizing anyone too seriously. They are still working on "Wizardry" in their therapy sessions, but the tone is more calm, more reflective, more reciprocal; both boys are moving on. Arnie is almost ready to return to public school, and Mitchell has made some friends outside of pair therapy. Although social relationships are unquestionably going to continue to be problematic for both boys, some of the profound and moving gains seen in pair therapy have proven to be generalizable to their relationships with both peers and adults outside this special setting. We don't claim that pair therapy alone is the "scientifically valid" cause for the changes, but we do feel that it is worth studying further how, when partners are deeply drawn into a challenging and compelling "quest," this becomes a context for fostering the integration and development of intimacy and autonomy processes in socially immature children and young adolescents and the movement toward a collaborative attitude.

Tomorrow

The field of child (psychosocial) development needs clinical investigators. In the field of medicine, the clinical investigator in a teaching hospital—with administrative, patient care, medical education, and research commitments—over time has brought medical research from a highly empirical but often isolated exercise to a successful, effective, beneficial, and highly respected position today, with vast opportunities for tomorrow. Child and adolescent psychosocial development needs "clinical-developmental" investigators with equivalent positions of responsibility in practical laboratories (the most obvious sites are "laboratory schools" and clinics) in order to be able to study the nature of socioemotional and cognitive development.

The clinical-developmental investigator is in a critical position to assess the quality of current research in child development and apply it to salient practical (educational/clinical) problems. But the bridge between basic child development research and practical applications is a road running two ways, of which work described in this essay is an example. Our (and others') basic research in child development points to the importance for psychosocial development of healthy peer relationships in childhood and adolescence (Parker and Asher, 1987). And just as theoretical opinion and developmental principles regarding the ontogeny of intimacy and autonomy functions suggested practical techniques and interventions, so have these practical clinical/research activities suggested developmental principles or refinements fruitful for study.

In essence, this chapter is a snapshot of a process that wants and warrants expansion. Perhaps one of the most exciting new sets of future research activities suggested here comes from thinking about the ideas and implications of the "developmental project." Where else might such projects be found? And how might they be used to understand the role the interaction between autonomy and intimacy processes plays in social development? If the trajectory of the individual's cognitive and personality development is inextricably intertwined with the development of his or her social relationships, as suggested here, then how are these relationships most fruitfully fostered in social contexts that themselves are developmental in organization and nature?

References

Blatt, S., and Shichman, S. "Two Primary Configurations of Psychopathology." *Psychoanalysis and Contemporary Thought,* 1983, *6* (2), 187–254.

Brenner, J., and Mueller, E. "Shared Meaning in Boy Toddlers' Peer Relations." *Child Development,* 1982, *53,* 380–391.

Cooper, C. R., Grotevant, H. D., and Condon, S. M. "Individuation and Connectedness in Family as a Context for Adolescent Identity Formation and Role-Taking Skills." In H. D. Grotevant and C. R. Cooper (eds.), *Adolescent Development in the Family.* New Directions for Child Development, no. 22. San Francisco: Jossey-Bass, 1983.

Erikson, E. *Childhood and Society.* New York: Norton, 1963.

Erikson, E. *Identity, Youth and Crisis.* New York: Norton, 1968.

Freud, A. *The Ego and the Mechanisms of Defense.* New York: International Universities Press, 1966.

Gilligan, C. *In a Different Voice: Psychological Theory and Women's Development.* Cambridge, Mass.: Harvard University Press, 1982.

Gottman, J. M. "How Children Become Friends." *Society for Research in Child Development Monograph,* 1983, *48* (3), 1–86.

Griffin, P., and Cole, M. "Current Activity for the Future: The Zo-Ped." In B. Rogoff and J. V. Wertsch (eds.), *Children's Learning in the "Zone of Proximal Development."* New Directions for Child Development, no. 23. San Francisco: Jossey-Bass, 1984.

Hinde, R. *Toward Understanding Relationships.* Orlando, Fla.: Academic Press, 1979.

Parker, J. G., and Asher, S. R. "Peer Relations and Later Personal Adjustment: Are Low-Accepted Children 'At Risk'?" *Psychological Bulletin,* 1987, *102* (3), 357–389.

Selman, R. L. *The Growth of Interpersonal Understanding:*

Developmental and Clinical Analyses. Orlando, Fla.: Academic Press, 1980.

Selman, R. L., and Schultz, L. H. "Children's Strategies for Interpersonal Negotiation with Peers: An Interpretive/Empirical Approach to the Study of Social Development." In T. Berndt and G. Ladd (eds.), *Peer Interaction.* New York: Wiley, forthcoming.

Selman, R. L., and Yeates, K. O. "Childhood Social Regulation of Intimacy and Autonomy: A Developmental-Constructionist Perspective." In W. M. Kurtines and J. L. Gewirtz (eds.), *Moral Development Through Social Interaction.* New York: Wiley, 1987.

Sroufe, L. A., and Fleeson, J. "Attachment and the Construction of Relationships." In W. W. Hartup and Z. Rubin (eds.), *Relationships and Development.* Hillsdale, N.J.: Erlbaum, 1986.

Stern, D. *The Interpersonal World of the Infant.* New York: Basic Books, 1985.

Sullivan, H. S. *The Interpersonal Theory of Psychiatry.* New York: Norton, 1953.

Vygotsky, L. S. *Mind in Society: The Development of Higher Psychological Processes.* (M. Cole, V. John-Steiner, S. Scribner, and E. Souberman, eds.) Cambridge, Mass.: Harvard University Press, 1978.

Werner, H. *The Comparative Psychology of Mental Development.* New York: International Universities Press, 1948.

White, K. M., Speisman, J. C., and Costos, D. "Young Adults and Their Parents: From Individuation to Mutuality." In H. D. Grotevant and C. R. Cooper (eds.), *Adolescent Development in the Family.* New Directions for Child Development, no. 22. San Francisco: Jossey-Bass, 1983.

Name Index

Subject Index

Affective warmth, and competent
children, 366, 367, 368, 370
Africa, and cross-cultural studies,
58-60, 63-64
Agency, in competent children, 350,
359, 370
Aggression, and interpersonal competence training, 402, 403
Agrarian peoples, cross-cultural
studies of, 58-60, 63, 64-65
Alabama, textbook decision in, 86
Alcoholism, and depression, 191
Altruism, and empathy and sympathy, 146-147, 148
American Psychiatric Association,
193, 195-196
American Psychological Association, 43, 222n
Anaphoric relationships, of utterances, 26
Anger: development to resentment
and jealousy from, 124-130; developmental differences in, 107;
facets of, 110-111; fear simultaneous with, 128; of infants,
107, 114-115, 128; prototypic
script for, 114-115; sensorimotor
action, representation, and abstraction for, 125-128
Anorexia nervosa, and hormonal
factors, 163
Antidevelopmentalism: arguments
of, 250-251; and creativity, 241-
242, 254-255; and social construction, 91-92
Aphasia, and modularity, 230-234
Asia, and cross-cultural studies, 58-
60. See also China; India; Japan
Assertiveness, social, and competent
children, 355, 357, 358, 359, 360,
363-364, 366
Attachment: of adolescents, 372,
383; and affective disorders, 190-
193; and competent children,
367, 372; disorganized/disor-
iented (Type D) category of, 185,
191; and empathy and sympathy,
145-146; and family development, 41; and peer relations, 318,

319, 320; types of, 191; and universality, 61-62
Attunement: in infant-parent interactions, 295, 300; sensitive, and
competent children, 368-369
Authoritarian parents, and competent children, 351-352, 353, 356,
359, 360
Authoritative parents, and competent children, 351, 353-354, 356,
358, 359, 360, 364, 369, 370-371
Authority: of parents for adolescents,
385; patterns of, 351-352
Autism, and drawing ability, 210,
212-213, 216
Autonomy. See Intimacy and autonomy

B

Baltimore, closeness study in, 383
Behavior genetic research, and family studies, 42
Berkeley, California, competent children study in, 349, 371
Biology: and change model, 70; and
creativity, 242; and empathy and
sympathy, 140; and family studies, 42, 44; and pubertal processes, 155-176
Bipolar disorder, and affective development, 193-195
Bonding, and competent children,
367
Boston, pair therapy in, 410
Boston University, 312n
Boys, pubertal processes in, 166, 167

C

California, competent children study
in, 349, 371
California Achievement Test/Form
C (CAT/C), 78-79
Capital. See Social capital
Carnegie Corporation, 222n
Cattell Fund, 107n
Causal inference, and higher-order
thinking, 277-280